DECOLONIZATION

The process of decolonization which started after World War I utterly reshaped the world. Rather than occurring as a coherent event, decolonization varied from country to country in its shape and duration, and has been evaluated in many different ways over time. But is decolonization complete? What replaces former colonial controls after independence? Are Western historical frameworks adequate to describe decolonization?

Decolonization brings together the most cutting-edge thinking by major historians of decolonization, including both analytical articles by contemporary historians, and writings by statesmen and intellectual leaders of the decolonization movement such as Ho Chi Minh and Jawaharlal Nehru. The chapters in this volume present a move away from both the older Western as well as nationalist views of decolonization, towards a deeper historical view of it as a wider and still unfinished process. This is a groundbreaking survey of a subject central to modern global history.

Prasenjit Duara is Professor of History and East Asian Studies at the University of Chicago. He is the author of *Culture, Power and the State: Rural Society in North China, 1900–1942* (1988), *Rescuing History from the Nation: Questioning Narratives of Modern China* (1997) and *Sovereignty and Authenticity: Manchukuo and the East Asian Modern* (2003).

Series editor **Jack R. Censer** is Professor of History at George Mason University.

REWRITING HISTORIES

Series editor: Jack R. Censer

T

DECOLONIZATION

Perspectives from now and then

Edited by Prasenjit Duara

Routledge
Taylor & Francis Group

LONDON AND NEW YORK

First published 2004
by Routledge
11 New Fetter Lane, London EC4P 4EE

Simultaneously published in the USA and Canada
by Routledge
29 West 35th Street, New York, NY 10001

Routledge is an imprint of the Taylor & Francis Group
© 2003 Prasenjit Duara

Typeset in Palatino by Taylor & Francis Ltd
Printed and bound in Great Britain by TJ International Ltd,
Padstow, Cornwall

British Library Cataloguing in Publication Data
A catalogue record for this book is available from the British Library

Library of Congress Cataloging in Publication Data

ISBN 0–415–24840–X (hbk)
ISBN 0–415–24841–8 (pbk)

CONTENTS

CONTENTS

CONTENTS

SERIES EDITOR'S PREFACE

Few subjects are as appropriate as decolonization for this series. In part, because of the increasing interconnection among all parts of the globe, the subject retains political ramifications. Whether colonization and decolonization have completed their course even remains under debate, and continues to influence the writing and revision of this phenomenon. This volume begins with the views of significant past participants in decolonization who sought to frame the process that would free their own areas from outside domination. Although scholars' views constitute the last two sections of this collection and all regard colonization negatively, they hold differing assumptions about the current place of the colonizers and the decolonized. Because of its limited embrace of old-style colonization but in its role in the modern world order, the place of the United States plays a significant and varying role in these analyses. With so many basic assumptions still undecided, this collection brings to the fore some of the best contributions in a field still much in the process of being rewritten. The vibrancy of the debates, coupled to theoretical awareness and careful research, makes this volume a guidepost for experienced as well as novice historians.

ACKNOWLEDGEMENTS

The publication of this book owes a great deal to series editor Jack Censer who persuaded me as to its feasibility and got me truly excited about its importance. His support and light handed direction have been exactly what I needed. All the contributors who wrote original peices or revised older ones for the volume, for the most part, accepted or negotiated my editorial scalpel with graciousness. The editorial team at Routledge headed by Vicky Peterson and including Sunje Redies, Alex Ballatine, Chantelle Johnson and Andy Soutter were generous, courteous and efficent and considerably eased the vexing business of producing a book. I extend my gratitude to all of you.

Note: Because of considerations of space and readability required of a Reader, most footnotes have been removed from the texts. Exceptions have been made for quotations.

Readers interested in pursuing the sources should turn to the original texts. A bibliography for further readings on the subject follows many of the articles.

We should like to thank the following copyright holders for permission to reproduce their work.

Introduction: Written for the volume by Prasenjit Duara

Chapter 1: Reprinted from Sun Yat-sen, *San Min Chu I The Three Principles of the People* trans. Frank W. Price, ed. L.T. Chen (Shanghai, China: China Committee, Institute of Pacific Relations 1927). Selections from Lecture 4, pp. 76-100

Chapter 2: Reprinted from Ho Chi-Minh, 'The Path that led me to Leninism' [April 1960] from Ho Chi-Minh, *Selected Articles and Speeches;* ed. and intro. Jack Woddis, pp. 156-158, by permission of International Publishers Co Inc

Chapter 3: Reprinted from Jawaharlal Nehru, *The Discovery of India* (1985) pp. 515-523, by permission of Jawaharlal Nehru Memorial Fund on behalf of Sonia Gandhi

Chapter 4: Reprinted from Frantz Fanon, 'Algeria Unveiled' from Frantz Fanon, *A Dying Colonialism* (1960) pp. 35-49, 58-64. Copyright © 1960 by Monthly Review Press, by permission of Monthly Review Foundation

Chapter 5: Reprinted from Jalal-al-I Ahmad, *Occidentosis: A Plague from the West* trans. R. Campbell; annotations and intro. Hamid Algar, Chapter 1, pp. 27-35, Berkeley, Mizan Press, 1984

Chapter 6: Reprinted from Kwame Nkrumah, *Consciencism: Philosophy and Ideology for Decolonization* (1970) pp. 56-77. Copyright © 1970 by Monthly Review Press, by permission of Monthly Review Foundation

Chapter 7: 'Contested Hegemony: The Great War and the Afro-Asian Assault on the Civilizing Mission Ideology' written for this volume by Michael Adas

Chapter 8: Reprinted from Patrick Wolfe, 'Imperialism and History: A Century of Theory from Marx to Postcolonialism' *American Historical Review*, vol. 102, no. 2, [April 1997], pp. 338-420 by permission of the American Historical Association

Chapter 9: Reprinted from Geoffrey Barraclough, *An Introduction to Contemporary History*, Penguin Books, 1967

Chapter 10: '"My ambition is much higher than independence": US Power, the UN World, the Nation-state, and their Critics' written for this volume by John D. Kelly and Martha Kaplan

Chapter 11: Reprinted from William Roger Louis and Ronald Robinson, 'Empire preserv'd: How Americans put anti-Communism before anti-imperialism', *Times Literary Supplement*, 5 May 1995, pp. 14-16

Chapter 12: Reprinted from Radha Kumar, 'The Troubled History of Partition', *Foreign Affairs*, 76:1, (1997) pp. 22-34. Copyright © 1997 by the Council on Foreign Relations, Inc, by permission of *Foreign Affairs*

Chapter 13: '"Don't Paint Nationalism Red!" National Revolution and Socialist Anti-Imperialism' written for this volume by Ronald Grigor Suny

Chapter 14: 'Islamic Renewal and the Failure of the West' written for this volume by John O. Voll

Chapter 15: Reprinted from Frederick Cooper, 'The Dialectics of Decolonization: Nationalism and Labor movements in Postwar French Africa' in Frederick Cooper and Ann Laura Taylor, eds, *Tensions of Empire: Colonial Cultures in a Bourgeois World* (1996) pp. 406-436. Copyright © 1960 by Monthly Review Press, by permission of Monthly Review Foundation

Chapter 16: Reprinted from Jiweon Shin, 'Social Construction of Idealized Images of Women in Colonial Korea: the "New Women" versus "Motherhood" in Tamara L. Hunt and Micheline R. Lessard, eds, *Women and the Colonial Gaze* (2002) pp. 162-173, by permission of Palgrave Macmillian and New York University Press

Chapter 17: 'National Divisions in Indochina's Decolonization' written for this volume by Stein Tønnesson

Chapter 18: Reprinted from Bruce Cumings, '*Colonial Formations and Deformations: Korea, Taiwan, and Vietnam in Parallax Visions: Making Sense of American-East Asian Relations at the End of the Century,*' pp. 69-97. Copyright, 1999, Duke University Press. All rights reserved. Used by permission of the publisher

CONTRIBUTORS TO PARTS II
AND III

Michael Adas is the Abraham E. Voorhees Professor of History at Rutgers University. He has written extensively on European colonialism and peasant protest movements, and more recently on technology and Western global dominance. His *Machines as the Measure of Men* (1989) focused on British and French variations on the latter of these themes, and he is now completing a new book entitled *Dominance by Design: Technological Imperatives and America's Civilizing Mission.*

Geoffrey Barraclough was Chichele Professor of Modern History at the University of Oxford. Among his many books are *Mediaeval Germany* (1938) and *European Unity in Thought and Action* (1963).

Frederic Cooper is Professor of African History at New York University. His most recent books are *Africa since 1940: The Past of the Present* (2002), *Beyond Slavery: Exploration of Race, Labor, and Citizenship* (with Thomas Holt and Rebecca Scott, 2000), *Decolonization and African Society: The Labor Question in French and British Africa* (1996), *Tensions of Empire: Colonial Cultures in a Bourgeois World* (co-edited with Ann Stoler, 1997), and *International Development and the Social Sciences: Essays in the History and Politics of Knowledge* (co-edited with Randall Packard, 1997).

Bruce Cumings is Norman and Edna Freehling Professor of International History and East Asian Political Economy at the University of Chicago. He is author or co-author of eight books, including a two-volume study, *Origins of the Korean War* (Princeton University Press, 1981, 1990), *War and Television* (Verso, 1992), *Korea's Place in the Sun: A Modern History* (Norton, 1997), *Parallax Visions: American/East Asian Relations at the End of the Century* (Duke University Press, 1998). He was elected to the American Academy of Arts and Sciences in 1999, and has been a recipient of fellowships from NEH, the MacArthur Foundation, and the Center for Advanced Study at Stanford.

Martha Kaplan is Professor of Anthropology at Vassar College. Among her publications are 'Panopticon in Poona: an essay on Foucault and colonialism' (*Cultural Anthropology* 10[1]: 85–98 [1995]), *Neither Cargo Nor Cult: Ritual Politics and the Colonial Imagination in Fiji* (Duke University Press, 1995) and *Represented Communities: Fiji and World Decolonization* (co-authored with John D. Kelly, University of Chicago Press, 2001).

John D. Kelly is Professor of Anthropology at the University of Chicago. His publications include *A Politics of Virtue: Hinduism, Sexuality and Countercolonial Discourse in Fiji* (University of Chicago Press, 1991), 'The other Leviathans: corporate investment and the construction of a sugar colony', in Pal Ahluwalia *et al.* (eds) *White and Deadly: Sugar and Colonialism* (Nova Science Publishers, 1999) and *Represented Communities: Fiji and World Decolonization* (co-authored with Martha Kaplan, University of Chicago Press, 2001).

Radha Kumar is a Senior Fellow of Peace and Conflict Studies at the Council on Foreign Relations. She is the author of *Divide and Fall: Bosnia and the Annals of Partition*.

Wm Roger Louis is Kerr Professor of English History and Culture at the University of Texas, Austin, and a Fellow of St Antony's College, Oxford. He is the author of *The British Empire in the Middle East* and Editor-in-Chief of the *Oxford History of the British Empire*.

Ronald Robinson is Emeritus Beit Professor of the History of the British Commonwealth, and Fellow of Balliol College, Oxford. He is the co-author (with John Gallagher and Alice Denny) of *Africa and the Victorians*.

Jiweon Shin has a Ph.D. in sociology from Harvard University and is currently teaching in the Social Studies Program, Harvard University. She has two main research projects at this point: the institutionalization of Christianity in Korea, Japan and Taiwan; and new women and motherhood in Korea and Japan. She has several articles out and under review.

Ronald Grigor Suny is Professor of Political Science at the University of Chicago, and is the author of *The Revenge of the Past: Nationalism, Revolution, and the Collapse of the Soviet Union* (Stanford University Press, 1993); and *The Soviet Experiment: Russia, the USSR, and the Successor States* (Oxford University Press, 1998). He is also the editor of *The Structure of Soviet History: Essays and Documents* (Oxford University Press, 2003); and co-editor of *Becoming National* (Oxford University Press, 1996) and *A State of Nations: Empire and Nation-making in the Age of Lenin and Stalin* (Oxford University Press, 2001).

He is currently working on a study of the young Stalin and the formation of the Soviet Union, and a series of essays on empire and nations.

Stein Tønnesson is director of the International Peace Research Institute, Oslo (PRIO). Before coming to PRIO in 2001, he was Professor of Human Development Studies at the Centre for Development and Environment, University of Oslo. He spent the years 1992–8 as Research Professor and Senior Research Fellow at the Nordic Institute of Asian Studies (NIAS) in Copenhagen, and has published widely on the contemporary history of Vietnam, nationalism and national identity in Asia, and the conflict in the South China Sea.

John O. Voll is Professor of Islamic History and Associate Director of the Center for Muslim-Christian Understanding of Georgetown University. He is a past president of the Middle East Studies Association, and author, co-author and editor of numerous books and articles, including *Islam: Continuity and Change in the Modern World* (2nd edn, 1994) and, with John L. Esposito, *Islam and Democracy* (1996) and *Makers of Contemporary Islam* (2001).

Patrick Wolfe is Victoria Research Fellow at Victoria University of Technology, Australia. He has written and taught on imperialism, race and the history of anthropology. His publications include *Settler Colonialism and the Transformation of Anthropology* (Cassell, 1999) and 'Land, labor, and difference: elementary structures of race' (*American Historical Review* 106 [2001]).

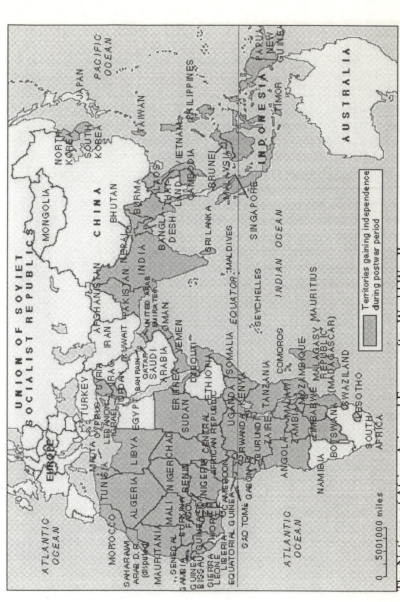

The Nations of Africa, Asia and Europe after World War II

1

INTRODUCTION

The decolonization of Asia and Africa in the twentieth century[1]

Prasenjit Duara

From a historian's perspective, decolonization was one of the most important political developments of the twentieth century because it turned the world into the stage of history. Until World War I, historical writing had been the work of the European conquerors that, in the words of Oswald Spengler, had made the world appear to 'revolve around the pole of this little part-world' that is Europe. With few exceptions, the regions outside Europe were seen to be inhabited by people without the kind of history capable of shaping the world. The process of decolonizaton, which began towards the end of World War I, was accompanied by the appearance of *national* historical consciousness in these regions, that is, the history, not of dynasties or the work of God/gods, but of a people as a whole. To be sure, historical writing continues to be filtered through national preoccupations, but the rapid spread of modern historical writing to most of the world also enabled us to see how happenings in one region – no matter how peripheral or advanced – were often linked to processes and events in other parts. It became possible to grasp, as did the leaders of decolonization, the entire globe as an interconnected entity for understanding and action.

There are remarkably few historical studies of decolonization as a whole, despite the importance of the subject. This is not entirely surprising because it is neither a coherent event such as the Russian Revolution, nor a well defined phenomenon like fascism. The timing and patterns of decolonization were extremely varied, and the goals of the movement in different countries were not always consistent with each other. Indeed, we have had to exclude from our consideration the pre-twentieth century independence movements in the Americas from European powers, as well as the later decolonization of the Pacific islands from powers such as New Zealand, Australia, Britain and the Netherlands starting in the 1960s. In both cases, the circumstances of decolonization were very different from the *core* period and region of our consideration: Asia and Africa from the early years of the twentieth century until the 1960s.

1

Within this approximate time and region, decolonization refers to the
[process whereby colonial powers transferred institutional and legal
control over their territories and dependencies to indigenously based,
formally sovereign, nation-states.] The political search for independence
often began during the inter-war years and fructified within fifteen years
of the end of World War II in 1945. It should be noted that there were
many formally independent countries, such as Iran and China, whose
leaders considered themselves to have been informally and quasi-legally
subordinated to colonial powers, and who viewed their efforts for
autonomy as part of the anti-imperialist movement (see Chapters 2 and 6
by Sun Yat-sen and Jalal Al-i Ahmad respectively). Therefore decolonization [represented not only the transference of legal sovereignty, but a
movement for moral justice and political solidarity against imperialism.]
It thus refers both to the anti-imperialist political movement and to an
emancipatory ideology which sought or claimed to liberate the nation
and humanity itself.

Even within these specifications, decolonization varied sufficiently
from country to country, and often within the same country, to make
generalizations quite risky. Take for instance, the case of China. Here was
a vigorous anti-imperialist movement directed against the Western
powers and Japan, based largely on an ethic of socialist emancipation.
Yet there was no felt need to critique the West culturally – to ideologically decolonize in the manner of a Frantz Fanon or Mahatma Gandhi –
since it had been only partially and informally colonized, and was occupied by an Asian power, Japan. Additionally, the meaning of
decolonization as a process has itself been differently evaluated over
time. Our historiographical understanding of decolonization during the
period when political independence from imperialist powers was taking
place was shaped considerably by the writings of nationalist statesmen
and historians, as well as a generation of Western historians who were
optimistic or sympathetic to the process. More recently, the debates
around post-colonialism have questioned the extent or thoroughness of
'decolonization' when independence from colonial powers meant the
establishment of nation-states closely modelled upon the very states that
undertook imperialism. Here again, the post-colonial critique has found
more or less sympathy in different places according to the historical
experiences of the people there. The volume will try to represent this
variation without losing sight of the core historical character of the
process.

If we can pinpoint a particular event to symbolize the beginnings of
this movement, it would be the victory of Japan over Czarist Russia in
the war of 1905, which was widely hailed as the first victory of the dominated peoples against an imperial power.] Sun Yat-sen, the father of
Chinese nationalism, reminisced about this event in a speech he made in

2

Japan in 1925. He was on a ship crossing the Suez Canal soon after news of the Japanese victory became known. When the ship was docked in the canal, a group of Arabs mistook him for a Japanese and enthusiastically flocked around him. Even upon discovering their mistake, they continued to celebrate their solidarity with him against the imperialist powers. In the speech, Sun developed the theme of a racial or colour war against the white race for whom 'blood is thicker than water' and urged the oppressed Asians of common colour and culture to unify and resist imperialism.

Similarly, the event symbolizing the culmination of this movement was the Bandung Conference, a meeting of the representatives of twenty-nine new nations of Asia and Africa, held in Bandung, Indonesia in 1955, fifty years after the Russo-Japanese war. The conference aimed to express solidarity against imperialism and racism and promote economic and cultural cooperation among these nations. China, India and Indonesia were key players in the meeting. The conference finally led to the non-aligned movement in 1961, a wider Third World force in which participants avowed their distance from the two superpowers – aligning themselves neither with the United States or Soviet Union – during the Cold War. However, conflicts developed among these non-aligned nations – for instance between India and China in 1962 – which eroded the solidarity of the Bandung spirit. With the dissolution of the socialist bloc and the end of the Cold War in 1989, the non-aligned movement – this in reality had included both truly neutral countries and those that were aligned with one or the other superpower – became irrelevant.

The imperialism we are concerned with in this volume was the imperialism of Western nation-states and later Japan that spread from roughly the mid-eighteenth century to Asia, Africa, and the Caribbean and Pacific islands. The brutal and dehumanizing conditions it imposed upon these places have been well documented, most graphically by the independence movements themselves. At the same time, as Karl Marx noted, this imperialism represented an incorporation of these regions into the modern capitalist system. As we shall see in the historiographical survey of imperialism conducted by Patrick Wolfe in Chapter 9 this volume, debates continue about the purposes and nature of this incorporation, but we may make a few general comments about it. First, the colonial projects of capitalist nation-states such as Britain, France, the Netherlands, and later Germany, Italy, the US and Japan, among others, were an integral part of the competition for control of global resources and markets. The ideology accompanying the intensification of competition in the late nineteenth and early twentieth century was Social Darwinism. This was an evolutionary view of the world that applied Darwin's theory of 'the survival of the fittest' to races and nations, and justified imperialist domination in terms of an understanding that a race

3

or nation that did not dominate would instead be dominated. Imperialist competition for a greater share of world resources, particularly on the part of late-comer nation-states such as Germany and Japan, was an important factor behind the two world wars of the twentieth century. Ironically, however, both wars accelerated decolonization considerably.

Second, from the perspective of the colonized, this incorporation inevitably involved the erosion of existing communities as they experienced the deepening impact of capitalism and alien cultural values. The extent to which these communities were able to adapt to the new circumstances depended upon the historical resources they were able to muster, as well as their position and role in the imperialist incorporation process. Thus it was not uncommon to find a dualistic type of society in the colonies: on the one hand, an adaptive and relatively modern, coastal, urban sector, integrated under however unequal terms, with metropolitan society. On the other hand, a vast hinterland where historical forms of social life, economic organization and exploitation continued to exist, but hardly as pristine 'tradition'. This is the phenomenon known in dependency theory as 'the articulation of modes of production', whereby modern capitalism utilizes non-capitalist modes of production and exploitation for the production of capitalist value. Whether responding to global prices or a plantation economy, these regions also serviced the modern capitalist sector of the metropolitan economy, but, typically, they received few of its benefits. In other words, the gap ought not to be seen merely as the difference between a traditional and a modern sector, but as different kinds of incorporation into the capitalist system. The gap between these two sectors and ways of life would often shape and bedevil the decolonization process.

Anti-imperialist nationalism emerged historically from the urban, coastal sector where modern, capitalist forms of knowledge, technology, capital and organization had spread more widely. Although there had been several major expressions of resistance to colonial powers organized around older, indigenous political patterns – such as the mid-nineteenth century Taiping Rebellion or the late-nineteenth century Boxer Uprising in China, the 1857 Rebellion in India, and the Senussi Uprising in Tunisia – as discussed by Geoffrey Barraclough in Part II, the successful movements of decolonization were almost invariably led by Westernized leaders from the modernized sectors of society. These were the would-be administrators and entrepreneurs who felt a very concrete ceiling over their heads, and educated Chinese who bristled at the signs declaring 'Dogs and Chinese not allowed' posted in public places in the foreign settlements in Shanghai and elsewhere. These were people who experienced constant denial and humiliation because of their colour or origins, but they were also people who, like Mahatma Gandhi, clearly recognized the contradictions these actions presented to the Western doctrines of humanism and rationality. Finally, they were the people who understood the modern world well enough to know how to mobilize the resources to topple colonial domination.

How did these modern nationalists and reformers mobilize the hinterlands and the lower classes of their society which were negatively affected by the modern incorporation and barely touched by modern ideas? For many in these communities, loyalty to the nation-state was an abstraction quite removed from their everyday consciousness, and modern programmes of secular society, national education or the nuclear family were quite inimical to their conceptions of a good society – which involved regional, linguistic, religious, caste, tribal and lineage solidarity – and religious life. On the other side, for the modernizing elites, the peasants and the 'people' lived in a world that was increasingly alien and distasteful to them, and the new language of modernity, historical progress, citizenship and the like increased the gap between the two still further.

To be sure, the process of transforming the hinterlands of Western nation-states in the nineteenth century was no less a forceful project of state- and nation-building. In the case of France, Eugen Weber has dubbed the process as the conversion of 'peasants into Frenchmen'. But there were also significant differences between the two areas. The process in Europe grew out of historical conditions within those regions, and was not so sharp and wrenching as the process in the colonies. Second, colonies were disadvantaged by the unfavourable circumstances of imperialist domination absent in the European case; and finally, the prior development of capitalism in Western societies led to accelerated rates of growth and development that made it harder and harder for the disadvantaged societies to catch up and extend growth to the hinterlands.

The great challenge faced by the decolonizers was not simply to bridge the gap between these rapidly diverging worlds, but to re-make hinterland society in their own image. This image derived both from their conception of humanistic reform as well as the need to create a sleek national body capable of surviving and succeeding in a world of competitive capitalism. The decolonization movement was thus always faced with two tasks which were often in tension with each other: to fulfil the promise of its humanistic ideals and modern citizenship and to create the conditions for international competitiveness. To the extent that these conditions required the production of a homogenized people, there was also often a violent transformation of the lives and world-views of people who were forced to adapt to a world in which the benefits to them were not always clear. The various nationalist movements combined different strategies or methods of force and violence with education and peaceful mobilization to achieve their goals. Thus leaders like Nkrumah and Gandhi were able to achieve rural mass mobilization relatively peacefully, but in the absence of significant land reform or economic integration, the gap persisted. Revolutionary nationalists like Mao Zedong or Ho Chi Minh succeeded in restructuring the inequities of rural society, but often at the cost of massive violence. Other nationalist movements, like that led by Sukarno in Indonesia, were prevented by the structure of Dutch colonial control from achieving any significant rural mobilization.

Nationalists in the colonies – as in earlier nationalisms of the West – often justified the process of mobilization and transformation of the people by narratives of national belonging, or belonging to what Benedict Anderson has called the 'imagined community of the nation'. The imagined community refers to the sense that people who are differentiated by distance, language, class and culture are enabled by modern means of communication (from print to screen) to imagine themselves as part of a single community or family. These nationalists posited an ancient, even primordial unity of the nation that had gone into a long era of forgetfulness or slumber during the middle period between the ancient and the modern. The alleged ancient unity of the nation granted nationalists and the nation-state the right to make these transformations, and they described the nationalism they were seeking to foster as a national 'awakening'.

To be sure, this is not to say that there are no indigenous foundations of modernity. Nationalist historians and others have discovered the 'sprouts of capitalism' and 'alternative modernities' not only in China, but in India, Southeast Asia and elsewhere. Research on the Indian Ocean and East Asia from various different perspectives – Japan, India, China, Southeast Asia, Africa, the Arabian peninsula – reveals a dynamic and cosmopolitan world of commerce and cultural flows that long preceded the Western arrival. However, the problem with the nationalist understanding is not that the research findings are wrong, but that these findings are located within an evolutionary paradigm containing the implicit (and sometimes explicit) argument that these developments would have ultimately led to modern capitalism and nationalism. This is an instance of how nationalists adopted the basic assumptions of the evolutionism of their colonial masters. One of the challenges of thinking historically about the problem of decolonization is to evaluate the importance of these historical developments without subscribing to the misguided evolutionary framework.

These long-term, often no longer extant, conditions must be separated from the more immediate conditions and circumstances which permitted decolonization or situated a society to quickly build a modern nation-state. Different societies were differently advantaged and disadvantaged with regard to this latter problem. Thus Japan's ability to rapidly build a modern nation-state in the Meiji Restoration (1868) had much to do with the presence of strong political and merchant elites. But it was also lucky in being relatively neglected by the imperialist powers; to be the last country to suffer the unequal treaties, and to be threatened by America, an emergent power with a rather different imperialist vision of the world. Indeed, after World War I, the circumstances for decolonization were generated as much from the international situation as any other. First, the Soviet Union and the United States of America emerged as new powers with little stake in the old international order based upon the European balance of power, and were indeed, opposed to formal imperialism. Then there was the intensification of imperialist rivalries occasioned by the nose-thumbing, new imperialism of Germany and Japan, which often caused the colonizers to grant concessions in their colonies or promote opposition in others. These circumstances did much to undermine the facade of unity so critical to colonial control and superiority.

World War II made conditions still more unfavourable for colonialism. The spectacle of the old colonial powers being overrun by the Axis forces in North Africa and particularly by Japan in Southeast Asia (and threatening British India), the establishment of formally independent states in Southeast Asia under the rhetoric of pan-Asianism, the prominence of leaders like Sukarno and the Burmese leader U Nu who would lead nationalist movements against the returning colonial powers in the Japanese-dominated wartime governments, and the further rise of the United States and Soviet Union, made eventual decolonization a matter of time in most parts of the world. Thus while the chapters in this volume focus on the domestic or regional factors behind decolonization, this larger international perspective has to be borne in mind.

The leadership of the modernizing nationalists implied as well that independence would not involve a return to the pre-modern ideals of the dynastic, imperial, religious, feudal or tribal systems. To be sure, as Frederick Cooper suggests in Chapter 16, national independence was not always the goal of the decolonizing movement. In the Japanese and French empires, there were efforts on the part of both colonizers and colonized to create ideals of 'imperial citizenship' where equality would prevail in a multinational community (of the ex-empire), but ingrained colonial attitudes and escalating demands for autonomy (and defeat in the Japanese case) nullified these political experiments. Thus it turned out that the decolonizing movements sought to fashion themselves in certain basic ways as modern nation-states in the manner of their imperialist oppressors. To what extent this would involve taking on some characteristics of the imperialist states themselves – acquiring neighbouring territories, exploiting the resources of peripheral regions within the nation – especially as they joined the competitive system of global capitalism, was yet to become clear. But what was clear to the nationalists is that they denounced imperialism and were determined to launch a new era of justice and equality both within their nations and in the world.

• As we shall see in the essays by the decolonizing leaders in Part I, the ideals of decolonization and the anti-imperialist movement were built upon two pillars: socialism and the discourse of alternative civilizations, or what I call the new discourse of civilization. These two aspects were much more closely and deeply intertwined in the twentieth century than we have customarily believed. By socialism, I refer specifically to the Leninist programme of anti-imperialism and socialist equality, as well as state and party command over society. Some societies like China, Vietnam, North Korea and Tanzania adopted the socialist programme more completely, but most other decolonizing societies also reflected more or less the socialist ideals of equality, market restrictions and state re-distribution programmes as the alternative to the imperialist capitalism under which they had suffered. Here we encounter these ideas among non-communists such as Sun Yat-sen and his successors in Republican China (1911–49), Jawaharlal Nehru in India, Kwame Nkrumah of Ghana, and Jalal Al-i Ahmad, an influential intellectual in Iran under the Shah.

One of the more important debates in the Third Communist International or Comintern, convened after the Russian Revolution, concerned the possibilities of developing socialist revolutions in the colonized world. In other words, they debated whether it was possible for decolonization to be accompanied by the birth not of a capitalist nation-state, but rather of an egalitarian socialist society. This debate became more serious as the tide of revolution began to ebb in Europe, and in a reversal of the Marxist doctrine, European communists and the Russian revolutionary leaders in particular, began to consider the possibility that the road to revolution would not emerge from Paris and London, the centres of capitalism, but rather from Shanghai and Calcutta at the peripheries of the world capitalist system. After all, even the Russian Revolution had taken place in one of the weakest countries of the capitalist world. Nonetheless, the communists recognized that the industrial working class or the proletariat in these countries often represented a tiny minority of the population, and the debate turned upon the extent to which communists ought to support the nationalist movements of 'progressive bourgeois nationalism' represented by leaders like Sun and Nehru. Ronald Suny has captured the essence of this debate in Chapter 14, and we need not elaborate it here except to note that while rhetorically, the Soviet Union and the Comintern backed the decolonization movement, practically, the interests of the Soviet state under Stalin often determined which anti-imperialist movements it would support.

The impact of socialist ideas and the support of the Soviet Union – even if it was only moral support sometimes – upon the independence movements in the different colonies and informal colonies was, of course, widely welcomed by a range of leaders including Ho Chi Minh, Nehru and Sun. At the same time, however, socialist ideas and support also produced serious tensions within the nationalist movements. In his essay on African working-class movements, Frederic Cooper analyses how this movement became subordinated to the nationalist forces and was steered away from purely socialist agendas. But decolonizing leaders continued to inject at least a modicum of socialist egalitarianism into the nationalist ideology and programme. This was also the case in many other countries, such as India, which under the leadership of Jawaharlal Nehru in the 1950s and 1960s, experimented with a 'mixed economy', combining state ownership of many economic enterprises with regulated private property. Even the KMT regime in Taiwan, which came firmly under US hegemony after it lost the mainland to the communists in 1949, retained the strong state control over the economy and society that it had developed from Nazi and Soviet models in the 1930s, until as late as the 1960s.

Conversely, in societies where socialist forces became dominant in the movement against imperialism, the leaders of the movement who based their organizational strength upon some combination of working-class movements and the land hunger of an impoverished peasantry, frequently had to appeal to a broader national coalition that included several elite and intermediate classes who were usually outside the scope of a purely socialist movement. The best example of this kind of 'united front' thinking was to be found in the Chinese communist movement, which increased its power relative to the Nationalist Kuomintang party of Sun Yat-sen and his successor Chiang Kai-shek, during the anti-Japanese war in the 1930s and 1940s. Indeed, the Chinese communists were successful in riding to power on a massive revolution significantly because they combined their organizational techniques and reform projects with a call for national salvation, not merely class war. In 1940, Mao Zedong wrote *On New Democracy*, in which he declared 'The Chinese democratic republic which we now desire to establish can only be a democratic republic under the joint dictatorship of all the anti-imperialist and anti-feudal people', and included in this common front, the proletariat, the peasantry, the intellectuals, the petty bourgeoisie and even sections of the capitalist bourgeoisie opposed to imperialism (Mao 2002: 89). Not long after achieving power in 1949, however, Mao became increasingly intolerant of anyone who did not abide by his particular vision of communism. In the Cultural Revolution of the 1960s, he demoralized an entire generation by destroying the very party that had been painstakingly built since the 1920s.

Just as socialism and workers' issues became inseparable from nationalism, so too did women's issues and women's rights movements. The relationship between the women's movement and the national movement is a complex and recently much debated topic that we can only introduce here. Two chapters deal with gender issues in this volume: one by the Algerian psychiatrist and thinker Frantz Fanon (Chapter 5) and another by a contemporary scholar Jiweon Shin, who has written about Korean women under Japanese colonialism in Chapter 17. Together the pieces convey many of the problems associated with the role of women and gender in the nationalist movements of decolonization. Fanon is widely regarded as among the most intellectually penetrating critic of colonialism, but he has also been taken to task for his understanding of women's roles, particularly in Islamic societies dominated by colonialism. The rights of native women were frequently championed by colonial powers and colonial reformers. Fanon grasps the ways in which colonial power seeks to invade the domestic realm of the colonized society by advocating the liberation of women and seeking to enlist their support for the colonial state, thus dividing the men and women of the nation. At the same time, feminists believe that this kind of critique of imperialism, which is by no means confined to Islamic society, but applies to nationalist movements in most other colonial societies in Africa, India, and East and Southeast Asia, tends at the same time to keep women within the structures of patriarchal domination.

To be sure, decolonizing nationalism did not envision a mere return to traditional patriarchy. The new woman was to be educated so that she could contribute to making the nation strong by rearing healthy children. Many women were also expected to be involved in the freedom struggle. But ideally, they were to be mothers of the nation, protecting and cherishing its inner values especially within the home, and not centrally involved in the public sphere. As such, women's questions, particularly relating to changes in gender relationships or to their desire to undertake roles equal or similar to men's, were subordinated to the overall needs of the nation as perceived by men. The new patriarchy, as Partha Chatterjee has observed for India, was not a traditional patriarchy, but a nationalist patriarchy. Of course, we can scarcely expect to find the same conceptions of gender in every anti-imperialist movement, and we also need to recognize that for many women the enhanced role of motherhood may have been deeply satisfying. Nonetheless, the idea that women's status and issues became the object of contestation between imperialists and male nationalists can be found across the territory of our inquiry, from Algeria to Korea.

The priority given to the nation – or should we say, to the dominant conception of the nation – over the agenda of workers, feminists, ethnic groups or others was of course achieved, in part, by the appeal to present a unified resistance to imperialism. Still more important was the assumption that the nation was founded upon historically deep traditions or an ancient civilization whose timeless values could not be easily challenged or changed. Resistance to any radical transformation of gender conceptions, in particular, was often grounded in such claims. The new discourse of civilization appeared and spread around the world at the end of World War I. The war threw European imperialism into an ideological crisis because its scale and brutality seemed, in the eyes of the colonized and many Western intellectuals, to expose European claims of civilizational superiority and 'the civilizing mission' as utterly hollow. As Michael Adas shows in Chapter 8, this sense of the failure of the West led to a psychological liberation for many intellectuals in the colonized world, and John Voll in Chapter 15 reveals a similar pattern for intellectuals in Islamic societies during a later period. At the heart of the critique of civilization launched by Western and non-Western intellectuals after the Great War, was the universalizing promise of the 'civilizing mission' – a mission which exemplified the desire not (simply) to conquer the Other, but to be desired by the Other. In this critique, Western civilization had forfeited the right to represent the highest goals or ultimate values of humanity, and was no longer worthy of being desired, or even recognized, by the Other. As the famous quip attributed to Mahatma Gandhi goes:

Journalist What do you think of Western civilization?
Gandhi   I think it would be a good idea.

In some ways, the idea that there were other civilizations had been around in the West for a long time. Yet by the nineteenth century, European civilization based on Enlightenment ideas of progress came to displace the idea that other civilizations mattered. Indeed, the absence of such an idea of civilization in a society was sufficient reason to justify colonization. The war, the changed balance of power in the world, and the critique of European civilization restored the idea that other civilizations were just as (or nearly as) legitimate, and decolonizing thinkers associated civilization with claims to sovereignty, thus reversing the terms of the European assertion that denied sovereignty because of the lack of civilization. The new discourse of civilization was a truly global intellectual product. Oswald Spengler's *The Decline of the West*, written just before World War I, and the postwar writings of Arnold Toynbee, converged with those of many Asian, and later, African, thinkers and writers. Among them were Okakura Tenshin and Okawa Shumei from Japan, Gu Hongming, Liang Qichao and Liang Shuming in the Chinese speaking world, Rabindranath Tagore and Mahatma Gandhi in India, and Léopold Senghor, Aimé Césaire and others of the Négritude movement.

The view that emerged from this discourse was the world could be saved from materialist greed and technological destructiveness by combining the spiritual and moral qualities of other – such as Islamic, Hindu, African, Buddhist or Confucian – civilizations. The validity of these civilizations was often established through three, sometimes combined, approaches. One was to find elements similar to European civilization within these societies: Confucian rationality, Buddhist humanism, Hindu logic, etc. Another found the opposite of the West in alternative civilizations which are 'peaceful' as opposed to 'warlike', 'spiritual' as opposed to 'material', 'ethical' as opposed to 'decadent', 'natural' as opposed to 'rational', 'timeless' as opposed to 'temporal', communal as opposed to competitive, and so on. Finally, these new nations would synthesize or harmonize these binaries and Western materialism would be balanced by Eastern spirituality and modernity redeemed.

In such ways, the discourse of multiple and alternative civilizations gave considerable authority and confidence to the critique of the Social Darwinist ideology that had fuelled imperialism and the imperialist idea of the civilizing mission. In each of the chapters of Part I, the reader will note how the nationalist leaders or intellectuals appeal not only to an egalitarian ideal deriving from the socialist tradition, but combine it with an appeal to unique civilizational traditions, whether these be pan-African communitarianism, timeless Indian or Chinese practices hidden among the ordinary people, or Islamic historical greatness. The mobilizational value of this rhetoric of civilization made it an empowering and enabling force in the battle against imperialism. By the same token, however, it also subordinated other claims for justice and equality to the nation as the representative of a civilization.

The ideals of egalitarianism, humanitarianism (or universalism) and the moral and spiritual values represented by the twin pillars of socialism and civilization discourse were frequently in tension with the programme of nation-making that decolonizing societies had to inevitably undertake. We have already alluded to several problems faced by modernizing nationalists, namely those connected with a hinterland society suspicious of modernizing projects, and with groups such as workers and women seeking greater rights. Added to these was a range of territorial and ethnic conflicts produced by the need to create a unified nation-state. Territorial maximization and the homogenization of the population were seen as necessary conditions for a strong nation-state capable of mobilizing its natural resources and population for the tasks of global competition. These goals would have been largely foreign to pre-colonial historical empires or other polities in these regions. With respect to ethnicity, several historical empires, such as the Ottoman, the Chinese or the Mughal, had fashioned strategies for the co-existence of different ethnic communities, although local conflicts and violence were scarcely absent. Moreover, the frontier and peripheral zones of these empires and polities were typically regarded as no-man's lands: dark, forbidding wildernesses inhabited by barbarian peoples. Political control over these areas was at best informal and frequently multiple and changing: different neighbouring polities might make claims to them if and when they could or cared to. Many communities in these regions remained largely untouched by state power.

During the period of colonial empires, several developments took place that were to leave a different heritage for decolonizing nations. First, as a modern state, the colonial state was built upon the imperative that *all* global resources be controlled by territorially sovereign polities, whether nations or empires. This logic transformed the fuzzy frontier zones of the historical empires into the militarized boundaries of the modern state. The rulers of modern empires, such as the British, the French or the Japanese, were often obsessed by the need to maximize their territories and militarize their boundaries, often in remote, unprofitable regions. Their actions provided the impetus for emergent nation-states like China, India, Nigeria, Iraq or Indonesia to maximize and militarize their own territories. Modern states have tended to incorporate contiguous, alien territories and peoples wherever possible, thereby blurring the practical distinction between imperialism and nationalism in these areas. This drive led not only to border conflicts among the new states, but also often meant the rapid deterioration of the environment – especially forests – and the elimination of the means of livelihood and cultures of indigenous peoples. In other places it often led to the alienation of larger populations, such as Kashmiri Muslims, the Tibetans, the Kurds or the East Timorese.

Second, the problem of ethnicity was frequently created and certainly compounded during the colonial period. Colonial states often created new categories of people – and even reified such categories as caste or tribe – for purposes of governance and to establish their power through a policy of divide and rule. In Africa, European colonialists reified a certain image of the tribe in order to co-opt chieftains whose power they had recently enlarged. The British in India favoured certain 'martial classes' from the north, such as Sikhs or Gurkhas, in opposition to the 'effeminate' and politically restive Bengali intellectuals. More consequential for the South Asian subcontinent was the division of electoral constituencies in the twentieth century along religious lines, which had the effect of exacerbating and deepening tensions between majority Hindus and Muslim elites who felt they would be dominated in a new Indian nation. Colonial policies encouraged and facilitated large-scale immigration from China, India and elsewhere to work on plantations and mines in Southeast Asia, the Caribbean and Africa. Colonial powers frequently used these immigrant communities as 'docile labour' or as junior partners of imperial rule – as merchants, intermediaries and functionaries – thus fomenting much ethnic strife between the local and diasporic communities, a strife that continues to the present.

Just as important as the policies of colonial states was the broader discourse of national rights that emanated from the Americas and the French Revolution intensified in nineteenth-century Europe, and was circulating globally by the early twentieth century. This discourse held that a people or nationality which could be shown to have had a long history (and civilization) had a *right* to a territory and a state of its own. This is a discourse that we have, of course, assumed all along to have lain at the base of the decolonization movement. But while the discourse certainly enabled decolonization, it also divided the movement as it exacerbated ethnic tensions and led ethnic groups to demand nationality rights and a territorial nation-state for themselves. The long drawn-out and violent decolonization of the French colony of Indochina was, as Stein Tønnesson has shown below, due not only to the tenacity of the French colonial rulers, the subsequent American support of the French, and collaboration by large groups of the colonized, it was also a consequence of the rivalry between different nationalists both within Vietnam and between the Vietnamese and the Cambodians and Laotians. In general, partitions of empire through the twentieth century in the Middle East, East Europe, Africa, South and Southeast Asia were a result as much of colonial desire to divide up spheres of influence (which continued under the Cold War empires) or to extricate the colonizers from increasingly sticky situations, as they were of ethno-national aspirations. As Radha Kumar shows in Chapter 13, rapidly devised colonial departure strategies of 'divide and quit' exacerbated many of the world's ethnic conflicts, and today represent a major legacy of the colonial period.

In the end, the principal tension between the ideals of the new nations and their practical projects arose from the demands made by the very system which they sought to join. This was the Westphalian/Vatellian system of states which had once been a club of exclusive – and imperialist – nations, but which after World War I was in the process of transforming itself into a 'family of nations', originally through the League of Nations, and after World War II, the United Nations. The United Nations crystallizes many of the ideals of the decolonizing era – a vision of global civilization, championing the rights of the oppressed, as well as the right of national self-determination. The United Nations also represented a means to address the conflicts and problems among nation-states. That such conflict persists between and within nation-states is perhaps testimony to the driving power of competitiveness that is the underlying reason for the very existence of the system. It was, after all, the competition between nations for a greater share of the world's resources that had led to the world wars of the twentieth century. A good deal of the resource-maximizing and mobilization strategies of new nations derived from this imperative as well.

Within the tensions of this larger context, how are we to interpret the decolonization movement of the twentieth century? In this volume itself we are able to trace several interpretive threads which should help us think our way. Geoffrey Barraclough's essay from the 1960s (Chapter 10) represents a sympathetic account of the movement. He recognizes the problems within the movements, but he is sensitive to the injustices and psychological injuries of colonialism. In a way, we might say, his piece is morally – if not always intellectually – continuous with the writings of the nationalist leaders themselves. Like many of them, for him, decolonization represents a new beginning of development and fulfilment of the individual and citizen. The chapters by John Kelly and Martha Kaplan and by Roger Louis and Ronald Robinson (Chapters 11 and 12) present a different view emerging from a global perspective. For Louis and Robinson, European – especially British – imperialism hardly disappeared after World War II. It transmuted into a neo-imperialism led by the United States of America with Britain as junior partner. They dominated the Cold War world by effectively controlling many formally sovereign nation-states through new forms of military and financial dependency. Kelly and Kaplan spell out the wider implications of this view, in which most of the decolonizing nations have become part of the 'Third World', formally sovereign in the nation-state system, but trapped by debt, alien institutions and cultural dependency in a world where many argue that the conditions for the great mass of people are not significantly better than in colonial times. They argue that decolonization mostly represented entry into a new world order dominated by the US, 'already tooled for purposes at best different than the aims of the anti-colonial movements, and at times, clearly obstructive of them'.

There is yet another interpretive thread. The East Asian countries have done notably better in developmental terms than the rest of the Southern World. We might say that they have been able to utilize certain institutional and historical advantages to mobilize the nation and prise themselves out of a peripheral and dominated status to become competitive players in the system, much as Japan had been able to do more than a century ago. In his comparative essay on Japanese colonialism (Chapter 19), Bruce Cumings reveals that in contrast to European colonies in the same region, such as Vietnam, the Japanese colonial state built a strong institutional and developmental infrastructure in Korea and Taiwan in the 1930s and 1940s. Of course, the recent growth of China, which did not see the same kind of development under Japanese occupation, suggests that Japanese colonialism was at best just one factor, and others, especially the dynamics of regional economic integration, have been just as important.

It may also be argued that East Asian development represented a new or emergent moment in imperialist ideology when, in response to rising nationalism and intensifying economic competition, the relationship with the colony was re-thought. The colony was to be viewed less as an object of exploitation than as a partner – a dependent partner for sure – that could be economically strengthened through investments and infrastructure-building and mobilized in the global competition for wealth and power. Certainly Hong Kong, the last – and fabulously successful – British colony decolonized in 1997, represents this transformation, as Britain came to see it less as a symbol of empire than a critical piece of its strategy to remain a global power after World War II. The economic development of the Japanese colonial empire also took place principally from the 1930s, after the establishment of the Japanese puppet state of Manchukuo in northeast China signalled an economic strategy of alliance and investment in these dependent states so that they could be more useful to the Japanese military's pursuit of world power.

While we may think of the East Asian case as a sign of possibilities and hope, it is also important to remember that these nations participate in a system that is becoming increasingly volatile, both economically and politically. The late-1990s economic crisis in Asia and the longer-term decline of Japan is a sharp reminder that capitalist competition produces risks and uncertainties that may be even less controllable now than they were in the twentieth century, when several global empires were brought to the ground.

For decolonized nations, we have seen that the Cold War often meant new forms of dependence upon either the dominant capitalist powers or the Soviet Union. Non-alignment in any absolute sense was a chimera. Still, many new nations were able to play off the competition between the two superpowers to some advantage. The relatively restricted power of multinational capital allowed the nation-state to regulate relationships between national society and global society, although this varied from nation to nation. Moreover, domestically, the nation-state form as an unprecedentedly strong interventionist and mobilizational agency was often able to achieve a measure of social justice and development. The higher ideals of justice, morality and equality that emerged in the course of the anti-imperialist movement still played an important role as regulatory or directive goals.

The end of the Cold War and the collapse of the socialist bloc and socialist ideology as a counter-weight to capitalism have produced a different scenario for these nations. They are confronted by a world dominated much more powerfully by multinational corporations, and they complain that these corporations and unfair trading practices in the mature capitalist economies continue to disadvantage their growth and competitiveness. Politically, they are more dependent on the US as hegemon and protector of the nation-state system which shows a dangerous tendency to exempt itself from the authority of the system. While it is arguable that some kind of equilibrium has developed between interdependence and hegemony within the nation-state system, discontent with the system is increasingly expressing itself from the interstices and the spaces between territorially bounded national units. Such movements of discontent, we have seen, are expressed in transnational ideologies with allegiance to the civilizational narratives and goals that were fostered in the encounter of imperialism and nationalism. The era of decolonization may be over, but the pains of that transition have found their way into the new era of globalization.

This volume has been organized into three parts of six chapters each. An introduction to each part discusses the relationship of each chapter with other chapters and with the wider themes of the book itself. Part I, 'In their own words', presents essays by the decolonizing leaders and thinkers. These represent a mixture of well known and relatively obscure pieces which discuss the ideals of the movement, the critique of colonial ideology, and the difficulties encountered in practical mobilization of the people. The chapters in Part II, 'Imperialism and nationalism', by contemporary scholars, discuss the role of imperialism and nationalism in the decolonization movement as global phenomena. The authors ask questions about the emergence of the movement in the changing role and understanding of imperialism and its ideology, such as the 'civilizing mission', about the role of peasant mobilization, ethno-nationalisms, and partitions, and finally, about the new nation-states and neo-imperialism or the imperialism of the 'new world order'. Part III, 'Regions and themes', also contains pieces by contemporary scholars which are thematically related to the rest of the book; but they address these problems from the viewpoint of a particular region. The relationship between decolonization and socialism is viewed from its point of emergence in the Soviet Union; the changing status of the West in the Middle East the tensions between the working-class movement and decolonization in Africa; the gender question in Korea; a comparison of the colonial experiences of East Asia and Vietnam; and the extended nature of decolonization in Vietnam, or the history of the Vietnam war are all discussed in this part.

Note

1   I would like to express my gratitude to Michael Adas, Frederick Cooper and Stein Tønnesson for their comments and advice.

References and further reading

Adas, Michael, Peter N. Stearns and Stuart B. Schwartz (2003) *Turbulent Passage: A Global History of the Twentieth Century*, New York: Longman.

Anderson, Benedict (1991) *Imagined Communities: Reflections on the Origins and Spread of Nationalism*, London: Verso.

Betts, Raymond F. (1998) *Decolonization*, London and New York: Routledge.

Chatterjee, Partha (1993) *The Nation and its Fragments: Colonial and Postcolonial Histories*, Princeton: Princeton University Press.

Duara, Prasenjit (2003) *Sovereignty and Authenticity: Manchukuo and the East Asian Modern*, Lanham: Rowman and Littlefield.

——(2000) 'The discourse of civilization and Pan-Asianism', *Journal of World History*, March.

Mao Zedong (2002) 'On new democracy' [15 January 1940], in Timothy Cheek, *Mao Zedong and China's Revolution: A Brief History with Documents*, New York: Bedford/St Martin's Press.

Marshall, Bruce D. (1973) *The French Colonial Myth and Constitution Making in the Fourth Republic*, New Haven and London: Yale University Press.

Spengler, Oswald (1962) *The Decline of the West*, abridged edn by Helmut Werner (English abridged edn prepared by Arthur Helps from the translation by Charles Francis Atkinson) New York: Alfred A. Knopf.

Weber, Eugen (1976) *Peasants into Frenchmen: The Modernization of Rural France, 1870–1914*, Stanford: Stanford University Press.

Part I

IN THEIR OWN WORDS

We can find the principal themes of the decolonization movement in the writings of these statesmen and intellectuals that span the time from Sun Yat-sen's 1924 lecture to Kwame Nkrumah's piece of 1964. They incorporate the vision of a promised new world as well as the fears of a post-colonial world still dominated by the political, technological and cultural dominance of the West, most evident in the writings of Jalal Al-i Ahmad which re-appeared in 1978 on the eve of the Islamic revolution in Iran. Between these two bookends lie a range of issues and problems. Among them is the cosmopolitanism of their thought which grew out of a belief in an egalitarian socialist future, a sense of solidarity with the oppressed peoples, and a growing sense of confidence in an age-old civilizational tradition. This cosmopolitanism permitted them to oppose Social Darwinism and the Western idea of an imperialist, material civilization.

At the same time, their ideas and actions also reveal a struggle to create a disciplined new nation, modelled, ironically, on the Western nation-state that they opposed. The emphasis in the essays on preserving and building this nationalism in the face of competing interests, loyalties and ideologies – be those communism, tribalism, or ethnic or gender differences – signals the challenge and predicament of these new nations. Their practical goal is to create a political structure capable of surviving and succeeding in a competitive world, but their cosmopolitan aspirations create ambivalence towards this world and their very goal.

Given the historical importance of each of these figures and their essays, I have prepared an introductory sketch of each person which precedes the essay.

* * *

2

SAN MIN CHU I (THE THREE PRINCIPLES OF THE PEOPLE)

Selections from Lecture 4[1]

Sun Yat-sen

Although Sun Yat-sen (1866–1925) never got the chance to occupy the presidency of the Chinese Republic (1912–49; he served as the provisional president for a few weeks), he is widely known as the 'father of modern China'. Many of his ideas are contained in his lectures on the 'Three principles of the people' from which we have culled the present selection. While Sun developed a devastating critique of Western imperialism in China, he was also keenly interested – perhaps more so than the other leaders presented here – in understanding how the West came to gain such enormous power in the world. Partly because of the prevalence of Social Darwinist ideas in East Asia from the late nineteenth century until the end of World War I, and partly because he represented a somewhat earlier generation of leaders who took this ideology more seriously, Sun saw the plight of the colonized and semi-colonized peoples of Asia and Africa in Social Darwinist terms. His lecture blends three kinds of language, that of Social Darwinism, the idea of a morally superior Chinese civilization, and the emergent idealism of the anti-imperialist movement. Like Nehru, Sun too emphasizes cosmopolitanism that grows out of nationalism.

* Sun Yat-sen San Min Chu I (The Three Principles of the People) Trans. Frank W Price. Shanghai, China Committee, Institute of Pacific Relations 1927. Selections from Lecture 4, pp 76-100.

* * *

The population of the world today is approximately a billion and a half. One fourth of this number live in China, which means that one out of every four persons in the world is a Chinese. The total population of the white races of Europe also amounts to 400 million. The white division of mankind, which is now the most flourishing, includes four races: in central and northern Europe, the Teutons, who have founded many states, the largest of which is Germany, others being Austria, Sweden, Norway, Holland, and Denmark; in eastern Europe, the Slavs, who also have founded a number of states, the largest being Russia, and, after the European War, the new countries of Czechoslovakia and Yugoslavia; in western Europe, the Saxons or Anglo-Saxons, who have founded two large states – England and the United States of America; in southern Europe, the Latins, who have founded several states, the largest being France, Italy, Spain, and Portugal, and who have migrated to South America forming states there just as the Anglo-Saxons migrated to North America and built up Canada and the United States. The white peoples of Europe, now numbering only 400 million persons, are divided into four great stocks which have established many states. Because the national spirit of the white race was highly developed, when they had filled up the European continent they expanded to North and South America in the Western Hemisphere and to Africa and Australia in the southern and eastern parts of the Eastern Hemisphere.

The Anglo-Saxons at present occupy more space on the globe than any other race. Although this race originated in Europe, the only European soil it holds are the British Isles: England, Scotland, and Ireland, which occupy about the same position in the Atlantic that Japan occupies in the Pacific. The Anglo-Saxons have extended their territory westward to North America, eastward to Australia and New Zealand, and southward to Africa until they possess more land and are wealthier and stronger than any other race. Before the European War the Teutons and the Slavs were the strongest races; moreover, by reason of the sagacity and ability of the Teutonic peoples, Germany was able to unite more than twenty small states into a great German confederation. At the beginning an agricultural nation, it developed into an industrial nation and through industrial prosperity its army and navy became exceedingly powerful.

Before the European War all the European nations had been poisoned by imperialism. What is imperialism? It is the policy of aggression against other countries by means of political force, or, in the Chinese phrase, 'long-range aggression'. As all the peoples of Europe were imbued with this policy, wars were continually breaking out; almost every decade had at least one small war and each century one big war. The greatest of all was the recent European War, which may be called the World War because it finally involved the whole world and pulled every nation and peoples into its vortex. The causes of the European War were, first, the rivalry between the Saxon and Teutonic races for control of the sea. Germany in her rise to greatness had developed her navy until she was the second sea power in the world; Great Britain wanted her own navy to rule the seas so she tried to destroy Germany, whose sea power was next to hers. From this struggle for first place on the sea came the war.

A second cause was each nation's struggle for more territory. In eastern Europe there is a weak state called Turkey. For the past hundred years the people of the world have called it the 'sick man of Europe'. Because the government was unenlightened and the sultan was despotic, it became extremely helpless and the European nations wanted to partition it. Because the Turkish question had not been solved for a century and every nation of Europe was trying to solve it, war resulted. The first cause of the European War, then, was the struggle between white races for supremacy; the second cause was the effort to solve critical world problems. If Germany had won the war, she would have held the supreme power on the sea after the war and Great Britain would have lost all her territory, breaking into pieces like the old Roman Empire. But the result of the war was defeat for Germany and the failure of her imperialistic designs.

The recent European War was the most dreadful war in the history of the world. Forty to fifty million men were under arms for a period of four years, and near the end of the war they still could not be divided into conquerors and vanquished.

[...]

During the war there was a great phrase, used by President Wilson and warmly received everywhere – 'self-determination of peoples'. Because Germany was striving by military force to crush the peoples of the European Entente, Wilson proposed destroying Germany's power and giving autonomy henceforth to the weaker and smaller peoples. His idea met a worldwide welcome, and although the common people of India still opposed Great Britain, their destroyer, yet many small peoples, when they heard Wilson say that the war was for the freedom of the weak and small peoples, gladly gave aid to Great Britain. Although Annam had been subjugated by France and the common people hated the French tyranny, yet during the war they still helped France to fight, also because they had heard of Wilson's just proposition. And the reason why other small peoples of Europe, such as Poland, Czechoslovakia and Romania, all enlisted on the side of the Entente against the Allied Powers, was because of the self-determination principle enunciated by President Wilson. China, too, under the inspiration of the United States, entered the war; although she sent no armies, yet she did contribute hundreds of thousands of labourers to dig trenches and to work behind the lines. As a result of the noble theme propounded by the Entente, all the oppressed peoples of Europe and of Asia finally joined together to help them in their struggle against the Allied Powers. At the same time Wilson proposed, to guard the future peace of the world, fourteen points, of which the most important was that each people should have the right of self-determination. When victory and defeat still hung in the balance, England and France heartily endorsed these points, but when victory was won and the Peace Conference was opened, England, France, and Italy realized that Wilson's proposal of freedom for nations conflicted too seriously with the interests of imperialism; and so, during the conference, they used all kinds of methods to explain away Wilson's principles. The result was a peace treaty with most unjust terms; the weaker, smaller nations not only did not secure self-determination and freedom but found themselves under an oppression more terrible than before. This shows that the strong states and the powerful races have already forced possession of the globe and that the rights and privileges of other states and nations are monopolized by them. Hoping to make themselves forever secure in their exclusive position and to prevent the smaller and weaker peoples from again reviving, they sing praises to cosmopolitanism, saying that nationalism is too narrow; really their espousal of internationalism is but imperialism and aggression in another guise.

But Wilson's proposals, once set forth, could not be recalled; each one of the weaker, smaller nations who had helped the Entente to defeat the Allied Powers and had hoped to attain freedom as a fruit of the victory was doomed to bitter disappointment by the results of the Peace Conference. Then Annam, Burma, Java, India, the Malay Archipelago, Turkey, Persia, Afghanistan, Egypt, and the scores of weak nations in Europe, were stirred with a great, new consciousness; they saw how completely they had been deceived by the Great Powers' advocacy of self-determination, and began independently and separately to carry out the principle of the 'self-determination of peoples'.

Many years of fierce warfare had not been able to destroy imperialism because this war was a conflict of imperialisms between states, not a struggle between savagery and civilization or between Might and Right. So the effect of the war was merely the overthrow of one imperialism by another imperialism; what survived was still imperialism. But from the war there was unconsciously born in the heart of mankind a great hope – the Russian Revolution. The Russian Revolution had begun much earlier, as far back as 1905, but had not accomplished its purpose. Now during the European War the efforts of the revolutionists were crowned with success. The reason for the outbreak of revolution again at this time was the great awakening of the people as a result of their war experience. Russia was formerly one of the Entente nations; when the Entente Powers were fighting Germany, Russia sent over 10 million soldiers into the field – not a puny force. Without Russia's part in the war, the

Entente's line on the Western Front would long before have been smashed by Germany; because Russia was embarrassing the Germans on the Eastern Front, the Entente Powers were able to break even with Germany for two or three years and finally turn defeat into victory. Just halfway through the war, Russia began to reflect, and she realized that in helping the Entente to fight Germany she was merely helping several brute forces to fight one brute force and that no good results would come of it in the end. A group of soldiers and citizens awoke, broke away from the Entente, and concluded a separate peace with Germany.

[...]

Of the billion and a half people in the world, the most powerful are the 400 million whites on the European and American continents; from this base the white races have started out to swallow up other races. The American red aborigines are gone, the African blacks will soon be exterminated, the brown race of India is in the process of dissolution, the yellow races of Asia are now being subjected to the white man's oppression and may, before long, be wiped out.

But the 150 million Russians, when their revolution succeeded, broke with the other white races and condemned the white man's imperialistic behaviour; now they are thinking of throwing in their lot with the weaker, smaller peoples of Asia in a struggle against the tyrannical races. So only 250 million of the tyrannical races are left, but they are still trying by inhuman methods and military force to subjugate the other 1,250 million. So hereafter mankind will be divided into two camps: on one side will be the 1,250 million; on the other side, the 250 million.

[...]

Now we want to revive China's lost nationalism and use the strength of our 400 millions to fight for mankind against injustice; this is our divine mission. The Powers are afraid that we will have such thoughts and are setting forth a specious doctrine. They are now advocating cosmopolitanism to inflame us, declaring that, as the civilization of the world advances and as mankind's vision enlarges, nationalism becomes too narrow, unsuited to the present age, and hence that we should espouse cosmopolitanism. In recent years some of China's youth, devotees of the new culture, have been opposing nationalism, led astray by this doctrine. But it is not a doctrine which wronged races should talk about. We, the wronged races, must first recover our position of national freedom and equality before we are fit to discuss cosmopolitanism. The illustration I used in my last lecture of the coolie who won first prize in the lottery has already made this very clear. The lottery ticket represents cosmopolitanism; the bamboo pole, nationalism. The coolie, on winning first prize, immediately threw away his pole just as we, fooled by the promises of cosmopolitanism, have discarded our nationalism. We must understand that cosmopolitanism grows out of nationalism; if we want to extend cosmopolitanism we must first establish strongly our own nationalism. If nationalism cannot become strong, cosmopolitanism certainly cannot prosper. Thus we see that cosmopolitanism is hidden in the heart of nationalism just as the ticket was hidden inside the bamboo pole; if we discard nationalism and go and talk cosmopolitanism we are just like the coolie who threw his bamboo pole into the sea.

We put the cart before the horse. I said before that our position is not equal to that of the Annamese or the Koreans; they are subject peoples and slaves while we cannot even be called slaves. Yet we discourse about cosmopolitanism and say that we do not need nationalism. Gentlemen, is this reasonable?

According to history, our 400 millions of Chinese have also come down the road of imperialism. Our forefathers constantly employed political force to encroach upon weaker and smaller nations; but economic force in those days was not a serious thing, so we were not guilty of economic oppression of other peoples. Then compare China's culture with Europe's ancient culture. The Golden Age of European culture was in the time of Greece and Rome, yet Rome at the height of its power was contemporaneous with as late a dynasty in China as the Han. At that time China's political thinking was very profound; many orators were earnestly opposing imperialism and much anti-imperialistic literature was produced, the most famous being 'Discussions on abandoning the Pearl Cliffs'. Such writings opposed China's efforts to expand her territory and her struggle over land with the southern barbarians, which shows that as early as the Han dynasty, China already discouraged war against outsiders and had developed the peace idea to broad proportions.

In the Sung dynasty, China was not only ceasing to encroach upon other peoples, but she was even being herself invaded by foreigners. The Sung dynasty was overthrown by the Mongols and the nation did not again revive until the Ming dynasty. After this restoration, China became much less aggressive. However, many small states in the South China Sea wanted to bring tribute and to adopt Chinese culture, giving voluntary adherence because of their admiration for our culture and not because of military pressure from China. The small countries in the Malay Archipelago and the South China Sea considered it a great honour for China to annex them and receive their tribute; China's refusal would have brought them disgrace.

The strongest powers in the world today have not succeeded in calling forth praise like this. Take America's treatment of the Philippines: allowing the Filipinos to organize their own Assembly and to have a share in the government; allowing them to appoint delegates to the Congress in Washington; not only not requiring a money tribute but subsidizing their main items of expenditure, building roads, and providing education for them. Such benevolent and magnanimous treatment can be considered the limit of generosity, yet the Filipinos even now do not consider it an honour to be Americanized and are every day asking for independence. Or take Nepal in India. The people of Nepal are called Gurkhalis, a very brave and warlike race; although England has conquered India she still fears the Gurkhalis. She treats them very generously, sending them money each year, just as the Sung dynasty in China, fearing the Kin Tartars, sent them funds, with this difference, that what the Sungs gave to the Kin Tartars was called a tribute, while England's gift to the Gurkhalis is probably called a gratuity. But up to the first year of our Republic, the Gurkhalis were still bringing their tribute to China, which proves that the small nations around China have not yet lost their hope for or faith in her.

[...]

Gentlemen, you know that revolution is naturally a thing of bloodshed. Thus, in the revolutions of Toqang and Wu, everyone said that the rebels were 'obedient to Heaven and well-pleasing to men', but as to the fighting it was said that they experienced 'battle staves floating on rivers of blood'. In the Revolution of 1911, when we overthrew the Manchus, how much blood was spilled? The reason for the small bloodshed then was the Chinese people's love of peace, an outstanding quality of the Chinese character. The Chinese are really the greatest lovers of peace in the world. I have constantly urged the people of the world to follow China's example; now the Slavic people of Russia are keeping pace with us and espousing the cause of peace after us, and their 100 millions want to cooperate with us.

Our 400 millions are not only a most peaceful but also a most civilized race. The new cultures which have flourished of late in Europe and which are called anarchism and communism are old things in China. For instance, Hwang-Lao's[2] political philosophy is really anarchism, and what is Lieh-tze's[3] dream of the land of the Hua-hsü people who lived in a natural state without ruler or laws but another theory of anarchism? Modern youths in China, who have not studied carefully these old Chinese theories, think that their ideas are the newest things in existence, unaware that, though they may be new in Europe, they are thousands of years old here. What Russia has been putting into practice is not pure communism but Marxism; Marxism is not real communism. What Proudhon and Bakunin advocated is the only real communism. Communism in other countries is still in the stage of discussion; it has not been fully tried out anywhere. But it was applied in China in the time of Hung Hsiu-chuan; his economic system was the real thing in communism and not mere theory.

European superiority to China is not in political philosophy but altogether in the field of material civilization. With the progress of European material civilization, all the daily provisions for clothing, food, housing and communication have become extremely convenient and timesaving, and the weapons of war – poison, gas and such – have become extraordinarily perfected and deadly. All these new inventions and weapons have come since the development of science. It was after the seventeenth and eighteenth centuries when Bacon, Newton and other great scholars advocated the use of observation, experiment and investigation of all things, that science came into being. So when we speak of Europe's scientific progress and of the advance of European material civilization, we are talking about something which has only 200 years' history. A few hundred years ago, Europe could not compare with China, so now if we want to learn from Europe we should learn what we ourselves lack – science – but not political philosophy. Europeans are still looking to China for the fundamentals of political philosophy. You all know that the best scholarship today is found in Germany. Yet German scholars are studying Chinese philosophy and even Indian Buddhist principles to supplement their partial conceptions of science. Cosmopolitanism has just flowered in Europe during this generation, but it was talked of 2,000 years ago in China. Europeans cannot yet discern our ancient civilization, yet many of our race have imagined a political world civilization; and as for international morality, our 400 millions have been devoted to the principle of world peace. But because of the loss of our nationalism, our ancient morality and civilization have not been able to manifest themselves and are now even declining.

The cosmopolitanism which Europeans are talking about today is really a principle supported by force without justice. The English expression 'might is right' means that fighting for acquisition is just. The Chinese mind has never regarded acquisition by war as right; it considers aggressive warfare barbarous. This pacifist morality is the true spirit of cosmopolitanism. Upon what foundation can we defend and build up this spirit? – Upon nationalism. Russia's 150 millions are the foundation of Europe's cosmopolitanism, and China's 400 millions are the foundation of Asia's cosmopolitanism. As a foundation is essential to expansion, so we must talk nationalism first if we want to talk cosmopolitanism. 'Those desiring to pacify the world must first govern their own state'. Let us revive our lost nationalism and make it shine with greater splendour, then we will have some ground for discussing internationalism.

17 February 1924

Notes

1   Sun Yat-sen (1927) *San Min Chu I* (The Three Principles of the People), trans. Frank W. Price, Shanghai: China Committee, Institute of Pacific Relations. Selections from Lecture 4, 76–100.
2   Hwangti and Laotze.
3   The name of a philosopher in the Chow dynasty.

3

THE PATH THAT LED ME TO LENINISM[1]

Ho Chi Minh

The short piece by Ho Chi Minh (1890–1969), Vietnamese nationalist leader and President of North Vietnam from 1954–69, reveals the influence of Parisian intellectual life on his thinking. It tracks his development from patriotism to socialism and communism and the manner in which he saw these ideologies as quite inseparable. Ho's views speak to the debates that raged in the Comintern (abbreviation of the Communist International, the name given to the Third International founded by Lenin in 1919) which are discussed by Ronald Suny in Chapter 14 of this volume. A description of Ho Chi Minh's role in the Vietnamese struggle against the French, and subsequently against the US-backed governments in the south, can be found in Stein Tønneson's essay, Chapter 18 of this volume.

* * *

After World War I, I made my living in Paris, now as a re-toucher at a photographer's, now as a painter of 'Chinese antiquities' (made in France!). I used to distribute leaflets denouncing the crimes committed by the French colonists in Vietnam.

At that time, I supported the October Revolution only instinctively, not yet grasping all its historic importance. I loved and admired Lenin because he was a great patriot who liberated his compatriots; until then, I had read none of his books.

The reason for my joining the French Socialist Party was that these 'ladies and gentlemen' – as I called my comrades at that moment – had shown their sympathy towards me, towards the struggle of the oppressed peoples. But I understood neither what was a party, a trade union, nor what was socialism nor communism.

Heated discussions were then taking place in the branches of the Socialist Party about the question whether the Socialist Party should remain in the Second International: should a Two and a Half International be founded or should the Socialist Party join Lenin's Third International? I attended the meetings regularly, twice or thrice a week, and attentively listened to the discussion. First, I could not understand thoroughly. Why were the discussions so heated? Either with the Second, Two and a Half or Third International, the revolution could be waged. What was the use of arguing? As for the First International, what had become of it?

What I wanted most to know – and this precisely was not debated in the meetings – was: which International sides with the peoples of colonial countries?

I raised this question – the most important in my opinion – in a meeting. Some comrades answered: It is the Third, not the Second International. And a comrade gave me Lenin's 'Thesis on the national and colonial questions' published by l'Humanité to read.

There were political terms difficult to understand in this thesis. But by dint of reading it again and again, finally I could grasp the main part of it. What emotion, enthusiasm, clear-sightedness and confidence it instilled into me! I wept for joy. Though sitting alone in my room, I shouted out aloud as if addressing large crowds: 'Dear martyrs, compatriots! This is what we need, this is the path to our liberation!'.

After that I had entire confidence in Lenin, in the Third International.

Formerly, during the meetings of the Party branch, I only listened to the discussion; I had a vague belief that all the speakers were logical, and could not differentiate as to who was right and who was wrong. But, from then on, I also plunged into the debates and discussed with fervour. Though I still lacked French words to express all my thoughts, I smashed the allegations attacking Lenin and the Third International with no less vigour. My only argument was: 'If you do not condemn colonialism, if you do not side with the colonial people, what kind of revolution are you waging?'.

Not only did I take part in the meetings of my own Party branch, but I also went to other Party branches to lay down 'my position'. Comrades Marcel Cachin, Vaillant Couturier, Monmousseau and many others helped me to broaden my knowledge. Finally, at the Tours Congress, I voted with them for our joining the Third International.

At first, patriotism, not yet communism, led me to have confidence in Lenin, in the Third International. Step by step, along the struggle, by studying Marxism-Leninism parallel with participation in practical activities, I gradually came upon the fact that only socialism and communism can liberate the oppressed nations and the working people throughout the world from slavery.

There is a legend, in our country as well as in China, of the miraculous 'Book of the wise'. When facing great difficulties, one opens it and finds a way out. Leninism is not only a miraculous 'Book of the wise', a compass for us Vietnamese revolutionaries and people; it is also the radiant sun illuminating our path to final victory, to socialism and communism.

Note

1   Ho Chi-minh, 'The path that led me to Leninism' [April 1960], in Ho Chi-minh (1969) *Selected Articles and Speeches*, ed. with introduction by Jack Woddis, New York: International Publishers, 156–8.

4

THE IMPORTANCE OF THE NATIONAL IDEA

Changes necessary in India[1]

Jawaharlal Nehru

Jawaharlal Nehru (1889–1964) was, together with Mahatma Gandhi, the most important leader of the Indian independence movement. He served as prime minister of India from independence in 1947 until his death. He was strongly influenced by socialist ideas and sought to develop India on a 'socialist pattern of society', although for much of the rest of the twentieth century, India remained a highly controlled capitalist economy popularly known as the 'license raj'. The extract from The Discovery of India (1946) included here reveals his ideas about the relationship between socialism, nationalism and the indigenous culture. While he recognizes the staying power of nationalism over socialism, he is also mindful that the experience of socialism makes nationalism more progressive and international, enabling people to become 'citizens of this wide and fascinating world'. Note also his admiration of China which was part of his commitment to internationalism; this admiration was sorely tested during the Sino-Indian border conflict in 1962.

* * *

A blind reverence for the past is bad and so also is a contempt for it, for no future can he founded on either of these. The present and the future inevitably grow out of the past and bear its stamp, and to forget this is to build without foundations and to cut off the roots of national growth. It is to ignore one of the most powerful forces that influence people. Nationalism is essentially a group memory of past achievements, traditions and experiences, and nationalism is stronger today than it has ever been. Many people thought that nationalism had had its day and must inevitably give place to the ever-growing international tendencies of the modern world. Socialism with its proletarian background derided national culture as something tied up with a decaying middle class. Capitalism itself became progressively international with its cartels and combines, and overflowed national boundaries. Trade and commerce, easy communications and rapid transport, the radio and cinema, all helped to create an international atmosphere and to produce the delusion that nationalism was doomed.

Yet whenever a crisis has arisen nationalism has emerged again and dominated the scene, and people have sought comfort and strength in their old traditions. One of the remarkable developments of the present age has been the rediscovery of the past and of the nation. This going back to national traditions has been most marked in the ranks of labour and the proletarian elements, who were supposed to be the foremost champions of international action. War or similar crisis dissolves their internationalism and they become subject to nationalist hates and fears even more than other groups. The most striking example of this is the recent development of the Soviet Union. Without giving up in any way its essential social and economic structure, it has become more nationalist-minded, and the appeal of the fatherland is now much greater than the appeal of the international proletariat. Famous figures in national history have again been revived and have become heroes of the Soviet people. The inspiring record of the Soviet people in this war, the strength and unity they have shown, are no doubt due to a social and economic structure which has resulted in social advances on a wide front, on planned production and consumption, on the development of science and its functions, and on the release of a vast quantity of new talent and capacity for leadership, as also on brilliant leadership. But it may also be partly due to a revival of national memories and traditions and a new awareness of the past, of which the present was felt to be a continuation. It would be wrong to imagine that this nationalist outlook of Russia is just a reversion to old-style nationalism. It is certainly not that. The tremendous experiences of the revolution and all that followed it cannot be forgotten, and the changes that resulted from it in social structure and mental adjustment must remain. That social structure leads inevitably to a certain international outlook. Nevertheless nationalism has reappeared in such a way as to fit in with the new environment and add to the strength of the people.

It is instructive to compare the development of the Soviet state with the varying fortunes of the communist parties in other countries. There was the first flush of enthusiasm among many people in all countries, and especially in proletarian ranks, soon after the Soviet revolution. Out of this grew communist groups and parties. Then conflicts arose between these groups and national labour parties. During the Soviet five-year plans there was another wave of interest and enthusiasm, and this probably affected middle-class intellectuals even more than labour. Again there was a reaction at the time of the purges in the Soviet Union. In some countries communist parties were suppressed, in others they made progress. But almost everywhere they came into conflict with organized national labour. Partly this was due to the conservatism of labour, but more so to a feeling that the Communist Party represented a foreign group and that they took their policies from Russia. The inherent nationalism of labour came in the way of its accepting the cooperation of the Communist Party even when many were favourably inclined towards communism. The many changes in Soviet policy, which could be understood in relation to Russia, became totally incomprehensible as policies favoured by communist parties elsewhere. They could only be understood on the basis that what may be good for Russia must necessarily be good for the rest of the world. These communist parties, though they consisted of some able and very earnest men and women, lost contact with the nationalist sentiments of the people and weakened accordingly. While the Soviet Union was forging new links with national tradition, the communist parties of other countries were drifting further away from it.

I cannot speak with much knowledge of what happened elsewhere, but I know that in India the Communist Party is completely divorced from, and is ignorant of, the national traditions that fill the minds of the people. It believes that communism necessarily implies a contempt for the past. So far as it is concerned, the history of the world began in November 1917, and everything that preceded this was preparatory and leading up to it. Normally speaking, in a country like India with large numbers of people on the verge of starvation and the economic structure cracking up, communism should have a wide appeal. In a sense there is that vague appeal, but the Communist Party cannot take advantage of it because it has cut itself off from the springs of national sentiment and speaks in a language which finds no echo in the hearts of the people. It remains an energetic, but small group, with no real roots.

It is not only the Communist Party in India that has failed in this respect. There are others who talk glibly of modernism and modern spirit and the essence of Western culture, and are at the same time ignorant of their own culture. Unlike the communists, they have no ideal that moves them and no driving force that carries them forward. They take the external forms and outer trappings of the West (and often some of the less desirable features), and imagine that they are in the vanguard of an advancing civilization. Naive and shallow and yet full of their own conceits, they live, chiefly in a few large cities, an artificial life which has no living contacts with the culture of the East or of the West.

National progress can, therefore, neither lie in a repetition of the past nor in its denial. New patterns must inevitably be adopted but they must be integrated with the old. Sometimes the new, though very different, appears in terms of pre-existing patterns, and thus creates a feeling of a continuous development from the past, a link in the long chain of the history of the race. Indian history is a striking record of changes introduced in this way, a continuous adaptation of old ideas to a changing environment, of old patterns to new. Because of this there is no sense of cultural break in it and there is that continuity, in spite of repeated change, from the far distant days of Mohenjodaro to our own age. There was a reverence for the past and for traditional forms, but there was also a freedom and flexibility of the mind and a tolerance of the spirit. So while forms often remained, the inner content continued to change. In no other way could that society have survived for thousands of years. Only a living and growing mind could overcome the rigidity of traditional forms, only those forms could give it continuity and stability.

Yet this balance may become precarious and one aspect may overshadow, and to some extent, suppress this other. In India there was an extraordinary freedom of the mind allied to certain rigid social forms. These forms ultimately influenced the freedom of the mind and made it in practice, if not in theory, more rigid and limited. In Western Europe there was no such freedom of the mind and there was also much less rigidity in social forms. Europe had a long struggle for the freedom of the mind and, as a consequence, social forms also changed.

In China the flexibility of the mind was even greater than in India, and for all her love of, and attachment to, tradition, that mind never lost its flexibility and essential tolerance. Tradition sometimes delayed changes but that mind was not afraid of change, though it retained the old patterns. Even more than in India, Chinese society built up a balance and an equilibrium which survived through many changes for thousands of years. Perhaps one of the great advantages that China has had over other countries is her entire freedom from dogma, from the narrow and limited religious outlook, and her reliance on reason and common sense. No other country has based its culture less on religion and more on morality and ethics and a deep understanding of the variety of human life.

In India, because of the recognized freedom of the mind, howsoever limited in practice, new ideas are not shut out. They are considered and can he accepted far more than in countries which have a more rigid and dogmatic outlook on life. The essential ideals of Indian culture are broad-based and can be adapted to almost any environment. The bitter conflict between science and religion which shook up Europe in the nineteenth century would have no reality in India, nor would change based on the applications of science bring any conflict with those ideals. Undoubtedly such changes would stir up, as they are stirring up, the mind of India, but instead of combating them or rejecting them it would rationalize them from its own ideological point of view and fit them into its mental framework. It is probable that in this process many vital changes may be introduced to the old outlook, but they will not be superimposed from outside and will seem rather to grow naturally from the cultural back-ground of the people. This is more difficult today than it might have been, because of the long period of arrested growth and the urgent necessity for big and qualitative changes.

Conflict, however, there will be, with much of the superstructure that has grown up round those basic ideals and which exist and stifles us today. That superstructure will inevitably have to go, because much of it is bad in itself and is contrary to the spirit of the age. Those who seek to retain it do an ill service to the basic ideals of Indian culture, for they mix up the good and the bad and thus endanger the former. It is no easy matter to separate the two or draw a hard and fast line between them, and here opinions will differ widely. But it is not necessary to draw any such theoretical and logical line; the logic of changing life and the march of events will gradually draw that line for us. Every kind of development – technological or philosophical – necessitates contact with life itself, with social needs, with the living movements of the world. Lack of this contact leads to stagnation and loss of vitality and creativeness. But if we maintain these contacts and are receptive to them, we shall adapt ourselves to the curve of life without losing the essential characteristic which we have valued.

Our approach to knowledge in the past was a synthetic one, but limited to India. That limitation continued and the synthetic approach gave place gradually to a more analytical one. We have now to lay greater stress on the synthetic aspect and make the whole world our field of study. This emphasis on synthesis is indeed necessary for every nation and individual if they are to grow out of the narrow grooves of thought and action in which most people have lived for so long. The develop-ment of science and its applications have made this possible for us, and yet the very excess of new knowledge has added to its difficulty. Specialization has led to a narrowing of individual life in a particular groove, and man's labour in industry is often confined to some infinites-imal part of the whole product. Specialization in knowledge and work will have to continue, but it seems more essential than ever that a synthetic view of human life and man's adventure through the ages should be encouraged. This view will have to take into consideration the past and time present, and include in its scope all countries and peoples. In this way perhaps we might develop, in addition to our own national backgrounds and cultures, an appreciation of others and a capacity to understand and cooperate with the peoples of other countries. Thus also we might succeed to some extent in building up integrated personalities instead of the lop-sided individuals of today. We might become, in Plato's words, 'spectators of all time and all being', drawing sustenance from the rich treasures that humanity has accumulated, adding to them, and applying them in building for the future.

It is a curious and significant fact that, in spite of all modern scientific progress and talk of internationalism, racialism and other separating factors are at least as much in evidence today, if not more so, than at any previous time in history. There is something lacking in all this progress, which can neither produce harmony between nations nor within the spirit of man. Perhaps more synthesis and a little humility towards the wisdom of the past, which, after all, is the accumulated experience of the human race, would help us to gain a new perspective and greater harmony. That is especially needed by those peoples who live a fevered life in the present only and have almost forgotten the past. But for countries like India a different emphasis is necessary, for we have too much of the past about us and have ignored the present. We have to get rid of that narrowing religious outlook, that obsession with the supernatural and metaphysical speculations, that loosening of the mind's discipline in religious ceremonial and mystical emotionalism, which come in the way of our understanding ourselves and the world. We have to come to grips with the present, this life, this world, this nature which surrounds us in its infinite variety. Some Hindus talk of going back to the Vedas; some Moslems dream of an Islamic theocracy. Idle fancies, for there is no going back to the past; there is no turning back even if this was thought desirable. There is only one-way traffic in Time.

India must therefore lessen her religiosity and turn to science. She must get rid of the exclusiveness in thought and social habit which has become like a prison to her, stunting her spirit and preventing growth. The idea of ceremonial purity has erected barriers against social intercourse and narrowed the sphere of social action. The day-to-day religion of the orthodox Hindu is more concerned with what to eat and what not to eat, who to eat with and from whom to keep away, than with spiritual values. The rules and regulations of the kitchen dominate his social life. The Moslem is fortunately free from these inhibitions, but he has his own narrow codes and ceremonials, a routine which he rigorously follows, forgetting the lesson of brotherhood which his religion taught him. His view of life is, perhaps, even more limited and sterile than the Hindu view, though the average Hindu today is a poor representative of the latter view, for he has lost that traditional freedom of thought and the background that enriches life in many ways.

Caste is the symbol and embodiment of this exclusiveness among the Hindus. It is sometimes said that the basic idea of caste might remain, but its subsequent harmful development and ramifications should go; that it should not depend on birth but on merit. This approach is irrelevant and merely confuses the issue. In a historical context a study of the growth of caste has some value, but we cannot obviously go back to the period when caste began; in the social organization of today it has no place left. If merit is the only criterion and opportunity is thrown open to everybody, then caste loses all its present-day distinguishing features and, in fact, ends. Caste has in the past not only led to the suppression of certain groups, but to a separation of theoretical and scholastic learning from craftsmanship, and a divorce of philosophy from actual life and its problems. It was an aristocratic approach based on traditionalism. This outlook has to change completely, for it is wholly opposed to modern conditions and the democratic ideal. The functional organization of social groups in India may continue, but even that will undergo a vast change as the nature of modern industry creates new functions and puts an end to many old ones. The tendency today everywhere is towards a functional organization of society, and the concept of abstract rights is giving place to that of functions. This is in harmony with the old Indian ideal.

The spirit of the age is in favour of equality, though practice denies it almost everywhere. We have got rid of slavery in the narrow sense of the word, that a man can be the property of another. But a new slavery, in some ways worse than the old, has taken its place all over the world. In the name of individual freedom, political and economic systems exploit human beings and treat them as commodities. And again, though an individual cannot be the property of another, a country and a nation can still be the property of another nation, and thus group slavery is tolerated. Racialism also is a distinguishing feature of our times, and we have not only master nations but also master races.

Yet the spirit of the age will triumph. In India, at any rate, we must aim at equality. That does not and cannot mean that everybody is physically or intellectually or spiritually equal or can be made so. But it does mean equal opportunities for all and no political, economic or social barrier in the way of any individual or group. It means a faith in humanity and a belief that there is no race or group that cannot advance and make good in its own way, given the chance to do so. It means a realization of the fact that the backwardness or degradation of any group is not due to inherent failings in it, but principally to lack of opportunities and long suppression by other groups. It should mean an understanding of the modern world wherein real progress and advance, whether national or international, have become very much a joint affair and a backward group pulls back others. Therefore, not only must equal opportunities he given to all, but special opportunities for educational, economic and cultural growth must be given to backward groups so as to enable them to catch up to those who are ahead of them. Any such attempt to open the doors of opportunity to all in India will release enormous energy and ability and transform the country with amazing speed.

If the spirit of the age demands equality, it must necessarily also demand an economic system which fits in with it and encourages it. The present colonial system in India is the very antithesis of it. Absolutism is not only based on inequality but must perpetuate it in every sphere of life. It suppresses the creative and regenerative forces of a nation, bottles up talent and capacity, and discourages the spirit of responsibility. Those who have to suffer under it, lose their sense of dignity and self-reliance. The problems of India, complicated as they seem, are essentially due to an attempt to advance while preserving the political and economic structure more or less intact. Political advance is made subject to the preservation of this structure and existing vested interests. The two are incompatible.

Political change there must be, but economic change is equally necessary. That change will have to be in the direction of a democratically planned collectivism. 'The choice', says R. H. Tawney, 'is not between competition and monopoly, but between monopoly which is irresponsible and private and a monopoly which is responsible and public'. Public monopolies are growing even in capitalist states and they will continue to grow. The conflict between the idea underlying them and private monopoly will continue till the latter is liquidated. A democratic collectivism need not mean an abolition of private property, but it will mean the public ownership of the basic and major industries. It will mean the cooperative or collective control of the land. In India especially it will be necessary to have, in addition to the big industries, cooperatively controlled small and village industries. Such a system of democratic collectivism will need careful and continuous planning and adaptation to the changing needs of the people. The aim should be the expansion of the productive capacity of the nation in every possible way, at the same time absorbing all the labour power of the nation in some activity or other and preventing unemployment. As far as possible there should be freedom to choose one's occupation. An equalization of income will not result from all this, but there will be far more equitable sharing and a progressive tendency towards equalization. In any event, the vast differences that exist today will disappear completely, and class distinctions, which are essentially based on differences in income, will begin to fade out.

Such a change would mean an upsetting of the present-day acquisitive society based primarily on the profit motive. The profit motive may still continue to some extent but it will not be the dominating urge, nor will it have the same scope as it has today. It would be absurd to say that the profit motive does not appeal to the average Indian, but it is nevertheless true that there is no such admiration for it in India as there is in the West. The possessor of money may be envied but he is not particularly respected or admired. Respect and admiration still go to the man or woman who is considered good and wise, and especially to those who sacrifice themselves or what they possess for the public good. The Indian outlook, even of the masses, has never approved of the spirit of acquisitiveness.

Collectivism involves communal undertakings and cooperative effort. This again is fully in harmony with old Indian social conceptions which were all based on the idea of the group. The decay of the group system under British rule, and especially of the self-governing village, has caused deep injury to the Indian masses, even more psychological than economic. Nothing positive came in its place, and they lost their spirit of independence, their sense of responsibility, and their capacity to cooperate together for common purposes. The village, which used to be an organic and vital unit, became progressively a derelict area, just a collection of mud huts and odd individuals. But still the village holds together by some invisible link and old memories revive. It should be easily possible to take advantage of these age-long traditions and to build up communal and cooperative concerns in the land and in small industry. The village can no longer be a self-contained economic unit (though it may often be intimately connected with a collective or cooperative farm), but it can very well be a governmental and electoral unit, each such unit functioning as a self-governing community within the larger political framework, and looking after the essential needs of the village. If it is treated to some extent as an electoral unit, this will simplify provincial and all-India elections considerably by reducing the number of direct electors. The village council, itself chosen by all the adult men and women of the village, could form these electors for the bigger elections. Indirect elections may have some disadvantages but, having regard to the background in India, I feel sure that the village should he treated as a unit. This will give a truer and more responsible representation.

In addition to this territorial representation, there should also be direct representation of the collectives and cooperatives on the land and in industry. Thus the democratic organization of the state will consist of both functional and territorial representatives, and will be based on local autonomy. Some such arrangement will be completely in harmony with India's past as well as with her present requirements. There will be no sense of break (except with the conditions created by British rule) and the mass mind will accept it as a continuation of the past which it still remembers and cherishes.

Such a development in India would be in tune with political and economic internationalism. It would breed no conflicts with other nations and would be a powerful factor for peace in Asia and the world. It would help in the realization of that one world towards which we are inevitably being driven, even though our passions delude us and our minds fail to understand it. The Indian people, freed from the terrible sense of oppression and frustration, will grow in stature again and lose their narrow nationalism and exclusiveness. Proud of their Indian heritage, they will open their minds and hearts to other peoples and other nations, and become citizens of this wide and fascinating world, marching onwards with others in that ancient quest in which their forefathers were the pioneers.

Note

1 Jawaharlal Nehru (1985) [1946] selections from chapter 10 of *The Discovery of India*, New Delhi: Oxford University Press, 515–23.

5

ALGERIA UNVEILED[1]

Frantz Fanon

Frantz Fanon (1925–61) was born in Martinique, educated in France, and worked as a psychiatrist in Algeria. He became a leader of the Algerian National Front and wrote several books, the most well known of which is The Wretched of the Earth *(1961). In the present essay, the principal subject is the status of women in colonial society, already discussed in the introduction. Fanon's essay might be productively read together with Jiweon Shin's article (Chapter 17) on the status of Korean women under Japanese colonialism. Apart from the gender issue, Fanon's essay also seeks to grasp the symbolic hegemony of colonialism and the ways to perceive resistance to it. He argues that while colonial powers seek to dominate cultural signs such as the veil, the resistance is also able to resignify the meaning of the veil (or its absence); it is thus able to elude and oppose this domination in a kind of semiotic guerilla war against the colonizer. More on Fanon's conception of the struggle against colonialism may be found in Chapter 11 by Kelly and Kaplan (which also contains an extended discussion of Gandhi).*

* * *

The way people clothe themselves, together with the traditions of dress and finery that custom implies, constitutes the most distinctive form of a society's uniqueness, that is to say the one that is the most immediately perceptible. Within the general pattern of a given costume, there are of course always modifications of detail, innovations which in highly developed societies are the mark of fashion. But the effect as a whole remains homogeneous, and great areas of civilization, immense cultural regions, can be grouped together on the basis of original, specific techniques of men's and women's dress.

It is by their apparel that types of society first become known, whether through written accounts and photographic records or motion pictures. Thus there are civilizations without neckties, civilizations with loincloths, and others without hats. The fact of belonging to a given cultural group is usually revealed by clothing traditions. In the Arab world, for example, the veil worn by women is at once noticed by the tourist. One may remain for a long time unaware of the fact that a Moslem does not eat pork or that he denies himself daily sexual relations during the month of Ramadan, but the veil worn by the women appears with such constancy that it generally suffices to characterize Arab society.

In the Arab Maghreb, the veil belongs to the clothing traditions of the Tunisian, Algerian, Moroccan and Libyan national societies. For the tourist and the foreigner, the veil demarcates both Algerian society and its feminine component. In the case of the Algerian man, on the other hand, regional modifications can be noted: the *fez* in urban centres, turbans and *djellabas*[2] in the countryside. The masculine garb allows a certain margin of choice, a modicum of heterogeneity. The woman seen in her white veil unifies the perception that one has of Algerian feminine society. Obviously what we have here is a uniform which tolerates no modification, no variant.

The *haïk*[3] very clearly demarcates the Algerian colonized society. It is of course possible to remain hesitant before a little girl, but all uncertainty vanishes at the time of puberty. With the veil, things become well defined and ordered. The Algerian woman, in the eyes of the observer, is unmistakably 'she who hides behind a veil'.

We shall see that this veil, one of the elements of the traditional Algerian garb, was to become the bone of contention in a grandiose battle, on account of which the occupation forces were to mobilize their most powerful and most varied resources, and in the course of which the colonized were to display a surprising force of inertia. Taken as a whole, colonial society, with its values, its areas of strength, and its philosophy, reacts to the veil in a rather homogeneous way. The decisive battle was launched before 1954, more precisely during the early 1930s.

The officials of the French administration in Algeria, committed to destroying the people's originality, and under instructions to bring about the disintegration, at whatever cost, of forms of existence likely to evoke a national reality directly or indirectly, were to concentrate their efforts on the wearing of the veil, which was looked upon at this juncture as a symbol of the status of the Algerian woman. Such a position is not the consequence of a chance intuition. It is on the basis of the analyses of sociologists and ethnologists that the specialists in so-called native affairs and the heads of the Arab Bureaus coordinated their work. At an initial stage, there was a pure and simple adoption of the well known formula, 'Let's win over the women and the rest will follow'. This definition of policy merely gave a scientific colouration to the 'discoveries' of the sociologists.

Beneath the patrilineal pattern of Algerian society, the specialists described a structure of matrilineal essence. Arab society has often been presented by Westerners as a formal society in which outside appearances are paramount. The Algerian woman, an intermediary between obscure forces and the group, appeared in this perspective to assume a primordial importance. Behind the visible, manifest patriarchy, the more significant existence of a basic matriarchy was affirmed. The role of the Algerian mother, that of the grandmother, the aunt and the 'old woman', were inventoried and defined.

This enabled the colonial administration to define a precise political doctrine: 'if we want to destroy the structure of Algerian society, its capacity for resistance, we must first of all conquer the women; we must go and find them behind the veil where they hide themselves and in the houses where the men keep them out of sight'. It is the situation of woman that was accordingly taken as the theme of action. The dominant administration solemnly undertook to defend this woman, pictured as humiliated, sequestered, cloistered. It described the immense possibilities of woman, unfortunately transformed by the Algerian man into an inert, demonetized, indeed dehumanized object. The behaviour of the Algerian was very firmly denounced and described as medieval and barbaric. With infinite science, a blanket indictment against the 'sadistic and vampirish' Algerian attitude toward women was prepared and drawn up. Around the family life of the Algerian, the occupier piled up a whole mass of judgments, appraisals, reasons, accumulated anecdotes and edifying examples, thus attempting to confine the Algerian within a circle of guilt.

Mutual aid societies and societies to promote solidarity with Algerian women sprang up in great number. Lamentations were organized. 'We want to make the Algerian ashamed of the fate that he metes out to women'. This was a period of effervescence, of putting into application a whole technique of infiltration, in the course of which droves of social workers and women directing charitable works descended on the Arab quarters.

The indigent and famished women were the first to be besieged. Every kilo of semolina distributed was accompanied by a dose of indignation against the veil and the cloister. The indignation was followed up by practical advice. Algerian women were invited to play 'a functional, capital role' in the transformation of their lot. They were pressed to say no to a centuries-old subjection. The immense role they were called upon to play was described to them. The colonial administration invested great sums in this combat. After it had been posited that the woman constituted the pivot of Algerian society, all efforts were made to obtain control over her. The Algerian, it was assured, would not stir, would resist the task of cultural destruction undertaken by the occupier, would oppose assimilation, so long as his woman had not reversed the stream. In the colonialist programme, it was the woman who was given the historic mission of shaking up the Algerian man. Converting the woman, winning her over to the foreign values, wrenching her free from her status, was at the same time achieving a real power over the man and attaining a practical, effective means of destructuring Algerian culture.

Still today, in 1959, the dream of a total domestication of Algerian society by means of 'unveiled women aiding and sheltering the occupier' continues to haunt the colonial authorities.

The Algerian men, for their part, are a target of criticism for their European comrades, or more officially for their bosses. There is not a European worker who does not sooner or later, in the give and take of relations on the job site, the shop or the office, ask the Algerian the ritual questions: 'Does your wife wear the veil? Why don't you take your wife to the movies, to the fights, to the café?'.

European bosses do not limit themselves to the disingenuous query or the glancing invitation. They use 'Indian cunning' to corner the Algerian and push him to painful decisions. In connection with a holiday – Christmas or New Year, or simply a social occasion with the firm – the boss will invite *the Algerian employee and his wife*. The invitation is not a collective one. Every Algerian is called in to the director's office and invited by name to come with 'your little family'. 'The firm being one big family, it would be unseemly for some to come without their wives, you understand?'. Before this formal summons, the Algerian sometimes experiences moments of difficulty. If he comes with his wife, it means admitting defeat, it means 'prostituting his wife', exhibiting her, abandoning a mode of resistance. On the other hand, going alone means refusing to give satisfaction to the boss; it means running the risk of being out of a job. The study of a case chosen at random – a description of the traps set by the European in order to bring the Algerian to expose himself, to declare: 'My wife wears a veil, she shall not go out', or else to betray: 'Since you want to see her, here she is', – would bring out the sadistic and perverse character of these contacts and relationships and would show in microcosm the tragedy of the colonial situation on the psychological level, the way the two systems directly confront each other, the epic of the colonized society, with its specific ways of existing, in the face of the colonialist hydra.

With the Algerian intellectual, the aggressiveness appears in its full intensity. The *fellah*, 'the passive slave of a rigidly structured group', is looked upon with a certain indulgence by the conqueror. The lawyer and the doctor, on the other hand, are severely frowned upon. These intellectuals, who keep their wives in a state of semi-slavery, are literally pointed to with an accusing finger. Colonial society blazes up vehemently against this inferior status of the Algerian woman. Its members worry and show concern for those unfortunate women, doomed 'to produce brats', kept behind walls, banned.

Before the Algerian intellectual, racialist arguments spring forth with special readiness. For all that he is a doctor, people will say, he still remains an Arab. 'You can't get away from nature'. Illustrations of this kind of race prejudice can be multiplied indefinitely. Clearly, the intellectual is reproached for limiting the extension of learned Western habits, for not playing his role as an active agent of upheaval of the colonized society, for not giving his wife the benefit of the privileges of a more worthy and meaningful life. In the large population centres it is altogether commonplace to hear a European confess acidly that he has never seen the wife of an Algerian he has known for twenty years. At a more diffuse, but highly revealing, level of apprehension, we find the bitter observation that 'we work in vain', that 'Islam holds its prey'.

The method of presenting the Algerian as a prey fought over with equal ferocity by Islam and France with its Western culture reveals the whole approach of the occupier, his philosophy and his policy. This expression indicates that the occupier, smarting from his failures, presents in a simplified and pejorative way the system of values by means of which the colonized person resists his innumerable offensives. What is in fact the assertion of a distinct identity, concern with keeping intact a few shreds of national existence, is attributed to religious, magical, fanatical behaviour.

This rejection of the conqueror assumes original forms, according to circumstances or to the type of colonial situation. On the whole, these forms of behaviour have been fairly well studied in the course of the past twenty years; it cannot be said, however, that the conclusions that have been reached are wholly valid. Specialists in basic education for underdeveloped countries, or technicians for the advancement of retarded societies, would do well to understand the sterile and harmful character of any endeavour which illuminates preferentially a given element of the colonized society. Even within the framework of a newly independent nation, one cannot attack this or that segment of the cultural whole without endangering the work undertaken (leaving aside the question of the native's psychological balance). More precisely, the phenomena of counter-acculturation must be understood as the organic impossibility of a culture to modify any one of its customs without at the same time re-evaluating its deepest values, its most stable models. To speak of counter-acculturation in a colonial situation is an absurdity. The phenomena of resistance observed in the colonized must be related to an attitude of counter-assimilation, of maintenance of a cultural, hence national, originality.

The occupying forces, in applying their maximum psychological attention to the veil worn by Algerian women, were obviously bound to achieve some results. Here and there it thus happened that a woman was 'saved', and symbolically unveiled.

These test-women, with bare faces and free bodies, henceforth circulated like sound currency in the European society of Algeria. These women were surrounded by an atmosphere of newness. The Europeans, over-excited and wholly given over to their victory, carried away in a kind of trance, would speak of the psychological phenomena of conversion. And in fact, in the European society, the agents of this conversion were held in esteem. They were envied. The benevolent attention of the administration was drawn to them.

After each success, the authorities were strengthened in their conviction that the Algerian woman would support Western penetration into the native society. Every rejected veil disclosed to the eyes of the colonialists horizons until then forbidden, and revealed to them, piece by piece, the flesh of Algeria laid bare. The occupier's aggressiveness, and hence his hopes, multiplied tenfold each time a new face was uncovered. Every new Algerian woman unveiled announced to the occupier an Algerian society whose systems of defence were in the process of dislocation, open and breached. Every veil that fell, every body that became liberated from the traditional embrace of the *haïk*, every face that offered itself to the bold and impatient glance of the occupier, was a negative expression of the fact that Algeria was beginning to deny herself and was accepting the rape of the colonizer. Algerian society with every abandoned veil seemed to express its willingness to attend the master's school and to decide to change its habits under the occupier's direction and patronage.

We have seen how colonial society, the colonial administration, perceives the veil, and we have sketched the dynamics of the efforts undertaken to fight it as an institution and the resistances developed by the colonized society. At the level of the individual, of the private European, it may be interesting to follow the multiple reactions provoked by the existence of the veil, which reveal the original way in which the Algerian woman manages to be present or absent.

For a European not directly involved in this work of conversion, what reactions are there to be recorded?

The dominant attitude appears to us to be a romantic exoticism, strongly tinged with sensuality.

And, to begin with, the veil hides a beauty.

A revealing reflection – among others – of this state of mind was communicated to us by a European visiting Algeria who, in the exercise of his profession (he was a lawyer), had had the opportunity of seeing a few Algerian women without the veil. These men, he said, speaking of the Algerians, are guilty of concealing so many strange beauties. It was his conclusion that a people with a cache of such prizes, of such perfections of nature, owes it to itself to show them, to exhibit them. If worst came to worst, he added, it ought to be possible to force them to do so.

A strand of hair, a bit of forehead, a segment of an 'overwhelmingly beautiful' face glimpsed in a streetcar or on a train, may suffice to keep alive and strengthen the European's persistence in his irrational conviction that the Algerian woman is the queen of all women.

But there is also in the European the crystallization of an aggressiveness, the strain of a kind of violence before the Algerian woman, Unveiling this woman is revealing her beauty; it is baring her secret, breaking her resistance, making her available for adventure. Hiding the face is also disguising a secret; it is also creating a world of mystery, of the hidden. In a confused way, the European experiences his relation with the Algerian woman at a highly complex level. There is in it the will to bring this woman within his reach, to make her a possible object of possession.

This woman who sees without being seen frustrates the colonizer. There is no reciprocity. She does not yield herself, does not give herself, does not offer herself. The Algerian has an attitude toward the Algerian woman which is on the whole clear. He does not see her. There is even a permanent intention not to perceive the feminine profile, not to pay attention to women. In the case of the Algerian, therefore, there is not, in the street or on a road, that behaviour characterizing a sexual encounter that is described in terms of the glance, of the physical bearing, the muscular tension, the signs of disturbance to which the phenomenology of encounters has accustomed us.

The European faced with an Algerian woman wants to see. He reacts in an aggressive way before this limitation of his perception. Frustration and aggressiveness, here too, evolve apace. Aggressiveness comes to light, in the first place, in structurally ambivalent attitudes and in the dream material that can be revealed in the European, whether he is normal or suffers from neuropathological disturbances.

In a medical consultation, for example, at the end of the morning, it is common to hear European doctors express their disappointment. The women who remove their veils before them are commonplace, vulgar; there is really nothing to make such a mystery of. One wonders what they are hiding.

European women settle the conflict in a much less roundabout way. They bluntly affirm that no one hides what is beautiful and discern in this strange custom an 'altogether feminine' intention of disguising imperfections. And they proceed to compare the strategy of the European woman, which is intended to correct, to embellish, to bring out (beauty treatments, hairdos, fashion), with that of the Algerian woman, who prefers to veil, to conceal, to cultivate the man's doubt and desire. On another level, it is claimed that the intention is to mislead the customer, and that the wrapping in which the 'merchandise' is presented does not really alter its nature, nor its value.

The content of the dreams of Europeans brings out other special themes. Jean-Paul Sartre, in his *Réflexions sur la question juive*, has shown that on the level of the unconscious, the Jewish woman almost always has an aura of rape about her.

The history of the French conquest in Algeria, including the overrunning of villages by the troops, the confiscation of property and the raping of women, the pillaging of a country, has contributed to the birth and the crystallization of the same dynamic image. At the level of the psychological strata of the occupier, the evocation of this freedom given to the sadism of the conqueror, to his eroticism, creates faults, fertile gaps through which both dreamlike forms of behaviour and, on certain occasions, criminal acts can emerge.

Thus the rape of the Algerian woman in the dream of a European is always preceded by a rending of the veil. We here witness a double deflowering. Likewise, the woman's conduct is never one of consent or acceptance, but of abject humility.

Whenever, in dreams having an erotic content, a European meets an Algerian woman, the specific features of his relations with the colonized society manifest themselves. These dreams evolve neither on the same erotic plane, nor at the same tempo, as those that involve a European woman.

With an Algerian woman, there is no progressive conquest, no mutual revelation. Straight off, with the maximum of violence, there is possession, rape, near-murder. The act assumes a para-neurotic brutality and sadism, even in a normal European. This brutality and this sadism are in fact emphasized by the frightened attitude of the Algerian woman. In the dream, the woman-victim screams, struggles like a doe, and as she weakens and faints, is penetrated, martyrized, ripped apart.

Attention must likewise be drawn to a characteristic of this dream content that appears important to us. The European never dreams of an Algerian woman taken in isolation. On the rare occasions when the encounter has become a binding relationship that can be regarded as a couple, it has quickly been transformed by the desperate flight of the woman who, inevitably, leads the male 'among women'. The European always dreams of a group of women, of a field of women, suggestive of the gynaeceum, the harem – exotic themes deeply rooted in the unconscious.

The European's aggressiveness will express itself likewise in contemplation of the Algerian woman's morality. Her timidity and her reserve are transformed in accordance with the commonplace laws of conflictual psychology into their opposite, and the Algerian woman becomes hypocritical, perverse, and even a veritable nymphomaniac.

We have seen that on the level of individuals the colonial strategy of destructuring Algerian society very quickly came to assign a prominent place to the Algerian woman. The colonialist's relentlessness, his methods of struggle, were bound to give rise to reactionary forms of behaviour on the part of the colonized. In the face of the violence of the occupier, the colonized found himself defining a principled position with respect to a formerly inert element of the native cultural configuration. It was the colonialist's frenzy to unveil the Algerian woman, it was his gamble on winning the battle of the veil at whatever cost, that were to provoke the native's bristling resistance. The deliberately aggressive intentions of the colonialist with respect to the *haïk* gave a new life to this dead element of the Algerian cultural stock – dead because stabilized, without any progressive change in form or colour. We here recognize one of the laws of the psychology of colonization. In an initial phase, it is the action, the plans of the occupier that determine the centres of resistance around which a people's will to survive becomes organized.

It is the white man who creates the Negro. But it is the Negro who creates negritude. To the colonialist offensive against the veil, the colonized opposes the cult of the veil. What was an undifferentiated element in a homogeneous whole acquires a taboo character, and the attitude of a given Algerian woman with respect to the veil will be constantly related to her overall attitude with respect to the foreign occupation. The colonized, in the face of the emphasis given by the colonialist to this or that aspect of his traditions, reacts very violently. The attention devoted to modifying this aspect, the emotion the conqueror puts into his pedagogical work, his prayers, his threats, weave a whole universe of resistances around this particular element of the culture. Holding out against the occupier on this precise element means inflicting upon him a spectacular setback; it means more particularly maintaining 'co-existence' as a form of conflict and latent warfare. It means keeping up the atmosphere of an armed truce.

Upon the outbreak of the struggle for liberation, the attitude of the Algerian woman, or of native society in general, with regard to the veil was to undergo important modifications. These innovations are of particular interest in view of the fact that they were at no time included in the programme of the struggle. The doctrine of the Revolution, the strategy of combat, never postulated the necessity for a revision of forms of behaviour with respect to the veil. We are able to affirm even now that when Algeria has gained her independence such questions will not be raised, for in the practice of the Revolution the people have understood that problems are resolved in the very movement that raises them.

Until 1955, the combat was waged exclusively by the men. The revolutionary characteristics of this combat, the necessity for absolute secrecy, obliged the militant to keep his woman in absolute ignorance. As the enemy gradually adapted himself to the forms of combat, new difficulties appeared which required original solutions. The decision to involve women as active elements of the Algerian Revolution was not reached lightly. In a sense, it was the very conception of the combat that had to be modified. The violence of the occupier, his ferocity, his delirious attachment to the national territory, induced the leaders no longer to exclude certain forms of combat. Progressively, the urgency of a total war made itself felt. But involving the women was not solely a response to the desire to mobilize the entire nation. The women's entry into the war had to be harmonized with respect for the revolutionary nature of the war. In other words, the women had to show as much spirit of sacrifice as the men. It was therefore necessary to have the same confidence in them as was required from seasoned militants who had served several prison sentences. A moral elevation and a strength of character that were altogether exceptional would therefore be required of the women. There was no lack of hesitations. The revolutionary wheels had assumed such proportions; the mechanism was running at a given rate. The machine would have to be complicated; in other words its network would have to be extended without affecting its efficiency. The women could not be conceived of as a replacement product, but as an element capable of adequately meeting the new tasks.

In the mountains, women helped the guerilla during halts or when convalescing after a wound or a case of typhoid contracted in the *djebel*.[4] But deciding to incorporate women as essential elements, to have the Revolution depend on their presence and their action in this or that sector, was obviously a wholly revolutionary step. To have the Revolution rest at any point on their activity was an important choice.
[...]
Carrying revolvers, grenades, hundreds of false identity cards or bombs, the unveiled Algerian woman moves like a fish in the Western waters. The soldiers, the French patrols, smile to her as she passes, compliments on her looks are heard here and there, but no one suspects that her suit-

cases contain the automatic pistol which will presently mow down four or five members of one of the patrols.

We must come back to that young girl, unveiled only yesterday, who walks with sure steps down the streets of the European city teeming with policemen, parachutists, militiamen. She no longer slinks along the walls as she tended to do before the Revolution. Constantly called upon to efface herself before a member of the dominant society, the Algerian woman avoided the middle of the sidewalk, which in all countries in the world belongs rightfully to those who command.

The shoulders of the unveiled Algerian woman are thrust back with easy freedom. She walks with a graceful, measured stride, neither too fast nor too slow. Her legs are bare, not confined by the veil, given back to themselves, and her hips are free.

The body of the young Algerian woman, in traditional society, is revealed to her by its coming to maturity and by the veil. The veil covers the body and disciplines it, tempers it, at the very time when it experiences its phase of greatest effervescence. The veil protects, reassures, isolates. One must have heard the confessions of Algerian women or have analysed the dream content of certain recently unveiled women to appreciate the importance of the veil for the body of the woman, Without the veil she has an impression of her body being cut up into bits, put adrift; the limbs seem to lengthen indefinitely. When the Algerian woman has to cross a street, for a long time she commits errors of judgment as to the exact distance to be negotiated. The unveiled body seems to escape, to dissolve. She has an impression of being improperly dressed, even of being naked. She experiences a sense of incompleteness with great intensity. She has the anxious feeling that something is unfinished, and along with this a frightful sensation of disintegrating. The absence of the veil distorts the Algerian woman's corporal pattern. She quickly has to invent new dimensions for her body, new means of muscular control. She has to create for herself an attitude of unveiled-woman-outside. She must overcome all timidity, all awkwardness (for she must pass for a European), and at the same time be careful not to overdo it, not to attract notice to herself. The Algerian woman who walks stark naked into the European city relearns her body, re-establishes it in a totally revolutionary fashion. This new dialectic of the body and of the world is primary in the case of one revolutionary woman.

But the Algerian woman is not only in conflict with her body. She is a link, sometimes an essential one, in the revolutionary machine. She carries weapons, knows important points of refuge. And it is in terms of the concrete dangers that she faces that we must gauge the insurmountable victories that she has had to win in order to be able to say to her chief, on her return: 'Mission accomplished. R.A.S.'.[5]

Another difficulty to which attention deserves to be called appeared during the first months of feminine activity. In the course of her comings and goings, it would happen that the unveiled Algerian woman was seen by a relative or a friend of the family. The father was sooner or later informed. He would naturally hesitate to believe such allegations. Then more reports would reach him. Different persons would claim to have seen 'Zohra or Fatima unveiled, walking like a...My Lord, protect us!...'. The father would then decide to demand explanations. He would hardly have begun to speak when he would stop. From the young girl's look of firmness the father would have understood that her commitment was of long standing. The old fear of dishonour was swept away by a new fear, fresh and cold – that of death in battle or of torture of the girl. Behind the girl, the whole family – even the Algerian father, the authority for all things, the founder of every value – following in her footsteps, becomes committed to the new Algeria.

Removed and reassumed again and again, the veil has been manipulated, transformed into a technique of camouflage, into a means of struggle. The virtually taboo character assumed by the veil in the colonial situation disappeared almost entirely in the course of the liberating struggle. Even Algerian women not actively integrated into the struggle formed the habit of abandoning the veil. It is true that under certain conditions, especially from 1957 on, the veil reappeared. The missions in fact became increasingly difficult. The adversary now knew, since certain militant women had spoken under torture, that a number of women very Europeanized in appearance were playing a fundamental role in the battle. Moreover, certain European women of Algeria were arrested, to the consternation of the adversary who discovered that his own system was breaking down. The discovery by the French authorities of the participation of Europeans in the liberation struggle marks a turning point in the Algerian Revolution. From that day, the French patrols challenged every person. Europeans and Algerians were equally suspect. All historic limits crumbled and disappeared. Any person carrying a package could be required to open it and show its contents. Anyone was entitled to question anyone as to the nature of a parcel carried in Algiers, Philippeville, or Batna. Under those conditions it became urgent to conceal the package from the eyes of the occupier and again to cover oneself with the protective *haïk*.

Here again, a new technique had to be learned: how to carry a rather heavy object dangerous to handle under the veil and still give the impression of having one's hands free, that there was nothing under this *haïk*, except a poor woman or an insignificant young girl. It was not enough to be veiled. One had to look so much like a 'fatma' that the soldier would be convinced that this woman was quite harmless.

Very difficult. Three metres ahead of you the police challenge a veiled woman who does not look particularly suspect. From the anguished expression of the unit leader you have guessed that she is carrying a bomb, or a sack of grenades, bound to her body by a whole system of strings and straps. For the hands must be free, exhibited bare, humbly and abjectly presented to the soldiers so that they will look no further. Showing empty and apparently mobile and free hands is the sign that disarms the enemy soldier.

The Algerian woman's body, which in an initial phase was pared down, now swelled. Whereas in the previous period the body had to be made slim and disciplined to make it attractive and seductive, it now had to be squashed, made shapeless and even ridiculous. This, as we have seen, is the phase during which she undertook to carry bombs, grenades, machine-gun clips.

The enemy, however, was alerted, and in the streets one witnessed what became a commonplace spectacle of Algerian women glued to the wall, over whose bodies the famous magnetic detectors, the 'frying pans', would be passed. Every veiled woman, every Algerian woman became suspect. There was no discrimination. This was the period during which men, women, children, the whole Algerian people, experienced at one and the same time their national vocation and the recasting of the new Algerian society.

Ignorant or feigning to be ignorant of these new forms of conduct, French colonialism, on the occasion of May 13th, re-enacted its old campaign of Westernizing the Algerian woman. Servants under the threat of being fired, poor women dragged from their homes, prostitutes, were brought to the public square and symbolically unveiled to the cries of 'Vive l'Algérie française!'. Before this new offensive old reactions reappeared. Spontaneously and without being told, the Algerian women who had long since dropped the veil once again donned the *haïk*, thus affirming that it was not true that woman liberated herself at the invitation of France and of General de Gaulle.

Behind these psychological reactions, beneath this immediate and almost unanimous response, we again see the overall attitude of rejection of the values of the occupier, even if these values objectively be worth choosing. It is because they fail to grasp this intellectual reality, this characteristic feature (the famous sensitivity of the colonized), that the colonizers rage at always 'doing them good in spite of themselves'. Colonialism wants everything to come from it. But the dominant psychological feature of the colonized is to withdraw before any invitation of the conqueror's. In organizing the famous cavalcade of 13 May, colonialism has obliged Algerian society to go back to methods of struggle already outmoded. In a certain sense, the different ceremonies have caused a turning back, a regression.

Colonialism must accept the fact that things happen without its control, without its direction. We are reminded of the words spoken in an international assembly by an African political figure. Responding to the standard excuse of the immaturity of colonial peoples and their incapacity to administer themselves, this man demanded for the underdeveloped peoples 'the right to govern themselves badly'. The doctrinal assertions of colonialism in its attempt to justify the maintenance of its domination almost always push the colonized to the position of making uncompromising, rigid, static counter-proposals.

After the 13th of May, the veil was resumed, but stripped once and for all of its exclusively traditional dimension.

There is thus a historic dynamism of the veil that is very concretely perceptible in the development of colonization in Algeria. In the beginning, the veil was a mechanism of resistance, but its value for the social group remained very strong. The veil was worn because tradition demanded a rigid separation of the sexes, but also because the occupier *was bent on unveiling Algeria*. In a second phase, the mutation occurred in connection with the Revolution and under special circumstances. The veil was abandoned in the course of revolutionary action. What had been used to block the psychological or political offensives of the occupier became a means, an instrument. The veil helped the Algerian woman to meet the new problems created by the struggle.

The colonialists are incapable of grasping the motivations of the colonized. It is the necessities of combat that give rise in Algerian society to new attitudes, to new modes of action, to new ways.

Notes

1 Frantz Fanon (1965) extracts from 'Algeria unveiled', in *A Dying Colonialism*, New York: Monthly Review Press, 35–64.
2 *Djellaba*: a long, hooded cloak (translator's note).
3 The *haïk*: the Arab name for the big square veil worn by Arab women, covering the face and the whole body (translator's note).
4 *Djebel*: mountain (translator's note).
5 *R.A.S.: rien à signaler* – a military abbreviation for 'nothing to report'.

6

DIAGNOSING AN ILLNESS[1]

Jalal Al-i Ahmad

Jalal Al-i Ahmad (1923–69), an Iranian teacher, anthropologist and writer, turned away from his early religious upbringing and became a Marxist. Subsequently, he returned to embrace Islam, but perhaps less from the point of view of the faithful than in an effort to find in Islam an alternative to Western culture and dominance. In this way, he was similar to many non-Western intellectuals, including Mahatma Gandhi, who also re-discovered his religious faith after considerable exposure and effort to embrace Western values. Although it first appeared in the early 1960s, the final version of Gharbzadagi *or* Occidentos is *(Western-struckness) from which this chapter is taken, was published in a final and uncensored version posthumously in 1978. Al-i Ahmad's radical message dominates the essay as he criticizes global inequality and the cultural relegation of the colonized people by the West to another time – of the past and of the primitive. He also considers the possible unity of the Third World. At the same time, there is a strong undercurrent in his writing of the need for cultural strength to resist Occidentosis, and he finds it 'in our Islamic totality', the only civilization left to survive the onslaught of the West. Readers will want to read this essay in conjunction with John Voll's (Chapter 15), which seeks to historicize the anti-Western strain in Islamic thinkers.*

* * *

I speak of 'occidentosis' as of tuberculosis. But perhaps it more closely resembles an infestation of weevils. Have you seen how they attack wheat? From the inside. The bran remains intact, but it is just a shell, like a cocoon left behind on a tree. At any rate, I am speaking of a disease: an accident from without, spreading in an environment rendered susceptible to it. Let us seek a diagnosis for this complaint and its causes – and, if possible, its cure.

Occidentosis has two poles or extremes – two ends of one continuum. One pole is the Occident, by which I mean all of Europe, Soviet Russia and North America, the developed and industrialized nations that can use machines to turn raw materials into more complex forms that can be marketed as goods. These raw materials are not only iron ore and oil, or gut, cotton, and gum tragacanth; they are also myths, dogmas, music, and the higher worlds. The other pole is Asia and Africa, or the backward, developing or non-industrial nations that have been made into consumers of Western goods. However, the raw materials for these goods come from the developing nations: oil from the shores of the Gulf, hemp and spices from India, jazz from Africa, silk and opium from China, anthropology from Oceania, sociology from Africa. These last two come from Latin America as well: from the Aztec and Inca peoples, sacrificed by the onslaught of Christianity. Everything in the developing nations comes from somewhere else. And we – the Iranians – fall into the category of the backward and developing nations: we have more points in common with them than points of difference.

It is beyond the scope of this book to define these two poles in terms of economy, politics, sociology or psychology, or as civilizations. This is exacting work for specialists. But I shall draw on general concepts from all these fields. All I will say here is that 'East' and 'West' are no longer geographical or political concepts to me. For a European or an American the West means Europe and America, and the East the USSR, China and the Eastern European nations. But for me, they are economic concepts. The West comprises the sated nations and the East, the hungry nations. To me, South Africa is part of the West. Most of the nations of Latin America are part of the East, although they are on the other side of the world. Although one must secure exact data on an earthquake from the university's seismograph, the peasant's horse (however far from thoroughbred) will have bolted to the safety of open land before the seismograph has recorded anything. I would at least sniff out rather more keenly than the shepherd's dog and see more clearly than a crow what others have closed their eyes to – or what they have seen no gain for themselves in considering.

Western nations generally have high wages, low mortality, low fertility, well organized social services, adequate foodstuffs (at least 3,000 calories per day), per capita annual income of at least 3,000 *tumans*, and nominal democracy (the heritage of the French Revolution). The second group of nations has these characteristics: low wages, high mortality, even higher fertility, social services nil (or for hire), inadequate foodstuffs (at most 1,000 calories per day), annual income less than 500 *tumans*, and no notion of democracy (the heritage of the first wave of imperialism).

Obviously, we belong to this second group, the hungry nations. The first group is all the sated nations, in accordance with Josué de Castro's definition in *The Geography of Hunger* (Boston MA, 1952). There is not only a great gap between the two groups, but, in the words of Tihor Mende, an unfillable chasm deepening and widening by the day. Thus wealth and poverty, power and impotence, knowledge and ignorance, prosperity and ruin, civilization and savagery, have been polarized in the world. One pole is held by the sated – the wealthy, the powerful, the makers and exporters of manufactures. The other pole is left to the hungry – the poor, the impotent, the importers and consumers. The heat of progress is in that ascending part of the world, and the pulse of stagnation is in this moribund part of the world. The difference arises not just from the dimension of time and place – it is not just a quantitative one. It is also qualitative, with two diverging poles: on the one hand, a world with its forward momentum grown terrifying and, on the other, a world that has yet to find a channel to guide its scattered motive forces, which run to waste. And both these worlds have a certain dynamic.[2]

Thus the day is past when we could divide the world into two blocs, East and West, or communist and non-communist. And although the constitutions of most of the world's governments begin with this great whitewash of the twentieth century, the flirtation of the United States and Soviet Russia (the two supposed unchallenged pivots of the two blocs) over the Suez Canal or Cuba showed that the masters of the camps can sit quite comfortably at the same table. The same may he said of the Nuclear Test Ban Treaty and other happenings. Thus our age, besides being no longer the age of class conflicts within borders or of national revolutions, is no longer the age of clashing 'isms' and ideologies. One must see what would-be corporate colonists and what supportive governments are secretly plotting under cover of every riot, *coup d'état* or uprising in Zanzibar, Syria or Uruguay; one can no longer see in the regional wars of our time even the ostensible contests of various beliefs. Nowadays, many not only see through the cover of the Second World War to the expansionism of the two contending alliances' industries, but see the underlying struggles over sugar, diamonds and oil, respectively in the cases of Cuba, the Congo, and the Suez Canal or Algeria. Many see in the bloodshed in Cyprus, Zanzibar, Aden or Vietnam the establishment of a bridgehead designed to secure commerce, the foremost determinant of the polities of states.

No longer is the spectre of communism dangled before the people in the West and that of the bourgeoisie and liberalism in the East. Now even kings can be ostensibly revolutionary, and Khrushchev can buy grain from America. Now all these 'isms' and ideologies are roads leading to the sublime realm of mechanization. The political compass of leftists and pseudo-leftists around the world has swung ninety degrees to the Far East, from Moscow to Beijing, because Soviet Russia is no longer the 'vanguard of the world revolution' but rather sits around the conference table with other members of the nuclear club. A direct hotline has been set up between the Kremlin and the White House. No longer is there a need for British intermediation.

Even those in power in Iran understand that the Soviet threat has declined. The plunder that Soviet Russia hoped to snatch was really just the leavings from the disastrous picnic of the First World War. Now is the era of de-Stalinization, and Radio Moscow has come out in support of the referendum of 6 Bahman! Communist China has taken the place of Soviet Russia because, just like the Russia of the 1930s, it summons all the world's hungry to unity in aspiring to utopia. And while Russia then had a population of a hundred-odd million, China today has 750 million people.

What Marx said is true today, that we have two worlds in conflict. But these two worlds stretch far more vastly than in his time, and the conflict has grown far more complex than the one of worker and employer. In our world, poor confront rich, and the vast earth is the arena. Our age is one of two worlds: one producing and exporting machines, the other importing and consuming them and wearing them out. The stage for this conflict is the global market. The weapons, apart from tanks, guns, bombers and missile launchers, themselves products of the West, are UNESCO, the FAO, the UN, ECAFE, and the other so-called international organizations. In fact, they are Western con artists come in new disguises to colonize this other world: to South America, to Asia, to Africa. Here is the basis for the occidentosis of all non-Western nations. I am not speaking of rejecting the machine or of banishing it, as the utopianists of the early nineteenth century sought to do. History has fated the world to fall prey to the machine. It is a question of how to encounter the machine and technology.

The important point is that we the people of the developing nations are not fabricating the machines. But, owing to economic and political determinants and to the global confrontation of rich and poor, we have had to be gentle and tractable consumers for the West's industrial goods, or at best contented assemblers at low wages of what comes from the West. And this has necessitated our conforming ourselves, our governments, our cultures, and our daily lives to the machine. All we are, we have had to conform to the measure of the machine. The one who created the machine has grown accustomed to this new god, its heaven and hell, over the course of two or three hundred years' gradual transformation. But what of the Kuwaiti who became acquainted with the machine only yesterday, or the Congolese, or myself as an Iranian? How are we to vault over this 300-year historical gap?

I shall pass over the others; let me consider Iran. We have been unable to preserve our own historico-cultural character in the face of the machine and its fateful onslaught. Rather, we have been routed.[3] We have been unable to take a considered stand in the face of this contemporary monster. So long as we do not comprehend the real essence, basis and philosophy of Western civilization, only aping the West outwardly and formally (by consuming its machines), we shall be like the ass going about in a lion's skin. We know what became of him. Although the one who created the machine now cries out that it is stifling him, we not only fail to repudiate our assuming the garb of machine tenders, we pride ourselves on it. For 200 years we have resembled the crow mimicking the partridge (always supposing that the West is a partridge and we are a crow). So long as we remain consumers, so long as we have not built the machine, we remain occidentotic. Our dilemma is that once we have built the machine, we will have become mechanotic, just like the West, crying out at the way technology and the machine have stampeded out of control.[4]

Let us concede that we did not have the initiative to familiarize ourselves with the machine a hundred years ago, as Japan did. Japan presumed to rival the West in mechanosis and to deal a blow to the czars (in 1905) and to America (in 1941) and, even earlier, to take markets from them. Finally the atom bomb taught them what a case of indigestion follows a feast of watermelons. And if the nations of the 'free world' have now opened some of their treasure hoard of global markets to Japan's goods, it is because they have investments in all her industries. Another explanation may be that they want to make good their military expenditures to defend those islands, for the leaders of Japan came to their senses after World War II and were very reluctant to spend money on armies and armaments. Perhaps also the average American wishes to salve the unease of conscience that drove the pilot of that infernal plane to madness.[5] The story of Ad and Thamud was repeated in Hiroshima and Nagasaki.

The 'West' began calling us (the area from the eastern Mediterranean to India) the 'East' just when it arose from its medieval hibernation, when it came in search of sun, spices, silk and other goods. First it came in the garb of pilgrims to the Christian holy places of the East (Bethlehem, Nazareth and so forth), and then in the armour of the crusaders. Next it came in the dress of merchants; then, under cover of cannon, as shippers of goods; and most recently as apostles for 'civilization'. This last name was really heaven-sent. *Istioqmar* ('colonization') is from the same root as *umran* ('settlement'). And whoever engages in *umran* is necessarily concerned with cities.

Of all the lands coming under these gentlemen's hammer, Africa proved the most malleable, the most encouraging. In addition to its having so many raw materials, including gold, diamonds, copper and ivory, in such abundance, its inhabitants had not created any urban centres or mass religions. Every tribe had its own god, its own chief, its own language. What a crazy quilt it was and so how eminently domitable! Most important, all the natives went about naked. In such heat, one cannot wear clothes. When Stanley, the relatively humane English globetrotter, returned home with this last bit of news, they threw celebrations in Manchester. If each man and woman in the Congo could be induced to buy the three yards of cloth a year required to make a shirt to wear to church services and so grow 'civilized', that would come to 320 million yards of cloth from the factories of Manchester.[6] And we know that the vanguard of colonialism is the Christian missionary. Beside every trade mission around the world they built a church, and by every sort of chicanery they drew the indigenous people into that church. And today, as colonialism is uprooted from those places, when each trade mission is boarded up, a church likewise closes.

Africa proved inviting to the gentlemen also because its peoples served as raw material for every sort of Western laboratory. Thousands of sciences – anthropology, sociology, ethnology, linguistics – were compiled on the basis of research in Africa and Australia. Professors of any of these fields in Cambridge, the Sorbonne or Leyden owe their chairs to these peoples. They see the other side of their urbanity in the African's primitiveness.

But we Middle Easterners were less receptive, less encouraging. Why? To bring the question closer to home, let me ask why we Muslims were less receptive. The question contains its own answer: in our Islamic totality, we seemed unsusceptible to study. Thus in encountering us, the West not only attacked this Islamic totality (in inciting the Shioqa to bloodshed in Safavid times, in playing us against the Ottomans, in encouraging Baha'ism in the middle of the Qajar era, in breaking up the Ottoman Empire after the First World War, in confronting the Shioqi clergy during the constitutionalist uprising, and so forth), but strived to hasten the dissolution from within of a totality only apparently unified. It sought to reduce us to a raw material like the people of Africa. Then it would take us to the laboratory. This explains why foremost among all the encyclopaedias written in the West is the *Encyclopaedia of Islam*. We remain asleep, but the Westerner has carried us off to the laboratory in this encyclopaedia.

India reminds one of Africa as a linguistic Tower of Babel and agglomeration of races and religions. Think of South America becoming

Christianized with one sweep of the Spanish sword or of Oceania, a collection of islands and thus ideal for stirring up dissensions. Thus only we in our Islamic totality, formal and real, obstructed the spread (through colonialism, effectively equivalent to Christianity) of European civilization, that is, the opening of new markets to the West's industries. The halt of Ottoman artillery before the gates of Vienna concluded a process that began in 732 CE in Andalusia.[7] How are we to regard these twelve centuries of struggle of East against West if not as the struggle of Islam against Christianity? In the present age, I, as an Asian, as a remnant of that Islamic totality, represent just what that African or that Australian represents as a remnant of primitiveness and savagery. We are all equally acceptable to Westerners, the makers of our machines, as contented museum pieces. We are to be objects of research in the museum or the laboratory, nothing more. Watch that you don't alter this raw material! I am not speaking now of their wanting Khuzistan's or Qatar's oil, Katanga's diamonds, or Kirman's chromite, unrefined. I am saying that I, as an Asian or an African, am supposed to preserve my manners, culture, music, religion, and so forth untouched, like an unearthed relic, so that the gentlemen can find and excavate them, so they can display them in a museum and say, 'Yes, another example of primitive life'.[8]

If we define occidentosis as the aggregate of events in the life, culture, civilization and mode of thought of a people having no supporting tradition, no historical continuity, no gradient of transformation, but having only what the machine brings them, it is clear that we are such a people. And because this discussion will relate primarily to the geographic, linguistic, cultural and religious background of its author, I might expand on the definition by saying that when we Iranians have the machine, that is, when we have built it, we will need its gifts less than its antecedents and adjuncts.

Occidentosis thus characterizes an era in which we have not yet acquired the machine, in which we are not yet versed in the mysteries of its structure. Occidentosis characterizes an era in which we have not yet grown familiar with the preliminaries to the machine, the new sciences and technologies. Occidentosis characterizes an era in which the logic of the marketplace and the movements of oil compel us to buy and consume the machine.

How did this era arrive? Why did we utterly fail to develop the machine, leaving it to others to so encompass its development that by the time we awakened, every oil rig had become a nail driven into our land? How did we grow occidentotic? Let us turn to history to find out.

Notes

1   Jalal Al-i Ahmad (1984) Chapter 1 of *Occidentosis: A Plague from the West*, trans. R. Campbell, annotations and introduction by Hamid Algar, Berkeley: Mizan Press, 27–35.
2   Paraphrased from Tihor Mende (1958) *Entre la peur et l'espoir: réflexions sur l'histoire d'aujourd'hui*, Paris.
3   I have given a precise example of what I mean in *Jazira-yi Kharg* [*Kharg Island*], Tehran, 1339/1960.
4   For example, see Georges Bernanos (1947) *La France contre les robots*, Paris.
5   Colonel Paul W. Tibbits Jr, who piloted the *Enola Gay* over Hiroshima. See Robert Laffont (ed.) *Avoir détruit Hiroshima*, a collection of the man's correspondence with an Austrian writer, with an introduction by Bertrand Russell. A translation of this book by Iraj Qarib was serialized in *Firdaus* magazine in 1342/1963.
6   David Livingstone and Henry Morton Stanley (1959) *Du Zimbèze au Tanganyika, 1858–1872*, Paris.
7   I refer to the defeat of Abd ar-Rahman the Umayyad (the first representative of the caliphal dynasty in Spain) at the hands of Charles Martel, French commander, at Poitiers, and hence the end of the expansion of the Caliphate in the West in the early eighth century CE. And remember that today 'Martell' is the name of a well known cognac!
8   Samin Baghchaban, my musicologist friend, has among his unpublished memoirs an account of the conference on music held in Tehran in March 1961:

> For [Alain] Daniélou [the French delegate] nothing was so interesting as how we lived in the Sassanian epoch; he, coming from the heart of the twentieth century, sought to use the most advanced recording equipment to find his way back to the Sassanian court and record the artistry of Barbod and Nekisa. Then, at the airport next to the Sassanian capital, built for the benefit of orientalists, experts on art, poetry, and music, he took an Air France jet back to Paris.

7

SOCIETY AND IDEOLOGY[1]

Kwame Nkrumah

Kwame Nkrumah (1909–72) led the British colony of Gold Coast to independence and became the President of the re-named Republic of Ghana from 1960 until 1966. Although as president he became increasingly dictatorial, he was able to gain considerable concessions and aid from both the Soviet Union and the United States. Nkrumah was also among the most passionate advocates of pan-Africanism. In the present essay, he tries to integrate the ideals of African communalism with socialism and materialism in order to oppose both colonialism and capitalism. As such he also tried to create the philosophical ground for pan-Africanism by reversing the imperialist association of tribalism and communalism with backwardness. Although pan-Africanism as a political force has been difficult to achieve, the Organization of African Unity (founded in 1963) has survived, and it played an important role in ending apartheid in South Africa.

* * *

Indeed it can be said that in every society there is to be found an ideology. In every society, there is at least one militant segment which is the dominant segment of that society. In communalistic societies, this segment coincides with the whole. This dominant segment has its fundamental principles, its beliefs about the nature of man, and the type of society which must be created for man. Its fundamental principles help in designing and controlling the type of organization which the dominant segment uses. And the same principles give rise to a network of purposes, which fix what compromises are possible or not possible. One can compromise over programme, but not over principle. Any compromise over principle is the same as an abandonment of it.

In societies where there are competing ideologies, it is still usual for one ideology to be dominant. This dominant ideology is that of the ruling group. Though the ideology is the key to the inward identity of its group, it is in intent solidarist. For an ideology does not seek merely to unite a section of the people; it seeks to unite the whole of the society in which it finds itself. In its effects, it certainly reaches the whole society, when it is dominant. For, besides seeking to establish common attitudes and purposes for the society, the dominant ideology is that which in the light of circumstances decides what forms institutions shall take, and in what channels the common effort is to be directed.

Just as there can be competing ideologies in the same society, so there can be opposing ideologies between different societies. However, while societies with different social systems can coexist, their ideologies cannot. There is such a thing as peaceful coexistence between states with different social systems; but as long as oppressive classes exist, there can be no such thing as peaceful coexistence between opposing ideologies.

Imperialism, which is the highest stage of capitalism, will continue to flourish in different forms as long as conditions permit it. Though its end is certain, it can only come about under pressure of nationalist awakening and an alliance of progressive forces which hasten its end and destroy its conditions of existence. It will end when there are no nations and peoples exploiting others; when there are no vested interests exploiting the earth, its fruits and resources for the benefit of a few against the well-being of the many.

When I say that in every society there is at least one ideology, I do not thereby imply that in every society a fully articulated set of statements is to be found. In fact, it is not ideology alone which can be so pervasive and at the same time largely covert.

In every society, there is to be found a morality; this hardly means that there is an *explicit* set of statements defining the morality. A morality is a network of principles and rules for the guidance and appraisal of conduct. And upon these rules and principles we constantly fall back. It is they which give support to our moral decisions and opinions. Very often we are quite definite about the moral quality of an act, but even when we are so definite, we are not necessarily ready with the reasons for this decision or opinion. It is not to be inferred from any such reticence, however, that there are no such reasons. We share within the same society a body of moral principles and rules garnered from our own experience and that of our forebears. The principles directing these experiences give us skill in forming moral opinions without our having to be articulate about the sources of the judgments.

[...]

The ideology of a society is total. It embraces the whole life of a people, and manifests itself in their class structure, history, literature, art, religion. It also acquires a philosophical statement. If an ideology is integrative in intent, that is to say, if it seeks to introduce a certain order which will unite the actions of millions towards specific and definite goals, then its instruments can also be seen as instruments of social control. It is even possible to look upon 'coercion' as a fundamental idea in society. This way of looking at society readily gives rise to the idea of a social contract. According to this idea, man lived, during certain dark ages in the dim past, outside the ambit of society. During those dark ages, man was alleged to have lived a poor, nasty, brutish, short and fearful life. Life, not surprisingly, soon became intolerable. And so the poor men came together, and subtly agreed upon a contract. By means of this contract they waived certain rights of theirs in order to invest a representative with legislative and executive powers of coercion over themselves.

We know that the social contract is quite unhistorical, for unless men already lived in a society, they could have no common language, and a common language is already a social fact, which is incompatible with the social contract. Nevertheless, howsoever it is that societies arose, the notion of a society implies organized obligation.

I have made mention of the way in which ideology requires definite ranges of behaviour. It is difficult, however, to fix the limits of these ranges. Still, the impression is not to be formed from this difficulty that the ranges are not definite. They are as definite as territories, even if, on occasion, border uncertainties arise between territories next to each other. Obviously, there are at least two senses of definiteness. The one sense is mathematical. In this sense, a range of conduct is definite if and only if every item of conduct either falls unambiguously inside it or falls unambiguously outside it. In the other sense, a range of conduct is definite if there are items of behaviour unambiguously falling inside it, and items of behaviour unambiguously falling outside it. Any ambiguity that there is must only be at the extremes. It is this possible fluidity at the extremes which makes growth and progress logically possible in human conduct.

Every society stresses its permissible ranges of conduct, and evolves instruments whereby it seeks to obtain conformity to such a range. It evolves these instruments because the unity out of diversity which a society represents is hardly automatic, calling as it does for means whereby unity might be secured, and, when secured, maintained. Though, in a formal sense, these means are means of 'coercion', in intent they are means of cohesion. They become means of cohesion by underlining common values, which themselves generate common interests, and hence common attitudes and common reactions. It is this community, this identity in the range of principles and values, in the range of interests, attitudes, and so of reactions, which lies at the bottom of social order. It is also this community which makes social sanction necessary, which inspires the physical institutions of society, like the police force, and decides the purposes for which they are called into being.

Indeed, when I spoke at the Law Conference at Accra in January 1962, I emphasized that law, with its executive arms, must be inspired at every level by the ideals of its society. Nevertheless, a society has a choice of instruments. By this, I do not merely mean that different societies can have different instruments. I mean that a society can, for example, decide that all its instruments of 'coercion' and unity shall be centralized. The logical extreme of this is where every permissive right is explicitly backed by an enactment, and where every social disapprobation is made explicit in a prohibitive enactment. This logical extreme of centralization is, needless to say, impossible to attain. But any society can attempt to approximate to it as much as it desires. A society, however, which approximates too closely to this extreme will engender such an unwieldy bureaucracy that the intention of bureaucracy will be annulled. Of course, ideally the intention of bureaucracy is to achieve impartiality and eschew the arbitrary. But when a society develops an unwieldy bureaucracy it has allowed this fear of the arbitrary to become pathological, and it is itself autocratic.

And yet, a society must count among its instruments of 'coercion' and cohesion, prohibitions and permissions which are made explicit in a statutory way. In many societies, there is in addition a whole gamut of instruments which are at once subtle and insidious. The sermon in the pulpit, the pressures of trade unionism, the opprobrium inflicted by the press, the ridicule of friends, the ostracism of colleagues; the sneer, the snub and countless other devices, these are all non-statutory instruments by means of which societies exert coercion, by means of which they achieve and preserve unity.

'Coercion' could unfortunately be rather painful, but it is signally effective in ensuring that individual behaviour does not become dangerously irresponsible. The individual is not an anarchic unit. He lives in orderly surroundings, and the achieving of these orderly surroundings calls for methods both explicit and subtle.

One of these subtle methods is to be found in the account of history.

The history of Africa, as presented by European scholars, has been encumbered with malicious myths. It was even denied that we were a historical people. It was said that whereas other continents had shaped history, and determined its course, Africa had stood still, held down by inertia; that Africa was only propelled into history by the European contact. African history was therefore presented as an extension of European history. Hegel's authority was lent to this a-historical hypothesis concerning Africa, which he himself unhappily helped to promote. And apologists of colonialism lost little time in seizing upon it and writing wildly thereon. In presenting the history of Africa as the history of the collapse of our traditional societies in the presence of the European advent, colonialism and imperialism employed their account of African history and anthropology as an instrument of their oppressive ideology.

Earlier on, such disparaging accounts had been given of African society and culture as to appear to justify slavery, and slavery, posed against these accounts, seemed a positive deliverance of our ancestors. Then the slave trade and slavery became illegal, the experts on Africa yielded to the new wind of change, and now began to present African culture and society as being so rudimentary and primitive that colonialism was a duty of Christianity and civilization. Even if we were no longer, on the evidence of the shape of our skulls, regarded as the missing link, unblessed with the arts of good government, material and spiritual progress, we were still regarded as representing the infancy of mankind. Our highly sophisticated culture was said to be simple and paralysed by inertia, and we had to be encumbered with tutelage. And this tutelage, it was thought, could only be implemented if we were first subjugated politically.

The history of a nation is, unfortunately, too easily written as the history of its dominant class. But if the history of a nation, or a people, cannot be found in the history of a class, how much less can the history of a continent be found in what is not even a part of it – Europe. Africa cannot be validly treated merely as the space in which Europe swelled up. If African history is interpreted in terms of the interests of European merchandise and capital, missionaries and administrators, it is no wonder that African nationalism is in the forms it takes regarded as a perversion and neo-colonialism as a virtue.

In the new African renaissance, we place great emphasis on the presentation of history. Our history needs to be written as the history of our society, not as the story of European adventures. African society must be treated as enjoying its own integrity; its history must be a mirror of that society, and the European contact must find its place in this history only as an African experience, even if as a crucial one. That is to say, the European contact needs to be assessed and judged from the point of view of the principles animating African society, and from the point of view of the harmony and progress of this society.

When history is presented in this way, it can become not an account of how those African students referred to in the introduction became more Europeanized than others; it can become a map of the growing tragedy and the final triumph of our society. In this way, African history can come to guide and direct African action; African history can thus become a pointer to the ideology which should guide and direct African reconstruction.

This connection between an ideological standpoint and the writing of history is a perennial one. A check on the work of the great historians, including Herodotus and Thucydides, quickly exposes their passionate concern with ideology. Their irresistible moral, political and sociological comments are particular manifestations of more general ideological standpoints. Classically, the great historians have been self-appointed public prosecutors, accusing on behalf of the past, admonishing on behalf of the future. Their accusations and admonishments have been set in a rigid framework of presuppositions, both about the nature of the good man and about the nature of the good society, in such a way that these presuppositions serve as intimations of an implicit ideology.

Even Ranke, the great nineteenth-century German historian, who boasted that his aim was not to sit in judgment on the past, but only to show us what really happened, was far from being a mere chronicler of the past. He was, in spite of his claims, an *engagé* historian. The key to the attitude which he strikes in his historical works lies first in his views on the necessity of strife for progress, and second in his ideas on the source of the state and the relation of the individual to the state. Dutifully grinding an axe for His Prussian Majesty, on the first point Ranke holds that it is precisely through one state seeking a hegemony of Europe, and thereby provoking a rivalry, that the civilization of the European state is maintained; on the second point he holds that the state, in being an idea of God, enjoys a spiritual personality, and hence that neither reform nor revolution is exportable, for this would do violence to the personality of the importing state. He also holds that it is only through the state to which an individual belongs that he can develop and preserve his fullness of being. And the ideal of liberty which he is able to propose to Prussian subjects is a spontaneous subjection to the state. Is it surprising that he should have 'explained' Luther's condemnation of the Peasants' War? Ranke, writing history, implements an ideological viewpoint which he at the same time seeks to conceal.

I have mentioned art as another of the subtle instruments of ideology. One can illustrate this in various ways. In the Medieval Age of Europe, when religion was considered to be the main preoccupation of life, all other concerns were subordinated to the religious, and actions tended to win approval to the extent that they supported religion, or at least were not in conflict with it. In the second chapter, I illustrated how economic activity was subordinated to the religious concern. Art, too, became infected by this idea; it accordingly specialized in Biblical illustration and apocalypses of paradise.

Today, in the socialist countries of Europe, where the range of conduct is fixed by socialist principles, that particular art which glorifies the socialist ideology is encouraged at the expense of that art which the supremacy of aristocrats or the bourgeoisie might inspire. The aristocracy in general encouraged a bucolic and a classical kind of art, its subjects appropriated from the class of gods and goddesses, and leisured, flute-playing shepherd boys. The bourgeoisie for their part injected a puritan strain into art, and in general directed it along lines of portraiture. Art has not, however, always propagated ideals within an already accepted ideology. It has sometimes thrived in the vanguard of reform or even revolution. Goya, for example, was responsible for significant conscience-stricken and protest painting in which by paint and brush he lambasted the brutalities of the nineteenth-century ruling classes. Here he was not defending an ideology, but was exposing one to attack.

In African art, too, society was often portrayed. It is the moral-philosophical preoccupation in terms of which this portrayal was done which explains its typical power. It is this also which explains the charac-teristic distortion of form in African art. In the portrayal of force, whether as forces of the world, of generation and death, or the force of destiny, it was essential that it should not be delineated as something assimilated and overcome. And this is the impression which the soft symmetries of lifelike art would have given. It is to avoid this impression of force over-come that African art resorted to distortion of forms.

By treating of such examples, one may illustrate subtle methods of 'coercion' and cohesion. To cope with the teddy-boy problem, many churches in Britain formed clubs. In these clubs they hoped to entice teddy boys by the provision of rock-and-roll music. Once these youths were so trapped, the churches expected so to influence, and so 'coerce' them as to reinstate their behaviour within the range of passable conduct. The churches used a non-subtle instrument which was at the same time not centralized.

In the Soviet Union, too, open and systematic ridicule was resorted to, and when this did not work well enough, teddy boys were moved from one area of the country to another. Through inconveniencing them, Soviet authorities sought by a non-statutory instrument to influence, and so 'coerce', teddy boys in order to bring their activities within the range of passable behaviour.

[...]

The need for subtle means of social cohesion lies in the fact that there is a large portion of life which is outside direct central intervention. In order that this portion of life should be filled with order, non-statutory methods are required. These non-statutory methods, by and large, are the subtle means of social cohesion. But different societies lay different emphases on these subtle means, even if the range of conformity which they seek is the same. The emphasis which a particular society lays on a given means depends on the experience, social-economic circumstances and the philosophical foundation of that society.

In Africa, this kind of emphasis must take objective account of our present situation at the return of political independence. From this point of view, there are three broad features to be distinguished here. African society has one segment which comprises our traditional way of life; it has a second segment which is filled by the presence of the Islamic tradition in Africa; it has a final segment which represents the infiltration of the Christian tradition and culture of Western Europe into Africa, using colonialism and neo-colonialism as its primary vehicles. These different segments are animated by competing ideologies. But since society implies a certain dynamic unity, there needs to emerge an ideology which, genuinely catering for the needs of all, will take the place of the competing ideologies, and so reflect the dynamic unity of society, and be the guide to society's continual progress.

The traditional face of Africa includes an attitude towards man which can only be described, in its social manifestation, as being socialist. This arises from the fact that man is regarded in Africa as primarily a spiritual being, a being endowed originally with a certain inward dignity, integrity and value. It stands refreshingly opposed to the Christian idea of the original sin and degradation of man.

This idea of the original value of man imposes duties of a socialist kind upon us. Herein lies the theoretical basis of African communalism. This theoretical basis expressed itself on the social level in terms of institutions such as the clan, underlining the initial equality of all and the responsibility of many for one. In this social situation, it was impossible for classes of a Marxian kind to arise. By a Marxian kind of class, I mean one which has a place in a horizontal social stratification. Here classes are related in such a way that there is a disproportion of economic and political power between them, In such a society there exist classes which are crushed, lacerated and ground down by the encumbrance of exploitation. One class sits upon the neck of another.

In the traditional African society, no sectional interest could be regarded as supreme; nor did legislative and executive power aid the interests of any particular group. The welfare of the people was supreme.

But colonialism came and changed all this. First, there were the necessities of the colonial administration to which I referred in the Introduction.

For its success, the colonial administration needed a cadre of Africans, who, by being introduced to a certain minimum of European education, became infected with European ideals, which they tacitly accepted as being valid for African societies, Because these African instruments of the colonial administration were seen by all to be closely associated with the new sources of power, they acquired a certain prestige and rank to which they were not entitled by the demands of the harmonious development of their own society.

In addition to them, groups of merchants and traders, lawyers, doctors, politicians and trade unionists emerged, who, armed with skills and levels of affluence which were gratifying to the colonial administration, initiated something parallel to the European middle class. There were also certain feudal-minded elements who became imbued with European ideals either through direct European education or through hobnobbing with the local colonial administration. They gave the impression that they could be relied upon implicitly as repositories of all those staid and conservative virtues indispensable to any exploiter administration. They, as it were, paid the registration fee for membership of a class which was now associated with social power and authority.

Such education as we were all given put before us right from our infancy ideals of the metropolitan countries, ideals which could seldom be seen as representing the scheme, the harmony and progress of African society. The scale and type of economic activity; the idea of the account-ability of the individual conscience introduced by the Christian religion; countless other silent influences; these have all made an indelible impression upon African society.

But neither economic nor political subjugation could be considered as being in tune with the traditional African egalitarian view of man and society. Colonialism had in any case to be done away with. The African Hercules has his club poised ready to smite any new head which the colonialist hydra may care to put out.

With true independence regained, however, a new harmony needs to he forged, a harmony that will allow the combined presence of traditional Africa, Islamic Africa and Euro-Christian Africa, so that this presence is in tune with the original humanist principles underlying African society. Our society is not the old society, but a new society enlarged by Islamic and Euro-Christian influences. A new emergent ideology is therefore required, an ideology which can solidify in a philosophical statement, but at the same time an ideology which will not abandon the original humanist principles of Africa.

Such a philosophical statement will be born out of the crisis of the African conscience confronted with the three strands of present African society. Such a philosophical statement I propose to name *philosophical consciencism*, for it will give the theoretical basis for an ideology whose aim shall be to contain the African experience of Islamic and Euro-Christian presence as well as the experience of the traditional African society, and, by gestation, employ them for the harmonious growth and development of that society.

Every society is placed in nature. And it seeks to influence nature, to impose such transformations upon nature, as will develop the environment of the society for its better fulfilment. The changed environment, in bringing about a better fulfilment of the society, thereby alters the society. Society placed in nature is therefore caught in the correlation of transformation with development. This correlation represents the toil of man both as a social being and as an individual. This kind of correlation has achieved expression in various social-political theories. For a social-politi cal theory has a section which determines the way in which social forces are to be deployed in order to increase the transformation of society.

[...]

Whereas capitalism is a development by refinement from slavery and feudalism, socialism does not contain the fundamental ingredient of capitalism, the principle of exploitation. Socialism stands for the negation of that very principle wherein capitalism has its being, lives, and thrives, that principle which links capitalism with slavery and feudalism.

If one seeks the social-political ancestor of socialism, one must go to communalism. Socialism has characteristics in common with communalism, just as capitalism is linked with feudalism and slavery. In socialism, the principles underlying communalism are given expression in modern circumstances. Thus, whereas communalism in an untechnical society can be *laissez-faire*, in a technical society where sophisticated means of production are at hand, if the underlying principles of communalism are not given centralized and correlated expression, class cleavages arise, which are the result of economic disparities, and accompanying political inequalities. Socialism, therefore, can be and is the defence of the principles of communalism in a modern setting. Socialism is a form of social organization which, guided by the principles underlying communism, adopts procedures and measures made necessary by demographic and technological developments.

These considerations throw great light on the bearing of revolution and reform on socialism. The passage from the ancestral line of slavery via feudalism and capitalism to socialism can only lie through revolution: it cannot lie through reform. For in reform, fundamental principles are held constant and the details of their expression modified. In the words of Marx, it leaves the pillars of the building intact. Indeed, sometimes, reform itself may be initiated by the necessities of preserving identical fundamental principles. Reform is a tactic of self-preservation.

Revolution is thus an indispensable avenue to socialism, where the antecedent social-political structure is animated by principles which are a negation of those of socialism, as in a capitalist structure (and therefore also in a colonialist structure, for a colonialist structure is essentially ancillary to capitalism). Indeed, I distinguish between two colonialisms, between a domestic one and an external one. Capitalism at home is domestic colonialism.

But because the spirit of communalism still exists to some extent in societies with a communalist past, socialism and communism are not in the strict sense of the word 'revolutionary' creeds. They may be described as restatements in contemporary idiom of the principles underlying communalism. On the other hand, in societies with no history of communalism, the creeds of socialism and communism are fully revolutionary, and the passage to socialism must be guided by the principles of scientific socialism.

[...]

The evil of capitalism consists in its alienation of the fruit of labour from those who with the toil of their body and the sweat of their brow produce this fruit. This aspect of capitalism makes it irreconcilable with those basic principles which animate the traditional African society. Capitalism is unjust; in our newly independent countries it is not only too complicated to be workable, it is also alien.

Under socialism, however, the study and mastery of nature has a humanist impulse, and is directed not towards a profiteering accomplishment, but the affording of ever-increasing satisfaction for the material and spiritual needs of the greatest number. Ideas of transformation and development, insofar as they relate to the purposes of society as a whole and not to an oligarch purpose, are properly speaking appropriate to socialism.

On the philosophical level, too, it is materialism, not idealism, that in one form or another will give the firmest conceptual basis to the restitution of Africa's egalitarian and humanist principles. Idealism breeds an oligarchy, and its social implication, as drawn out in my second chapter, is obnoxious to African society. It is materialism, with its monistic and naturalistic account of nature, which will balk arbitrariness, inequality and injustice. How materialism suggests a socialist philosophy I have explained in my second chapter.

In sum, the restitution of Africa's humanist and egalitarian principles of society requires socialism; it is materialism that ensures the only effective transformation of nature, and socialism that derives the highest development from this transformation.

Note

1   Kwame Nkrumah (1970) selections from Chapter 3 of *Consciencism: Philosophy and Ideology for Decolonization*, New York: Monthly Review Press, 56–77.

Part II

IMPERIALISM AND NATIONALISM

Many of the issues brought up in this part cannot be meaningfully separated from those in Part III, but the essays in this section foreground the comparative or theoretical dimension, whereas those in the next part examine these problems in a regional context. The essays here explore the twin political forces that conditioned and shaped the decolonization movement more than any other: imperialism and nationalism.

The opening piece by Michael Adas records a critical turning point in the discourse of imperialism. In the aftermath of World War I, the emergent decolonizing movement turned on its head the 'civilizing mission' that had been the pivotal ideology of imperialism. Adas shows how the horrors of war catalysed the critique of the civilizing mission among numerous thinkers in Asia and Africa, thus undermining its moral authority and launching a fully fledged attack upon the ideas of racial and technological superiority. This richly documented article can be compared with John Voll's essay in Part III (Chapter 15) which also traces the decolonization of the mind that takes place in the Islamic world.

Adas brings together the two terms of this section – imperialism and nationalism. The subsequent essay by Patrick Wolfe surveys the changing conceptions of imperialism – within both the Marxist and non-Marxist traditions – from the late nineteenth century until the present time. We should note that these conceptions directly influenced most of the leaders and thinkers of the decolonization movement, including each of the figures in Part I. Thus while Leninist ideas had an impact on such thinkers as Ho Chi Minh, Nehru, and even Sun Yat-sen, we can see some versions of dependency theory – which are closely related to ideas of neo-imperialism – in figures like Nkrumah, Fanon and Al-i Ahmad. Interestingly, the famous Robinson (and Gallagher) thesis on imperialism that Wolfe discusses was propounded by the same Ronald Robinson who writes in this volume about neo-imperialism.

The second half of Wolfe's essay introduces the contemporary post-colonial critiques of imperialism. The intellectuals associated with these critiques – such as Edward Said or Ashish Nandy – may be seen as the intellectual successors to the anti-imperialist thinkers of the colonial world. These thinkers seek to critique our present-day assumptions about race, gender and modernity as being continuous with the colonial period. They argue that a discourse which presents the decolonizing nation as the mirror opposite of the colonial risks reproducing the basic form of the colonial representation. They try to show how both colonizer and colonized were shaped by contemporary political and economic forces, and how each contributed to the production of the other. These theorists also explore colonial gender conceptions that earlier troubled Fanon (in this volume) and others. Wolfe's own concern is to bridge the gap between the cultural or representational (e.g. colonial-contemporary representations of masculinity or a 'backward race') emphasis of post-colonial theories with the older political-economic analyses of imperialism. He concludes with his own studies of race relations in the world, relations which were shaped simultaneously by the imperialist division of labour and by the cultural representations arising from the specific circumstances of this division.

Turning to nationalism, Geoffrey Barraclough's chapter from his 1964 book An Introduction to Contemporary History *(Chapter 10 of the present volume) represents perhaps one of the more inclusive and sympathetic studies of the decolonization movement during its time. Barraclough attends to the novel and historical dimensions of the movement as it awakens and mobilizes the peasant masses to political consciousness. He also presents us with a comparative study of the movement in its different phases, enumerating the strengths and weaknesses of the movement in places like India, China, North Africa and elsewhere. As such, it provides the background for several of the more specialized essays which appear later in the volume.*

Barraclough's vision of the decolonization movement may be interpreted as a culmination of the self-liberation of the colonized peoples, who are now able to build a bright future for themselves. Writing almost twenty years later, Benedict Anderson's highly influential and superb study of nationalism, Imagined Communities, *reiterates a similar (though by no means identical) view of Third World nationalism. In their contribution to this volume, John Kelly and Martha Kaplan seek to go beyond the Barraclough-Anderson type of vision to suggest that nationalism in the Third World did not necessarily result in self-liberation, but often turned out to be an entry into a new form of domination through the nation-state model. The authors argue that the trappings of the nation-state represented a kind of outfit to equip these societies to enter a new world order dominated by the United States and the United Nations. Kelly and Kaplan conclude their provocative analysis with an extended discussion of Frantz Fanon and Mahatma Gandhi, who, they demonstrate, reveal two different, although equally prescient, understandings of the contradictions of this new world order.*

The essay by William Roger Louis and Ronald Robinson that follows, furnishes the historical details by which 'the British imperial system was neo-colonized more intensively under new management' of a British-American alliance after World War II. The authors cover Africa and the Middle East in particular (whereas Stein Tønnesson's essay in Part III [Chapter 18] addresses America's role in Southeast Asia during the long Vietnam war). Their description of the neo-imperialist interventions in the Middle East during the Cold War is particularly relevant for our understanding of the more recent interventions by 'the alliance' in the region.

The last chapter of Part II, by Radha Kumar (Chapter 13), deals with the 'partitions' that accompanied the disintegration of empires, from the post-World War I era to the post-World War II decolonizations, and beyond to the contemporary 'decolonization' of the Soviet empire. The essay focuses on the contemporary division of Yugoslavia after 1989, and particularly on the partition of Bosnia in 1996; but in doing so it draws attention to the entire history of partition in the twentieth century. The newly emergent nationalist doctrine of ethnic purity or dominance among decolonizing movements within colonial empires, and the imperative among colonial powers to abandon sticky conflicts through a quick solution that Kumar calls 'divide and quit', has left a legacy that continues to haunt both the ex-colonizers and ex-colonized well into the twenty-first century. It may well be the most lasting political legacy of modern colonialism and decolonization, a legacy that the United Nations has been hitherto at best only able to contain.

* * *

8

CONTESTED HEGEMONY

The Great War and the Afro-Asian assault on the civilizing mission ideology

Michael Adas

The civilizing mission has been traditionally seen as an ideology by which late-nineteenth-century Europeans rationalized their colonial domination of the rest of humankind. Formulations of this ideology varied widely, from those of thinkers or colonial administrators who stressed the internal pacification and political order that European colonization extended to 'barbaric' and 'savage' peoples suffering from incessant warfare and despotic rule, to those of missionaries and reformers who saw religious conversion and education as the keys to European efforts to 'uplift' ignorant and backward peoples. But by the late nineteenth century, most of the fully elaborated variations on the civilizing mission theme were grounded in presuppositions that suggest that it had become a good deal more than a way of salving the consciences of those engaged in the imperialist enterprise. Those who advocated colonial expansion as a way of promoting good government, economic improvement or Christian proselytization, agreed that a vast and ever-widening gap had opened between the level of development achieved by Western European societies (and their North American offshoots) and that attained by any of the other peoples of the globe. Variations on the civilizing mission theme became the premier means by which European politicians and colonial officials, as well as popularizers and propagandists, identified the areas of human endeavour in which European superiority had been incontestably established and calibrated the varying degrees to which different non-European societies lagged behind those of Western Europe. Those who contributed to the civilizing mission discourse, whether through official policy statements or in novels and other fictional works, also sought to identify the reasons for Europe's superior advance relative to African backwardness or Asian stagnation, and the implications of these findings for international relations and colonial policy.

Much of the civilizing mission discourse was obviously self-serving. But the perceived gap between Western Europe's material development and that of the rest of the world appeared to validate the pronouncements of the colonial civilizers. Late Victorians were convinced that the standards by which they gauged their superiority and justified their global hegemony were both empirically verifiable and increasingly obvious. Before the outbreak of the Great War in 1914, these measures of human achievement were contested only by dissident (and marginalized) intellectuals, and occasionally by disaffected colonial officials. The overwhelming majority of thinkers and political leaders who concerned themselves with colonial issues had little doubt that the scientific and industrial revolutions – at that point still confined to Europe and North America – *had* elevated Western societies far above all others in the understanding and mastery of the material world. Gauges of superiority and inferiority, such as differences in physical appearance and religious beliefs, that had dominated European thinking in the early centuries of overseas expansion, remained important. But by the second half of the nineteenth century, European thinkers, whether they were racists or anti-racists, expansionists or anti-imperialists, or on the political left or right, shared the conviction that through their scientific discoveries and inventions, Westerners had gained an understanding of the workings of the physical world and an ability to tap its resources that were vastly superior to anything achieved by other peoples, past or present.

Many advocates of the civilizing mission ideology sought to capture the attributes that separated industrialized Western societies from those of the colonized peoples by contrasting Europeans (or Americans) with the dominated 'others' with reference to a standard set of binary opposites that had racial, gender and class dimensions. Europeans were, for example, seen to be scientific, energetic, disciplined, progressive and punctual, while Africans and Asians were dismissed as superstitious, indolent, reactionary, out of control and oblivious to time. These dichotomous comparisons were, of course, blatantly essentialist. But the late Victorians were prone to generalizing and stereotyping. They were also determined to classify and categorize all manner of things in the mundane world, and fond of constructing elaborate hypothetical hierarchies of humankind.

For virtually all late-Victorian champions of the civilizing mission, the more colonized peoples and cultures were seen to exhibit such traits as fatalism, passivity and excessive emotionalism, the further down they were placed on imaginary scales of human capacity and evolutionary development, and thus the greater the challenge of civilizing them. For even the best-intentioned Western social theorists and colonial administrators, difference meant inferiority. But there was considerable disagreement between a rather substantial racist majority, which viewed these attributes as innate and permanent (or at least requiring long periods of time for evolutionary remediation), and a minority of colonial reformers, who believed that substantial progress could be made in civil

79

izing stagnant or barbarian peoples like the Chinese or Indians within a generation, and that even savage peoples like the Africans or Amerindians could advance over several generations. Those who held to the social evolutionist dogmas interpolated from rather dubious readings of Darwin's writings were convinced that the most benighted of the savage races were doomed to extinction. Some observers, such as the Reverend Frederick Farrar, thought the demise of these lowly peoples who had 'not added one iota to the knowledge, the arts, the sciences, the manufactures, the morals of the world'[1] quite consistent with the workings of nature and God.

Whatever their level of material advancement, 'races', such as the Sikhs of India or the Bedouin peoples of the African Sahel, that were deemed to be martial – thus presumably energetic, active, disciplined, in control, expansive and adaptive – were ranked high in late-Victorian hierarchies of human types. The colonizers' valorization of martial peoples underscores the decidedly masculine bias of the desirable attributes associated with the civilizing mission ideology. Colonial administrations, such as the legendary Indian Civil Service, were staffed entirely by males until World War II, when a shortage of manpower pushed at least the British to recruit women into the colonial service for the first time. The club-centric, sports-obsessed, hard-drinking enclave culture of the European colonizers celebrated muscular, self-controlled, direct and energetic males. Wives and eligible young females were allowed into these masculine bastions. But their behaviour was controlled and their activities constricted by the fiercely enforced social conventions and the physical layout of European quarters that metaphorically and literally set the boundaries of European communities in colonized areas. Within the colonizers' enclaves, the logic of the separate spheres for men and women prevailed, undergirded by a set of paired, dichotomous attributes similar to that associated with the civilizing mission ideology. Thus such lionized colonial proconsuls as Evelyn Baring (the first Earl of Cromer), who ruled Egypt like a monarch for over two decades, saw no contradiction between their efforts to 'liberate' Muslim women from the veil and *purdah* in the colonies and the influential support that they gave to anti-suffragist organizations in Great Britain.

As T. B. Macaulay's often-quoted 1840 caricature of the Bengalis as soft, devious, servile, indolent and effeminate suggests, feminine qualities were often associated in colonial thinking with dominated, inferior races. Some writers stressed the similarities in the mental makeup of European women and Africans or other colonized peoples; others argued that key female attributes corresponded to those ascribed to the lower orders of humanity. Again, the paired oppositions central to the civilizing mission ideology figured prominently in the comparisons. Though clearly (and necessarily) superior in moral attributes, European women – like the colonized peoples – were intuitive, emotional, passive, bound to tradition, and always late. In addition, the assumption that scientific discovery and invention had been historically monopolized by males (despite the accomplishments of contemporaries such as Marie Curie) was taken as proof that women were temperamentally and intellectually unsuited to pursuits, such as engineering and scientific research, that advocates of the civilizing mission ideology viewed as key indicators of the level of societal development. These views not only served to fix the image and position of the European *mem sahib* as passive, domestic, apolitical and vulnerable; they made it all but impossible for indigenous women in colonized societies to obtain serious education in the sciences or technical training. As Ester Boserup has demonstrated, institutions and instruction designed to disseminate Western scientific knowledge or tools and techniques among colonized peoples, were directed almost totally toward the male portion of subject populations.

The virtues that the colonizers valorized through the civilizing mission ideology were overwhelmingly bourgeois. Rationality, empiricism, progressivism, systematic (hence scientific) inquiry, industriousness and adaptability were all hallmarks of the capitalist industrial order. New conceptions of time and space, that had both made possible and were reinforced by that order, informed such key civilizing mission attributes as hard work, discipline, curiosity, punctuality, honest dealing and taking control – the latter rather distinct from the self-control so valued by aristocrats. Implicit in the valorization of these bourgeois traits was approbation of a wider range of processes, attitudes and behaviour that was not usually explicitly discussed in the tomes and tracts of the colonial proponents of the civilizing mission ideology. Ubiquitous complaints by colonial officials regarding the colonized's lack of foresight, their penchant for 'squandering' earnings on rites of passage ceremonies or religious devotion, and their resistance to work discipline and overtime, suggested they lacked proclivities and abilities that were essential to the mastery of the industrial, capitalist order of the West. Implicitly then, and occasionally explicitly, advocates of the civilizing mission ideology identified the accumulation and reinvestment of wealth, the capacity to anticipate and forecast future trends, and the drive for unbounded productivity and the provision of material abundance as key attributes of the 'energetic, reliable, improving'[2] Western bourgeoisie that had been mainly responsible for the scientific and industrial revolutions and European global hegemony.

In the decades before the Great War, white European males reached the pinnacle of their power and global influence. The civilizing mission ideology both celebrated their ascendancy and set the agenda they intended to pursue for dominated peoples throughout the world.

The attributes that male European colonizers ascribed to themselves and sought – to widely varying degrees in different colonial settings and at different social levels – to inculcate in their African or Asian subjects, were informed by the underlying scientific and technological gauges of human capacity and social development that were central to the civilizing mission ideology. Both the attributes and the ideology of the dominant in turn shaped European perceptions of and interaction with the colonized peoples of Africa and Asia in a variety of ways. Many apologists for colonial expansion, for example, argued that it was the duty of the more inventive and inquisitive Europeans to conquer and develop the lands of backward or primitive peoples who did not have the knowledge or the tools to exploit the vast resources that surrounded them. Having achieved political control, it was incumbent upon the Western colonizers to replace corrupt and wasteful indigenous regimes with honest and efficient bureaucracies, to reorganize the societies of subjugated peoples in ways the Europeans deemed more rational and more nurturing of individual initiative and enterprise, and to restructure the physical environment of colonized lands in order to bring them into line with European conceptions of time and space.

The Europeans' superior inventiveness and understanding of the natural world also justified the allotment of tasks in the global economy envisioned by proponents of the civilizing mission. Industrialized Western nations would provide monetary and machine capital and entrepreneurial and managerial skills, while formally colonized and informally dominated overseas territories would supply the primary products, cheap labour and abundant land that could be developed by Western machines, techniques and enterprise. Apologists for imperialism argued that Western peoples were entrusted with a mission to civilize because they were active, energetic and committed to efficiency and progress. It was therefore their duty to put indolent, tradition-bound and fatalistic peoples to work, to discipline them (whether they be labourers, soldiers, domestic servants or clerks), and to inculcate within them (insofar as their innate capacities permitted) the rationality, precision and foresight that were seen as vital sources of Europe's rise to global hegemony.

In the pre-World War era, the great majority of Western-educated collaborateur and comprador classes in the colonies readily conceded the West's scientific, technological and overall material superiority. Spokesmen for these classes – often even those who had already begun to agitate for an end to colonial rule – clamoured for more Western education and an acceleration of the process of diffusion of Western science and technology in colonized societies. In Bengal in eastern India in the 1860s, for example, a gathering of Indian notables heartily applauded K. M. Banerjea's call for the British to increase opportunities for Indians to receive advanced instruction in the Western sciences. Banerjea dismissed those who defended 'Oriental' learning by asking which of them would trust the work of a doctor, engineer or architect who knew only the mathematics and mechanics of the Sanskrit *Sutras*. What is noteworthy here is not only Banerjea's confusion of Buddhist (hence Pali) *Sutras* and Sanskrit *Shastras*, but his internalization of the Western Orientalists' essentialist conception of Asian thinking and learning as a single 'Oriental' whole that had stagnated and fallen behind the West in science and mathematics. Just over two decades later, the prominent Bengali reformer and educator, Keshub Chunder Sen, acknowledged that the diffusion of Western science that had accompanied the British colonization of India had made it possible for the Indians to overcome 'ignorance and error' and share the Europeans' quest to explore 'the deepest mysteries of the physical world'.[3]

Thus, despite the Hindu Renaissance that was centered in these decades in Bengal, as S. K. Saha has observed, the presidency's capital, Calcutta, had been reduced to an intellectual outpost of Europe. But English-educated Indians revered not just Western scientific and technological achievements; they accepted their colonial masters' assumption that responsible, cultivated individuals privileged rationality, empiricism, punctuality, progress and the other attributes deemed virtuous by proponents of the civilizing mission ideology. Just how widely these values had been propagated in the Indian middle classes is suggested by anthropological research carried out among Indian merchant communities in central Africa in the 1960s. Responses to questions relating to the Indians' attitudes toward the African majority in the countries in which they resided, revealed that the migrant merchants considered their hosts 'illiterate and incomprehensible savages', who were lazy and without foresight, childlike in their thinking and thus incapable of logical deductions, and self-indulgent and morally reprobate.[4]

As the recollections of one of Zimbabwe's Western-educated, nationalist leaders, Ndabaningi Sithole, make clear, the colonized of sub-Saharan Africa were even more impressed by the Europeans' mastery of the material world than their Indian counterparts. Because many African peoples had often been relatively isolated before the abrupt arrival of European explorers, missionaries and conquerors in the last decades of the nineteenth century, early encounters with these agents of expansive, industrial societies were deeply disorienting and demoralizing:

> The first time he ever came into contact with the white man the African was overwhelmed, overawed, puzzled, perplexed, mystified, and dazzled....Motor cars, motor cycles, bicycles, gramophones, telegraphy, the telephone, glittering Western

clothes, new ways of ploughing and planting, added to the African's sense of curiosity and novelty. Never before had the African seen such things. They were beyond his comprehension; they were outside the realm of his experience. He saw. He wondered. He mused. Here then the African came into contact with two-legged gods who chose to dwell among people instead of in the distant mountains.[5]

In part because European observers took these responses by (what they perceived to be) materially impoverished African peoples as evidence of the latter's racial incapacity for rational thought, discipline, scientific investigation and technological innovation, there were few opportunities before World War I for colonized Africans to pursue serious training in the sciences, medicine or engineering, especially at the post-secondary level. Technological diffusion was also limited, and the technical training of Africans confined largely to the operation and maintenance of the most elementary machines. Nonetheless, the prescriptions offered by French- and English-educated Africans for the revival of a continent shattered by centuries of the slave trade, shared the assumption of the European colonizers that extensive Western assistance would be essential for Africa's uplift. The Abbé Boilat, for example, a mulatto missionary and educator, worked for the establishment of a secondary school at St Louis in Senegal, where Western mathematics and sciences would be taught to the sons of the local elite. Boilat also dreamed of an African college that would train indigenous doctors, magistrates and engineers who would assist the French in extending their empire in the interior of the continent.

Although the Edinburgh-educated surgeon J. A. Horton was less sanguine than Boilat about the aptitude of his fellow Africans for higher education in the Western sciences, he was equally convinced that European tutelage was essential if Africa was to be rescued from chaos and barbarism. Horton viewed 'metallurgy and other useful arts' as the key to civilized development, and argued that if they wished to advance, Africans must acquire the learning and techniques of more advanced peoples like the Europeans. Even the Caribbean-born Edward Blyden, one of the staunchest defenders of African culture and historical achievements in the pre-war decades, conceded that Africa's recovery from the ravages of the slave trade depended upon assistance from nations 'now foremost in civilization and science' and the return of educated blacks from the United States and Latin America. Blyden charged that if Africa had been integrated into the world market system through regular commerce rather than the slave trade, it would have developed the sort of agriculture and manufacturing and imported steam engines, printing presses and other machines by which the 'comfort, progress, and usefulness of mankind are secured'.[6]

There were those who contested the self-satisfied, ethnocentric and frequently arrogant presuppositions that informed the civilizing mission ideology in the decades before World War I. The emergence of Japan as an industrial power undermined the widely held conviction that the Europeans' scientific and technological attainments were uniquely Western or dependent on the innate capacities of the white or Caucasian races. Conversely, the modernists' 'discovery' of 'primitive' art and the well publicized conversion of a number of rather prominent European intellectuals to Hinduism, Buddhism and other Asian religions suggested the possibility of viable alternatives to European epistemologies, modes of behaviour, and ways of organizing societies and the natural world. Some European thinkers, perhaps most famously Paul Valéry and Herman Hesse, actually questioned Western values themselves. They asked whether the obsessive drive for increased productivity and profits, and the excessive consumerism that they saw as the hallmarks of Western civilization, were leading humanity in directions that were conducive to social well-being and spiritual fulfilment.

Before the outbreak of the war in 1914, these critiques and alternative visions were largely marginalized, dismissed by mainstream politicians and the educated public as the rantings of gloomy radicals and eccentric mystics. But the coming of the Great War and the appalling casualties that resulted from the trench stalemate on the Western Front made a mockery of the European conceit that discovery and invention were necessarily progressive and beneficial to humanity. The mechanized slaughter and the conditions under which the youth of Europe fought the war generated profound challenges to the ideals and assumptions upon which the Europeans had for over a century based their sense of racial superiority, and from which they had fashioned that ideological testament to their unmatched hubris, the civilizing mission. Years of carnage in the very heartlands of European civilization demonstrated that Europeans were at least as susceptible to instinctual, irrational responses and primeval drives as the peoples they colonized. The savagery that the war unleashed within Europe, Sigmund Freud observed, should caution the Europeans against assuming that their 'fellow-citizens' of the world had 'sunk so low' as they had once believed, because the conflict had made it clear that the Europeans themselves had 'never risen as high'.[7]

Remarkably (or so it seemed to many at the time), the crisis passed, the empire survived, and the British and French emerged victorious from the war. In fact, in the years following the end of the conflict in 1918, the empires of both powers expanded considerably as Germany's colonies and Turkey's territories in the Levant were divided between them. Although recruiting British youths into the Indian Civil Service and its African counterparts became more difficult, and such influential proponents of French expansionism as Henri Massis conceded that the Europeans' prestige as civilizers had fallen sharply among the colonized peoples, serious efforts were made to revive the badly battered civilizing mission ideology. Colonial apologists, such as Etienne Richet and Albert Bayet, employed new, less obviously hegemonic slogans that emphasized the need for 'mutual cooperation' between colonizers and colonized and programmes for 'development' based on 'free exchanges of views' and 'mutual respect'. But the central tenets of the colonizers' ideology remained the same: European domination of African and Asian peoples was justified by the diffusion of the superior science, technology, epistemologies and modes of organization that it facilitated. Though the engineer and the businessman may have replaced the district officer and the missionary as the chief agents of the mission to civilize, it continued to be envisioned as an unequal exchange between the advanced, rational, industrious, efficient and mature societies of the West and the backward, ignorant, indolent and childlike peoples of Africa, Asia and the Pacific.

For many European intellectuals and a handful of maverick politicians, however, post-war efforts to restore credibility to the civilizing mission ideology were exercises in futility. These critics argued that the war had destroyed any pretence the Europeans might have of moral superiority or their conceit that they were innately more rational than non-Western peoples. They charged that the years of massive and purposeless slaughter in the trenches had made a shambles of proofs of Western superiority based on claims to higher levels of scientific understanding and technological advancement. For four long years, colonized peoples in West and East Africa, the Middle East and in Europe itself had witnessed the spectacle of Europeans waging war and killing each other. Subjugated peoples from Algeria to Indochina had also been enraged by the duplicity and escalating demands of their European overlords; they had seen their colonies nearly emptied of European officials and soldiers who were desperately needed in other theatres of the conflict; and they had been recruited to fight and kill the European adversaries of their French or British rulers. The sorry spectacle of the suicidal European cataclysm, and the shortages and hardships it inflicted on colonized areas, sparked widespread regional protest and resistance to Western domination that assumed genuinely global dimensions by the last years of the conflict. Though these challenges never seriously threatened the European colonial order as a whole, they forced substantial wartime concessions from the victorious British and French in many parts of their empires. Equally critically, they gave great impetus to the contestation of the central tenets of the civilizing mission ideology that Asian and African intellectuals had only begun to question in the decades before the outbreak of the war. Necessarily combined with an ever-bolder defence of the societal norms, cultures and capacities of the colonized peoples, this assault on the civilizing mission played a major role in the psychological liberation of the intellectual and political elites of subjugated societies. And that liberation was perhaps the single most important consequence of the wartime crisis in terms of the long-term process of decolonization. It was essential to the success of efforts of leaders like Gandhi and Nkrumah to mobilize mass-based, anti-colonial resistance and sustain the longer-term drives for independence that would bring an end to centuries of European global hegemony following yet another global conflict between 1937 and 1945.

Mounted by Asian and African thinkers and activists who often received little publicity in Europe or the United States, pre-World War I challenges to assumptions of Western superiority enshrined in the civilizing mission ideology were highly essentialist, mainly reactive rather than proactive, and framed by Western gauges of human achievement and worth. The most extensive and trenchant critiques in the case of India were articulated by the Hindu revivalist Swami Vivekananda (Naren Datta), who had won some measure of fame in the West with a brilliant lecture on Vedanta philosophy at the Conference of World Religions held in conjunction with the Chicago World's Fair in 1893. Vivekananda was fond of pitting a highly essentialized spiritual 'East' against an equally essentialized materialistic 'West'. And like the earlier holymen-activists of the Arya Dharm, he claimed that most of the scientific discoveries attributed to Western scientists in the modern era had been pioneered or at least anticipated by the sages of the Vedic age. Vivekananda asserted that after mastering epistemologies devised to explore the mundane world, the ancient Indians (and by inference their modern descendants) had moved on to more exalted, transcendent realms – a line of argument that clearly influenced the thinking of the French philosopher René Guenon, in the post-war decades. Vivekananda cautioned his Indian countrymen against the indiscriminate adoption of the values, ways and material culture of the West, a warning that was powerfully echoed at another level by the writings of Ananda Coomaraswamy, who, like William Morris and his circle in England, called for a concerted effort to preserve and restore the ancient craft skills of the Indian peoples, which he likened to those of Medieval Europe. In what has been seen as a premonition of the coming global conflict, Vivekananda predicted, decades before 1914, that unless the West tempered its obsessive materialistic pursuits by adopting the spiritualism of the East, it would 'degenerate and fall to pieces'.[8]

Many of Vivekananda's themes had been taken up in the pre-war years by two rather different sage-philosophers, Rabindranath Tagore and Aurobindo Ghose, who like Vivekananda were both Bengalis who had been extensively exposed to Western learning and culture in their youth. Tagore emerged during the war years as the most eloquent and influential critic of the West, and a gentle advocate of Indian alternatives to remedy the profound distortions and excesses in Western culture that the war had so painfully revealed. But in the pre-war decades, knowledge in the West of the concerns of the Hindu revivalists regarding the directions that European civilization was leading the rest of humanity, was confined largely to literary and artistic circles, particularly to those like the Theosophists, who were organized around efforts to acquire and propagate ancient Indian philosophies. Popularists like Hermann Keyserling had begun in the years before the war to disseminate a rather garbled version of Hinduism to a growing audience in the West. But few Europeans gave credence to the notion that Indian or Chinese learning or values, or those of any other non-Western culture for that matter, might provide meaningful correctives or alternatives to the epistemologies and modes of organization and social interaction dominant in the West. The war changed all of this rather dramatically. Shocked by the self-destructive frenzy that gripped European civilization, Western intellectuals sought answers to what had gone wrong, and some – albeit a small but influential minority – turned to Indian thinkers like Tagore for tutelage.

In many ways Tagore was the model guru. Born into one of the most intellectually distinguished of modern Bengali families, he was educated privately and consequently allowed to blend Western and Indian learning in his youthful studies. From his father Devendranath, the founder of the reformist Brahmo Samaj, Rabindranath inherited a deep spiritualism and a sense of the social ills that needed to be combated in his colonized homeland. Both concerns were central to his prolific writings that included poems, novels, plays and essays. Though more of a mystic than activist, Tagore promoted community development projects on his family estates. And he later founded an experimental school and university at Shantiniketan, his country refuge, which visitors from the West likened to a holyman's *ashram*. Although Tagore had attracted a number of artistic friends in Europe and America during his travels abroad in the decades before the war, and his poetry and novels were admired by Yeats, Auden and other prominent Western authors, he received international recognition only after winning the Nobel Prize for literature in 1913, the first Asian or African author to be so honoured.

The timing was fortuitous. When the war broke out in the following year, Tagore was well positioned to express the dismay and disbelief that so many Western-educated Africans and Asians felt regarding Europe's bitter and seemingly endless inter-tribal slaughter. He expressed this disenchantment as a loyal subject of King George and the British Empire – which may also help to explain why he received such a careful hearing from educated British, French and American audiences during and after the war. During the first months of the war, Tagore learned that he had made a bit of money on one of the poems he had sent to his friend

William Rothenstein to be published in London. He instructed Rothenstein to use the proceeds to 'buy something' for 'our' soldiers in France; a gesture which he hoped would 'remind them of the anxious love of their countrymen in the distant home'.[9] But loyalty to the British did not deter Tagore from speaking out against the irrationality and cruelty of the conflict, and using it as the starting point for a wide-ranging critique of the values and institutions of the West. The more perceptive of his Western readers, and the more attentive members of the audiences who attended his well publicized lectures in Europe, the United States and Japan, could not miss his much more subversive subtexts: such a civilization was not fit to govern and decide the future of most of the rest of humanity; the colonized peoples must draw on their own cultural resources and take charge of their own destinies.

In his reflections on the meanings of the war, Tagore returned again and again to the ways in which it had undermined the civilizing mission ideology that had justified and often determined the course of Western global hegemony. Like Valéry, Hesse and other critics of the West from within, Tagore explored the ways in which the war had inverted the attributes of the dominant and revealed what the colonizers had trumpeted as unprecedented virtues to be fatal vices. Some of the inversions were incidental, such as Tagore's characterization of the damage to the cathedral town of Rheims as 'savage', and others were little more than brief allusions, to science, for example, as feminine (the direct antithesis of the masculine metaphors employed in the West), and to Europe as a woman and a child. But many of the inversions were explored in some detail. In a number of his essays and lectures, Tagore scrutinized at some length the colonizers' frequent invocation of material achievement as empirical proof of their racial superiority and fitness to rule less advanced peoples. He charged that the moral and spiritual side of the Europeans' nature had been sapped by their material self-indulgence. As a result, they had lost all sense of restraint (or self-control), as was amply evidenced by the barbaric excesses of trench warfare. Because improvement had come for the Europeans to mean little more than material increase, they could not begin to understand – or teach others – how to lead genuinely fulfilling lives. The much-touted discipline that was thought to be exemplified by their educational systems produced, he averred, little more than dull repetition and stunted minds. The unceasing scramble for profit and material gain that drove Western societies had resulted in a 'winning at any cost' mentality that abrogated ethical principles and made a victim of truth, as wartime propaganda had so dramatically demonstrated.

Like Mohandas Gandhi in roughly the same period, Rabindranath Tagore expressed considerable discomfort with railways and other Western devices that advocates of the civilizing mission had celebrated as the key agents of the Europeans' victory over time and space. Forced to rush his meal at a railway restaurant and bewildered by the fast pace at which cinema images flickered across the screen, Tagore concluded that the accelerated pace of living made possible by Western machines contributed to disorientation and constant frustration, to individuals and societies out of sync with the rhythms of nature, each other and their own bodies. He reversed the familiar, environmental-determinist notion that the fast thinking and acting – hence decisive and aggressive – peoples of the colder northern regions were superior to the languid, congenitally unpunctual peoples of the south. The former, Tagore averred, had lost the capacity for aesthetic appreciation, contemplation and self-reflection. Without these, they were not fit to shape the future course of human development, much less rule the rest of humankind.

In two allegorical plays written in 1922, Tagore built a more general critique of the science- and industry-dominated societies of the West. The first, entitled *Muktadhara*, was translated into French as *La Machine*, and published in 1929 with a lengthy introduction, filled with anti-industrial polemic, by Marc Elmer. The second, *Raketh Karabi*, was translated into English as *Red Oleanders*. Both plays detail the sorry plight of small kingdoms that come to be dominated by machines. In each case, the misery and oppression they cause spark revolts aimed at destroying the machines and the evil ministers who direct their operations. Like Vivekananda before him, Tagore warned that science and technology alone were not capable of sustaining civilized life. Like Vivekananda, he cautioned his Indian countrymen against an uncritical adoption of all that was Western, and insisted that the West needed to learn patience and self-restraint from India, to acquire the spirituality that India had historically nurtured and shared with all humankind. With the other major holymen-activists of the Hindu revival, Tagore pitted the oneness and cosmopolitanism of Indian civilization against the arrogance and chauvinism of European nationalism. He argued that the nationalist mode of political organization that the Europeans had long seen as one of the key sources of their global dominion, had proved the tragic flaw that had sealed their descent into war. Unlike Gandhi, Tagore did not reject the industrial civilization of Europe and North America *per se*, but concluded that if it was to endure, the West must draw on the learning of the 'East', which had so much to share. He urged his countrymen to give generously and to recognize the homage that the Europeans paid to India by turning to it for succour in a time of great crisis.

In sharp contrast to Tagore, Aurobindo Ghose felt no obligation to support the British in the Great War. Educated in the best English-language schools in India and later at St Paul's School and Cambridge University in Britain, Ghose's life had veered from brilliant student and a stint as a petty bureaucrat in one of India's princely states, to a meteoric career as a revolutionary nationalist that ended with a two-year prison sentence, and finally to an *ashram* in (French-controlled) Pondicherry in southeast India. Finding refuge in the latter, he began his life-long quest for realization, and soon established himself as one of India's most prolific philosophers and revered holymen. Aurobindo was convinced that the war would bring an end to European political domination and cultural hegemony throughout Asia. In his view, the conflict had laid bare, for all humanity to see, the moral and intellectual bankruptcy of the West. Fixing on the trope of disease, he depicted Europe as 'weak', 'dissolute', 'delirious', 'impotent' and 'broken'. He believed that the war had dealt a 'death blow' to Europe's moral authority, but that its physical capacity to dominate had not yet dissipated. With the alternative for humanity represented by the militarist, materialist West discredited, Aurobindo reasoned, a new world was waiting to be born. And India – with its rich and ancient spiritual legacy – would play a pivotal role in bringing that world into being.

Of all of the Indian critics of the West, Aurobindo was the only one to probe explicitly the capitalist underpinnings of its insatiable drive for power and wealth, and the contradictions that had brought on the war and ensuing global crisis. Aurobindo mocked Woodrow Wilson's version of a new world order, with its betrayal of wartime promises of self-determination for the colonized peoples. Though he felt that the Bolshevik Revolution had the potential to correct some of the worse abuses of capitalism, Aurobindo concluded that socialism alone could not bring about the process of regeneration that humanity needed to escape the *kali yuga* or age of decline and destruction in which it was ensnared. Only Indian spiritualism and a 'resurgent Asia' could check socialism's tendency to increase the 'mechanical burden of humanity', and usher in a new age of international peace and social harmony.

Although he was soon to become the pivotal leader of India's drive for independence, Mohandas Gandhi was not a major contributor to the cross-cultural discourse on the meanings of World War I for European global dominance. Despite his emergence in the decade before the war as major protest leader in the civil disobedience struggles against the pass laws in South Africa, Gandhi, like Tagore, felt that he must do 'his bit' to support the imperial war effort. He served for some months as an ambulance driver, and later sought to assist British efforts to recruit Indians into the military. When the contradiction between his support of the war and his advocacy of non-violent resistance was pointed out, Gandhi simply replied that he could not expect to enjoy the benefits of being a citizen of the British Empire without coming to its defence in a time of crisis. But he clearly saw that the war had brutally revealed the limits of Western civilization as a model for the rest of humanity. Even before the war, particularly in a 1909 pamphlet entitled *Hind Swaraj*, he had begun to dismiss Western industrial civilization in the absolute terms that were characteristic of his youthful thinking on these issues. Like the holymen-activists who had come before him, and drawing on prominent critics of industrialism and materialism such as Tolstoy and Thoreau, Gandhi concluded that it was folly to confuse material advance with social or personal progress. But he went beyond his predecessors in detailing alternative modes of production, social organization and approaches to nature that might replace those associated with the dominant West. The war strengthened his resolve to resist the spread of industrialization in India, and turned him into a staunch advocate of handicraft revival and village-focused community development. Though often neglected in works that focus on his remarkable impact on India's drive for independence, these commitments – fed by his witnessing of the catastrophic Great War – were central to Gandhi's own sense of mission. As he made clear in an article on 'Young India' in 1926, freedom would be illusory if the Indian people merely drove away their British rulers and adopted their fervently nationalistic, industrial civilization wholesale. He urged his countrymen to see that

> India's destiny lies not along the bloody way of the West...but along the bloodless way of peace that comes from a simple and godly life. India is in danger of losing her soul. She cannot lose it and live. She must not, therefore, lazily and helplessly say: 'I cannot escape the onrush from the West'. She must be strong enough to resist it for her own sake and that of the world.[10]

Because most of sub-Saharan Africa had come under European colonial rule only a matter of decades before 1914, the continent's Western-educated classes were a good deal smaller than their counterparts in India. With important exceptions, such as the Sengalese of the *Quatre Communes*, African professionals and intellectuals tended to have fewer avenues of access to institutions of higher learning in Europe, and fewer opportunities for artistic and literary collaboration with their British, French or German counterparts than the Indians. For these reasons, and because the new Western-educated classes of Africa were fragmented like the patchwork of colonial preserves that the continent had become by the end of the Europeans' late-nineteenth-century scramble for territory, African responses to the Great War were initially less focused and forceful than those of Indian thinkers like Tagore and Aurobindo. Only well over a decade after the conflict had ended did they coalesce in a sustained and cogent interrogation of the imperialist apologetics of the civilizing mission ideology. But the delay in the African response cannot be attributed to an absence of popular discontent or disillusioned intellectuals in either the British or French colonies.

In the years following the war, anthropologists serving as colonial administrators and European journalists warned of a 'most alarming' loss of confidence in their European overlords on the part of the Africans. They reported widespread bitterness over the post-Versailles denial of promises made to the colonized peoples under the duress of war, and a general sense that the mad spectacle of the conflict had disabused the Africans of their pre-war assumption that the Europeans were more rational and in control – hence more civilized.

These frustrations and a bitter satire of the Europeans' pretensions to superior civilization were evident in René Maran's novel, *Batouala*, which was published in 1921 and was the first novel by an author of African descent to win the prestigious Prix Goncourt in the following year. An *évolué* from Martinique, Maran had been educated from childhood in French schools and had served for decades in the French colonial service. His account of the lives of the people of Ubangui-Shari, the locale in central Africa where the novel takes place, tends to vacillate between highly romanticized vignettes of the lives of African villagers and essentialized depictions of the 'natives' as lazy, promiscuous and fatalistic that are worthy of a European *colon*. But Maran's skilful exposé of the empty promises of civilizing colonizers added an influential African voice to the chorus of dissent that began to drown out Europeans' trumpeting of the glbloal mission in the post-war years.

Although Maran's protagonist, Batouala, admits to an 'admiring terror' of the Europeans' technology – including their bicycles and false teeth – he clearly regards them as flawed humans rather than demigods with supernatural powers. In a series of daring inversions, Maran's characters compare their superior bodily hygiene to the sweaty, smelly bodies of the colonizers; their affinity with their natural surroundings to the Europeans 'worry about everything which lives, crawls, or moves around [them]'; and their 'white' lies to the exploitative falsehoods of the colonizers:

> The 'boundjous' (white people) are worth nothing. They don't like us. They came to our land just to suppress us. They treat us like liars! Our lies don't hurt anybody. Yes, at times we elaborate on the truth; that's because truth almost always needs to be embellished; it is because cassava without salt doesn't have any taste.
>
> Them, they lie for nothing. They lie as one breathes, with method and memory. And by their lies they establish their superiority over us.[11]

In the rest of the tale that Maran relates, the vaunted colonizers' mission to civilize is revealed as little more than a string of conscious deceptions and broken promises. In exchange for corvée labour and increasingly heavy taxes, Batouala and his people have been promised 'roads, bridges and machines which move by fire on iron rails'. But the people of Ubangui-Shari have seen none of these improvements – taxes, Batouala grumbles, have gone only to fill the 'pockets of our comman-dants'. The colonizers have done little more than exploit the Africans, whom they contemptuously regard as slaves or beasts of burden. In their arrogant efforts to suppress the exuberant celebrations and sensual plea-sures enjoyed by Batouala and his fellow villagers, the Europeans are destroying the paradisiacal existence the African villagers had once enjoyed.[12]

Maran's essentialized treatment of Africa and Africans is more or less a twentieth-century rendition of the noble savage trope that had long been employed by European travellers and intellectuals. In many ways a testament to the thoroughness of his assimilation into French culture, Maran's depiction of the 'natives' of Ubangui-Shari might have been written by a compassionate colonial official who had dabbled in ethnology during his tour of duty. In fact, it is probable that he was influ-enced by the work of anthropologist colleagues in the colonial civil service, and the pioneering studies of the Sierra Leonean, James Africanus Horton, and his West Indian-born countryman Edward Blyden. He would certainly have been familiar with the West African ethnologies compiled by the French anthropologist Maurice Delafosse. Delafosse's works in particular had done much to force a rethinking of Western (and Western-educated African) attitudes toward Africa in the decades before and after the First World War. The revision of earlier assessments of African achievement was also powerfully influenced by the 'discovery' of African art in the pre-war decades by avant-garde European artists of the stature of Derain, Braque, Matisse and Picasso. The powerful impact of African masks and sculpture on cubism, abstract expressionism and other modernist artistic movements bolstered once-despairing African intellectuals in their efforts to fight the racist dismissals of African culture and achievement that had been common-place in nineteenth-century accounts of the 'dark continent'. The accolades of the European arbiters of high culture energized the dele-gates who journeyed to Paris in 1919 from all the lands of the slave diaspora and Africa itself for the Second Pan-African Congress, convened by W. E. B. Dubois in 1919. Though most of those attending from colonized areas urged a conciliatory and decidedly moderate approach to the post-war settlement, many took up Dubois' call to combat racism and linked that struggle to the need to remake the image of Africa that had long been dominant in the West. With its explicit chal-lenges to the assumptions of the civilizing mission ideology and its acclaim by the French literary establishment, Maran's *Batouala* proved a pivotal, if somewhat eccentric work.

The extent of Maran's influence on the progenitors of the Négritude movement that dominated the thinking of African intellectuals in French-speaking colonies from the late 1930s onward has been a matter of some dispute. But both Maran's efforts to reconstruct pre-colonial life and culture and his challenges to the colonizers' arguments for continuing their domination in Africa, which were grounded in the civilizing mission ideology, figure importantly in the work of the most influential of the Négritude poets. Maran's background as an *évolué* and a scion of the slave diaspora also reflected the convergence of trans-continental influences, energy and creativity that converged in the Pan-African Congresses in the 1920s and in the Négritude movement in the following decade.

As Léopold Senghor fondly recalls in his reflections on his intellectual development and philosophical concerns, the circle of Négritude writers began to coalesce in Paris in the early 1930s. He credits Aimé Césaire, a poet from Martinique, for the name of the movement, and sees its genesis in the contributions to the short-lived journal *L'Etudiant Noir* and the lively exchanges among the expatriate students and intellectuals drawn to the great universities of Paris from throughout the empire in the inter-war decades. Most of the poems that articulated the major themes of Négritude were published after World War II, beginning with the seminal 1948 *Anthologie de la nouvelle poésie négre et malgache de langue française*. But a number of works that were privately circulated in the late 1930s and Aimé Césaire's *Cahier d'un retour au pays natal*, first published in fragments in 1938, suggest the continuing power of recollections of the trauma of the First World War in the African awakening.

In Senghor's evocative 'Neige sur Paris',[13] the poet awakes to find the city covered with newly fallen snow. Though encouraged by the thought that the pure white snow might help to soften the deep divisions that threaten to plunge Europe once again into war and heal the wounds of a Spain already 'torn apart' by civil war, Senghor conjures up the 'white hands' that conquered Africa, enslaved its peoples and cut down its forests for 'railway sleepers'. He mocks the mission of the colonizers as indifferent to the destruction of the great forests as they are to the suffering they have inflicted on the African people:

> They cut down the forests of Africa to save Civilization, for there was a shortage of human raw-material.

And he laments the betrayal of his people by those posing as peacemakers, suggesting the ignoble machinations of the Western leaders at Versailles:

Lord, I know I will not bring out my store of hatred against the
diplomats who flash their long teeth
And tomorrow will barter black flesh.

In 'For Koras and Balafong', which he dedicated to René Maran,
Senghor flees from the factory chimneys and violent conflict of Europe to
the refuge of his childhood home, the land of the Serer, south of Dakar
along the coast of Senegal. Throughout the poem he celebrates the music
and dance, the sensuality and beauty of his people and their communion
with the natural world – all central themes in the corpus of Négritude
writings. But like Maran, he turns these into inversions of the European
societies from which he has fled and which have been defiled by the
violence of the Great War. His journey to the land of his ancestors is

guided through thorns and signs by Verdun, yes Verdun
the dog that kept guard over the innocence of Europe.

In his travels, Senghor passes the Somme, the Seine, the Rhine and the
'savage Slav rivers' all 'red under the Archangel's sword'. Amid the
rhythmic sounds of African celebration, he hears

Like the summons to judgment, the burst of the trumpet over the
snowy graveyards of Europe.

He implores the earth of his desert land to wash him clean 'from all
contagions of civilized man', and prays to the black African night to
deliver him from

arguments and sophistries of salons, from
pirouetting pretexts, from calculated hatred and humane
butchery.

These final passages recall the powerful inversions that provide some of
the most memorable passages in the verse of Senghor's collaborators and
cofounders of the Négritude movement in the 1930s. There is Léon
Damas' iconoclastic rejection of the costume of his assimilated self:

I feel ridiculous
in their shoes
in their evening suits,
in their starched shirts,
in their hard collars
in their monocles
in their bowler hats.[14]

And in Aimé Césaire's *Cahier d'un retour au pays natal*, perhaps the most stirring of the Négritude writers' defiant mockeries of the standards by which the Europeans have for centuries disparaged their people and justified their dominance over them:

> Heia [praise] for those who have never invented anything
> those who never explored anything
> those who never tamed anything
> those who give themselves up to the essence of all things
> ignorant of surfaces but struck by the movement of all things
> free of the desire to tame but familiar with the play of the world[15]

The discourse centred on the meanings of the Great War for the future of the science- and technology-oriented civilization pioneered in the West was, I believe, the first genuinely global intellectual exchange. Though the African slave trade had prompted intellectual responses from throughout the Atlantic basin, the post-World War I discourse was the product of the interchange between thinkers from the Americas, Europe, Africa and Asia. At one level, the post-war discourse became a site for the contestation of the presuppositions of the civilizing mission ideology that had undergirded the West's global hegemony. At another, it raised fundamental questions about the effects of industrialization in the West itself, as well as the ways in which that process was being transferred to colonized areas in Asia and Africa. For nearly two decades, philosophers, social commentators and political activists scrutinized the ends to which scientific learning and technological innovation had been put since the industrial watershed. Their profound doubts about the long-term effects of the process itself on human development would not be matched until the rise of the global environmentalist discourse that began in the 1960s and continues to the present.

Although unprecedented in its global dimensions, in the colonized areas of Africa and Asia post-war challenges to the industrial order and the civilizing mission ideology were confined largely to the Western-educated elite. Colonized intellectuals, with such notable (and partial) exceptions as Tagore and Aurobindo, critiqued the hegemonic assumptions of the West in European languages for audiences that consisted largely of Western-educated professionals, politicians and academics. Even those who wrote in Asian or African languages were also compelled to publish and speak in 'strong' languages like English or French if they wished to participate in the post-war discourse. And as Ngugi wa Thiong'o reminds us, the cage of language set the limits and had much to do with fixing the agenda of that interchange.[16] Not only did Indian and African intellectuals draw on the arguments of Western thinkers, such as Tolstoy, Bergson, Thoreau and Valéry, but the issues they addressed were largely defined by European and, to a lesser extent, American participants in the global discourse. In this sense, the post-war Indian and African assault on the civilizing mission was as reactive as Antenor Firmin's nineteenth-century refutations of 'scientific' proofs for African racial inferiority or Edward Blyden's defence of African culture. Even the essentialized stress on the spirituality of Indian civilization or the naturalness of African culture was grounded in tropes employed for centuries by European travellers, novelists and Orientalists. As the reception of Maran and Tagore (or Vivekananda before them and Senghor afterwards) also suggests, Robert Hughes' 'cultural cringe'[17] was very much in evidence. European approbation had much to do with the hearing that Asian or African thinkers received not only in the West, but among the Western-educated, elite circles they addressed in colonial settings.

Although the terms of the discourse between colonizer and colonized remained the same in many respects, the Great War had done much to alter its tone and meaning for Indian and African participants. The crisis of the West and the appalling flaws in Western civilization that it revealed did much to break the psychological bondage of the colonized elite, which, as Ashis Nandy has argued,[18] was at once the most insidious and demoralizing of the colonizers' hegemonic devices. The war provided myriad openings for the reassertion – often in the guise of reinvention – of colonized cultures that were dramatically manifested in the inversions in the post-war writings of Indian and African thinkers of the attributes valorized by the pre-war champions of the civilizing mission. The crisis of the Great War gave credence to Gandhi's contention that the path for humanity cleared by the industrial West was neither morally nor socially enabling nor ultimately sustainable. And though the circle in which the post-war discourse unfolded was initially small, in the following decades it contributed much to the counter-hegemonic ideas of the Western-educated intellectuals of Asia and Africa; ideas that were taken up by the peasants and urban labourers who joined them in the revolt against the European colonial order.

Notes

1 'Aptitudes of the races', *Transactions of the Ethnological Society of London* 5 (1867): 120.
2 William Greg, as quoted in John C. Greene (1981) *Science, Ideology and World View*, Berkeley: University of California Press, 108.
3 'Asia's message to Europe', in *Keshub Sen's Chunder Lectures in India*, vol. 2, London: Cassell, 1901, 51, 61.
4 Floyd and Lillian Dotson (1968) *The Indian Minority of Zambia, Rhodesia, and Malawi*, New Haven: Yale University Press, 262–8, 320.
5 In *African Nationalism*, London: Oxford University Press, 1969, 157.

6 'Hope for Africa: a discourse', *Colonization Journal* (August 1861): 7–8; and 'The Negro in ancient history', in *The People of Africa*, New York, 1871, 23–4, 34.

7 'Reflections on war and death' (1915), reprinted in Philip Reiff (ed.) (1963) *Character and Culture*, New York: Collier, 118. For a fuller discussion of these themes, see Michael Adas (1989) *Machines as the Measure of Men: Science, Technology and Ideologies of Western Dominance*, Ithaca NY: Cornell University Press, ch. 6.

8 From his *Lectures from Colombo to Almora*, quoted in V. S. Narvane (1964) *Modern Indian Thought*, Bombay: Asia Publishing House, 106. See also *Collected Works*, vol. 4, 410–11.

9 Mary M. Lago (ed.) (1972) *Imperfect Encounter: Letters of William Rothenstein and Rabindranath Tagore*, Cambridge MA: Harvard University Press, 189, 191.

10 Quoted in Gandhi, *Socialism of My Conception*, 175.

11 *Batouala*, trans. Barbara Beck and Alexandre Mboukou, London: Heinemann, 1973, 74.

12 *Ibid.*, 29–31, 47–50, 75–6.

13 Quoted portions are taken from the superb translation of 'Snow upon Paris' by John Reed and Clive Wake in Senghor (1964) *Selected Poems*, Oxford: Oxford University Press.

14 From 'Solde', published in *Pigments* (Paris, 1962) and quoted in Abiola Irele (1965) 'Négritude or Black cultural nationalism', *The Journal of Modern African Studies* 3(3): 503.

15 From *Cahier d'un retour au pays natal*, translated as *Return to My Native Land* by John Berger and Anna Bostock, Harmondsworth: Penguin, 1969, 75.

16 *Decolonising the Mind: The Politics of Language in African Literature*, London: Heinemann, 1986.

17 'The decline of the city of Mahagonny', *The New Republic*, 28 June 1990, 27–8.

18 *The Intimate Enemy: Loss and Recovery of Self Under Colonialism*, Delhi: Oxford University Press, 1983, esp. xi–xiii.

Further reading

Michael Adas (1989) *Machines as the Measure of Men: Science, Technology and Ideologies of Western Domination*, Ithaca NY: Cornell University Press.

Sigmund Freud, 'Reflections on war and death' (1963) [1915] in Philip Reiff (ed.) *Character and Culture*, New York: Collier.

Mohandas Gandhi (1957) *An Autobiography: The Story of My Experiments with Truth*, Boston MA: Beacon.

Aurobindo Ghose (n.d.) *War and Self-Determination*, Calcutta: Saronjini Ghose.

John C. Greene (1981) *Science, Ideology and World View*, Berkeley: University of California Press.

Benjamin Kidd (1898) *The Control of the Tropics*, London: Macmillan.

Ira Klein (1973) 'Indian nationalism and anti-industrialization: the roots of Gandhian economics', *South Asia* 3.

Henri Massis (1927) *Defence of the West*, London: Faber.

Ashis Nandy (1983) *The Intimate Enemy: Loss and Recovery of Self Under Colonialism*, Delhi: Oxford University Press.

Leopold Sedar Senghor (1964) *Collected Poems*, trans. John Reed and Clive Wake, Oxford: Oxford University Press.

Ndabaningi Sithole (1963) *African Nationalism*, London: Oxford University Press.

Paul Sorum (1977) *Intellectuals and Decolonization in France*, Chapel Hill: University of North Carolina Press.

Rabindranath Tagore (1962) *Diary of a Westward Voyage*, Bombay: Asia Publishing House.

Ngugi was Thiong'o (1986) *Decolonizing the Mind: The Politics of Language in African Literature*, London: Heinemann.

9

THE WORLD OF HISTORY AND THE WORLD-AS-HISTORY

Twentieth-century theories of imperialism[1]

Patrick Wolfe

Theories of imperialism emanating from outside the Marxist tradition have generally presented themselves as exceptions. This might well have surprised Karl Marx, who preceded the great global controversy on imperialism and never used the term himself. Yet this did not stop the majority of theorists of imperialism from claiming to be furthering his ideas. To trace the historical career of the term, therefore, it is as well to start with Marx. Marx saw capitalism as condemned to succumb to its own internal contradictions. Yet it is important to recognize that, rather than simply denouncing capitalism, he admired its achievements, which he viewed as necessary for the transition to socialism. Though the profit motive was bound to produce class war, the same process would also stretch capitalism to the limits of its material and technological potential. Historical development was, therefore, as much qualitative as quantitative.

For Marx, the global pre-eminence of the West (in his time, this still effectively meant Europe) flowed from the dialectic of class conflict, whose history he devoted his life to tracing and furthering. The historical development of other societies could not follow the same path, however, since, in their case, Europe was already there, exerting a transformative influence. Hence Marx's famous assertion, which was to prove embarrassing to Marxist liberation movements in the twentieth century, that England had a dual mission in India. On the one hand, colonial intrusion and the reorganization of native society to serve the requirements of European capital had occasioned untold destruction. On the other hand, though – and much more positively – European capitalism, with its railroads, industrial infrastructure and communication systems, had introduced a dynamic historical spark that would rouse Indian society from its timeless stagnation and set it on the path of historical development, a course that would eventually lead through capitalism and produce India's own transition to socialism.

In the decade following Marx's death in 1883, capitalism developed rapidly, only the consequences were not as he had foreseen. Rather than carving up each other, corporate monopolies began to carve up the market, with cooperative trusts, oil cartels and empire-wide closed shops becoming the order of the day. This trend flew in the face of some of Marx's key predictions, so it is not surprising that the first major theoretical response to it should have come not from within Marxism but from within the world of liberal capitalism itself. In the United States, with the possibilities of frontier expansion exhausted, the era that saw Rockefeller's formation of the Standard Oil Trust in 1888, the recession of the 1890s, and the Spanish-American War produced a range of American proposals for exploiting the opportunities that monopolization held out. In global terms, however, the most influential response to the developing situation was the English liberal J. A. Hobson's book *Imperialism*, which appeared in 1902 and shaped subsequent debating on imperialism as a result of the profound effect that it had on the thinking of Lenin.

Hobson's starting point, which was to shape the whole of subsequent debating on imperialism, was the problem of the economic surplus that capitalism generated. An ever more competitive economy demanded downsizing and new technologies, with the result that industrial productivity was boosted beyond the domestic market's capacity to consume its output. This left a glut of unconsumed commodities which cancelled out profits (the thesis was known as 'underconsumptionism'). The solution lay in undeveloped markets overseas. For Hobson, imperialism's primary function was as an outlet for domestic surplus, with Western governments vying to secure colonies that could restrict market access to their own national companies. Since this only benefited a wealthy few and directed national expenditure toward colonial wars and away from socially beneficial undertakings, Hobson recommended that imperialism be discontinued in favour of an income redistribution that would produce a more equitable and domestically viable form of capitalism.

The great Marxist-Leninist debate on imperialism shuffled the foregoing concepts and derived a range of strategic implications from them. Given its emancipatory aspirations, however, the communist movement could hardly remain limited to the imperialists' point of view. Initially surfacing at the Amsterdam and Stuttgart congresses of the Second International, in 1904 and 1907 respectively, but achieving full expression a decade or so later in the 1920 Comintern theses of M. N. Roy, founder of the Communist Party of India, the view was put that, rather than leading the rest of the world, the revolution in Europe would require a prior revolution in the colonies. This conclusion followed from the observation that the capitalist class could buy off the European proletariat, and thus postpone the revolution in Europe, by intensifying exploitation in the colonies. This consequence of imperialism was widely accepted, not only by prominent Marxist theoreticians such as Karl Kautsky and

Rosa Luxemburg, but by arch-imperialists such as Cecil Rhodes and Joseph Chamberlain. Though the implications that these varied figures attached to it differed widely, the crucial feature of their common perception was its denial of a barrier between the metropolitan and the colonial (or 'the West and the rest'), which they recognized as integrated aspects of a world-wide system. This theme would be considerably elaborated in later twentieth-century thinking on imperialism and globalization.

Of perhaps even greater significance for later – indeed, for some of the most recent – writing on imperialism is Roy's conclusion, which the orthodox theorists of imperialism rejected, that the colonized could initiate their own revolution. At the 1920 Comintern, Lenin – whose 1916 classic, *Imperialism, the Highest Stage of Capitalism*, enjoys unrivalled status in the annals of theories of imperialism – made some concessions to Roy's position, building in an accommodation to Asia that a Russian revolutionary could hardly avoid. Lenin argued that the small but politically conscious Russian proletariat could form a revolutionary 'vanguard' that would lead the feudal masses of Russia's Asian empire to skip the capitalist phase of history and proceed straight to a socialist revolution. Lenin was an activist. In the practical struggle against imperialism, life had become too short to wait for Europe.

That Asia should figure at all was a fateful sign of things to come. Mao Zedong's peasants, agents and bearers of their own revolution, gathered just over the historical horizon, whilst, further on, Frantz Fanon would declare Europe to be so corrupting that the natives whom it touched could but betray the anticolonial movement. In the crucible of the struggle against imperialism, Europe would cease to be a historical role-model and become an obstacle. This occurred in a world that had changed utterly since the late nineteenth century, when Marx had been fresh in his grave and the 'scramble for Africa' was proceeding apace. In the post-World War II era of decolonization, neocolonialism and development, dependency theory would insist that economic backwardness in the Third World resulted from the presence rather than the absence of capitalism, thus turning Marxism on its head. This was despite the fact that the theory's proponents either styled themselves as Marxists or closely aligned themselves with Marxism in theory and in practice. In turning to dependency theory, then, we turn to a new style of theory for a new style of imperialism, one that increasingly dispensed with the formality of colonial rule.

[...]

Dependency theory combined North- and South-American strands. The common target was the theory and ideology of modernization – broadly, the claim that incorporation into Western capitalism would help poorer economies to emulate the success of the West. In the United States, long-time collaborators Paul Baran and Paul Sweezy developed the contention

that monopoly capitalism had stultifying rather than dynamic consequences for economic development. Third World markets were not so
much profitable in their own right as on account of the massive state
expenditure that was required to arm and maintain Western-friendly
puppet governments in power. Somewhat later than Baran and Sweezy,
and from the hemisphere below, André Gunder Frank, Theotonio Dos
Santos and others asserted that 'underdevelopment' in Latin America
was not a frustration but an outcome of capitalist development. Though
complementary, the northern and southern theories emerged in quite
different contexts. Within Europe, the success of fascism had provided
Marxists with a major distraction from overseas concerns, so theories of
imperialism had received little elaboration since the death of Lenin. As
US hegemony was consolidated in the wake of World War II, the Cold
War and McCarthyism, on the other hand, it was understandable that, in
1957, at the height of the Eisenhower years, a beleagured American
Marxist such as Baran should recall the Great Depression and warn that
all was not as it seemed; that monopoly capitalism was bound to
produce stagnation in both the domestic and foreign economies. In
contrast, the Latin American dependency theorists (*dependencistas*) of the
1960s and 1970s did not have a domestic boom to explain away. Rather,
the era of Third World development that had been inaugurated along
with the World Bank and the International Monetary Fund at Bretton
Woods in 1944 had produced an appalling affinity between development
programmes and mass poverty. This new, US-dominated regime of
deprivation in Latin America differed in quality and extent from the type
of exploitation that had characterized European domination of the sub-
continent. Dependency theory expressed its proponents' anger at the gap
between the rhetoric of modernization and the reality of exploitation.

The basic premise of dependency theory was historical: the history
of the West was unrepeatable. In holding out capitalist development as
a process of catching up, modernization theory ignored the fact that,
when the West had been undergoing its own historical development,
there had not been another 'West' already there. Rather, there had been
colonies, whose exploitation had historically produced – and in less
formal ways, continued to produce – the dominance of the West.
Accordingly, in representing Western development as a model that the
Third World could repeat, modernization theory suppressed the fact
that development and underdevelopment were not two distinct states
but a *relationship*. Underdevelopment was not separate from capitalism, a condition that lived on in backward regions that had yet to
develop. Rather, it was central to capitalism, sustaining the developed
status of the dominant economies. If there were any areas of the globe
that had yet to be touched by capitalism, their independence of the
international division of labour would be *un*development, an island

within history, rather than *under*development, the life-blood of international capitalism.

A distinctive feature of dependency theory was the hierarchical model whereby a metropolis (also known as 'centre', 'core', etc.) dominated a number of usually neighbouring satellites (the 'periphery'). In addition to dominating its satellites, a metropolis was itself satellite to a higher-order metropolis further up the chain of dependency, say a state or regional capital, and so on up to the final metropolis, the imperial centre. Apart from the very lowest and the very highest links in the chain, therefore, each level had a dual aspect, functioning both as metropolis and as satellite.

In dependency theory, power was conceived as travelling downwards: to depend was to subserve. In consequence, there was little sense of the metropolis' own dependence on the compliance of its satellites. Moreover, scant attention was paid to ideological and cultural issues. At various points, the theory was potently suggestive in regard to such matters, only to hurry back to raw economics as if questions of culture or consciousness were a frivolous indulgence. This applies particularly to the client or collaborationist role of Third World elites, whom Frank deftly disparaged as *lumpenbourgeoisie*. They were the crux of the whole system, acquiescing in their own exploitation from above in return for the balance left over from what they had siphoned off from below – including, of course, the military, political and economic support that the metropolis committed to maintaining them in power. This deeply ambivalent condition cries out for ideological analysis.

Shying away from ideological and cultural issues, however, dependency theory failed to account for the extent to which *lumpenbourgeois* leaderships could employ the rhetoric of national independence to mobilize popular support for programmes that actually intensified national dependency. The theory's inattention to this ideological paradox rendered impractical the solution to dependency ('autocentric' or independent development) that its proponents advocated. This outcome was aggravated by the fact that, for all its radicalism, the theory never questioned the concept or value of development in its own right. Rather than imagining alternatives to development, the *dependencistas* sought to orchestrate a takeover bid. Having so stressed the limits of local agency in the face of the enormous power of international capitalism, however, their theory undermined in advance its own commitment to enabling satellites to break free and keep their surpluses to themselves.

[...]

As noted, dependency was conceived as a one-way process – spreading out from the West, it reduced the whole periphery (the singular is significant) to undifferentiated subordination. Small wonder that other schools of thought have since stressed variety and particularity. Ronald Robinson

and Jack Gallagher's distinctively British theory of 'excentric' development, which was enunciated in the context of decolonization and the
Nasserite revolution in Egypt, tended to make local factors a law unto
themselves. Though Robinson and Gallagher acknowledged that
European imperialism had been partly motivated by economic and political pressures that arose from within Europe, in their writings these were
dwarfed by local factors that originated in the colonies and threatened
imperial interests. In this, their rejection of the Marxist tradition was
explicit, as was their promotion of political and diplomatic considerations over economic ones. Their case was built on a rereading of the
late-nineteenth-century 'scramble for Africa'. In keeping with Marxist
premises, this had generally been depicted as a contest between the
major European powers for formal control of markets that capitalism had
already at least initially opened up. Robinson and Gallagher reversed
this schedule, placing colonial annexations before the development of
markets. According to them, the British government's imperial policy
had been light-handed and, where possible, informal in the nineteenth
century, a strategy that relied on the offices of native or, better still,
white-settler collaborators. The sudden rush of colonial annexations in
Africa in the 1880s and 1890s did not result from a change to this general
policy, but from a fear that nationalist successes in Egypt and South
Africa might jeopardize wider imperial interests, in particular the trade
routes to India (the Suez Canal) and to Australasia (the Cape). Britain's
occupation of Egypt prompted France to annex large portions of West
Africa so as to prevent the British from achieving cross-continental domination. Franco-British rivalry spiralled across the African interior, a
situation that the German leader Bismarck was not slow to exploit.
Robinson and Gallagher concluded that the European powers had
scrambled *in* rather than *for* Africa, their primary concern being to deny
each other colonial possessions rather than to aggrandize themselves.
Once they had acquired their African colonies, however, they became
obliged to make them pay their way. Hence trade followed the flag.

Robinson and Gallagher's reversal of Eurocentrism – which, today,
seems congenial to post-colonialism – was welcomed in conservative
circles as providing an alternative to Marxism. The enthusiasm with
which some proclaimed the theory to be 'Afrocentric' was, however,
misplaced. The imperial interests that motivated British takeovers in
Egypt and southern Africa did not arise from within Africa. Rather,
Africa provided an arena for the European powers to fight out wider
imperial concerns. Moreover, Robinson and Gallagher's 'collaborator'
category grouped white settlers together with tribal federations, Muslim
mujahideen and other indigenous entities, a conflation achieved by
treating those who resided in a sphere of colonial influence as indiscrimi-
nately belonging there. In many cases, white settlers were not so much

106

collaborators with European power as proxies for it. In other words, Robinson and Gallagher's departure from Europe was merely geographical. In social, economic and political terms, their analysis remained resolutely Eurocentric, a quality reflected in their fondness for colonial boys'-club rhetoric.

[...]

In its stress on empire-wide factors, Robinson and Gallagher's theory begged the basic question of globalization: how are we to conceive of a system that has no outer edge, nothing lying beyond it? This question grows ever more insistent in a decentred era that we might term virtual imperialism, when capital flashes about the globe at fibre-optic speed, prompting a 'race to the bottom' in labour and human-rights standards as transnational corporations seek out low wages, tax and tariff advantages, currency disparities and other advantages that depend on the very nation-state boundaries that their exploitation transcends. In this connection, there is no denying the profound impact of cyberspace and satellite communications. Nonetheless, we should question the technological determinism that credits these important developments with bringing about a complete break with the past. Throughout the twentieth century, imperialism was theorized as a global phenomenon cross-cut by other universal factors, in particular class, nation, race and gender. Moreover, Lenin's dating of imperialism from the end of the nineteenth century has by no means stood unchallenged, with writers such as Eric Wolf stressing the global significance of the late eighteenth century (the Industrial Revolution), those such as Immanuel Wallerstein and Samir Amin stressing the late fifteenth century (Columbus) and the renovated Frank plumping (at the last count) for 2,500 BC. The choice of late fifteenth, late eighteenth or late nineteenth century correlates with the emergence of mercantile, industrial and finance forms of capital respectively. Whichever one prefers, though, the point is that globality is not merely a postmodern condition.

A world system dating from the end of the fifteenth century had been prefigured in dependency theory. In the classic Latin-American case, indigenous Amerindean economies had been converted into dependencies whose exploitation was subsequently to underpin the development of mercantile capitalism (Portugal and Spain), then industrial capitalism (Britain) and, most recently, monopoly/finance capitalism (the United States). This historical scheme conflicted with the orthodox Marxist definition of capitalism as being constituted on the basis of wage labour.

For Wallerstein, the father of world-systems theory, nation-states, which are crucial to the unequal exchanges whereby centre ('core'), periphery and 'semi-periphery' relations are constituted, are cut across by the international division of labour. Though the regional distribution of wealth and power shifts over time, the *dependencia*-style linkage

PATRICK WOLFE

between development at the core and underdevelopment in the
periphery (a relationship that is termed 'uneven development') remains
integral to the system and persists through alternating periods of growth
and contraction. A problem with taking the whole world as one's unit of
analysis is, however, the dispersal of agency that can result. Lacking a
stable location, the core is hard to track down and threatens to degenerate into a reified abstraction. This tendency is apparent in Michael
Hardt and Antonio Negri's influential recent book *Empire*. As a number
of critics have pointed out, in presenting imperialism as having been
replaced by 'empire', a universal order that knows neither boundaries
nor limits, Hardt and Negri's book disguises the global dominance of the
United States.
[...]
Defined as a single division of labour cutting through multiple polities
and cultures, a world-system need not, however, cover the whole globe.
Nor need it be capitalist. Developing this aspect of the theory, Samir
Amin has contended that the notion of a universal history originating in
European capitalism's unprecedented unification of the globe is
misleading and Eurocentric. Prior to the sixteenth century, groups of
societies were linked by trade into regional and perhaps world systems.
Of a number of proto-capitalist regional systems (Indian, Arab-Islamic or
Mediterranean, Chinese, barbarian-Christian), all operating on a tributary basis (i.e. power was the source of wealth), barbarian Christendom
was distinguished by its relative lack of administrative centralization. In
combination with the colonization of the Americas, this produced wage-
labour-based European capitalism (i.e. wealth became the source of
power). Though historically novel, this system established itself on
proto-capitalist foundations that were not unique to Europe. Once
European capitalism had emerged, however, it stifled further development on the part of the other proto-capitalist systems.

Amin's analysis combines Marxist rigour in relation to wage labour
with the post-colonial sensibility of an Egyptian scholar at home in Paris
and in Senegal. Compared to the dependency/world-systems tradition
as a whole, his theory is refreshingly attuned to cultural and ideological
questions, placing the theoretical politics of the Western academy (as in
the critique of Eurocentrism) in the context of the historical development of world-systems. On the basis of his observation that the great
philosophical and religious movements of Antiquity emerged in concert
with the consolidation of the great tributary societies, Amin locates the
break between Antiquity and the Middle Ages not, as the Eurocentric
scheme of things would have it, at the end of the Roman Empire in the
West, but from the time of Alexander's unification of the Hellenic East
('The choice of the conventional division at the end of the Roman
Empire betrays a deeply rooted preconception that the Christian era

108

marks a qualitative decisive break in world history, when in fact it does not').

[...]

At first sight, Amin's Marxist blending of cultural and material factors might seem to distinguish his approach from critiques of Eurocentrism that have been couched in the idiom of text or discourse analysis. Yet we should recall that Marx himself was unfailingly attentive to questions of ideology and consciousness. Furthermore, the fact that Michel Foucault appropriated the term 'discourse' from linguistics should not lead us to forget that, in his hands, the concept encompassed institutional configurations as solid as the prison or the asylum (as practices go, few can be more material than architecture). Despite this, though, it is fair to state that, with the advent of poststructuralist methods, the dominant focus in scholarly discussions of imperialism shifted dramatically from material/economic to representational questions. While it is easy enough to lament this development, as many have, it should be noted that the introduction of a concern with symbolic meanings has produced an illuminating discourse on race, an issue that, bizarre as it may seem, had largely been left unexamined in traditional accounts of imperialism. Thus it is worth considering the historical conditions under which issues of race and representation should have come to acquire a hold on scholarly discourse.

One of the principal factors in contemporary global discourse is the extent to which imperialism has been 'deterritorialized'. This is an extremely complex and still emerging phenomenon. All the same, it is increasingly apparent that the escalating volume, speed and intensity with which capital, information, commodities, weapons, technologies and people move about the globe constitutes a situation that can no longer be analysed on the basis of traditional geographical categories. As imperialism has come home to roost in the form of labour, refugee and other migrations, the metropolis has followed in the demographic footsteps of the periphery, with major Western cities taking on the creolized, multi-ethnic look of a nineteenth-century colonial centre like Rio, New Orleans or Singapore. In traditional theories of imperialism, race was relatively redundant, since domination had most obviously been structured by spatial distance (the West dominated the non-West). Today, however, post-colonial theory confronts a pattern of urban segregation within the West whereby race redraws colonial boundaries within the confines of the post-imperial city.

Marxism's ingrained colour-blindness is characteristic of economic thinking as a whole, which generally lacks categories with which to specify racial, ethnic or cultural differences. When it comes to tabulating difference as a whole, the most developed academic discipline is linguistics. Borrowing from linguistics to find ways to express the racial, ethnic and cultural differences on which colonialism relied, poststructuralist approaches to imperialism turned domination into a kind of language. In the process, race became a distinctly representational – even aesthetic – concept, regardless of the physicality of its conventional signs. The aesthetic quality of much post-colonial analysis has made it a safe enterprise for the US academy to foster – after all, post-colonialism has had little to say about the World Bank or the International Monetary Fund. As we shall see, though, this did not need to be the case and has not always been the case. Indeed, the very distinction between the representational and the material is a false one, for the simple reason that representations inform the (mis)understandings that prompt practical activity. Post-colonial theory offers suggestive ways for historians to open up some of the ideological dimensions of the complex field of imperialism, but this should not be allowed to suppress other dimensions.

The linkage of Marx and Foucault in this context is not accidental. Though appealing to kindred political instincts, their approaches are largely incompatible. A consequence has been an uneasy division of radical loyalties in the Western academy. Within Western Europe, the circumstances of the late 1960s (in particular, the Soviet invasion of Czechoslovakia and the events of May 1968 in France) undid communism's revolutionary credentials. In the Third World, on the other hand, Marxism's role in decolonization – and, above all, the triumph of the Viet Cong – gave it continuing vitality in oppositional discourse. Unlike many of their Western counterparts, therefore, Third World intellectuals who embraced poststructuralism were unlikely to see this as requiring them to renounce Marxism. This was the case even though most of those involved were based in the West. Rather than viewing the incompatibility between Marxism and poststructuralism as necessitating a choice between them, Western post-colonialism has derived much of its disruptive energy from a provisional juggling of the two. Edward Said's *Orientalism* (which, along with the work of Frantz Fanon, enjoys foundational status in post-colonialism) is a case in point. A prefatory quotation from *The Eighteenth Brumaire of Louis Bonaparte* dramatizes Marx's own complicity in Orientalism ('They cannot represent themselves; they must be represented'). Yet no sooner has the introduction got under way than Foucault's concept of discourse is yoked to Gramsci's thoroughly Marxist concept of hegemony, as if the incompatibility between the theories did not present an obstacle. In terms of scholarly outcomes, however, it seems safe to say that it has not presented an obstacle. Moreover, using Foucault – who rejected the humanist notion of subjectivity – without (say) Gramsci would have discounted subjectivity to an extent that would have taken the colonizer out of colonialism. In this as in other respects, Said knew what he was doing.

In contrast to Marxist thought – which, with varying degrees of subtlety, posits a gap between reality and (mis)representation – Foucault's concept of discourse is constitutive (or, as he put it, 'positive'). As opposed to a distortion put about by the powerful, discourse produces realities – regulating, ordering and conditioning the possibilities of practical existence. Thus Foucault's concept of discourse is not simply about ideas or abstract representations. Rather, discourse shapes the structures, institutions and routines of social life. This basic distinction has crucial implications for post-colonialism. In particular, it means that, when Said termed Orientalism a discourse, he meant much more than just that the Western academy had disseminated misleading ideas about the Islamic Middle East:

> Orientalism [is] a Western style for dominating, restructuring and having authority over the Orient…[an] enormously systematic discipline by which European culture was able to manage – and even produce – the Orient politically, sociologically, militarily, ideologically, scientifically and imaginatively during the post-Enlightenment period.

In underwriting Orientalism, then, the Western academy was, in a very wide sense, *making* the Middle East, a scenario that credited certain academics with extraordinary power. This consequence flowed from Said's harnessing Foucauldian positivity to a Marxist concept of ideology. As a result, rather than a mutual process, discourse became unidirectional, something that the colonizers wielded. It would be hard to imagine a more fertile flaw.

[…]

Nineteenth-century anthropology depicted humanity as an all-encompassing evolutionary hierarchy with white westerners at the top. As such, it ideally complemented the colonial project. An anthropological display was automatically a statement about rank. For instance, commercial fairs that provided competing industrial nations with opportunities to demonstrate the superior efficiency of their products typically included anthropological displays that illustrated the world-historical development of the advanced technologies in question. These displays were organized on the evolutionist principle that 'their' present was 'our' past – that non-European peoples variously occupied the series of developmental niches through which European society had historically raised itself. Thus space and time became one: to travel beyond the bounds of European civilization was to travel back in time.

In positioning European spectators at the apex of human history, imperialist showbusiness potently brought together nationalism and imperialism. The psychosocial dimension – how these experiences made

Europeans feel like lords of creation – cannot be expressed by traditional approaches in which ideology is seen simply as misinformation. Thus many recent analyses have turned to poststructuralism for ways to describe the fuller discursive production of imperial selfhood. For instance, Timothy Mitchell's *Colonising Egypt* contrasted the European concept of representation underlying the great exhibitions and world fairs of the nineteenth century to the different cultural responses of Egyptian visitors to the Egyptian exhibit at the Paris exhibition. Not only did the Egyptians confront images of themselves within the exhibition; once back outside in the 'real' world of nineteenth-century Paris, they found themselves immersed in a sea of imagery ('exotic' commodity displays in shopping arcades, etc.) that popularized the anthropological doctrines that had informed the exhibition. Reciprocally, when Europeans who had been to the exhibition visited the 'real' Egypt, they found a disorderly confusion that challenged them to establish a commanding vantage point for themselves; to impose European form on the unruly Oriental content.

Mitchell's inclusion of the Egyptian visitors' reactions emphasizes the Eurocentrism of analyses that present the colonial encounter as a one-way projection of the Western will to power. As observed, domination is a relationship. Europe became what it was through its unequal exchanges with the rest of the world; the Englishman's sweet tooth required the slave triangle. Fifteen years after *Orientalism*, Said moved to remedy the book's one-sidedness by demonstrating that the development of European culture – right down to the genteel provincial reaches of Jane Austen's *Mansfield Park* – would not have been possible without imperialism. Whether or not an effective antidote to Eurocentrism is more Eurocentrism, Said's shift reflects the development, largely in response to *Orientalism*, of a widespread concern with Europe's recip-rocal dependence on those whom it subordinated. Ideologically, the development of European culture required imperialism in a manner analogous to the way in which, materially and economically, Manchester cotton mills required the coercion of labour in Louisiana, India and Egypt.

[...]

When it comes to the tricky question of colonial identities, a similar pattern applies: the fact that Europe and its colonized others were co-produced in and through their unequal interactions means that, through making these others the objects of its action, Europe constructed itself as subject. From the Enlightenment on, this subjectivity took the form of a universal taken-for-grantedness whereby the European norm was held to reflect the natural order, with the result that difference or divergence from that norm came to be stigmatized as defective, degraded or patho-logical. Backed up by the awesome power of Western military and technological achievements, this ethnocentric view was very persuasive – to the extent that it could infect the self-esteem of colonized people themselves. To resist this kind of power, and its continuing legacy of Western racism, it is necessary to denaturalize the Western world-view, to show how certain ideals that it holds out as universal are actually products of the West's own particular historical and cultural experience. Hence the concerted poststructuralist assault on ostensibly universal Western concepts such as Progress, the Nation, the Citizen, etc.

So far as historians are concerned, this assault would seem to have reached an end of sorts in Dipesh Chakrabarty's disconcerting conclusion that Europe is the subject of history – that the very activity of writing history itself, regardless of its contents or emphases, is inherently and inescapably a Western kind of thing to do. In its positive or critical aspect, Chakrabarty's apparently pessimistic thesis encourages an invigorating politics, the project of 'provincializing Europe', of unseating European history from the centre of human development and reinscribing it as one history among – and, crucially, produced in concert with – other histories. Chakrabarty's position is informed by the *Subaltern Studies* collective's long-standing concern with retrieving the voices of oppressed and marginalized natives from between the lines ('against the grain') of colonial – and, for that matter, elite native – discourse about them.

Subaltern discourse – the perspective of an illiterate nineteenth-century plantation worker, for instance, or, to bring it into the present, of a credit-baited Third World female outworker for a transnational corporation – is not simply a mirror-image of imperialist discourse. Hindu/Muslim antagonism in India, for example, is not just a feudal survival that confronts post-colonial modernity with its opposite. Rather, it is an integral component of modern Indian society, concretely grounded in the complex modern consciences of those who participate in it (the point recalls the distinction between un- and under-development). To try to express the reality of actual subaltern consciousness rather than repeat the clichés and stereotypes ('noble savage', 'lazy native', 'mystic oriental', 'muslim fanatic', etc.) that imperialist discourse ceaselessly disseminates, it is necessary to avoid the dualistic either/or, black-and-white (the in-house term is 'binary') approach to imperialism, which can only represent the colonized as that which the West is not.

To adopt Homi Bhabha's much-adopted terminology, the complex modern condition that transcends colonialism's binary oppositions can be expressed as 'hybridity'. In Bhabha's writing, the concept of hybridity assumes the (post-)colonial co-production of Europe and its others, going beyond notions of colonial discourse as a one-way projection to open up the multiple complexities of the colonial encounter. Hybridity confronts the colonizer with the threat of recognition; the colonized other is like, but only partially like, the colonizing self – 'almost the same but not quite/white'. Anxiously seeking to shore up the unreliable racial differences that were supposed to keep the colonized inferior to their white masters, colonial discourse betrayed a profound ambivalence. On the one hand, it strove to domesticate – which is to say, to assimilate – the native; on the other, it was brought undone by resemblance, by the slightness of the difference between 'being English and being Anglicized' that this assimilation brought about. Racial imitation was a profoundly threatening form of flattery. The scornful colonial stereotype of the Indian mimicking Englishness attested to the colonizer's fear of the brownness that mocked even as it mimicked. Recognizable in a brown skin, Englishness broke down.

[...]

In its primary form, hybridity is, of course, only too material an outcome of the practical confusion of colonial dualities. Wherever they have gone, male colonizers have impregnated colonized women. This notwithstanding, issues of gender and sexuality, especially homosexuality, have until relatively recently been marginalized in scholarly discussions of imperialism. Over the past decade or so, however, our understanding of the complexities of the colonial encounter has been enriched and transformed by an emergent body of work whose significance can hardly be overstated. To survey this work would require a chapter on its own. I shall merely indicate a few directions here.

In relation to imperialism as much as to other issues, feminist scholarship has been obliged to labour the most elementary of points before being able to move on to more demanding questions. Thus feminists have had to remind us (or, at least, too many of us) that women were there too, and that women have colonized and been colonized in different ways to men. Much of this work has been recuperative, re-reading the imperial archive to uncover its female dimension. White women in the colonies have emerged in all their variety, exploding the stereotypical catalogue of *memsahibs*, travellers and missionary wives. Attempts by female scholars from the West to recover Third World women's experiences from between the lines of patriarchal colonial discourse have, however, provoked controversy. A number of scholars have objected that the sharing of gender does not entitle Western women to claim a sharing of experience substantial enough to transcend colonial divisions from which they themselves have historically benefited. Moreover, in taking up the cudgels on behalf of colonized women, Western feminists have resuscitated a stock justification for colonialism, 'white men saving brown women from brown men'. As Gayatri Spivak, who coined this deft phrase, has argued (her example being *sati* in British India), the championing of native women's rights provided colonial authorities with a pretext for imposing their own order on native society.

Who, then, can speak for subaltern women who lack access to the academy? The very existence of an academic discourse on colonial discourse attests to the hazards of this type of ventriloquism.

Gender is not, however, restricted to women. Rather, as Joan Scott has influentially stated, it is a way of encoding power relations. Following up some hints in Said's *Orientalism*, a number of scholars have analysed the inherent genderedness of the colonial project. This has been most apparent when colonialism has functioned as a discourse on land, which, in settler colonies in particular, has figured as waiting to be penetrated, opened up, made fertile, and so on ('Guiana...', as Raleigh remarked, 'hath yet her maydenhead'). As gender provides a model and precedent for the dominated, so, by the same logic, does it construct the dominator as male – or, in Catherine Hall's more complete formulation, which restores race as well as gender to the account, as white, male and middle-class.

To begin to evoke the multifaceted fulness of imperialism, then, we not only have to bring it home, wherever that may be. We also have to trace its complex psychosocial operations – not just around the three-some of race, class and gender but, as noted, around (homo)sexualities and, it seems to me, the psychology of violence. Moreover, we also need to be rigorous in regard to different types of colonial relationships. As a historian of European/indigenous relations in Australia, for instance, I find that, suggestive though recent writing on imperialism can be, much of it fails to engage with Australian conditions for the simple reason that, unlike Bhabha's India (though like Said's Palestine), Australia is a settler colony. For all the homage it pays to difference, post-colonial theory has largely failed to accommodate such basic structural distinctions. Historians have also tended to remain blinded by the nation-state, mistaking the international for the imperial, with the result that certain global relationships of exploitation, historical building-blocks of the international division of labour, have become relegated to the parochial enclaves of domestic history-writing. A major example is racism in the United States, especially where it affects black people, as it so conspicuously does. Most accounts (there are exceptions) trace this repulsive tradition forwards from slavery, through Reconstruction and the dark days of Jim Crow to the Civil Rights movement and beyond (the sequence is a familiar one) as if it were a purely home-grown phenomenon. But, as Eric Williams famously argued in his 1944 book *Capitalism and Slavery*, as Marx had observed nearly a century earlier, and as we have had occasion to note here, plantation slavery was foundational to the world-historical process of capitalist expansion and makes little sense in isolation from that wider context. Thus it would not be surprising if my earlier remarks about the racial segregation of the post- imperial city seemed anachronistic to US readers. In the nineteenth-century

United States, the empire did not have to come home to roost. It was already there, and in very large numbers, a situation that lent particular intensity to the drive for segregation that followed the achievement of formal emancipation, a century before this was achieved by the bulk of Europe's overseas colonies.

In short, race and racism are not uniform or singular. Rather, they are locally varying legacies of distinct imperial histories. At this point, the ideological and the material become inseparable. For instance, the narrative of the dying race, which harmonizes with the project of removing natives from the land, is congenial to settler-colonization. It is incompatible with slavery, where labour is at a premium. Though black, therefore, Australian Aborigines have been ideologically represented as dying rather than as endowed with a natural sense of rhythm. On the same basis, the colonization of North American Indians has been structurally distinct from the colonization of black people in the United States. In the main, North American Indians were cleared from their land rather than exploited for their labour, their place being taken by displaced blacks who provided labour to be mixed with the expropriated land. Thus the two colonial relationships were (are) fundamentally opposed. The implications of this distinction flow through, particularly insofar as they affect the different constructions of 'miscegenation' that have been applied to the two communities. Briefly, while the 'one-drop' rule has meant that the category 'black' can withstand unlimited admixture, the category 'Red' has been highly vulnerable to dilution. This is consistent with a situation in which, whilst black labour was commodified (so that white plantation owners fathered black children), Red labour was not even acknowledged (so that white fathers generated 'half-breeds' whose indigeneity was compromised). In Australia, the structural counterparts to black slaves were white convicts, which has meant that racial coding and questions of emancipation have operated quite differently between the two countries. Where the respective indigenous populations have been concerned, however, there are substantial similarities between the racial calculations on which official policies toward them have been predicated. Such discursive distinctions, which cut through nation-state boundaries and are immune to the deterritorialization of imperialism, are clearly of considerable historical significance. They only make sense in relation to the material conditions that historically shaped the different colonial relationships concerned. If we wish to produce histories that tell us enough about imperialism to suggest ways of resisting it, we should start with these conditions.

Note

1   A fully referenced, significantly denser earlier version of this chapter was published as: 'History and theory: a century of theory, from Marx to post-colonialism', *American Historical Review* 102(1997): 388–420.

Further reading (in order of topics discussed in the chapter)

Brewer, A. (1990) *Marxist Theories of Imperialism: A Critical Survey*, 2nd edn, New York.

Hobson, J. A. (1902) *Imperialism: A Study*, London.

Lenin, N. (V. I.) (1970) [1916] *Imperialism, the Highest Stage of Capitalism*, Moscow.

Frank, A. G. (1969) *Capitalism and Underdevelopment in Latin America*, New York.

Escobar, A. (1993) *Encountering Development: The Making and Unmaking of the Third World*, Princeton.

Louis, W. R. (ed.) (1976) *Imperialism: The Robinson and Gallagher Controversy*, New York.

Amin, S. (1974) *Accumulation on a World Scale*, New York.

——(1977) *Imperialism and Unequal Development*, New York.

Wallerstein, I. (1974) *The Modern World-System*, New York.

——(1979) *The Capitalist World-Economy: Essays by Immanuel Wallerstein*, Cambridge.

Amin, S. (1989) *Eurocentrism*, New York.

Held, D. and A. McGrew (eds) (2000) *The Global Transformations Reader: An Introduction to the Globalization Debate*, Oxford.

Hardt, M. and A. Negri (2000) *Empire*, Cambridge MA.

Said, E. W. (1979) *Orientalism*, London.

Chakrabarty, D. (2000) *Provincializing Europe: Postcolonial Thought and Historical Difference*, Princeton.

Chatterjee, P. (1986) *Nationalist Thought and the Colonial World: A Derivative Discourse*, London.

Bhabha, H. K. (1994) *The Location of Culture*, New York.

Stoler, A. L. (2002) *Carnal Knowledge and Imperial Power: Race and the Intimate in Colonial Rule*, Berkeley.

Spivak, G. C. (1988) *In Other Worlds: Essays in Cultural Politics*, London.

10

THE REVOLT AGAINST THE WEST[1]

Geoffrey Barraclough

The reaction of Asia and Africa to European hegemony

'The problem of the twentieth century', said the famous American Negro leader, William E. Burghardt Du Bois, in 1900, 'is the problem of the colour line – the relation of the darker to the lighter races of men in Asia and Africa, in America and the islands of the sea'.[2] It was a remarkable prophecy. The history of the twentieth century has been marked at one and the same time by the impact of the West on Asia and Africa and by the revolt of Asia and Africa against the West. The impact was the result, above all else, of Western science and industry, which, having transformed Western society, began in an increasing tempo to have the same disruptive and creative effects on societies in other continents; the revolt was a reaction against the imperialism which reached its peak in the fourth quarter of the nineteenth century. When the twentieth century opened, European power in Asia and Africa stood at its zenith; no nation, it seemed, could withstand the superiority of European arms and commerce. Sixty years later only the vestiges of European domination remained. Between 1945 and 1960 no less than forty countries with a population of 800 millions – more than a quarter of the world's inhabitants – revolted against colonialism and won their independence. Never before in the whole of human history had so revolutionary a reversal occurred with such rapidity. The change in the position of the peoples of Asia and Africa and in their relations with Europe was the surest sign of the advent of a new era, and when the history of the first half of the twentieth century – which, for most historians, is still dominated by European wars and European problems, by Fascism and National Socialism, and Mussolini, Hitler and Stalin – comes to be written in a longer perspective, there is little doubt that no single theme will prove to be of greater importance than the revolt against the West.

It is, of course, true that the emancipation of Asia and Africa and the development of the European crisis went hand-in-hand. Among the factors which facilitated the rise of independence movements in Asia and

Africa, we must include the weakening of the grip of the European powers, largely as a consequence of their own discords and rivalries and of the wastage of resources in which their wars resulted. From the time of the First World War the incipient nationalist movements in the non-European world profited substantially from the rivalries among the colonial powers, and the sudden collapse of the European empires after 1947 was to a large extent a consequence of external pressures and of the impact of world polities. In Asia neither the British nor the French nor the Dutch ever recovered from the blows inflicted by Japan between 1941 and 1945; while in Africa and the Middle East they were checked and forced into retreat by pressures from the United States – acting directly and through the United Nations – which had a strong anti-colonial tradition of its own and was unwilling to stand aside while colonialism drove the peoples of Asia and Africa over to the side of the Soviet Union.

Nationalism came to Asia a century later than it came to Europe and to black Africa fifty years later than to Asia. Two external events in the early years of the twentieth century were a powerful stimulus in its rise. The first was the victory of Japan over Russia in the war of 1904–5 – a victory hailed by dependent peoples everywhere as a blow to European ascendancy and proof that European arms were not invincible. Its impact was redoubled when, ten years later, the Japanese defeated the Germans in Shantung; and the successful campaigns of Kemal Ataturk against France in 1920 and Greece in 1922 were greeted in the same way as Asian victories over Western military power. The second event was the Russian revolution of 1905 – a revolution which produced scarcely an echo in Europe but which, seen as a struggle for liberation from despotism, had an electrifying effect throughout Asia. The wave of unrest extended as far as Vietnam, and its impact, in sparking off the Persian revolution of 1906, the Turkish revolution of 1908 and the Chinese revolution of 1911, and in the new impetus it gave to the Indian Congress movement in 1907, was such that its consequences in Asia have been compared with those of the French revolution of 1789 in Europe. The result was that, by 1914, in most countries of Asia and the Arab world, but not yet in tropical Africa, there were radical or revolutionary groups ready to take advantage of the conflict between the European powers to secure concessions by threats or pressure or bargaining.

After war broke out the European powers themselves encouraged nationalist movements in colonial territories in order to embarrass their enemies. The Germans, for example, incited the nationalists of the Maghreb to take up arms against France, while the British and French with greater success stirred up Arab nationalism in Syria, in Mesopotamia and in the Arab peninsula against the Turks. They were also forced by the pressure of events to make concessions to their own subject peoples. In India, for example, the famous declaration by the

British government on 20 August 1917, promising 'the gradual development of self-governing institutions', was a direct consequence of the Russian revolution which threatened to open the way for a Turkish and German advance on India at a time when the Bolsheviks were calling on the Asian peoples to overthrow the 'robbers and enslavers' of their countries. By the end of the First World War the cracks in the edifice of European imperialism in Asia and Africa were already assuming serious proportions, and there were limits, as the British found in Egypt after 1919, to what repression and military measures could achieve. Troops brought in from Syria broke the back of the Egyptian insurrection, but, as Allenby soon discovered, the problem of administering a restive country still remained. The troops could not be everywhere. Even when France, a generation later, diverted the bulk of its colonial army – 25 per cent of all French officers and 40 per cent of the non-commissioned officers – to the struggle with the nationalists in Indochina, it was as much as it could do to retain control of the big towns and main roads.

The world war also helped in the dissemination of Western ideas. War-aims propaganda could not be confined to Europe. Wilson's Fourteen Points, Lloyd George's declaration in 1918 that the principle of self-determination was as applicable to colonies as it was to occupied European territories, Lenin's denunciations of imperialism and the example of the Russian revolutionaries in declaring that the subject peoples of the Czarist empire were free to secede, all set up a ferment that was world-wide. Troops drafted to Europe from Indochina by the French and from India by the British returned home with new notions of democracy, self-government, and national independence, and a firm resolve no longer to accept the old status of inferiority; among them was the future Chinese communist leader, Chou En-lai. A further factor fanning European feeling was the failure of the European powers to carry out their wartime pledges. In the Near East and China the disclosure of the secret wartime agreements – the Sykes-Picot agreement between England and France to carve up the Ottoman empire and the agreement of February 1917 to hand over the former German possessions in China to Japan – discredited the Western powers and provoked violent reactions. In China, the immediate outcome was the 'Fourth of May Movement' of 1919, a decisive turning-point in the Chinese revolution. In the Arab world the impetus to nationalism was equally strong. It was no accident that it was in 1919 that the Wafd party was founded in Egypt, or that in Tunisia it was in the same year that the Destour party, before coming out into the open as a legal organization in 1920, took shape as a clandestine underground group. In Indonesia the same period saw the transformation of Sarekat Islam, founded in 1911 with limited and only semi-political objectives, into a mass movement demanding complete independence, to be obtained, if necessary, by force, and with a membership rising from 360,000 in 1916 to almost 2.5 million in 1919.

The year 1919 also witnessed the convening of the first Pan-African Congress, which met in Paris with the object of impressing on members of the Peace Conference the right of Africans to participate in government. Its practical results, it is hardly necessary to say, were nil, for in tropical and central Africa, where most of the territories had only come under European domination after 1885, it was many years before the effects of European intervention in the form of roads and railways, industrial exploitation of mineral resources, the beginnings of Western education and the like, produced substantial changes. In India, Malaya and the Dutch East Indies, the First World War inaugurated a period of rapid economic development; in Africa south of the Sahara similar developments hardly got under way before the Second World War. Nevertheless the Pan-African Congress of 1919, followed by others in 1921, 1923 and 1927, was indicative of the awakening which the ferment of the First World War stimulated and of the way ideas of self-governm ent and self-determination were spreading. Every blow struck for independence reverberated over an ever-widening field, and there was a new sensitivity in each part of the dependent world to political developments in the others. The achievements of the Indian Congress were followed with lively attention. Gandhi's strategy of passive resistance was quickly adopted as a model, and similar organizations were built up in Africa and elsewhere as the hard core of revolt. The Bolsheviks, who were aware of the revolutionary potentialities of Asia, did their best to keep up the ferment, and the Congress of the Peoples of the East, which they organized in Baku in 1920, brought together delegates from thirty-seven nationalities. In the Moslem world, Pan-Islamic movements formed a link between countries as far apart as the Dutch East Indies, French North Africa and India, and facilitated cooperation between different nationalist groups.

In this way the national movements of Asia and Africa gradually developed into a universal revolt against the West, a rejection of Western domination which found expression in the Afro-Asian conference at Bandung in 1955. The Bandung Conference symbolized the new-found solidarity of Asia and Africa against Europe; as Nehru said, it expressed the 'new dynamism' that had developed in the two continents during the preceding half-century.[3] Even as late as 1950, experienced Western observers – Margery Perham, for example – were expounding the comforting doctrine that, whatever the position might be in Asia, the day was still far distant when the African peoples would be capable of organizing independent states and, by implication, that imperial control and an enlightened, paternalistic colonial administration would continue to be necessary for an indefinite period. No prediction could have been

121

more fallacious. When the victory of Indian nationalism in 1947 and the collapse of European empires in Asia were followed by the failure of England and France in their war with Egypt, a new wave of nationalism pierced the barrier of the Sahara and swept across tropical Africa. After the Suez war of 1956 it was clear – to governments in Europe, if not to intransigent minorities of white colonies in Africa – that the imperialist age had ended, and the European powers hastened, under pressure from outside and from within, to disburden themselves of colonies which had become a liability rather than an asset.

There is no doubt that external pressures, and the changing position of the European powers in the world, contributed to this great reversal. But pressures from outside, though they go far to explain the precipitate withdrawal at the end, only hastened a process of crumbling that had long been gathering pace; they could not have produced the result they did, if there had not been revolutionary nationalist movements within the colonial territories poised ready to take advantage of the difficulties in which the imperialist governments found themselves. More fundamental in the long run than the pressures resulting from the interplay of power politics were two other factors. The first was the assimilation by Asians and Africans of Western ideas, techniques and institutions, which could be turned against the occupying powers – a process in which they proved far more adept than most Europeans had anticipated. The second was the vitality and capacity for self-renewal of societies which Europeans had too easily dismissed as stagnant, decrepit or moribund. It was these factors, together with the formation of an elite which knew how to exploit them, that resulted in the ending of European rule.

[...]

From the very beginning of the new imperialism in 1882 there were a few individuals with close knowledge of the Orient who foresaw this result. Hart in China, the French consul in Cairo, warned the Western governments of the dangers of the course they were embarking on and predicted the growth of an 'anti-European movement' 'destined to turn into fanaticism' and 'find expression in the wildest rage'.[4] At the time of the French advance in Indochina in 1885, Jules Delafosse told the French Chamber that they were 'dreaming of a utopia' and that, before fifty years had passed, there would 'not be a single colony left in Asia'.[5] But it is not easy to see how or where the European thrust, carried forward by its own inner logic, could have been voluntarily halted. Obsessed by their own rivalries, none of the European powers was prepared to stand aside while others extended their territories, or to withdraw and leave a void into which a potential enemy might move.

Against the gathering force of Asian and African nationalism the European powers found themselves, in the final analysis, with no effective defence. Considering their overwhelming superiority in arms and equipment, and their vast technological advantage, this was perhaps the most paradoxical aspect of the situation. The explanation, in the last resort, was demographic. How, for example, in the face of sustained civil disobedience, could Britain assure the long-term stability of its Asian possessions when, as we have seen, the British in Asia numbered scarcely more than 300,000 out of a population of roughly 334 million? Only where there was a substantial stratum of white settlers, as in South Africa and Algeria, was repression and the use of force an effective answer; the same factor and the advantage of a contiguous frontier was one reason – though it was not the only one – accounting for the relative success of Russian colonization in Asia. But such conditions were the exception, and elsewhere the imperial powers were forced back on a policy of compromise and concession. Sometimes the concessions were the product of genuine enlightenment, for there were always elements in Western society ready to raise their voice, on humanitarian and other grounds, against any form of colonial exploitation, and they were often able to bring effective pressure to bear; but in general they were the inescapable consequence of a situation which left the governing powers with no practicable alternative.

Though there were many local variants, the expedients to which the colonial powers resorted in order to preserve their supremacy followed a few simple patterns. First, there was the policy of indirect rule, support for princes and chiefs who were prepared in their own interest to collaborate with the occupying powers, which the British used in West Africa, the French in Indochina and the Dutch in Indonesia. It had been an element of Western policy ever since the European powers had thrown themselves behind the Manchu dynasty in its struggle with the Taiping rebels in China in the middle of the nineteenth century, and it implied for the most part maintenance of traditional societies as a bulwark against Westernization and the disaffection it was liable to engender. Almost the reverse was the policy employed by the French in North Africa, where the danger seemed to come from conservative tribal and religious forces and where it therefore seemed sound tactics to build up a Western educated elite of *évoulués* which, it was hoped, would side with the progressive colonial power against reactionary nationalism. This was also, in effect, the assumption behind the Morley-Minto reforms of 1909 in India, which were postulated upon the existence of 'a class of persons, Indian in blood and colour, but English in taste, in opinion, in morals, and in intellect',[6] on which the government relied for support. Finally, there was the policy of offering internal self-government by instalments in the hope of staving off demands for independence – the policy of the Government of India Act of 1919 – or even of appearing to satisfy nationalist demands by granting quasi-independence but reserving essential rights – the solution sought by the British in Egypt and Iraq in 1922.

Over the short term these expedients often had a fair measure of success; in Iraq, for example, they ensured the maintenance of British influence until 1958. But it was also clear from an early date that they offered no solution and were only postponing the final reckoning. It has often been said that the mistake of the imperialist powers was that the concessions they made to nationalist demands were 'always too small and too late to satisfy'. This may be true so far as it goes; but if it is meant to imply that nationalism in Asia and Africa could have been satisfied by concessions short of full independence, it is necessary to add that this is an unverifiable assumption. There were certainly elements everywhere ready, not only for egoistic reasons, to cooperate with the imperialist powers, at least on a temporary basis; Dr Kwegyir Aggrey, the first African assistant vice-principal of Achimota College, for example – an outstanding personality, whom subsequent nationalist leaders such as Kwame Nkrumah looked up to with affectionate devotion – sincerely believed in cooperation. But there is no reason to think that the situation could have been stabilized on this basis. The European powers, when they intervened in Asia and Africa, were caught in a dialectic of their own making; every action they took for the purpose of governing and developing the territories they had annexed made the maintenance of their own position more difficult, and there appears to have been no line of policy by which they could have escaped this fatal predicament. Nowhere, perhaps, is this more striking than in the history of British India after 1876. Here nothing is clearer than the ineffectiveness of what at the time seemed bold and radical changes of policy. Neither Lytton's conservatism, nor Curzon's paternalism, nor the liberalism of Ripon or Minto, deflected Indian nationalism from its course in any substantial way, and this was because ultimately nationalism was a response not to policies but to facts.

In these circumstances there is little point in discussing at length the different approaches of the different European powers to the problem of governing their colonial dependencies. At one stage the relative merits and demerits of 'association' and 'assimilation', of 'direct' and 'indirect' rule, and of other alternative systems, seemed to be a matter of immediate, practical concern. Today it is evident that the distinctions for the most part were 'legal rather than practical'. 'In practice association merely meant domination', and Léopold Senghor, the Senegalese leader, put his finger on the central defect of theories of assimilation when he said that what was needed – but not forthcoming – was 'assimiler, non être assimilés'.[7] If the immediate effect of indirect rule was to mitigate the impact of colonialism, it is also true that, by granting recognition to certain chiefs or princes only, and not to others, colonial governments tended over the longer run to create new, rigid patterns and to isolate the ruler, as an agent of the imperial authority, from his subjects. Consequently the effect of 'colonial rule in any form or shape' was to cause 'a displacement of authority working against the traditional ruler'.[8] Where the Western powers attempted to prop up existing dynasties as bulwarks against middle-class nationalism – for example, in Egypt – they only succeeded in discrediting them and involving them in the collapse of Western positions; where they sought the cooperation of Westernized elites, they weakened the only forces which had any lasting interest in maintaining European rule. Even on the lowest level of self-interest, the time was bound to come when Westernized businessmen in India or China or West Africa, who for a period might be ready to accept Western rule for the commercial and industrial advantages it brought, would see more profit in displacing the foreigner and establishing a monopolistic position of their own, and when Westernized politicians would rebel against having to continue to share the spoils of office with the officials of the occupying power. But opposition to Western imperialism was never, of course, simply an expression of crude self-interest. The desire for independence was pursued for the most part with unselfish devotion; and since European rule, however tempered by concessions it might be, necessarily implied dependence of some sort or other, the manoeuvres and contortions the imperialist powers went through until the very end, the offers and concessions and compromises they went on making in the hope of finding some formula which would save their own paramountcy while at the same time satisfying nationalist ambitions, were entirely unconvincing. At the same time they had to contend with the example of the 'white' dominions and *colons* who, however resolutely they might affirm their own superiority over the native population, were no less determined to assert their independent interests. In the end, the differentiation between the 'white' and 'coloured' dependencies, so popular at the beginning of the twentieth century, became increasingly difficult to maintain; and once India, in 1947, had secured parity of treatment, the dam was irrevocably breached.

[...]

The same inner logic which carried European expansion to the bounds of the earth, not only invoked opposition and rebellion among the peoples brought under European rule, but also put new weapons in their hands. Both in Asia and in Africa, European intervention had three necessary consequences. First, it acted as a solvent of the traditional social order; second, it brought about substantial economic changes; finally, it led to the rise of Western educated elites which took the lead in transforming the existing resentment against the foreigner and foreign superiority into organized nationalist movements on a massive scale. All of these developments were necessary and unavoidable if the colonial powers wished – as naturally they did wish – to exploit their colonial acquisitions, or even, in most cases, if the colonies were to be made to pay their own way. Once the decision to intervene was taken, inaction was impossible; and action of any sort, even the loosest form of indirect rule, resulted in the crystallization of anti-Western forces. What has been said of the Dutch in Indonesia applied to the colonial powers generally: 'the means chosen to defend the colonial regime…developed into one of the most potent of the forces undermining that regime'.[9]

[…]

The development of the nationalist movements in Asia and Africa occurred in three stages. The first can be identified with the 'proto-nationalism' we have already considered. It was still preoccupied with saving what could be saved of the old, and one of its main characteristics was the attempt to re-examine and reformulate the indigenous culture under the impact of Western innovation. The second stage was the rise of a new leadership of liberal tendencies, usually with middle-class partici-pation – a change of leadership and objectives not inappropriately described by Marxist historiography as 'bourgeois nationalism'. Finally, there was the broadening of the basis of resistance to the foreign colonial power by the organization of a mass following among peasants and workers and the forging of links between the leaders and the people. Not surprisingly these developments proceeded at different paces in different countries, and could be complicated by the impact of an exceptional personality, such as Gandhi, who fitted uneasily into any recognized category of revolutionary leadership. They took place more slowly in countries such as India, which pioneered the revolutionary techniques, and more quickly in countries where nationalist movements developing after the process of decolonization had begun could benefit from the precedent and example of the older areas of discontent. In Burma, for example, nationalist developments which in India lasted for almost three quarters of a century were telescoped into the decade between 1935 and 1945, while in the Belgian Congo, less than four years before it became independent in 1960, Lumumba was still content to ask for 'rather more liberal measures' for the small Congolese elite within the framework of Belgian colonialism, and it was not until 1958 that he founded the first mass party on a territorial basis, the *Mouvement National Congolais*. Nevertheless there is a clear pattern running through the nationalist movements, and the sequence observable in Asia and Africa seems in all essentials to be the same; in most cases, also, the three stages of develop-ment can be identified with the policies and actions of specific leaders.

The process of change is clearest in India. Here the representative names are Gokhale, Tilak and Gandhi, and the stages of development correspond fairly accurately to the three periods in the history of Congress: 1885–1905, 1905–19, 1920–47. In its earlier phase Congress was little more than a large-scale debating society of upper-class member-ship, content to pass resolutions proposing specific piecemeal reforms, and Gokhale, like other early Congress leaders, accepted British rule as 'the inscrutable dispensation of providence', merely asking for greater liberalism in practice and a larger share in government for educated Indians. With Tilak, after his rise to prominence between 1905 and 1909, this upper-middle-class reformism was abruptly challenged. Tilak rejected liberal reform under British overlordship, and demanded nothing less than independence; he also rejected constitutionalism and advocated violent methods. Yet on social questions Tilak was essentially conservative, while his nationalism – unlike that, for example, of the elder Nehru – was backward-looking, postulated upon a purified Hindu ethic which he opposed to that of the West. Tilak, in fact, marked an intermediate stage – the stage of nationalist agitation on a relatively narrow middle-class basis, with the disaffected students as a spearhead and little effort at systematic mobilization of the masses.

What propelled the Congress movement into a new stage was the return of Gandhi to India in 1915, his assumption of leadership in the following year, the substitution for non-cooperation, which affected only a few special groups – lawyers, civil servants, teachers and the like – of mass civil disobedience, which brought in the whole population, and the reorganization of Congress by the Nagpur constitution of 1920, as a result of which it became an integrated party with links from the village to the district and province and thence to the top. This is not the place to discuss Gandhi's complex and in many ways enigmatic character. Over the long run it was perhaps his greatest achievement to reconcile and hold together the many disparate interests of which Congress was composed – a task it is highly improbable that anyone else could have accomplished. But there is no doubt that his outstanding contribution in the phase immediately following the First World War was to bring Congress to the masses and thus to make it into a mass movement. It was when Gandhi launched his first national civil disobedience campaign in 1920 that 'India entered the age of mass politics'. He did not, of course, work single-handed, and the efforts of his lieutenants, particularly Vallabhai Patel and Jawaharlal Nehru, should not be under-estimated. It was Patel, a superb political manager, who organized the Kheda and Bardoli campaigns which galvanized the peasant masses into action; it was Nehru who combated the right-wing elements in Congress and maintained the impetus to social reform without which popular support might have flagged. But although it was the new radical elite which took in hand the task of organizing the masses politically, it is fair to say that it was Gandhi who made them aware of the importance of the masses. One significant result was that a nationalist movement which had originated in Bengal and long retained a Bengali imprint spread throughout the whole sub-continent and became, except in areas dominated by the Moslem League, an all-Indian movement; another was that

Congress, which at the time of the First World War was 'a floating but vocal elite with few real ties to its followers', had acquired by the time of the Second World War 'an effective organizational structure reaching from the Working Committee down through several levels of territorial organization to the villages'.[10]

The pattern we can trace in India can be seen, not without appreciable variations, in China. Here the three stages of nationalist development may be identified with Kang Yu-wei, Sun Yat-sen, and Mao Tse-tung, their sequence represented by the Hundred Days (1898), the revolution of 1911, and the reform and reorganization of the Kuomintang in 1924.

Unlike Kang Yu-wei, who hoped to reform China within the framework of the Manchu monarchy, Sun Yat-sen was a true revolutionary. It is true that, in 1892 or 1894, he had founded a reformist society, which aimed no higher than the establishment of constitutional monarchy; but after the disillusionment of 1898 and the bloody suppression of the Boxer revolt in 1900, Sun definitely threw over constitutional methods and in 1905 organized a revolutionary group which was the forerunner of the National Party, or Kuomintang. Its objectives were essentially political – the expulsion of the Manchus and the establishment of a republic – and although as early as 1907 Sun made reference to the third of his famous three principles, 'the People's Livelihood' (*Min sheng chu-i*), social problems and particularly the agrarian question played little part in practice in his programme at this stage.

Sun was, in fact, a liberal and an intellectual, who believed that China's political salvation lay in the attainment of democracy on the Western model; before 1919, he was not hostile to the Western powers and was prepared to leave the unequal treaties intact. But the failure of the republic after 1911 showed the limitations of this 'moderate' approach. It also revealed Sun's essential greatness as a leader. In terms of actual achievement Sun counted for little during the first ten years of the republic; he had difficulty in retaining a foothold in Canton and the principal role in the revolutionary movement appeared to be passing to the leaders of the Fourth of May movement. But Sun was one of those rare men – in this respect not unlike Gladstone – who became more radical with age. Disillusioned with the Western powers, and stimulated by the nationalist enthusiasm of the Fourth of May movement and the workers' strikes which followed on 5 June, Sun reorganized his party at the end of 1919, made contact with the Russian Bolsheviks, and set to work to revise his programme. From this time, Sun was a pronounced and open anti-imperialist, preaching passive resistance on the Indian model and a boycott of foreign goods. More important, he now placed the economic question at the head of his programme, allied himself with the Chinese Communist Party, which was busy under Mao Tse-tung organizing the peasants of Hunan, and carried through a major reorganization of the Kuomintang with the object of turning it into a mass party with a revolutionary army as its spearhead.

This reorganization of 1924 was a turning-point in the Chinese revolutionary movement. It marked the arrival of the third stage, namely the combination of nationalism and social reform and the broadening of the basis of resistance by the mobilization of the peasant masses. From this point, however, the revolutionary movement in China diverged from that of India. The death of Sun Yat-sen in 1925 meant that there was no one to hold together, as Gandhi did in India, the divergent elements in the national party; in China the businessmen, financiers and landlords on the right wing of the movement allied themselves with the army under Chiang Kai-shek and turned against the communists and the left. The rest is well known. Encouraged and financed by a group of Shanghai businessmen, Chiang in 1927 liquidated all communists within reach, finally forcing the remnant to withdraw in 1934–5 to a remote area in the northwest where they were out of reach of the national armies. The Kuomintang itself, under the control of reactionary groups, put aside all thought of land reform, and gradually the initiative passed to the communists under Mao. Their strength lay in the fact that they did not shrink from social revolution. In his testament, composed a few days before his death, Sun Yat-sen had written that forty years' experience had taught him that China would only attain independence and equality when the masses were awakened. Because Mao succeeded in translating this conviction into practice, it was he, rather than Chiang, who emerged as Sun's true heir. 'Whoever wins the support of the peasants', Mao declared, 'will win China; whoever solves the land question will win the peasants'.[11]

In the agrarian revolution they launched in 1927 in the rural border areas of Kiangsi and Hunan, and which ten years later they carried from their mountain retreat at Yenan into northern Hopei and Shansi, the communists provided the peasants with a leadership and organization without precedent in Chinese history. They organized local government by soviets, in which the poor and landless peasants had the major voice; they distributed land taken from the landlords to this rural proletariat; they welded them into a revolutionary army waging guerrilla warfare against the privileged groups and classes. In short, they tapped the great human reservoir of China, and in this way they carried through an irreversible social transformation, which brought the work begun by Sun to its logical conclusion. 'The political significance of mass organization', it has truly been said, 'was the primary factor that determined the success of the communists and the failure of the Kuomintang'.[12]

It would take us too far to follow, even in bare outline, the course of development in other countries in Asia and in the Arab lands of the Middle East and North Africa. The picture they present would not differ greatly in substance, though in the case of the later nationalist movements, where the sequence tended to be telescoped and affected by external events, divergences might be considerable.

It is important to bear in mind the indigenous roots of Asian and African nationalism. The will, the courage, the readiness to undergo persecution – in short, the deep human personal motivation behind the revolt against the West – owed little, if anything, to Western example. But will, determination and courage alone were not enough. As the great viceroy, Li Hung-chang, pointed out at the time of the Boxer rebellion, resistance to the West was worse than useless until conditions changed. The history of the twentieth century has been the history of this change in conditions. Its result has been a revolution in the relative position of Asia and Africa in the world which is almost certainly the most significant revolution of our time. The resurgence of Asia and Africa has given a quality to contemporary history different from anything that has gone before; the collapse of empire is one of its themes, but the other, and more significant, is the advance of the peoples of Asia and Africa – and, more slowly but no less surely, of Latin America – to a place of new dignity in the world.

Notes

1 Geoffrey Barraclough (1973) selections from Chapter 6, 'The revolt against the West', in *An Introduction to Contemporary History*, Harmondsworth, 153–98.
2 Cf. Colin Legum (1962) *Pan-Africanism*, London, 25.
3 For the Bandung conference, cf. *Survey of International Affairs, 1955–1956*, London, 1960, 59–65, where the main documentary sources are referred to.
4 Cf. M. Bruce (1958) *The Shaping of the Modern World*, London, 817; *New Cambridge Modern History*, vol. XI, Cambridge, 597.
5 J. Romein (1962) *The Asian Century: A History of Modern Nationalism in Asia*, London, 12–13.
6 Cf. *New Cambridge Modern History*, vol. XII, 215.
7 Cf. A. J. Hanna (1961) *European Rule in Africa*, London, 24–5.
8 F. Mansur (1962) *Process of Independence*, London, 26.
9 G. M. Kahin (1952) *Nationalism and Revolution in Indonesia*, Ithaca NY, 44.
10 R. L. Park and I. Tinker (1959) *Leadership and Political Institutions in India*, Princeton, 185.
11 Cf. Shao Chuan Leng and Norman D. Palmer (1961) *Sun Yat-sen and Communism*, London, 157.
12 Ping-chia Kuo (1960) *China, New Age and New Outlook*, revised edn, Harmondsworth, 63.

'MY AMBITION IS MUCH HIGHER THAN INDEPENDENCE'

US Power, the UN world, the nation-state, and their critics[1]

John D. Kelly and Martha Kaplan

In the twentieth century Europe's empires were disassembled. Well over a hundred new nation-states were constituted out of the fragments of the empires, more than tripling the number of nation-states in the United Nations. Were these decolonized nation-states 'the last wave' of something? Were they the final stage in the global diffusion of a modular form of national social organization, the globalization of 'the nation' as an idea? Were they the completion of the organization of the world into one kind of political culture, one kind of imagined, and now real, community? Or, how else can we imagine, understand, represent decolonization? Was it the end of something, or the beginning? And how has it been imagined, understood, and represented by those who engineered it and those who experienced it?

This essay has two parts: first, a critique of the 'last wave' approach to decolonization, and second, a reconsideration of the dialogue emerging in the era of decolonization between UN planners and their critics. Benedict Anderson provides the image of decolonization as 'the last wave' of a global diffusion of a modern culture of nationalism. We will argue that decolonization is instead the actual historical beginning of the nation-state, a globalized outcome of the rise of US power during and after World War II. This new understanding of the chronology of the nation-state – which challenges many more models of nation-state history than Anderson's alone – can also lead us to our second topic, a better understanding of the origins of the nation-state, and its characteristics, critics and alternatives in the dialogues of decolonization.

While US leaders from the Roosevelt and Truman administrations were heavily involved in the planning and instituting of the various bodies of the new United Nations, the crucial institution for the organization of a world of nation-states, leaders of anticolonial movements throughout the world had to engage with this 'new world order' even while actual decolonization appeared to be the successful conclusion of their anticolonial struggles. Intellectual and political leaders of anticolonial movements – in this essay we will discuss Frantz Fanon and Mohandas Gandhi in particular – were, in fact, clear-eyed in their criticism of the emergent UN world order precisely as their anticolonial movements faced the new challenge of articulating into a United Nations world. If we do not take the emergence of the 'nation-state' and the other political institutions of the UN world as inevitable features of a modern stage of world history, then recovering and reconsidering such political insights is vital now. The UN world and its nation-states emerged as alternatives to the European empires, but were not in fact planned by the leadership of anticolonial movements, and to understand the order and limits of 'nation-states', and US power now, we need to understand this disjuncture and all of its consequences.

The last wave or a new world order?

Imagined Communities, Benedict Anderson's volume of reflections on the origin and spread of nationalism, locates decolonization as the height of a larger tide: 'After the cataclysm of World War II the nation-state tide reached full flood' (1983: 104). As Anderson tells the story, in Europe's colonies, the advancing educational systems spread news among the colonized elites about the historic successes of European national liberation movements. These colonized elites were simultaneously privileged and limited by empires. Exposed to European life, then restricted from it, but also granted bureaucratic posts and powers that traversed and sometimes encompassed their entire home colony, these colonized intellectuals took inspiration from their European predecessors in the theory and practice of national liberation, argues Anderson:

> They had access, inside the classroom and outside, to models of nation, nation-ness, and nationalism distilled from the turbulent, chaotic experiences of more than a century of American and European history. These models, in turn, helped to give shape to a thousand inchoate dreams.
>
> (Anderson 1983: 128)

These colonized intelligentsia, Anderson argues, copied, adapted, and improved upon these models, propagated the national form of imagined community among their people, and led them to inhabit a nation of their own while the elite gained control of their very own state.

Thus, according to Anderson, at decolonization 'a thousand inchoate

最高潮

dreams' first gained shape, and new nations came into being outside the restrictions and discriminations of Europe's empires. Anderson's argument includes many other elements – notably a causal explanation for this spread focused on the operations and implications of what he calls 'print capitalism', i.e. the spread of publishing of newspapers, novels, and other forms of information that standardize the experience and imagination of peoples. But here let us stay focused on the story of culmination, his major theme. Colonized intelligentsia by coming into their own as the elite liberating a new nation, culminate the global spread of a culture of nationalism. They are a wave of their own, the last wave. Their successful beginnings end a global process.

Anderson's reflections invite us all to imagine ourselves and our world as the culmination of something. He is no triumphalist, which is to say that he does not celebrate this culmination as an achievement of a way of life we should all be happy to embrace. Quite the contrary. The first edition of *Imagined Communities* concludes by quoting Walter Benjamin's description of the present from the point of view of 'the angel of history', the present in relation to the past as 'one single catastrophe which keeps piling wreckage upon wreckage' (1983: 147) at the feet of an angel blown helplessly into the future. Anderson does not celebrate the triumph of the nation as a type of imagined community, but he does insist upon it. He criticizes Nairn and all others who theorize nationalism as a pathology or side-track to global history, and asserts a Marxist dialectic in which the forces of capitalism, especially what he calls print capitalism, culminate in the realization of the national imaginary. And Anderson is far less sanguine than many current theorists (e.g. Hobsbawm 1990) that we are near the end of the era of nation-states. The mood of his dialectical reflection is resigned. He begins and ends his text with his sense of scandal that self-describing revolutionary socialist states could launch nationalist wars against each other, especially in Indo-China. His angel of history is clearly as appalled by the failures of self-proclaimed socialisms as it is by the successes of nationalists. Here, Anderson is much more pessimistic than is Walter Benjamin, the social critic from whom he borrowed the image of this angel of history. In his own dialectical theory, Walter Benjamin more than balanced the pessimism of his angel with hopes for a history-redeeming Messiah (see Kelly and Kaplan 2001). But Anderson's angel is his conclusion.[2] Giving his revision of the dialectic the mood of Weber's iron cage, Anderson finds that the nation-state, not socialism, is the real culmination of a grand dialectic to human history.

And we doubt this. This essay will try to persuade you otherwise. Even though much that is deep rooted historically does culminate in the twentieth century nation-state (especially a specifically US anti-imperial agenda, and the European idea that an active nation can express collect ive political will), we will try to persuade you that much more can be gained by seeing what is novel, specifically motivated and contingent about the nation-state and its emergence in the period of decolonization. Something new was invented, planned, disseminated, made real in the wake of World War II. Scholars out to save the dialectic, striving to rebuild a vision of history with a unified grand meaning, even if a fatal one, can find a way to view it only as a synthesis of deep inevitablilities. But much critical possibility is lost when we thereby underestimate its novelty, the specificity of the purposes behind it and the contingency to so much of its structure. Against Anderson's story of decolonization as a culmination, a modularized European political form finally grasped and embraced by the educated among history's stragglers, we propose that you understand decolonization as the process recasting the world as United Nations, the creation of a UN world, a collection of formally symmetric nation-states. Against the image of the ex-colonies as the last wave, the image of inchoate dreams at the ends of the earth finally gaining solid form, we suggest that the colonies being decolonized were the main stage of the United Nations plan in practice, places where history was made but not just as anyone, least of all the local elites, pleased. In the ex-colonies, decolonization meant the disestablishment of imperial social structures. Entrenched, imperially nurtured, unequal group differences came to clash variously with new democratic schema. But even where elites did successfully take control of this process, and grasp control of the new state, by adapting and articulating a useful version of the past, present and future of their place as a nation, there was more than this role adaptation and inhabitance at issue and at stake. Decolonization was not only the exiting of imperial structure and the extension of a modularized dream. It was not just about giving form or expression to political will, but also about limiting it.

The nation-state was imposed in the twentieth century, made obligatory globally in the wake of World War II, as a barrier to war, a tool not only for the expression of national will but as a means to radically limit national aspirations. There was a problem, and it became the solution. Our world tends to take for granted the delegitimization of war between nation-states, this banning of all war between states and between nations, but it is an extraordinary accomplishment. By one estimate, there were approximately 20 million war dead from 1850 to 1900 (of a world population below 2 billion) and 58 million from 1900 to 1950 (of a world population still below 3 billion), but since 1950, with all the civil conflicts and even genocides of the 1990s included, perhaps 17 million war dead for a world of over 5 billion. Endemic civil wars, and perhaps most tellingly, so-called ethnic cleansing, are also part of the world of the nation-state. But criticism of the nation-state and the UN era should start with recognition of its general success in banning state-sponsored mili-

134

tary conquest, a major limitation of all political will. In the eighteenth and nineteenth centuries, the British and other European imperial nations took weapons and armies out of the hands of joint-stock companies and other mercantile and subject groups, after disasters in the Caribbean, India and elsewhere. They made the exercise of police and military force a more absolute state monopoly, and at the same time expanded the national army to an unprecedented scale and power, as Anderson rightly emphasizes. In the twentieth century the United States, triumphant, appalled and arrogant after the two ruinous world wars, led the effort to take the right to military action away from nations and states as well.

Enabled by the zone of relative peace created in the UN world, scholars of nations and states have recently tended to take the end of conquest for granted, to neglect or downplay the controlled use of military force that has historically been vital to the careers of both nations and states in actual history. We think this has led them, also, to underestimate the crucial transformations of both nations and states worked out and imposed upon the world in the aftermath of World War II, to neglect the recency of key features of the 'nation-state', that relate primarily to restriction of powers over death.

Of course, hatred of war and its grim tolls of death and destruction is probably as close to perennial as warfare itself has been. But the early-to-mid-twentieth century saw more warfare, of greater destructive intensity, than at any other time in world history. Even before the rise of nuclear weapons, futurists such as H. G. Wells were predicting with urgency a stark choice for the world: either establishment of a global ban on the use of advanced military weaponry, or the end of civilization. The sense became widespread that the world needed some kind of order, or, to use the phrase that Wells retooled from its Christian millennial roots, a 'new world order'. The Roosevelt White House, in the US, shared this sensibility, believing that the 'great power' rivalries connected to the European empires were an endless source of destructive political and economic conflict, and that something had to be done to replace 'great powers' with multilateralism and open doors to everywhere. Thus the US leadership planned for the replacement of all bilateral economic negotiation with a large and complex apparatus of new global institutions – a World Bank, an International Monetary Fund, Global Agreements on Tariffs and Trade, and an International Trade Organization (later WTO) – institutions that in reality, even while they invented themselves, restricted dramatically the possibilities of self-determination that the nation-state was said to embody. Above all, the US planned for a new, better, more inclusive and above all more vigorously anti-war league of nations, an association to be given the name of the association of states opposed to the Axis powers in World War II, an association to be titled 'the United Nations'. The rise of nuclear weapons affirmed this priority to the limitation of war powers. Harry Truman's first public appearance as President of the United States came on 26 June 1945. By this date, 'United Nations' firebombs had already destroyed Berlin and Tokyo, and US plans to use atomic weapons were in place. Truman was at the Opera House in San Francisco, for the official signing of the Charter for the new, permanent United Nations. 'They were there, he told the delegates, to keep the world at peace. "And free from the fear of war", he declared emphatically, both hands chopping the air, palms inward, in rhythm with the words "free", "fear" and "war"' (McCullough 1992: 401).

Not the actual origins of the 'nation-state'

Most discussions of the nation-state begin by describing its origins in Europe and then discuss its spread elsewhere. In contrast, we observe that the very term 'nation-state' does not come into general usage until after World War II, and that it arose in the global context of decolonization. Thus, while this section begins with a discussion of uses of the term 'nation' and even 'national state' in Europe from the nineteenth century on, our point is to show how European conceptions of nation and even national state were different, sharply different, from the 'nation-state' that emerged, both in concept and in reality, in the UN world. In short, the 'nations' in the age of empires were different from the 'nation-states' of the UN era.

The rise of the 'nation-state' takes place precisely as empires were delegitimized. Up until World War II, empires were the favoured vehicle whereby many European 'nations' competed with each other, emulated Rome, and colonized the world. It is useful to think about what 'nations' meant in Europe's imperial era, so that it will be clearer how different the post-World War II nation-states really are. European political theory in the imperial era was commonly conducted with a basically Greek and Roman political vocabulary, with distinctions made between empires and republics, and monarchical, aristocratic and democratic forms of government. Other basic contrasts were added to the scheme; some defined as Enlightenment ideas, such as the liberal versus the socialist visions of justice in property rights, individual versus collective. Within Europe's eighteenth- and nineteenth-century history, national imperial political development was uneven and, ironically, it was at the margins, in efforts to develop national polities for Italy and Germany, that much of the discussion of the virtues of the specifically national state took place. Different political theorists imagined different characteristics, histories and futures for national states, mixed variously with the other categories, and what became pieces of the nation-state to come certainly emerged from prominent theorists, including, via the spread of romanticism, British and French theorists as well as German and Italian. The national state, even where favoured, was not always thought intrinsically republican and liberal-democratic in its foundations, let alone anti-war; the most generally held view of the national state in late-nineteenth-century Europe probably found it a type of state suited to competition, conflict and conquest, a vehicle for expressing and extending, not limiting, national will. The political imagery for ruling nations harked back to Napoleon and to imperial Rome, and even when states were explicitly republics, they found nothing contradictory in also being imperial, conquering, colonizing and ruling other nations and peoples in far-flung empires. To the nineteenth-century European world, nation was also, commonly, equated with 'race' (even in dictionary definitions), and by the end of the nineteenth century, a rising 'social Darwinism' conflated Darwin's biology with the rivalries of collective human political interests. Wars between nations seemed natural and sharp competition between them almost inevitable, and aggressiveness and determination of will were widely admired as valuable attributes of national character.

The nation-state actually emerges

In the twentieth century, and more specifically by the end of the unprecedentedly destructive World War I, it seemed more prudent to European diplomats to follow the suggestions of US President Woodrow Wilson in the shaping of the Treaty of Versailles, and to connect the settlement of that war to the construction of a peace-protecting 'League of Nations'. The United States certainly shared Europe's penchant for overlapping nation conceptually with race, especially the white race for the Americans, and social Darwinism was at least as popular in the United States as in Europe. And the US was equally committed to an essentially Roman imaginary of empires and republics, monarchies the norm and republican democracies the exception. But from its early days the United States was a determined republic in a world of European empires. What began as a determination to hold off the Europeans from the space of its own 'manifest destiny', from the days of the Monroe doctrine on, developed by the beginning of the twentieth century into plans for deep, horizontal global symmetries of self-determination, combined not merely with economic open doors but economic doors to be held open. Woodrow Wilson's commitments to the self-determination of nations and 'a world made safe for democracy' combined neatly with naval planner Alfred Thayer Mahan's insistence on developing global military power, not to conquer and colonize other places but to ensure that doors stayed open and US interests were to be respected.

The dictionaries of the English language, collectively, tell a curious story about the origins of 'the nation-state'. Almost all definitions trace its origins to Enlightenment-era European republics or earlier, even to the seventeenth century. But the term does not enter the major English-language dictionaries until after 1950 (and is in all of them by 1970). In the same period in which the dictionaries enormously overhaul their definitions of 'nation' to excise all equations with race, they work hard to naturalize and historicize a connection of nation, not to race and physical nature, but to states and political order. To understand these connections, and the true birth of the 'nation-state' with the UN world at the end of World War II, we have to understand the national state as recognized and only imperfectly limited in the doomed, post-World War I League of Nations.

The word 'nation-state' first entered English-language usage, according to the *Oxford English Dictionary*, in and after 1918 in discussions of the Treaty of Versailles. The idea that legitimate states were democracies, manifesting the will of nations, was explicit in Wilson's famous fourteen points, and thus implicitly the idea that the nations came first and made the states. But no conclusion was drawn about the inevitability of self-determination, also, for colonized people outside of Europe. The Versailles negotiations focused on the proper boundaries of European polities – as Hobsbawm has emphasized, the form of nationally bounded democracy began to be imposed on people for the first time at Versailles, with the breakup of the vanquished Austro-Hungarian empire into such ill fated national states as 'Czechoslovakia' and 'Yugoslavia' – and the relations between European states, especially the reparations due to settle debts of defeat in the war. The League of Nations also, in its own terms, attended to the rights of colonized people, inventing a system of League 'mandates' entrusting the governing of distant places and peoples to specific member nations, in place of actual conquest and ownership. The League's planners claimed to respect national right to self-determination, but the terminologies owed much to the kind of liberalism articulated by John Stuart Mill, setting the capacity for self-determination within histories of civilization, and regarding it as a duty of the civilized peoples of the world to rule the primitive and barbarian peoples and raise them to the level of civility that was a precondition for national self-government. Ho Chi Minh went to Versailles to discuss Vietnamese independence, but Woodrow Wilson refused to meet with him, unwilling to spare the time; the declaration of independence for Vietnam that Ho later engineered, modelled on the US Declaration of Independence, was largely ignored by European and US governments.

Much then changed for the colonized world, in the course and in the wake of World War II. There was, from the centre, 'a political revolution' in the words of imperial historian and political scientist William Roger

Louis (1978: 92). The new UN set up a new trusteeship system, but one that was to decolonize quickly. And though decolonization happened faster, no doubt, than the architects of the UN system had expected, it was in fact the premise of the newer system. As Louis explains, starting with the League of Nation's mandate system:

> In 1919 the non-western peoples who comprised the 'sacred trust' were blocked into types of 'A', 'B', and 'C'. The 'A' peoples of the Middle East were those who appeared to be capable of standing on their own after a period of tutelage. The 'B' mandates were those of tropical Africa, whose inhabitants were destined for an indefinite period of guardianship. The 'C' mandates of South-West Africa and the Pacific Islands consisted of people so 'primitive' that they probably never would be capable of governing themselves. The 'A', 'B' and 'C' classifications may be taken as concepts of the non-western world. Different civilizations had various stages of development. By 1945 these crude concepts had vanished. 'Non-self-governing territories' became the phrase used to describe colonial dependencies. Preparation for independence became the explicit goal of the trustee system.
>
> (Louis 1978: 92)

Much was connected to this globalization of the premise of the nation-state. Overwhelming other factors were the Roosevelt and Truman administrations' commitments to ending empires, reducing 'great power' politics and locking in global free trade as vital to world peace (and prosperity on capitalist terms, not least for capitalist centres). In other words, the US was in the first instance at least as interested in reducing the economic and political powers of European empires as it was in advancing the causes of downtrodden, colonized nations. Another specific factor connects to the appalling consequences of enacted racism on all sides during World War II itself. As John Dower (1986) has documented, World War II was viewed by all its participant great powers as a 'race war', especially in the Pacific. After the war, it was above all the Holocaust that defined the evil of racism for the post-war world, but cognizance of the consequences of racial hatred in the Pacific added to the sense that in a new world order, in the UN world, political hatreds and passions especially on racial lines had to be opposed, limited, even banned from legitimate politics. In this context, then, the revolution in definition of trusteeships and the alacrity with which the UN world anticipated and welcomed the process of decolonization was not surprising – though not every European empire went quietly.

JOHN D. KELLY AND MARTHA KAPLAN

The dialogics of decolonization: the US plan and anticolonial movements

Nations dream of being free, argued Benedict Anderson (1983: 16; 1991: 7), depicting decolonization and its new nations as the last wave of peoples fixing their previously 'inchoate' hopes into this dream of freedom. Harry Truman made fundamentally the same premise the core of his famous Truman Doctrine, determining that, in several southern and eastern European hot spots, peoples longed to be free, while communist totalitarian infiltrators were coercing or tricking the war-weary away from their natural destiny as free democratic nation-states. Truman's doctrine opened a new door, to the paradox of American intervention into other nations and states in order to ensure that natural processes proceeded without interference. Many writers have emphasized the need to study decolonization in the context of the 'Cold War' rivalries especially between the USA and the USSR; we suggest that the Cold War needs to be reconsidered within the larger processes of decolonization and the rise of the nation-state. In the period in which the UN world took shape, the US and the Europeans still focused on their own political rivalries, and imagined world history destined to follow the tracks of one of two rival European political-economic ideologies, while the Truman Doctrine's contradictions were actually one manifestation of the larger paradox of decolonization. In the era of decolonization, departing colonizers assisted in the processes of constitution-writing, often holding the constitutional conference conveniently in the imperial capital. The creation of circuits of actual democratic sovereignty, with a nation of people with rights legitimating and even constituting its state, happened via chains of events far from resembling the social contract implied by the nation-state doctrine. That a new kind of 'Great Game' emerged among European rivals, out to win the hearts and minds of the elites of the so-called new nations, is clear, and that this rivalry had devastating results in a series of decolonizing civil wars, from Korea to Malaya to Indochina to Central America and many points in Africa, is also clear. And finally, that a third global bloodbath was avoided by adherence to the rules against conquest intrinsic to the UN world (buttressed no doubt by military reality, the threat of nuclear 'mutually assured destruction') should also be emphasized. But within and beyond all of these Cold War realities we should look at the more basic political contradictions of the new order of nation-states, the gaps between the political freedoms implied and the political limits experienced, and their continuing, possibly even accelerating consequences after capitalist-liberal-democratic victory in the Cold War.

There could have been no era of decolonization without the pressure on the European empires of sustained anticolonial movements. In a recent book (Kelly and Kaplan 2001) we have reviewed one particular

140

history of anticolonial discourse and protest (that of the colony of Fiji) in its intersection with the emergence of the UN world and the distinctiveness of the American plan behind it, in the context of European nationalisms, republics and empires. But the history of anticolonial nationalisms and other anticolonial movements, from the successful New World republican movements, to the rise of the non-Western great power, Japan, to the nineteenth-century emergence of anticolonial movements in Asia and Africa, is more complex and various than the history of nationalisms in Europe, and cannot be succinctly narrated as a whole. We hope that other chapters in this volume will address such histories in more detail. Here, let us plunge into the middle of several different histories, at the time of the emergence of the UN world, to see what difference it made. Our general theme is that nothing then, and really nothing yet, has truly articulated or aligned the varied goals of anticolonial movements with those of the UN world, this latter considered as an engine for limiting political will and securing peace between nations and states. This is the predicament of post-coloniality – not so much, as so many theorists of the post-colonial have sought to define it, the incompleteness of decolonization or the continuing importance of inherited colonial relationships, but this, the fact that decolonization as actually experienced was entry into a new world order already tooled for purposes at best differing from the aims of the anticolonial movements, and at times clearly obstructive of them.

Anticolonial movements, these other enemies of the European empires, were secondary in the logic of World War II to the European great powers. But even though their existence was a condition of possibility for the success of the American plan for reorganizing the world, a condition of possibility for the willingness of some of the Europeans, especially the British and the Dutch, to give up their empires, and even though they were the cause of the most severe problems for the French, the Portuguese and the rest of the world where the French and Portuguese resisted decolonization, they shaped little of the contours of the UN world. Whether as successful as Gandhi and the Indian National Congress or as resisted as the Vietnamese under Ho Chi Minh, the anticolonial movements and their political histories and aspirations were not already aligned with the American plan for UN nation-states – even when, as in the case of Ho Chi Minh, they had deliberately sought to be. The American plan for the UN, with its focus on the limitation of war, had more sympathy for parties of order than parties of struggle, even before and outside the dynamics of the Cold War.

Thus not only specifically anticolonial movements, but all movements for social reform, religious revival, any kind of specific political telos or utopia, sectarian religious assertion or new hybrid social movement, ran into specific limits, restrictions and even fears as the inner political logic

JOHN D. KELLY AND MARTHA KAPLAN

of each new nation-state was arranged by ex-colonial powers and other
outside consultants, as the constraints of the UN world were articulated
and imposed. James Ferguson has quite elegantly called the complex,
global apparatuses of development aid, in particular, 'the anti-politics
machine'. In the UN world generally, devoted as it was to freeing the
world from the fear of war, *all* that a political agent in any 'new nation'
could rightly aspire to was his or her national interest, and that interest
could only, responsibly, be this dream of 'being free', to again quote but
recast Anderson's observation. Far from Anderson's image of peoples
whose inchoate dreams finally found form in nationalism, the social and
political movements of the decolonized nation-states have been highly
various in their dreams, and have been repeatedly forced to attempt to fit
their dreams and goals into the limits of the nation-state form, to become
nations or part of a nation, content with local sovereignty and the project
of national development. And time has not caused the crucial gaps in
perspective to close. For example, for more than fifty years now, the
United States and India have had strained and stressed diplomatic relations. As Himadeep Muppidi has recently shown, India's relations with
the United States have been significantly worse than they have been with
the USSR and Russia, despite the fact that India sided with the US on
important questions at least as often as it has sided against it, and despite
the fact that India made it clear diplomatically, early on in its existence,
that it would not join with either the Soviet bloc or the US, and that it
sought a third path allied with neither power. The Soviets, Muppidi
shows, were able to commiserate with India over its struggles with
global capitalism, and unlike the United States, were able to recognize
India for its independence struggle. The United States, on the other
hand, while pleased to recognize India for its cultural differences, its
distinctive civilization, and its regional situation and interests, has never
been able to found its relations with India on acknowledgement of the
dramatic successes of its anticolonial movements, to find common
ground with India as anti-imperial. Instead of recognizing common
ground in a shared heritage of anticolonial struggle, the United States
persistently proposes itself to be a senior, wiser adviser, ready to help a
junior nation in need of modernization and development.

Conclusions: the end of the beginning of the nation-state

None of this means, as Benedict Anderson correctly observes, that we are
at the end of the era of nationalisms or indeed of nation-states. It is worth
recalling, again, how successful the UN world has been at preventing
large-scale war and death, and also that the tide of civil war and violence
is rising. And, to repeat for a final time, the nation-state is actually quite
recent in its tooling, a mandate against empires. We find ourselves not at

the beginning of the end of the era of nation-states, but at the end of the beginning. The UN world as it has developed has become increasingly demanding, at least in its formal structures, about what is necessary for good order in a nation-state, proposing itself to be against all totalitarian, dictatorial and otherwise anti-democratic states, and in favour of large numbers of specific sorts of rights for citizens within all nation-states. Of course the large and increasing number of rights-defining UN covenants can be used as resources by and for some seeking rights within nation-states, for example in Fiji (see Kelly and Kaplan 2001). The UN world grows increasingly specific and delimiting of the sovereignty it will recognize; its very specificity in demands for constitutional democracy and regard for long lists of civil and political rights ironically restricts the very self-constitutive process it determines itself to be fostering.

There is much evidence, in the contemporary world, of disquiet with the UN world, evidence of resistance to the limits of the nation-state as the vehicle for the realization of political dreams and will. One phenomenon is a new general pattern to diasporas. The world has long known diasporic movements of people in the original sense of dispersions of populations, especially in flight from persecution, even in flight from genocide, seeking not merely improved life-chances but above all the chance to continue bare life. Under all forms of capitalism the world has known various forms of labour diaspora, workers enslaved, indentured or free migrating to work in distant environs. Under most forms of capitalism, free migrations, often permanent and successive, have been a vehicle for the pursuit of increased life-chances for working-class people. Working-class migrations have been known from all corners of the planet. But in the era of nation-states, an interesting and different pattern to migration has emerged: elite diasporas. On a vector especially from impoverished homelands to metropolitan hostlands, people of the high, often the highest educational and status levels, have been migrating in increasing numbers in recent decades, often accepting temporary or even permanent loss of professional status in order to secure a different social place and future for their families and children. The elites of the poorest of the decolonized nation-states do not express their political will and agency by staying at home and putting their all into the development of their home nation. Often they provide financial and other forms of support for homelands they remember well. But there is no doubt that their migration also expresses a will to seek greater life-chances elsewhere than in 'their' nation-state.

And an equal lack of faith in the redemptive or even ameliorative power of the world's poorer nation-states is also, sometimes and increasingly, expressed in election rioting in several locales the world over. As Stanley Tambiah has recently demonstrated (Tambiah 1996), rioting connected to elections need not always be interpreted as an effort to

143

control or protest the actual pattern of voting, to capture control of the state or to intimidate its officers into specific courses of action. Tambiah documents, especially in cycles of rioting before rather than after elections, a distinct phenomenon, what he calls 'leveling crowds', not out to change the elections but to protest the perceived injustices that result from them and other structures of political favour. Tambiah describes ethnically or religiously self-defined crowds, in several nation-states in South Asia and elsewhere, that, ominously, seek mainly to destroy the privileges gained by others in ways perceived as unjust, crowds that seek to level downward the social field rather than to advance their own cause or to build anything new by political means.

So, at both the top and bottom of the class and status scales of many decolonized nation-states, one can see ample symptoms of failure of these states to deliver sufficient benefits to keep their citizens committed to them as political self-expressions and affiliations. Further, the model of 'leveling crowds' could probably be extended to explain the aims, also, of some terrorist organizations and movements. On top of these, we should also remember the world's several sites where endemic ethnic conflict has led to semi-permanent UN 'peacekeeping'. Some of them, for example Bosnia or Israel, fit the profile of territories of mixed nationality that Mill declared unsuited for national states. But other sites of the chronic failure of nation-states to achieve local peace also exist (China and Taiwan, North and South Korea, Haiti), leading one to doubt that pre-existing national consciousness stands as the only cause for such failures. If anything is general about 'peacekeeping', it is that it raises all the dilemmas, in microcosm, of intervention in the internal affairs of alleged nation-states. During the years of the Clinton presidency, the United States repeatedly preached the theme of impressing investors, a need for all nation-states to seek prosperity by creating local conditions suited to taking best advantage of the world's footloose and flowing investment capital. In the presidency of George W. Bush, and not only after 9/11, more is said about security, less about the need for rights in national and international law, and one sees an increasingly visible, and openly aggressive, hand of US intervention, more interested in sustaining its own freedoms, security and prosperity than in finding global solutions to anything.

Many critics in the US, Europe and elsewhere have described US power in the UN world as imperial. This description captures many aspects of US global domination, but on crucial matters it is highly imprecise. We suggest that it is high time for recognition and criticism of the specifically post-colonial and anti-imperial, as well as the neo-imperial, aspects of US power; that its forms of domination need their own, new names, that nothing like 'neo-imperialism', or for that matter 'modernity', will suffice. Otherwise, the prescriptions will simply be for more anti-imperialism, more decolonization, more post- or anti- or alternative modernity as the sufficient goal, more dreams of freedom as the panacea. The limited liabilities that are built into the UN world, the traps for places and peoples without capital or valuable resources intrinsic to the politics of freedom and self-determination, need to be recognized.

We want to finish more optimistically, with two important critical voices from the outset of the era of decolonization, addressing problems, limits and alternatives to the UN world.

The dialogics of decolonization: two critical perspectives

Frantz Fanon was a practicing psychoanalyst and student of the works of Jean-Paul Sartre. He was born in Martinique, fought for France during World War II, and after obtaining his education in the late 1940s and early 1950s, moved to Algeria, where he was the only racially non-white psychiatrist in the main hospital of Algeria's capital, Algiers, when, in the late 1950s, the colonial French government accelerated its campaigns to suppress Algeria's anticolonial movement. As the violence grew into open civil war, Fanon found himself treating both French police torturers and Algerian torture victims, the latter through translators. He finally quit his hospital work, but only with great regret, recognizing the number of patients he stranded in the act. He had determined that there was no way, under the conditions of colonialism and of open civil war, that he could solve the problems of his patients within the repressive regime of the colonial state. He found his way to centres of the rebellion and became a journalist for the Algerian rebels, and thereafter published works theorizing anticolonial rebellion, its means, needs and prospects.

Much has been written about Fanon and his radical calls for anticolonial violence. Fanon anticipated that anticolonial violence would be revolutionary, that it would create the 'new men', and bring forth the next stage in a global Hegelian dialectic; and the many things written about this vision include an elegant, and to our minds persuasive, caution against seeking too much in Fanon's broad arguments (Gates 1991). But in his perceptions of the US and the emerging UN, Fanon was acute. In the emerging Cold War, Fanon argued, 'the Americans take their role of patron of international capitalism very seriously' (1968: 79), advising their allies to decolonize and select their new governments in a friendly and controlled fashion. Especially when faced with the spectre of violence from the colonized, he argued, not only the Americans but the colonial governments themselves had come to call for decolonization, fearing more radical liberation movements such as that faced by the French in Indochina, especially after the successful rebel siege of Dien Bien Phu.

aware of manifold Dien Bien Phus…a veritable panic takes hold of the colonialist governments in turn. Their purpose is to capture the vanguard, to turn the movement of liberation toward the right, and to disarm the people: quick, quick, let's decolonize…for God's sake let's decolonize quick.…To the strategy of Dien Bien Phu, defined by the colonized peoples, the colonialist replies by the strategy of encirclement – based on the respect of the sovereignty of states.

(Fanon 1968: 70–1)

We think Fanon overestimated both the therapeutic and revolutionary prospects of violence, and underestimated the role of the Americans' anti-great power, new world order politics (as against fear of colonial rebellions) in defining this strategy of encirclement. But there is no doubt about his critical estimation of the difference between this form of decolonization and any viable long-term outcome:

The apotheosis of independence is transformed into the curse of independence.…In plain words, the colonial power says, 'Since you want independence, take it and starve'. The nationalist leaders have no choice but to turn to their people and ask from them a gigantic effort. A regime of austerity is imposed on these starving men…an autarkic regime is set up…which toils to exhaustion.

Other countries of the Third World refuse to undergo this ordeal and agree to get over it by accepting the conditions of the former guardian power [and, we would add, of the US, the new guardian power].…The former dominated country becomes an economically dependent country…

Thus we see that the accession to independence of the colonial countries places an important question before the world, for the national liberation of the colonized countries unveils their true economic state and makes it seem even more unendurable. The fundamental duel which seemed to be that between colonialism and anticolonialism, and indeed between capitalism and socialism, is already losing some of its importance. What counts today, the question looming over the horizon, is the need for a redistribution of wealth. Humanity must reply to this question, or be shaken to pieces by it.

(Fanon 1968: 97–8)

In short, Fanon saw the problem, this 'curse of independence', and its inability to address the most crucial political relationships and economic problems. But his thinking often returned to solutions of violent, radical liberation. For a critique of this solution, both in means and ends, we turn to Gandhi.

Politically active from the 1900s, among South Asian migrants to South Africa, through a long career serving and promoting the Indian National Congress in India, from the 1910s to his death in 1948, Mohandas Gandhi was both a moral, theological and above all political theorist, and a consummately effective politician, contributing more than any other polemicist or tactician to the successful campaigns to drive the British out of India (although, while Gandhi's campaigns were no doubt a condition of possibility for British willingness to decolonize under American pressure after World War II, one wonders what would have happened without that American pressure). Gandhi early on articulated his core political goals of *swaraj*, not merely independence but 'self-rule', and *satyagraha*, 'insistence on the truth' as the crucial political strategy. By Gandhi's reckoning *swaraj* meant self-control, self-mastery and self-discipline as much as it did self-rule or indeed self-determination: his goal was nothing like the individualistic pursuit of happiness, but instead more akin to the good-works branches of Christian ethics, perfect freedom in service to others. The strategies of *satyagraha* were, he thought, as radical, direct and potentially revolutionary as any scheme for violence, but required sacrifice of self rather than others, in efforts to persuade and reform rather than coerce or remove opponents. Gandhi applied his strictures first of all to himself. He amazed his followers, for example, in the 1920s when he refused to continue leading a series of boycotts, strikes and protests that, some historians feel, might well have driven the British to quit India long before India's eventual independence in 1947. After a massacre of police by some of his followers, Gandhi decided that India was not yet ready for independence, and he wanted from his followers and countrymen more political training, discipline and awareness before he would lead further campaigns.

Gandhi hoped, persistently throughout his life, to encourage a stronger sense of duty among all people. In a fascinating political exchange during World War II, in 1940, Gandhi refused to endorse H. G. Wells' scheme for a Universal Declaration of Human Rights. Wells' plan eventually bore fruit in the UN declaration of 1948. But Gandhi wrote to Wells bluntly that 'you have begun at the wrong end'. What was needed was a charter of the duties of humanity, Gandhi argued: 'I promise that the rights will follow as spring follows winter' (quoted in Wells 1940: 122). But Gandhi found his calls for duty over rights, self-discipline over self-gratification, and the politics of truth over the politics of self-interest, increasingly out of step with world political trends as the twentieth century progressed. By the time of the signing of the UN Charter in 1945, he was a strong and clear-eyed critic. His point of greatest sympathy was the search for a non-violent future – but Gandhi's schemes stressed especially self-renunciation of violence, concerned not just about security but about the effects of violent tactics on the perpetrators, individual or national in scale. He emphasized the need for equity and justice as well as freedom for colonized people, a future world not merely of free nations but of an end to domination, and predicted that true peace would depend upon achievements of justice as well as liberty. For example, he wrote on 17 April 1945, a week before the San Francisco conference convened, that:

> I reiterate my conviction that there will be no peace for the Allies or the world unless they shed their belief in the efficacy of war and its accompanying terrible deception and fraud and are determined to hammer out real peace based on freedom and equality of all races and nations. Exploitation and domination of one nation over another can have no place in a world striving to put an end to all wars.
>
> (Gandhi 1986: II, 497)

Gandhi often wrote that his form of nationalism was intrinsically internationalist. He wrote in 1928, 'My ambition is much higher than independence. Through the deliverance of India, I seek to deliver the so-called weaker races of the earth from the crushing heels of Western exploitation' (1987: III, 255). But the means would be not force but persuasion, not mere constitution of independence, but recognition of interdependence, not the mere balancing of interests but the pursuit of justice.

At its core, the nation-state concept is antithetical to the position of imperial lawgiver, the quasi-Roman model whereby any sacred, conquering, or otherwise higher power, whether individual or group, is able to legitimately give terms of law and order to others, and thereby put them into debt to the lawgivers. Lawgiving schemes constitute and perpetuate moral inequality in the guise of creating a realm of legal government. In the nation-state as liberal utopia, the law begins not as a gift but as a social contract, among the people of the nation and then between the nation and the state, in which debt, if accrued at all, runs from state to nation for the right and privilege of rule. The irony of the UN world is the incompleteness by which actual nation-states can realize the logic of sovereignty by social contract, when so much of their form of independence is determined, in effect given, by the forms and even the agents of international and transnational law. Thus the neo-imperialism, in a scheme that otherwise constitutes freedoms and limits responsibilities and liabilities. Gandhi prescribed a solution for this morass, not in the need for greater independence for the ex-colonized, but in greater initiative on their part in the constitution of the actual future order, both at home and abroad. Thus his intrinsically international nationalism, his

favouring of recognition of interdependence as a crucial part of independence. 'It is, therefore, not out of expedience that I oppose independence
as my goal', he wrote in 1928. 'I want India to come to her own and that
state cannot be better defined by any single word than *"swaraj"*....India's
coming to her own will mean every nation doing likewise' (1987: III,
255). But of course, in the fashion that decolonization occurred in fact,
India was able to take little initiative, a British diplomat even drawing
the borders of the partition of colonial India into the new states of India
and Pakistan. A school of historians that has come to be called *Subaltern
Studies* was founded on the need to study the failure of post-colonial
India 'to come to its own' (Guha 1982: 7). A prominent member of that
school, Partha Chatterjee, has observed acidly of the 'last wave' image of
decolonizing nationalism, that it proposes that 'Europe and the
Americas, the only true subjects of history, have thought out on our
behalf not only the script of colonial enlightenment and exploitation, but
also that of our anticolonial resistance and postcolonial misery'
(Chatterjee 1993: 5). What makes Gandhi's politics particularly interesting, despite the limitations of its righteous didacticism, is that it did
not follow the scripts of any of the major European forms of political
thought, from utilitarian liberalism through various romantic nationalisms even to the many forms of socialism. Palpably, its successes did
not extend to refounding the global order. That was achieved by a very
different plan, the American plan for a global order of nation-states,
founded on formal, not substantive, equalities of rights. The flaws of the
American plan are now apparent because of its success, and marked by
such phenomena as elite diasporas from poor nation-states to wealthier
ones, levelling crowds in among the chronically impoverished, and
morasses of 'peacekeeping' in locales where the nation-state has failed,
for many reasons, to come into its own. We want to conclude by
observing that a fourth set of phenomena is also visible in contemporary
politics, the so-called 'new social movements' that traverse the ordinary
politics of nation and state and exceed their boundaries with their globally connected and collected political will, making very general claims
for feminism, for environmentalism, for indigenous rights and for
human rights. Though they often speak in terms of rights, these movements in their insistence on the truth, their non-violence, and their calls
for recognition of interdependences and for assumption of duties, are
clearly the inheritors of Gandhi's politics, among many inspirations – as
when Martin Luther King brought Gandhi's politics to bear on problems
of civil rights in the US. Another of the *Subaltern Studies* historians has
warned that history always comes to be narrated, 'first in Europe, then
elsewhere' (Chakrabarty 2000). But in fact we are describing a political
imaginary whose dialogical roots and branches run outside as well as
within, against as well as along, the lines of the past, present and future

of the West. On the one hand, the UN world is largely rooted in specifically anti-European-imperial US plans and powers, and on the other hand, social movements have, in this Gandhian manner, begun to successfully collect and deploy political will beyond the forms and boundaries of empires and republics, and even of nations and states.

Notes

1   Although this essay was first written for this volume, for a fuller statement of the position and further references, readers should consult the authors' *Represented Communities: Fiji and World Decolonization* (University of Chicago Press, 2001).
2   Literally the conclusion of the first edition of his text.

References and further reading

Anderson, Benedict (1991) [1983] *Imagined Communities*, revised edn, London: Verso.

Chakrabarty, Dipesh (2000) *Provincializing Europe: Postcolonial Thought and Historical Difference*, Princeton: Princeton University Press.

Chatterjee, Partha (1993) *The Nation and Its Fragments: Colonial and Postcolonial Histories*, Princeton: Princeton University Press.

Dower, John (1986) *War Without Mercy*, New York: Pantheon Books.

Fanon, Frantz (1968) *The Wretched of the Earth*, New York: Grove Press.

Ferguson, James (1997) 'Paradoxes of sovereignty and independence: "real" and "pseudo" nation-states and the depoliticization of poverty', in Karen Fog Olwig and Kirsten Hastrup (eds) *Siting Culture: The Shifting Anthropological Object*, London: Routledge.

Gandhi, M. K. (1986) *The Moral and Political Writings of Mahatma Gandhi, Volume II: Truth and Non-Violence*, ed. Raghavan Iyer, Oxford: Oxford University Press.

——(1987) *The Moral and Political Writings of Mahatma Gandhi, Volume III: Non-Violent Resistance and Social Transformation*, ed. Raghavan Iyer, Oxford: Oxford University Press.

Guha, Ranajit (1982) 'On some aspects of the historiography of colonial India', in *Subaltern Studies*, vol. I, Delhi: Oxford University Press, 1–8.

Gates, Henry Louis Jr (1991) 'Critical Fanonism', *Critical Inquiry* 17: 457–70.

Hobsbawm, Eric (1990) *Nations and Nationalism since 1780*, Cambridge: Cambridge University Press.

Kelly, John D. and Martha Kaplan (2001) *Represented Communities: Fiji and World Decolonization*, Chicago: University of Chicago Press.

Louis, William Roger (1978) *Imperialism at Bay: The United States and the Decolonisation of the British Empire 1941–1945*, Oxford: Clarendon Press.

McCullough, David G. (1992) *Truman*, New York: Simon and Schuster.

Mill, John Stuart (1977) [1861] 'Considerations on representative government', in *Essays on Politics and Society by John Stuart Mill*, Toronto: University of Toronto Press/Routledge and Kegan Paul.

Muppidi, Himadeep (1999) 'Postcoloniality and the production of international insecurity: the persistent puzzle of US-Indian relations', in Jutta Weldes, Mark

Lafey, Hugh Gusterson and Raymond Duvall (eds) *Cultures of Insecurity: States, Communities, and the Production of Danger*, Minneapolis: University of Minnesota Press.

Tambiah, Stanley J. (1996) *Leveling Crowds: Ethnonationalist Conflicts and Collective Violence in South Asia*, Berkeley: University of California Press.

Wells, H. G. (1940) *The New World Order: Whether It Is Attainable, how It Can Be Attained, and what Sort of World a World at Peace Will Have To Be*, New York: Knopf.

12

EMPIRE PRESERV'D

How the Americans put anti-communism before anti-imperialism[1]

William Roger Louis and Ronald Robinson

In commemorating the end of the Second World War, historians are bound to reflect that the year of victory marked the end of a specifically British empire and the beginning of what became, in effect, an Anglo-American imperial system. Many historians have always assumed that the United States, with its historic anticolonial tradition, helped to bring about that empire's liquidation. Yet one of the remarkable features of the archival evidence still being divulged, is the extent to which American assistance sustained the British empire, enabling it to revive before it collapsed. Neither side cared to publicize the fact that British imperial power depended substantially on American support. The United States was concerned to avoid the taint of imperialism, while Britain wanted to keep the prestige of empire untarnished. An imperial coalition was as unnatural for the Americans as it was demeaning for the British. Yet it ought to become a commonplace that the post-war British empire was more than British and less than an imperium. As it survived, so it was transformed as part of the Allied front in the Cold War.

Neglecting the American reinforcement, historians often single out British enfeeblement as a prime cause of the empire's demise. The presumption is that an imperial state caved in at the centre like Gibbon's Rome, with infirmity in the metropole and insurgency in the provinces. For the 'Gibbonians', the empire therefore ends with political independence. Dependent though the new states remained in other ways, they are said to have been 'decolonized'. Historians of the Cold War take more account of 'invisible' empires, but the imperial effects of the transatlantic alliance are not their concern, except for some writers who suspect that the expansion of American capitalist imperialism swallowed up the empire. Far from being decolonized, in this view, the British imperial system was neo-colonized more intensively under new management.

The difficulty of attributing the fall to British decline is that it leads us into paradox. Colonial emancipation is not necessarily a sign of metropolitan weakness. Virtual independence was conceded to Canadian,

152

Australasian and South African nationalists before 1914, when Britain was at her strongest. When she was much weaker during the inter-war years, the empire reached its greatest extent, with the addition of much of the Middle East, and more of Africa. By 1940, when there was scarcely strength to defend the home islands, the British were able to crack down on nationalists in India, Egypt and Iran, and mobilize the empire for war. When peace came, a bankrupt metropole managed to reconstruct the imperial system in the familiar Victorian style of trade without rule where possible, rule for trade where necessary. The 'imperialism of free trade', or rather, of the sterling area, continued. Weak or strong, the metropole was clearly not the only source of imperial strength.

Before 1939, the international, financial and commodity markets of London held the system together. More than a mere project of the British state, imperial sway derived mainly from the sharing of business profits and of political power with indigenous elites overseas. At the colonial level, the system relied on unequal accommodations with client rulers or proto-nationalists who were willing to enhance British power locally with their own authority when it was to their own advantage. Yet local bargains could not be struck to imperial advantage if other great powers competed in the bidding: international alliances – at least 'hands-off' arrangements – were essential if the empire were to be defended and its balance-sheets kept out of the red. Whitehall monitored what was, in effect, a self-generating and self-financing system. The object was not that Britain should sustain the empire but that the empire should sustain Britain. Imperial upkeep required the tolerance of the British voter; the empire should not be maintained at the expense of home comforts.

After 1945, with the balance of pre-war accommodations overthrown, a different Britain reformed the empire in a changed world. Attlee's government faced an economic Dunkirk in the shape of towering trade deficits and debts to the United States and to the sterling area. The British were no longer the creditors but the debtors of the empire. To reduce the meagre food ration was not practical politics. The Cabinet had to choose between financing domestic recovery and imperial commitment. There was no resource but to go cap-in-hand for a large dollar loan, which John Maynard Keynes at the Treasury described as 'primarily required to meet the political and military expenditure overseas'.

On what terms would Washington with its plans for global free trade agree to underwrite Britain and the empire? In return for a loan of $3.75 billion, which the Canadians brought up to $5 billion, the British were forced to make the pound convertible into the dollar within twelve months. The imperial economy, in effect, was to be dismantled. Meanwhile, nationalist protests against stringent economic controls erupted throughout the dependent empire. Imperial contracts, or agreements both implicit and explicit, were falling apart at all levels in 1945–7, as Attlee recognized. 'It may be', the prime minister foresaw in March 1946, 'we shall have to consider the British Isles as an easterly extension of a strategic [arc] the centre of which is the American continent rather than as a Power looking eastwards through the Mediterranean to India and the East'. Attlee and some of his colleagues contemplated an empire reduced to Africa, the Caribbean and the Pacific islands. 'We cannot afford the great sums of money for the large forces involved', he wrote.

British recovery depended largely on the cohesion of the sterling area. From the economic standpoint, Hilton Poynton of the Colonial Office commented: 'The point surely is that the USA must help the British empire to under-write the world'. The issue remained in doubt up to the end of 1947. By that time, the Americans were doing a great deal to prop up the empire, especially in the eastern Mediterranean and the Middle East. In the interval between the end of the Second World War and the beginning of the Cold War, the British withdrew from Greece and gave up their Turkish commitment. They left India, Burma and Ceylon, and they were soon to abdicate in Palestine. President Truman's intervention on behalf of the Zionists led to an American-sponsored Israel taking over much of the British mandate in 1948.

As the Cold War intensified, competition between the two super-powers came to the rescue of the empire. After the fiasco of the sterling convertibility crisis in 1947, Washington accepted the necessity of the discriminatory imperial economy. Under the Truman Doctrine, American power reinforced the traditional imperial 'Great Game', in its Middle Eastern dimension, of checking Russian advances. After 1947, American dollars underwrote both Britain and the empire. Marshall Plan aid and eventually the Mutual Security programme met the otherwise prohibitive charge on the balance of payments of sustaining British power overseas up to 1952 and at need thereafter. Whitehall relied largely on the sterling countries between Suez and Singapore for the dollar earnings required to make up the British trade deficit. The potential of Africa's minerals and vegetable products was also linked to British recovery. With India and Pakistan hived off and Palestine shrugged aside, the empire reasserted itself in the Middle East and Africa.

Much of the pre-war empire survived locally, to be slotted into the post-war design. Even so, local continuities masked the basic discontinuity. As Ernest Bevin, the foreign secretary, stated in 1949:

Western Europe, including its dependent overseas territories, is now patently dependent on American aid. The United States recognises that the United Kingdom and the Commonwealth are essential to her defence and safety. Already it is, apart from the economic field, a case of partial inter-dependence rather than of complete dependence. As time goes by [in the next ten to twenty years] the elements of dependence ought to diminish and those of interdependence to increase.

Under the impact of Mao's triumph in China and the Korean War, the Anglo-American coalition extended, though with many a rift, from Europe and the Middle East to South- and Southeast Asia. India remained an important member of the Commonwealth. From 1949 onwards, the Pentagon joined the War Office in the traditional imperial Great Game of securing the Indian sub-continent's frontiers from Kabul and Herat to Rangoon and Singapore. As a member of the US State Department put it, Curzon's strategy in 1889 for containing Russian expansion in Central Asia applied 'very much today'. In competition with Soviet aid, American assistance to India and Pakistan soon surpassed that of the British. Similarly, in the ANZUS pact of 1951, the American 'offshore-island' chain around communist China took in the Australasian Commonwealth.

In Southeast Asia and Africa, the Americans feared that the only alternative to imperial rule would be chaos or communism. The revitalization of Western Europe depended upon the economic attachment of colonial and ex-colonial areas. To ride rough-shod over European imperial pride would strain vital NATO alliances. Ideally, the United States preferred 'independence' and covert influence to colonialism. In practice, the Americans gave priority to anti-communism over anticolonialism.

During 1951–7, first prime minister Churchill, and then his successor Eden, fell increasingly out of step with their wartime comrade Eisenhower. American financial aid dwindled. Despite British economic recovery, exports could not balance overseas payments under the overload of debt, social welfare and massive rearmament. Two solutions were discussed in 1952. One was to expand exports to hard currency markets by £600 million a year at the expense of power abroad and austerity at home. The other solution was, through tighter imperial control, to develop dollar earnings and savings in the sterling system. Harold Macmillan stated in a secret Cabinet memorandum: 'This is the choice – the slide into a shoddy and slushy Socialism [as a second-rate power], or the march to the third British Empire'. According to Macmillan: 'Our economic survival in the next year or two will largely depend upon world confidence in sterling'. This in turn depended on marching to the imperial drum.

The march to a third British empire led to increasing friction with the United States, especially in the Middle East. Economic anxiety nerved the British government to confront 'nationalists sapping at our position as a world power', whereas American officials favoured the substitution of direct American alliances for British influence. Churchill and Eden protested that the Americans were wooing Arab nationalists away from Soviet blandishments at imperial expense. Despite the British perception, Eisenhower, like Truman before him, was certain that Anglo-American coordination was necessary in the Middle East. The British seemed to have little choice. Vulnerable to Soviet pressure, they had to keep in line with American Cold War strategy, just as American strategy had to align on the strong points of the British empire. If either side tried to go it alone in Iran, Egypt or elsewhere, as Acheson's successor, John Foster Dulles, admitted, it would have the effect 'of tearing the free world coalition to pieces'. It was not the Americans but the British who decided to go it alone in the Middle East.

By 1956, both the British and Americans viewed Nasser as an involuntary pawn of the Russians. He incited the Arab states to rise against Western domination. From March, the British Cabinet set in train plans to destroy him. Three months later, the Anglo-American offer for the Aswan dam was cancelled. In riposte, on 26 July after the last British troops had left the Suez base, Nasser nationalized the Suez Canal Company, the final emblem of his country's bondage. The result was explosive. The canal carried two thirds of Europe's oil supply.

The Americans too hoped for Nasser's downfall. But as Eden was repeatedly told from April 1956 onwards, they were unalterably opposed to military intervention. Dulles suspected a British attempt to manoeuvre Washington into reasserting British imperial supremacy in the Middle East. If Egypt were invaded, the president predicted, every Arab state would swing towards Moscow. The Great Game was now being played for the highest stakes in the Cold War. Eden's ministers agreed with the Bank of England that Egyptian 'piracy' of the Canal 'imperils the survival of the UK and the Commonwealth, and represents a very great danger to sterling'. An expedition was prepared 'to bring about the fall of Nasser and create a government in Egypt which will work satisfactorily with ourselves and other powers'. The British took it for granted that their ally would gladly accept and pay for a *fait accompli*. Keeping Washington in the dark, the British now decided to go it alone, or rather, with the French and the Israelis. On 5 November 1956, an Anglo-French expedition landed on the Suez Canal in the guise of peacekeepers to stop a second Israeli-Egyptian war.

In the event, the canal was blocked. Pipelines were sabotaged. Oil ceased to flow. Far from saving sterling, the intervention set off a disastrous run on the pound. As the reserves ran out, Macmillan (then chancellor of the exchequer) presented two alternatives: either to float the pound – a 'catastrophe affecting not merely the British cost of living but also all our external economic relations', or to ask for massive American aid. Only after Eden had agreed to leave Egypt unconditionally did Eisenhower rescue the pound, with a billion dollars from the

IMF and Export-Import Bank. During the crisis, Khrushchev rattled the nuclear sabre over London and Paris. Eisenhower shielded his errant allies with a similar threat against Moscow. British dependence was military no less than economic.

It was the Americans, not the Russians, who had vetoed the Anglo-French effort at imperial reassertion in the Middle East and North Africa. At the peak of the crisis, Dulles told the National Security Council, in a now famous comment, that for many years the United States had been 'walking a tightrope' between backing Europe's empires and trying to win the friendship of countries escaping from colonialism. Unless the United States now asserted leadership, all those countries would turn to the Soviet Union. Eisenhower asked: 'How can we possibly support Britain and France if in doing so we lose the whole Arab world?'. The Americans insisted that their major European allies give priority to the Cold War over the empires. Yet the prize of Arab friendship eluded the righteous. The Arabs gave the credit for defeating imperialism mostly to the Egyptians and the Russians. Nasser was exalted. It was Eden who was toppled. American anti-imperialism in the Middle East provoked anti-Americanism in Europe and threw NATO into disarray.

A triumph for the non-aligned nations, the Suez fiasco was a disaster for the British empire. It ended British aspirations to imperial dominance in the Middle East. It showed that international confidence in the sterling empire still rested on the alignment of Anglo-American arms. Once and for all, it was established that Britain had to work in concert with the United States in the 'peripheral regions' no less than in Europe, or suffer humiliating consequences. What Dulles called the 'violent family quarrel' over Suez had exposed the American essentials underlying British power for all to see.

At meetings with Eisenhower in 1957 in Bermuda and later in Washington, Macmillan (who had become prime minister) spoke of Britain as a 'junior partner'. Now it was Eisenhower's turn to fulminate against 'the struggle of Nasser to get control of these petroleum supplies – to get the income and power to destroy the Western world'. The British saw the irony in all that, but the new Conservative government set its sights on an empire in the post-colonial world. Influence had to be won by converting discontented subjects into loyal allies.

During the scramble into Africa in the 1890s, Lord Salisbury had worked at keeping hostile powers away from the Upper Nile region. Six decades later, the British were pursuing a similar plan in the colonial scramble out of Africa. Only the method and the enemies had changed. Macmillan's government aimed at erecting buffer states against 'the southward drive of Nasser and the Russians' towards a projected British trans-African lifeline to Aden and Singapore. British officials concentrated on independence for tropical Africa after 1957 – but an independence that would prolong the imperial sway and secure British economic and strategic assets. It was urgent to exchange colonial control for informal empire. To turn this trick, the last acres of independence in the colonial hand would have to be played. In West Africa, Ghana achieved political independence in 1957. The acceleration in dismantling the empire defied timetables. British officials approached the crisis of African independence with no solid belief in the potential of black nationalism among so many divided ethnic communities. What impressed them was the speed with which handfuls of urban nationalists were stirring up popular black resentment against white rule. African nationalism was spreading from the Niger to the Zambezi and the Nile. It could be contained at local level, but the use of force would be self-defeating. As the Colonial Office noted,

> It would be difficult for us to create some new authoritarian force artificially, and if we tried to do so to the exclusion of people like Nkrumah [in Ghana] or Awolowo [in Nigeria] or Nyerere [in Tanganyika] it would probably lead to the creation of a revolutionary force against the set-up that we had created.

The archives clearly establish that both Washington and London agreed that tropical Africa was by no means ready for independence. None the less, the goodwill of amenable national leaders had to be won before independence, if they were to be allied after independence.

By the late 1950s, British hopes for the economic future veered away from the empire towards Europe. Sterling was on the verge of full convertibility. The preferences and financial controls of the imperial economy had given way to freer world trade. In 1957, Macmillan had requested a 'profit and loss account' for the colonies that had found, ambiguously, that British trade might be better served if independence came sooner rather than later. Two years later, colonial controls were clearly no longer indispensable for metropolitan prosperity. The inevitable political informalization of the empire in its final stages went hand-in-hand with the economic informalization of the sterling area.

The economics of dependence after political independence was the key to the British plan for African informal empire. Since 1957, British and American officials had agreed that the African dependencies must evolve 'toward stable self-government or independence' as rapidly as possible 'in such a way that these successor governments are willing and able to preserve their economic and political ties with the West'. An ambitious plan for Africa would be underwritten by the Americans. It was all to the good that the United States had few economic interests and large Cold War stakes in the continent. The British would share the profits of American investment. They were relying a great deal on the United States, financially and strategically, for their imperial future in Africa. The new African informal empire would be increasingly Anglo-American rather than British.

Everything at this point depended on winning and keeping African as well as American goodwill. All would be lost, the Colonial Office feared in 1959, unless the struggle for independence between black majorities and white minorities in Kenya and the Central African Federation could be resolved. Yet Macmillan and the colonial secretary, Alan Lennox-Boyd, were determined that British authority in East Africa would prevail for at least another decade. British Central Africa presented the gravest prospects of racial conflict. If white domination were maintained by force, the whole of the British position in Africa would be shaken to its foundations. With the possible domino effects of pan-Africanism, questions of local racial collaboration broadened into great matters of continental balance that involved not merely Britain but Europe and the United States.

In January 1960, the prime minister set out on a tour of African capitals in search of African partners. Macmillan assured the new rulers in Lagos and Accra that the British were on the side of black Africa. In Cape Town and Salisbury, he warned the Europeans against resisting the 'winds of change' from the north. The intransigent premier of the Federation, Roy Welensky, suspected that if need be, Macmillan would break up the Federation to appease pan-Africanism. African appeasement was certainly Macmillan's overriding aim. It seemed to him that 'the Africans are not the problem in Africa, it is the Europeans who are the problem'. Macmillan wanted to avoid a British Algeria in Central Africa.

The new colonial secretary, Iain Macleod, remarked that the pace of events 'in Somalia, Tanganyika, Uganda, and above all the Congo' had accelerated the colonial retreat. The British were scrambling out of colonialism before anarchy attracted Soviet penetration in conjunction with pan-Africanism and pan-Arabism. The Congo crisis of 1960–2 showed that the interdependent interests of the Western allies could all be lost if they failed to act in concert. Post-colonial sway in Africa would have to be planned as part of the Western coalition under American leadership. The Congo became, for better or worse, a vast client state of the United States. The Congolese type of breakdown, however, was soon matched in the Nigerian civil war, and later with Sino-Soviet intervention in Portuguese Africa and Rhodesia. Latter-day Lumumbas abounded. Castro, as Macmillan remarked, became Eisenhower's and Kennedy's Nasser, and Panama their Suez.

If the assessments of Attlee and his Treasury advisers in 1945 are to be believed, the collaborative basis of the pre-war empire went down in the

Second World War. The post-war system was regenerated on American wealth and power. Measured against this reinforcement, the loss of India in the imperial Great Game seems almost minor. With economic recovery and a brief respite from overseas payments deficits, the system under Churchill and Eden regained a tentative dynamism of its own, until in 1956 Eisenhower jolted Eden into recognizing the American dimension of imperial dynamics. Up to the late 1950s, British prosperity relied on an imperial economy whose discriminatory nature required American toleration, dollar underwriting and strategic protection. In all these ways, the post-war empire represented not a continuation but at once a more formidable and more vulnerable innovation. If the system were to succeed in securing and developing the sterling area, it had to operate as a project of the Anglo-American coalition. Such was the common prayer in Whitehall and Downing Street from Attlee to Macmillan.

It follows that the dismantling of the visible empire is not to be explained in monolithic terms of metropolitan infirmity. With American support or acquiescence, the British had resources enough to deal with local insurgency. Coercion was often threatened. Force was used in Cyprus, Aden and Malaya with Washington's blessing, and without it in Kenya, Suez and the Buraimi oasis. The Americans restored much of the British oil fief in Iran, and they refrained from interfering in Iraq and the Gulf emirates. In British calculations, the need to head off resistance for winning local collaboration governed the colonial retreat at different speeds in different territories. Just as local imperial authority had multiplied through divided indigenous alliances, so it dwindled in the face of popular national organization.

It should be a commonplace, therefore, that the post-war empire was more than British and less than an imperium. As it survived, so it operated more like an Anglo-American multinational company that, after taking over other peoples' countries, was hiving them off again, one by one, as subsidiaries, or associated concerns. In this at least, the empire after 1945 hewed to its original mid-Victorian design. Like the Americans, the Cobdenites in their day had worked for a revolutionary commercial republic of the world held together by economic attraction rather than by political subordination. Long before Truman and Eisenhower, Palmerston and even Gladstone had discovered that the international economy required imperial protection. Combining the two principles, Victorian imperialism withdrew from countries as reliable economic links and national organizations emerged, while it extended into others in need of development. Such was the genius of British free-trade imperialism.

The formal empire contracted in the post-war years, as it had once expanded, as a variable function of integrating countries in the international capitalist economy. Under Anglo-American auspices, the remains of the system were progressively nationalized and, in tropical Africa if not in India, and the Middle East, informalized. After 1956, the British fell in with the American design for Western alliances with freer trade and free institutions. In competition with communist political economies, the 1960s were dedicated to Third World development under the aegis of the United Nations and the World Bank. As things turned out, the new world order needed a good deal of old-fashioned imperial and financial intervention along with the economic attraction. Such was the imperialism of decolonization. Visible empires may be abolished: the thraldom of international economy remains. But there was no conspiracy to take over the empire. American influence expanded by imperial default and by the invitation of nationalists who required American help to fulfil their aspirations for independence. It was almost as if the colonial frontier of the first transatlantic British empire had become the centre of the third.

Note

1   William Roger Louis and Ronald Robinson (1995) 'Empire preserv'd: how the Americans put anti-communism before anti-imperialism', *Times Literary Supplement*, 5 May, 14–16. For the archival evidence supporting this essay, see the article by the two authors in the *Journal of Imperial and Commonwealth History* 22(3).

13

THE TROUBLED HISTORY OF PARTITION[1]

Radha Kumar

Bosnia goes the way of Cyprus

The September 1996 elections in Bosnia highlighted what was until then an implicit aspect of the current peace: it is more likely to move Bosnia toward the ethnic states for which the war was fought than to re-establ ish the multi-ethnic Bosnia that once was. Indeed, as the Dayton process unfolds, it becomes clearer that the peace agreement signed in November 1995 after three and a half years of war was something historically familiar: a so-called peace accord that is in reality a partition agreement with an exit clause for outside powers.

At the same time, while key aspects of the document, such as the creation of two 'entities' with virtually separate legislatures, administrations and armies, tend toward partition, the pact attempts to get around some of the more hostile legacies of partition through a common economic space and arms control, and it creates structures that could reverse the partition process by returning refugees and rebuilding civil society. So far, these structures have been dormant, and the holding of national elections in a still highly uncertain peace marks the tilt toward partition. As was widely predicted, the Bosnians gave their ethnic leaders new mandates, and Bosnia took another step toward partition. However, the postponement of the municipal elections due to irregularities in voter registration means the international community is not yet in a position to accept partition as the democratically expressed will of the people.

The Bosnian war and the Dayton peace agreement have reignited a debate on whether partition is an effective solution to ethnic conflict. Although Bosnia is the starting point, the arguments in this debate have broad resonance at a time in which the rapid spread of ethnic and communal wars east and south of Bosnia is of increasing concern to the international community. Defenders of partition make an argument that runs as follows. When an ethnic war is far advanced, partition is probably the most humane form of intervention because it attempts to achieve through negotiation what would otherwise be achieved through fighting; it circumvents the conflict and saves lives. It might even save a country from disappearing altogether, because an impartial intervenor will attempt to secure the rights of each contending ethnic group, whereas in war the stronger groups might oust the weaker ones. In fact, its advocates say, the ideal strategy for resolving an ethnic conflict is to intervene and take partition to its logical conclusion by dividing a country along its communal battle lines and helping make the resulting territories ethnically homogeneous through organized population transfers. This will ensure that partition is more than a temporary means of containing conflict. Less thorough partitions, however, can still be a lasting means of containment.[2]

Partition, however, has its own sordid history, not arising as a means of realizing national self-determination, but imposed as a way for outside powers to unshoulder colonies or divide up spheres of influence – a strategy of divide and quit. Although described as the lesser of two evils, the partitions in Cyprus, India, Palestine and Ireland, rather than separating irreconcilable ethnic groups, fomented further violence and forced mass migration. Even where partition enabled outside powers to leave, as in India, it also led to a disastrous war. Often thought of as a provisional solution, it has been unable to contain the fragmentation it triggers among dispersed or overlapping ethnic groups that are not confined by neat geographic boundaries, and it gives birth to weak civil institutions demanding supervision. Similar conditions ensure that the partition of Bosnia, which from the start should have been reintegrated, will also amount only to a policy of divide and be forced to stay. The Dayton accords should not evoke memories of Munich, but rather of Cyprus.

The road to quitting

The argument for ethnic partition is not new, but its terms changed considerably over this century before settling upon the current rationale of the lesser of two evils. Before World War I, most partitions were effected for the needs of empire, to strengthen rule or simplify administration. After 1918, however, colonial empires were increasingly challenged, and subsequent partitions took place as part of a devolution of authority or a Cold War policy of spheres of influence. There were two distinct rationales for the partitions resulting from the fall of colonial empires: Wilsonian national self-determination, applied to Poland and Romania, and the British colonial policy of identifying irreconcilable nationhoods, applied in Ireland, India, and, as a delayed response, Cyprus and Palestine. Though both rationales took ethnic identity as an important determinant of political rights, Wilsonian policy supported ethnic self-determination as freedom from colonial rule, while the British reluctantly espoused partition as a lesser evil than constant civil war.

After the last attempt to ratify a partition – Cyprus after the Turkish invasion in 1974 – the notion that partition was an effective solution to ethnic conflict fell into disuse for a quarter-century. Paradoxically, its revival followed hard on the heels of German reunification and the potential integration of Europe that it heralded. In the first phase of the revival of partition theory, Wilsonian self-determination was invoked more often than the lesser-evil argument. Indeed, the prevailing feeling was that the end of the Cold War – and the relatively peaceful dissolution of the Soviet Union – meant that separations could be negotiated. In the early 1990s the most frequently cited example of a peaceful negotiated division was Czechoslovakia's 'velvet divorce'. When asked on *The News Hour with Jim Lehrer* in November 1995 whether the Dayton agreement was a partition, assistant secretary of state Richard C. Holbrooke said he preferred the example of Czechoslovakia's voluntary dissolution. But fewer people now refer to the Czech split. That the Czech Republic and Slovakia were relatively homogeneous and that dissolution of the federation did not require an alteration of internal borders or a substantial displacement of people makes the comparison with Bosnia untenable. A comparison between Bosnia and the partitions of Ireland, India and Cyprus, or the incomplete partition of Palestine, would be better, because each involved ethnically mixed and dispersed populations and each was held to be a pragmatic recognition of irreconcilable ethnic identities.

It is worth examining these partitions' relevance to Bosnia in more detail. All relied heavily on the lesser-evil argument, but in at least two of them the decision for partition was prompted not by a desire for peace and self-determination, but because the colonial power, Britain, wanted to withdraw. The recognition of irreconcilable nationhoods followed as a consequence – it would he easier to withdraw quickly if the aims of the ethnic leaders were fulfilled by territorial grants. Looking back on the 1947 partition of India in 1961, former civil servant Penderel Moon summed up as 'divide and quit', in a book of the same name, the British policy of pushing partition through without establishing the boundaries of new states or planning for the wars that might ensue; it was the post-World War II imperative of quitting that drove the decision to divide, he said. It was arguably the post-World War I imperative of quitting the Irish conflict that led the British to espouse a partition of Ireland.

That both divisions were driven by considerations extraneous to the needs and desires of the people displaced does not necessarily mean that partition was not a solution to their conflicts. However, as in India and Ireland, partition has more often been a backdrop to war than its culmination in peace; although it may originate in a situation of conflict, its effect has been to stimulate further and even fresh conflict. Indeed, India's experience raises the question of whether a peaceful transition to partition is possible. India's political leadership agreed to partition the country before the spread of large-scale conflict; the 1947 partition agreement between the Indian National Congress and the Muslim League was intended partly to prevent the spread of communal riots from Bengal in eastern India to northwestern India, which was also to be divided. But the riots that followed in 1947–8 left more than a million people dead in six months and displaced upwards of 15 million.

Moreover, partition arises in high-level negotiations long before it becomes evident on the ground. The British partition of Ireland in 1921 was a late addition to negotiations for home rule during the 1919–21 Anglo-Irish war for independence, but partition had been on the drawing board since 1912, when it was suggested by a group of Conservative and Liberal MPs that Protestant-majority counties be excluded from the proposed Irish Home Rule bill. Calls for partition were renewed in 1914, 1916 and 1919; the offer of a double partition of Ireland and Ulster based on religion led to the spread of conflict between English and Irish across the south, west, and north of Ireland, escalating to guerrilla warfare when Catholic rebels formed the Irish Republican Army in 1919. Nor did the war end in 1921 when Britain negotiated a treaty with Sinn Fein, the political arm of the IRA, offering dominion status to southern Ireland in return for a separate Ulster under British administration. The decision to accept partition led to a split in Sinn Fein, and internecine conflict was added to communal conflict, ending two years later with the defeat of the faction led by Eamon De Valera. It took almost four years of war to achieve the partition of Ireland; and those four years were themselves a culminating phase in a movement toward partition that had begun ten years earlier.

Significantly, the British rejected the partition option in Palestine in the same years that they espoused it in India. The two reasons they gave were infeasibility and the risk of a military conflict that would involve an expanded British presence. Although partition had been proposed in 1937 by the Peel Commission, which concluded that cooperation between Jews and Arabs in a Palestinian state was impossible, and had been the subject of debate in Britain throughout the 1930s, in 1946 the British members of the Anglo-American Committee of Inquiry argued that because ethnic groups were so dispersed, partition would entail massive forced population transfers, and that the territories created – a tiny Arab state, a Jewish state in two parts, and three blocs under continuing British administration – would be infeasible. Moreover, they said, moves toward partition could cause a war. In 1947 the British referred the dispute to the United Nations. The Security Council opted for partition, with a special UN regime for Jerusalem and a continuing economic union for the whole of Palestine. The plan required Britain to undertake a substantial role in its implementation, but after the Ministry of Defence forecast that Britain's military presence would have to be reinforced in the wars that would follow, Britain announced that it would withdraw in May 1948. In April the Jewish Agency, which represented the Jewish community under the British mandate, announced that it would declare a Jewish state when the British withdrew. War broke out, resulting in a kind of skewed partition by which one new state was created but not the other. Subsequently there have been three Arab-Israeli wars, and the issue of territorial feasibility continues to dog the peace process.

In many ways Cyprus offers the most striking parallels to Bosnia, and its history again raises the question of whether a peaceful transition to partition is possible. Although the British proposed the partition of the island in a divide-and-rule move in 1956, they subsequently rejected the plan on the same grounds as in Palestine – infeasibility and the risk of conflict. The British-brokered constitution of 1960 that made Cyprus independent was an attempt to avert division of the island between ethnic Turks and ethnic Greeks, but the idea that ethnic politics could be contained by providing for ethnic representation at every level proved a failure. The constitutional creation of separate municipalities and a distribution between the two ethnic groups in the presidency, legislature, civil service, police and army added communal (that is, inter-religious) conflict to internecine conflict. In 1963 the 'Green Line', the first partition boundary to be drawn, divided Greek and Turkish Cypriots in Nicosia, the capital. Ethnic conflict only intensified, and a Turkish Cypriot decla-ration of support for partition followed in 1964. Although UN troops arrived that year, tensions escalated, with a counter-declaration of unifi-cation by Greece and Cyprus in 1966, a military coup in Greece, renewed conflict in Cyprus, a Turkish Cypriot announcement in 1967 of a provi-sional administration, increasing Greek support for the radical Greek underground in Cyprus, and finally a Turkish invasion in 1974 that rein-forced the *de facto* partition of the island. Thus it took fourteen years to establish what continues to be a shaky partition of Cyprus.

Fomenting conflict

How successful have these partitions been at reducing conflict and permitting outside powers to end their involvement? It is not clear that the partitions of Ireland and Cyprus can be said to have worked, even in the lesser-evil sense. Although the former was a move to divide and quit – in which all sides accepted division as the price of self-determination – the British are embroiled in a military operation in Northern Ireland that continues seventy years later. The military presence curtailed the toil that communal conflict might otherwise have taken; indeed, it could be argued that it contained the Irish conflict and kept deaths to a minimum. But it also brought the conflict to the heart of Britain as the IRA mounted terrorist attacks in London to increase pressure for a British withdrawal, and it could just as well be argued that, from the British point of view, independence would have been a more effective way to contain the conflict because it would have thrown the onus of peacekeeping onto the Irish; moreover, it might have encouraged regional compromises rather than a prolonged stalemate.

The partition of Cyprus can only be described as a partition by default that the UN presence inadvertently aided. The conflict following independence in 1960 was compounded by the fact that Turkey, Greece and Britain were appointed protecting powers by the constitution. The formal structure this gave to a wider engagement in the conflict drew both the Greek and Turkish armies in, and permitted international acceptance of Turkey's invasion in 1974 and what was until then a *de facto* partition. While casualties have been restricted since then, the division of Cyprus is little more than a long standoff that remains volatile and continues to require the presence of UN troops. Nor can the conflict be confined to Cyprus. Over the twenty years since partition, its short fuse is evident. A violent demonstration by Cypriots in August 1996 resulted in Greece and Turkey threatening war. The costs of containment, therefore, include permanent vigilance on the part of NATO and the Atlantic allies.

In many ways, despite the violence and displacements it produced, India's was the most successful ethnic partition, both because it allowed the British to quit and because the conflicts that ensued were by and large contained. But this had less to do with the wisdom of ethnic separation than with other factors, among them the subcontinent's distance from Europe. Unlike Ireland, Cyprus and Bosnia, the Indian subcontinent is so large that a dozen or more new states could have been created. The deployment of the ethnic two-nation theory, however, which holds that Hindus and Muslims could not live together, had a paradoxical effect – the new state created, Pakistan, was divided into two parts by roughly 2,000 miles of Indian territory. The subsequent separation of those parts points up the inadequacy of the principle of ethnic separation for effecting stable territories. In the late 1960s, resentment at West Pakistani political and economic dominance led to a regional Bengali movement for independence, a war between the two parts in which India intervened in support of the Bengalis, and the birth of Bangladesh in 1971.

In regions of multiple ethnicities – where, for example, the same individual might have loyalties to one community defined by its religion and another by its language – attempts to make one ethnic identity dominant can trigger further fragmentation and conflict. The temporary success of the Indian People's Party in whipping up Hindu nationalism during the destruction of the Babri mosque in Ayodhya and in the riots that followed in the winter of 1992–3 ultimately led to the party's isolation and failure to form a government after the 1996 elections. The case of Kashmir is more poignant. Since 1947, India and Pakistan have been embroiled in a conflict that has twice flared into war, over what has been described, in a phrase dear to politicians on both sides, as 'the unfinished business of partition': Kashmir. On ethnic grounds it can be argued that the conflict has continued because India retained the Muslim-majority Kashmir Valley, which should have gone to Pakistan. But following ethnic dividing lines could well entail a further three-way partition of the state – the valley, Buddhist Ladakh, and multi-ethnic Jammu – which would not only set the stage for intensified conflict and ethnic cleansing, as much of Jammu lies between Pakistan and the valley, but would also dissolve Kashmir.

Balkan bedlam

Bosnia-Herzegovina, like these other partitioned territories, has problems of dispersed populations and continuing fragmentation, which the Dayton agreement shows little promise of resolving. It is difficult to contain a conflict when partition is still in progress. Thus NATO and Implementation Force (IFOR) officials under its auspices increasingly worry that hasty implementation of civilian aspects of the agreement such as elections might renew the conflict; instead of reversing partition or facilitating its peaceful execution, the prelude to the elections brought renewed low-level conflict in August. To this extent the Bosnian elections are to the Dayton process what last year's Israeli elections were to the Palestinian peace process: they prove that partition is still incomplete on the ground. Nearly half the pre-1992 population of Bosnia is still living as refugees outside Bosnia. Ethnically homogeneous territories can be created only if the refugees are refused repatriation to the towns and villages from which they were driven, which puts pressure on their host countries not to enforce repatriation. The refugees have become a key constituency that is used both to further and to challenge the consolidation of such ethnic territories, as in the Serb efforts to force refugees to vote from towns other than their pre-war residences, and the subsequent threat of Bosnian Muslims to boycott the elections.

Both IFOR and the risibly named Office of the High Representative, which oversees the civilian implementation of Dayton under former Swedish prime minister Carl Bildt, make no secret of a concern the elections highlighted: the third partition that always hovered in Dayton's wings, between the Herzegovinian Croats and Bosnian Muslims now living together in the Bosnian Federation. Since the 1994 agreement signed in Washington that established the federation – which was intended to limit Bosnia's partition but produced a constitution remarkably similar to the 1960 Cyprus constitution – Herzegovinian Croats have asked: If a two-way partition is acceptable, why not a three-way one? Unsurprisingly, the answer, that Croatia has already been offered a far more substantial quid pro quo than Serbia and that a tiny and probably landlocked Muslim Bosnia would perpetuate Muslim resentment, does not satisfy Herzegovinians. But Muslim resentment should at least give partition revivalists pause for thought. Indeed, their argument that the United States should jettison the federation in favour of a tripartite partition begs both the resentment issue and a related matter that Bosnian nationalists have raised: that they be given Serbia's predominantly Muslim Sandjak province as territorial compensation. Moreover, their argument ignores the problematic relationship between Croatian and Herzegovinian Croats, whose distrust of each other rivals that between Croats and Muslims.

NATO and IFOR have also pointed out an even more crucial concern: a partition dependent on the awkward boundary line between the Bosnian Federation and the Republika Srpska, the Bosnian Serb entity, can last only so long as a large international force is there to enforce it. It is not Mostar in the federation but Banja Luka in the Serb entity that may bring the simmering partition war to a head. One look at the map of the Republika Srpska shows why. Like Pakistan after the partition of India, the Serb entity is divided into two parts, connected only by the narrow Posavina corridor, in which the disputed town of Brcko is key; Serb attempts to rig local elections there were a major factor in the postponement of municipal elections in Bosnia last year. Additionally, the two main parts of the Serb entity lean in opposite directions, Banja Luka toward Zagreb and the eastern strip toward Belgrade. Normalization would again pull Banja Luka toward Zagreb economically and diminish its links to the east. That might mean a further division of the Republika Srpska, rather like the division of Pakistan that created Bangladesh, in which the Serb republic would be reduced to a strip of eastern Bosnia. Banja Luka, therefore, must be forced to look eastward, and is – with tacit US support, if Richard Holbrooke's recent suggestions that the Bosnian Serbs make Banja Luka their capital are anything to go by. But Banja Luka's isolation amid federation territory can be maintained only if Serb leaders keep the city in a state of anarchy and mafia rule, like Mostar. Banja Luka's location, however, makes this task much more difficult because Mostar, which remains integrated with Croatia despite being incorporated into the Bosnian Federation, is close to the Croatian border. It is debatable whether anything short of a fortified wall will keep Banja Luka isolated.

Thus, while elections may well be a step toward ratifying partitions politically, efforts to consolidate a partition will not only perpetuate conflict but will eventually show that Bosnia can be successfully divided into two only if the Republika Srpska is further partitioned with the western part reintegrated into Bosnia and the eastern part joining Serbia. Paradoxically, this may be the only way of ensuring stable partition under the Dayton agreement, as the reintegration of Banja Luka will help keep the Croats in the federation. But if a multi-ethnic Bosnia can be re-created in one part, then why not in the whole, especially since a farther partition will renew conflict around Gorazde in eastern Bosnia?

All the king's horses

As pressure mounts to accept the September elections as a mandate for partition, more emphasis is being placed on the reintegration option of the Dayton agreement, which assumes that economic interests and the provisions for a common economic space will erode the partition lines by making them irrelevant. It is being argued that the partial partition the Dayton agreement partly accepts is only a means of buying time for Bosnia to undergo this process. Historically, however, the failure to inject substantial and timely aid has only hardened ethnic divisions.

Partition has rarely been seen as anything other than a temporary solution to a crisis, which can be reversed as the crisis recedes. However, ethnic partitions have never been reversed; their implementation has inexorably driven communities further apart. Sinn Fein's acquiescence to the partition of Ireland was on the condition that there be a referendum on unification; the referendum did not take place, and now that negotiations on the status of Northern Ireland have been revived, Sinn Fein faces the ironic possibility that Ireland may no longer want unification.

Ethnic partition can often hamper the development of post-war economies. Although economic cooperation could improve South Asia's economics enormously, the ongoing conflict between India and Pakistan over Kashmir has impeded attempts to build it. The Dayton agreement's hope that economic interests will militate against ethnic boundaries was also voiced in Ireland and Palestine. Irish nationalists and the UN mediators in Palestine both hoped that mutual dependence, geographic proximity and the benefits of shared infrastructure would gradually dissipate the aftermath of ethnic partition. Indeed, the UN plan for the partition of Palestine was based explicitly on the premise that economic union would compensate for the difficulties of the proposed territories. Instead, partition's legacies thwarted economic union and kept both Ireland and what was left of Palestine in poverty.

If the lessons of these examples are noteworthy, it may be because Bosnia will constitute a turning point in partition theory. The fact that NATO is preparing for an extended presence indicates that the alliance recognizes the unlikely success of a divide and quit approach in this situation. Though divide and quit was a motive in Britain's support for partition in Ireland, Palestine and India, it got Britain out quickly only in India, and that was because South Asia is distant from Britain. From the sequence of events in Bosnia, it is clear that European and American leaders, and the rest of the international community, were prepared to accept partition if it would curtail Western intervention in the conflict and limit Western involvement in the region. But as the partition process unfolds, it is being recognized that divide and quit might turn into divide and be forced to stay. Unlike Somalia or Rwanda, Bosnia is a high-profile intervention because the Balkans have played an important and generally unwelcome part in European security. So far, the West has not been able to walk away from this war, and each halfhearted intervention, however delusory, has led to more rather than less involvement. As the realization takes hold that a Bosnian partition may mean an indefinitely prolonged commitment to a chronically volatile region, investment in reintegration may be discovered to be an easier route to withdrawal.

Notes

1   Radha Kumar (1997) 'The troubled history of partition', *Foreign Affairs* Jan/Feb: 22–34.
2   For examples of this view, see John J. Mearsheimer (1993) 'Shrink Bosnia to save it', *New York Times*, 31 March, A23; Mearsheimer and Stephen Van Evera (1995) 'When peace means war', *The New Republic*, 18 December, 16–21; Chaim Kaufmann (1996) 'Possible and impossible solutions to ethnic civil wars', *International Security*, spring, 136–75. Kaufmann goes so far as to suggest that after an international military takeover, international forces should intern 'civilians of the enemy ethnic group' and 'exchange' them once peace is established.

Part III

REGIONS AND THEMES

Ronald Suny's essay (Chapter 14) opens Part III with a discussion of the role of the Russian Revolution in the anti-imperialist movement that it inspired during its immediate aftermath. Suny's perspective is particularly interesting because he joins what we have customarily treated separately, namely the decolonization of the tsarist empire which the revolution fostered and the global anti-imperialist movement. The symbolic and political impact of the Russian Revolution on the global decolonization movement has been plain to see in the writings of the leaders in Part I. Suny suggests that the Soviet leadership's early commitment to federalism and nationalism in the Soviet republics and neighbouring states was soon overtaken by the imperatives of Soviet state-building. Under Stalin, communist organizations in many of the decolonizing societies became puppets dancing to the tune of the Soviet state. Nehru's jibe at the isolation of the Communist Party of India in Part I reflects this sentiment. The Communist Party of China, which maintained a certain distance from Soviet policies with the ascendancy of Mao in the early 1930s, eventually severed ties with the Soviet Union in the 1960s, calling it a 'social imperialist' state. Ironically, the collapse of the Soviet Union in 1989 may be seen to have unleashed yet another process of decolonization in a state which in many ways initiated the process seventy years before.

John Voll's essay (Chapter 15) explores the other major source of inspiration for the decolonizing movement: civilizational discourse. Voll tracks the changing relationship between Islamic reformers and the idea of the West since the nineteenth century. Contrary to those – on both sides – who sought to pit opposition to Western ideas and practices in the Islamic world as an eternal civilizational conflict, Voll believes that this opposition is by no means age-old or unchanging. He seeks to grasp this opposition in relation to the new conception of the 'failure of the West' in the post-World War II period, a conception that is best understood in the context of the assimilation of Western ideas and institutions, rather than deriving from some essential ideas in Islam. A figure who perhaps best exemplifies this argument is Jalal Al-i Ahmad, whose work we encountered in Part I.

The next three chapters focus on the politics of the decolonizing movement. The emergence of a unified national movement – or failing which, the appearance of a unified nationalism – was seen as crucial to the nationalist confrontation of colonial power, and was also a pre-condition for the nationalists' claim to sovereignty in the world. Frederick Cooper's closely argued piece (Chapter 16) shows how the industrial working class in Francophone Africa had been able to make use of the imperial rhetoric about the fundamental unity of the French empire to claim equal pay and rights for all workers within the empire. But just as it was developing the techniques and awareness of workers' rights across states, the working-class movement became subordinated to the African nationalist movements. Moreover as the French government became more willing to devolve power to African political leaders rather than have to respond to the demands for social equality within the empire, the vibrant working-class movement with a distinct vision of justice and rights became silenced.

Jiweon Shin's chapter on colonial and nationalist images of the 'ideal woman' during the period of Japanese colonial rule in Korea (Chapter 17) studies another expression of the nationalist urge to subsume particular interests or consciousness – in this case, women's roles – to its goals. Korean nationalists were not well disposed to the idea of the New Woman of the 1920s promoted by Japanese cultural policies. This woman asserted her independence from nationalist conceptions of roles and goals, and Korean conservatives and nationalists succeeded in de-legitimating this image during the decade of the 1930s. This essay, of course, speaks directly to the issues posed by Fanon's piece in Part I regarding the extent to which women were considered embodiments of a culture to be preserved in the face of colonial attacks. It also echoes Fanon's understanding of how symbolic subversions by the colonized often take place within the dominant categories of the colonizer; here, through the colonial image of the 'ideal mother'.

The political tensions that developed within modern colonial empires ensured that the transfer of power was rarely smooth. Ethnicity, language, religion, (which were often hierarchically balanced in pre-modern empires) and different political visions (especially communist and anti-communist visions) divided the emergent national movements, leading frequently to the kinds of partition discussed by Radha Kumar in Part II. Stein Tønnesson's comprehensive essay on decolonization in French Indochina (Chapter 18) reveals how internal factors such as divisions between ethnic groups and political formations became intertwined with external factors – French and US policies – to drag out decolonization into an extended process of division and warfare. Tønnesson describes the entire history of this political process between 1945 and 1975 – which we may consider the long history of the Vietnam War – and thus allows us to see the ways in which the neo-imperialism of the US was continuous and discontinuous with the earlier French imperialism. The Vietnam war, one of the most dramatic and meaningful episodes of decolonization, was perhaps more instrumental than any other in producing the idea that the US was a neo-

imper ialist power and that imperialism was not over but had entered a new phase. The defeat of the US here also played a role in the changed view of the West as a 'failure' in the Islamic world and elsewhere.

The final essay in this volume (Chapter 19) by Bruce Cumings presents a view, rather different from all we have seen so far, of colonialism and decolonization based on the region he has studied, namely the Japanese colonial empire in East Asia. Comparing the economic experience of Korea and Taiwan under Japanese colonialism during the inter-war years with the Vietnamese experience under French rule, Cumings finds the Japanese colonies far better prepared for modern industrialization than Vietnam. He claims that the Japanese 'were imperialists but also capitalists, colonizers but also modernizers, every bit as interested as a Frederic Taylor in laying an industrial grid and disciplining, training and surveilling the workforce'. Thus the post-war economic development of East Asia has as much to do with its distinctive colonial past as with any other factor. Cumings' chapter raises the question as to why Japanese imperialism was different. He himself points to the European tradition of statism that Japan and others in East Asia imbibed. At the same time, as we have noted in the introduction to this volume, it was also tied to the Japanese re-conceptualization of imperialism during the inter-war period that in some ways prefigured the post-World War II US-dominated conceptions of the 'new world order' discussed by Kelly and Kaplan and others.

* * *

14

'DON'T PAINT NATIONALISM RED!'

National revolution and socialist anti-imperialism[1]

Ronald Grigor Suny

At the turn of the twentieth century the great land empires of Europe and the Middle East – tsarist Russia, the Ottoman empire and Austro-Hungary – were each faced by the dilemma of how to preserve their imperial state in the face of oppositional, potentially separatist nation-alisms of their constituent peoples. Imperial forms of nationalism failed to preserve these contiguous empires, and the catastrophe of World War I ended with their collapse and dissolution. The Habsburg realm broke up into small states, each defined and dominated by a single ruling nation; the Ottoman empire lost its Arab lands, and a Turkish national state emerged in Anatolia. Russia alone survived the war as a large multina-tional state, but one that in the view of its new communist rulers was neither a nation-state nor a colonial empire. The transformation of the Russian empire into the Soviet multinational state was at one and the same time a successful state-making enterprise and a failure of the maxi-malist, internationalist and anti-imperialist vision of its founders.

Prisonhouse of nations

In tsarist Russia the word 'empire' (*imperiia*) had a positive valence. The emperor was an all-powerful sovereign whose will was limited only by God and nature. The Russian empire was the largest country on the globe, and monarchs and intellectuals lauded the variety of its peoples as a great virtue. The empire, like all other empires, was built on the prin-ciple of difference and inequality between those who ruled and those whom they ruled. From at least the moment of Ivan IV's conquest of Kazan in the mid-sixteenth century, when Russia ceased to be a relatively homogeneous ethnic polity and became a multinational one, the relations between the governing elite, made up largely of ethnic Russians and Russified non-Russians, and the subordinate non-Russian peoples (as well as the bulk of ethnic Russians) were always unequal ones of subordination and superordination. Though access to the elite was never closed off entirely to non-Russians, those with Russian cultural competence held a privileged access to power and prestige. The degree of difficulty for upward social movement differed among the non-Russian peoples. While Baltic Germans had relatively easy entrée to the circles of power, other peoples, notably the Jews, Muslims of Central Asia, and Armenians after 1885, found their ways blocked. These tsarist practices that both distinguished the core ethno-religious community, the Russians, from the peripheral 'others' and kept the latter in a subordinated relationship to the core nationality, paralleled the hierarchies that kept the gentry and the simple *narod* (people) in their respective places. Imperial power was based on both horizontal distinctions between peoples and vertical differences between social estates (*sosloviia*).

As long as tsars were able to maintain their aura of legitimacy, the multinationality of the empire could act as a bond holding the empire together. Imperial power was justified because of difference; some people were intended and entitled to rule over others by virtue of their superiority. More pragmatically, a great and diverse state like Russia required the particular state form of autocracy to keep the various social and ethnic groups in place. Inequities and diversity, along with ideologies accepting and rationalizing them, were key structural and discursive impediments to the development of alternative political forms. The conservative support of basically inequitable, 'imperial' relations between peoples made devolution into more liberal constitutional forms difficult, and rendered democratic reforms utopian for much of the imperial period. Alhough some Russian political leaders recognized, reluctantly, that maintaining the empire precluded the likelihood of a representative political system, others, from Liberals to Bolsheviks, attempted to force a marriage between the unitary state that tsarism had created and some form of democratic politics.

The variety of political entities within the Russian empire, from the Grand Duchy of Finland and the Viceroyalty of Caucasia to the khanates of Bukhara and Khiva, were indelible reminders of the stages of expansion that continued until the last days of Romanov rule. Held together both by military force and the idea of loyalty to the tsar, the empire was not conceived in ethnic terms (*russkaia imperiia*) but as a cosmopolitan collection of peoples and polities (*rossiiskaia imperiia*) under a single sovereign. The ruling elite was equally cosmopolitan, Russian-speaking to be sure, but made up of members of many nationalities – Poles, Germans, assimilated Georgians and Tatars, among others – who once they had become loyal servitors of the emperor lost much of their identification with the people from which they had come. Ethnic elites were coopted into imperial service, and for much of the eighteenth and nineteenth centuries Russian policy was extraordinarily successful in deracinating those who might have been the leaders of resistance to central state rule.

Non-Russian peoples were governed in a contradictory system that involved indirect rule in some places, direct military government through local elites assimilated into the Russian administrative system in others, and various forms of constitutionalism (in the Grand Duchy of Finland and, until 1863, the Kingdom of Poland). Among the effects of tsarism was imposition of a new state order on societies that had little contact with strong state structures, new regulations and laws, the spread of serfdom to certain regions, such as Georgia, and the enforcement of new taxation. This administrative 'Russification', the extension of bureaucratic absolutism over non-Russian subjects, was accompanied by a spontaneous self-Russification that many non-Russians found advantageous in the first two thirds of the nineteenth century. But after 1881, when the government adopted a more stridently anti-national and anti-Semitic set of policies that threatened a forced cultural homogenization, ethnicities, like the Armenians, that had been Russophilic turned hostile to the tsarist regime. By World War I much of the support for tsarism had eroded among workers and intellectuals. On the edges of the empire a deep alienation from Russian authority grew among Caucasian and Central Asian Muslims, Poles, Finns, and other peoples.

Constituting a liberal order

The February Revolution of 1917 that brought down tsarism and inaugurated a brief experiment in liberal government was marked by an extraordinary confidence in the power of juridical solutions to ameliorate deep social and ethnic conflicts. The evils that had led to class and nationality hostilities were laid at the doorstep of tsarism, and newly-empowered politicians argued that proper legislation in a Western, liberal direction would remove obstacles to resolving conflicts. In one of its first acts (on 8 March) the Provisional Government restored the constitution of the Grand Duchy of Finland. The manifesto emphasized the illegality of tsarist regulations that contradicted the laws of Finland. Four days later newspapers announced that the government intended to abolish all legal restrictions based on religion, nationality and 'class' (here referring primarily to *soslovie* and *chin*). When Prime Minister Lvov signed the law on 20 March, it was greeted by an editorial in the conservative *Novoe vremia* (New Times) that expressed both the fear that 'the developing centrifugal forces and separatist aspirations of the nationalities that compose Russia' presented a 'real danger of the gradual decomposition of the state into its component parts' and the hope that '[n]ow all obstacles to mutual understanding among the peoples of Russia have withered away in the light of liberty dawning over the country'.[2] Such optimism that 'liberty will unite' demonstrated faith in juridical solutions, but also prepared the ground for bitter disappointment when problems associated with nationality proved to be far more intractable than imagined.

Toward the end of March, when the government worked out its provisions for local self-government, the principle of nationality was taken into consideration in two ways. In forming the provinces of Estland and Lifland, 'the natural boundaries' between them were to be delimited according to ethnicity. But in extending the *zemstva* (local representative assemblies) to Siberia and Arkhangel'sk province, the government exempted those areas occupied by the nomadic Samoeds, various other *inorodtsy* (foreign peoples), and Cossacks, for whom special regulations and institutions would be implemented. Special laws were issued for Turkestan (where local authorities would decide if *zemstva* were appropriate for various districts and peoples), the Kalmyk steppe and the lands of the Kyrgyz Inner Horde. Plans for extending *zemstva* to Transcaucasia and the Cossack regions of southern Russia were still being formulated when the Provisional Government was overthrown.

Nationality was clearly a consideration in the formulation of policy, but the government and the principal parties with influence within and over it were much more concerned about the unity of the state in a time of acute danger. Rather than acceptance of the radical implications of the principle of national self-determination, liberal and conservative politicians maintained a paternalistic attitude toward most of the non-Russian peoples. And moderate socialists were willing to go along with the government's consistent delaying of hard choices until the convening of the Constituent Assembly. The leading liberal party, the Kadets, opposed national territorial political autonomy, a federal structure for the new Russia, and any form of separatism. Representation would be geographic, rather than based on nationality. Proclaiming themselves for 'Russia, one and indivisible', the Kadets saw manifestations of nationalism as signs of pro-German disloyalty. Pavl Miliukov told his fellow Kadets in May that

the Party of the People's Freedom will endeavor to find a solution that, while giving an opportunity to the various regions of Russia to create their local autonomy on the principle of local legislation, will not at the same time destroy the unity of the Russian State. The preservation of the unity of the Russian State is the limiting factor conditioning the decisions of the Party. The division of the country into sovereign, independent units is considered by the Party as absolutely inadmissible.[3]

The Kadets saw themselves as the champions of equal rights of people, rather than peoples, but wanted a unitary Russian state. Miliukov supported Russian hegemony in a multinational state, though he wanted to end nationality restrictions such as those imposed under tsarism, for they inhibited the process of natural assimilation of minorities. Even more conservative than the Provisional Government, which promised independence for Poland, the Kadets were prepared to grant only autonomy to Poland and drew the line at Ukraine. Miliukov and Kokoshkin told a delegation from the Ukrainian National Congress in late April that territorial autonomy was a danger to Russia's unity and that Ukrainians were not ready for independence. For Russian liberals decolonization meant the end of legal discriminations against non-Russians, but not recognition of ethnic distinction or political autonomy.

To a greater degree than their leaders in the capital, provincial Kadets saw the February Revolution 'as a means of 'liberating' non-Russian nationalities; and despite the party program's adherence to a non-federal, centralized system of government, some Kadets expressed themselves locally in favor of a new republican federation'.[4] 'To some extent', William G. Rosenberg writes,

> the rights of Ukrainians, Georgians, and other national minorities were subordinated in Kadet practice to those of Great Russians, a posture of internal imperialism which had long characterized the tsarist regime itself, and which would cause Kadet leaders no end of difficulty in 1917, even within the ranks of their own party.[5]

By the autumn of 1917, not surprisingly, leading Kadets had become political allies of the Cossacks, the traditional defenders of Russian statehood.

Just as on the issues of war and peace and questions of political and social legislation, so on the problem of the non-Russians, the leading political organ of the lower classes, the Petrograd soviet, was seldom in agreement with the government. Even during the period of coalition, from May to October 1917, the representatives of the moderate socialist parties developed a distinctive policy toward non-Russians that reflected both the pre-revolutionary positions of their parties and a greater sensitivity to the aspirations of the non-Russians. The Party of Socialist Revolutionaries, the leading organization of pro-peasant socialists, had declared at its first congress, in Imatra, Finland in 1906, the 'unconditional right' of national self-determination, which included the right to political separation from Russia. Though some isolated voices called for subordination of the rights of nations to the mission of the socialist revolution, they were effectively silenced by an overwhelming majority. While the 'national question' was not a major concern for the neopopulists, the party was clear about its commitment to federalism – in contrast to the Marxist Social Democrats, who supported a unitary state – and its opposition to coercion in order to preserve the empire. But, as Oliver Radkey writes,

> In 1906 the SRs were a party without responsibility; in 1917 they had achieved responsibility; and, as they surveyed the nationalities problem from the vantage-ground of offices of state, they came to conceive of it in a less generous spirit than during the years preceding the triumph of the revolution.[6]

In 1917 the SR party continued to favour federalism, but now opposed separation. At the third party congress, in May 1917, the rapporteur on state organization, the right SR M. V. Vishniak envisioned Russia as Switzerland writ large, a federal state with a collegial executive, but, nevertheless, a single state – a *Bundesstaat* rather than a *Staatenbund*. Maximal national autonomy would be accommodated within the federation (even separate coinage and postal systems, but without tariff barriers), but secession was impermissible. Within these limits autonomy would be determined on the basis of mutual agreements. Only Poland was to be granted independence; Finland would remain tied to Russia for strategic reasons. When questioned about this anomalous treatment of Finland, Vishniak answered that Finnish independence would set a dangerous precedent and encourage separatist pretensions of other nationalities. On the national question the party as a whole followed the line of the right and rejected the left's support for secession. Even the centrist Viktor Chernov agreed that the All-Russian Constituent Assembly would first have to lay down the criteria within which national assemblies could elaborate their own claims to autonomy.

The Social Democrats were committed to national self-determination, and Vladimir Lenin, leader of its radical Bolshevik wing, took that slogan farthest – to separation from the empire. In contrast to the Jewish Bund and the Armenian Dashnaktsutiun, which advocated the Austro-Marxist position of extraterritorial national-cultural autonomy for ethnicities (each nationality represented in parliament no matter where its members lived), the Bolsheviks rejected the idea of cultural autonomy in favor of non-ethnic regional autonomy. Lenin also was firm through 1917 in his resistance to federalism. In the revolutionary year the Bolshevik position gave nationalities a stark choice: either full independence and separation from the rest of Russia or becoming part of a unitary socialist state with all cultural and civil rights guaranteed for working people. Lenin believed that national separatism would be reduced by Russian tolerance and support for full national self-determination to the point of independence.

Both the Provisional Government and the Petrograd soviet were committed to formal and complete independence for Poland. Since the German army was in control of most of Poland by early 1917, political support for Polish independence in no way threatened the war effort. But the concession to Poland only increased the appetites of the Finns and the Ukrainians, and the inherent conflict between the principle of national self-determination and the commitment of the leading political actors to the unity of the Russian state emerged into open political struggle within the first weeks of the revolution.

The manifesto of the government restoring Finland's constitution recognized the full 'internal independence' of the former Grand Duchy, but began by asserting that the Petrograd government was 'vested with plenary power'.[7] The Social Democratic leadership of the Finnish parliament soon proposed that with the fall of the monarchy sovereignty should pass to the Finnish government, while conceding that the Provisional Government would continue to decide foreign and military policy for the time being. The future Bolshevik Otto Kuusinen concluded that this draft constitution gave Finland all that it could wish for and was better than independence. The reaction in Petrograd to the Finnish move, however, was quick, sharp, and negative. Russian policy, as initially formulated by Alexander Kerensky, rejected any firm pronouncement on the ultimate status of Finland until the convening of the All-Russian Constituent Assembly.

The government's position was ultimately supported by moderate socialists (the SRs and the less radical Social Democrats, the Mensheviks) in the soviets. When in early April the Finnish Social Democrats met with the Russian Menshevik leaders, the latter recognized Finland's right to self-determination but held that only the Constituent Assembly could ultimately determine the issue. The only major party to support Finland's full independence was the Bolsheviks. As early as 11 March, Lenin, still in Switzerland, had argued that 'the Russian proletariat will guarantee to a Finnish republic complete freedom, including the freedom to secede'. Lenin told the Seventh Conference of the Bolsheviks in April: 'Our attitude toward the separatist movement is indifferent, neutral....We are for Finland receiving complete freedom because then there will be greater trust in Russian democracy, and the Finns will not separate'.

The attitude of the Petrograd authorities stimulated even more support for independence in Finland, and through May and June the Finnish Social Democrats pushed for a law (the *valtalaki*) that ascribed sovereignty to the Finnish Seim. The Russian socialists, however, hoped to delay the final disposition of Finland until the Constituent Assembly. The First All-Russian Congress of Soviets adopted a broad resolution on the national question, proclaiming its support of decentralization of the state and broad political autonomy for regions that differ ethnically and socio-economically from one another. It called on the government to issue a declaration recognizing the right of self-determination of all peoples, including separation, but left the final disposition of the various regions to be realized through a covenant with the national Constituent Assembly. Until the very last days of its existence, the Provisional Government refused to concede full independence to Finland, and proved willing to use the army to enforce its policy in Finland.

The Provisional Government subordinated the principles of self-determination and democratic choice to preservation of the territory of the late empire. Resolution of the question of autonomy or independence was postponed, and moderate socialists in the soviets concurred with the government's strategy. In 1917 most of the peoples of the Russian empire were not yet determined to secede from the new democratic state. Their faith lay in a constitutional solution within a renewed multinational state, which overrode the risky choice of going it alone in time of war. In Kiev, however, a locally elected assembly, the Rada, issued its First Universal, declaring autonomy for Ukraine and itself the supreme political authority. Late in June, delegates from the government conferred in Kiev with representatives of the Rada, and after heated discussions the Petrograd delegation reluctantly decided to recognize the Rada's competence to work out reforms in Ukraine and run the region until the convocation of the Constituent Assembly. This attempt at compromise led to the so-called 'July Crisis' in Petrograd, when several members of the Kadet party resigned from the government in protest over the concessions made in favour of autonomy for Ukraine. The resolution of the Ukrainian question would have to wait until after the October Revolution, and then be further delayed by foreign intervention and civil war. Similarly, the Finns waited until after the coming to power of the Bolsheviks in November to declare their independence. There a bitter and bloody struggle between pro-German nationalists and pro-Soviet socialists deeply divided the country and ultimately ended with White Terror against the supporters of the left. Throughout Russia the brief experiment in an institutional solution to the national question had failed. Both liberals and socialists believed in national self-determination as a political language, but when non-Russians opted for separation they almost always asserted interests of state over principle.

Fighting nationalism with federalism

Once the Bolsheviks took power in Petrograd in October 1917, Russia began to fragment into independent states. With the outbreak of civil war in mid-1918, semi-independent governments sprang up in the borderlands. The Bolsheviks, like the liberals and moderate socialists, wanted to preserve the great state, but for both ideological and pragmatic reasons they were willing to permit national self-determination, including separation from Russia. Lenin's hope was that permitting separatism would actually prevent it. In the euphoria of revolution and the confidence that came with surviving civil war, Lenin and the Bolsheviks gave in to their most cherished hopes: that the world would soon be made anew by international revolution. National borders would be swept away, and a new organization of human society would gradually replace capitalism and bourgeois parliamentarianism. Already in the appeal 'To All Muslim Toilers of Russia and the East', issued just one month after the Bolsheviks came to power in November 1917, the powerful rhetoric of self-determination, liberation, independence and anti-imperialism established a unity of the struggle against colonial and national oppression. For the next three years the Red Army was engaged in a simultaneous battle against 'bourgeois nationalists' and 'foreign interventionists'. Anti-imperialism was not distinguished from the drive to 'liberate' the former subject peoples of the Russian empire. But before the forces of nationa lism and imperialism could be defeated, pragmatism demanded that new states be formed. Soviet republics like the Russian Federation, Ukraine and Belorussia could safeguard proletarian power until allied revolutions in Europe and Asia could come to the aid of the Russian Revolution.

Soviet Russia was conceived not as an ordinary national state but as the first stone in a future multinational socialist edifice. The reach of the Russian Revolution was to be limitless. What its enemies would later build into a potent ideological image of a drive toward world domination was in its incarnation an effort directed primarily against British imperialism. It brought Lenin and his comrades into a series of peculiar alliances with the fallen Turkish leader Enver Pasha, King Amanullah of Afghanistan, the rebel Kuchuk Khan in northern Persia, Kemal Pasha in Anatolia, and other non-socialist nationalists. The empires of the Europeans in Asia, the semi-colonial periphery of Persia, China and Turkey (in Lenin's conceptualization), and the newly independent 'nationalist' states – like the Caucasian (Armenia, Azerbaijan and Georgia) and Baltic (Estonia, Latvia and Lithuania) republics – established after the October Revolution, dependent as they were on the presence and support of European power, all were linked in a single understanding as the last props of a moribund capitalism. With a confidence born of recent victories and faith in a Marxist eschatology, and with an opportunism rooted in the limited resources at hand, the Bolsheviks used all the means available to realize their dream of international revolution. For communists of the civil-war period, internationalism was less the servant of the Soviet states than the Soviet states were the servant of internationalism.

From the very beginning, the pull between socialism and nationalism was a struggle between supporters of the Soviet government and foreign interventionists who hoped to gain allies in the war against the Reds. A pristine nationalism, able to establish a firm base of support in the ethnic population and to hold on to political independence without foreign help, was difficult to find in the peripheries of the Russian empire. Bolshevism, anarchism, or various forms of peasant socialism were stronger contenders for the loyalties of many borderland peoples, and often the nationalists were limited to the urban settings and to intellectuals. Two fiercely antagonistic discourses contended in a battle of rhetoric and violence: nationalists appealed to the West to defend their right to national self-determination against a renewed Russian threat, whereas communists portrayed the nationalists and their foreign backers as part of an imperialist endeavour to contain or destroy Bolshevism and the coming international revolution.

Nationalism was relatively weak during the first revolutionary year, still largely centred in the ethnic intelligentsia, among students and the lower middle classes of the towns, with at best a fleeting following among broader strata. Among Belorussians, Lithuanians and Azerbaijanis, rather than a sense of nationality, the paramount identification was with people nearby with whom one shared social and religious communality. For these peoples, neither nationalism nor socialism was able to mobilize large numbers into the political struggles that would decide their future. For several other nationalities, among them the Latvians and Georgians, class-based socialist movements were far more potent than political nationalism. For still other nationalities, like the Ukrainians and the Estonians, nationality competed with a sense of class for primary loyalty of the workers and peasants, with neither winning a dominant position. Among Armenians a socialist-nationalist party, the Dashnaktsutiun, dominated, and faced by the threat of annihilation at the hands of Ottoman Turks, Armenians rallied around an inclusive, all-class nationalism.[8]

For Lenin and the Bolsheviks, policy toward the non-Russian peoples was inseparable from the anti-imperialist struggle. Nationality policy and anti-colonialism were intimately linked. The principle of national self-determination, long a socialist programme, was supposed to be consistent with the struggle for socialism, and yet at the same time it played into the hands of anti-socialist nationalists for whom the nation was the highest priority. The Bolsheviks' pre-revolutionary thinking on the national question did not survive their taking power. A few months after the October Revolution, the Bolsheviks conceded that the new Soviet state would be both federative, at least in name and theory, and based on ethnic political units. Even diasporic communities were given cultural and educational institutions, and in many cases their own political bodies. Indeed, for more than a decade following the civil war, nationalities like the Jews and Armenians, and the Ukrainians in Russia, enjoyed extraterritorial privileges, with their own schools and soviets operating in republics of other nationalities. Soviet practice combined ideological desiderata, such as the struggle against Russian chauvinism, with practical considerations of state unity. The aim was to erode separatist nationalism while developing class loyalties. But the concessions to the national principle led not, as Lenin expected, to the disappearance of ethnic cultural affiliations but to the consolidation of nationality. Rather than a melting pot, the Soviet Union became the incubator of new nations.

Though many of his comrades consistently favoured subordinating nationalism strictly to class considerations, Lenin was both aware of the power of nationalism (even as he hoped to harness it to the proletarian revolution) and ready to concede the need to ally with 'bourgeois nationalists'. For Lenin, nationalism and separatism were neither natural nor inevitable, but were contingent on the sense of oppression that nationalities experienced from imperialism. He remained convinced that nationalism reflected only the interests of the bourgeoisie, that the proletariat's true interests were supranational, and that the end of colonialism would diminish the power of nationalist sentiments.[9] In contrast to his party comrades on the left, he refused to oppose the independence of Finland, Poland and Ukraine. Though he hoped that such separations could be avoided and reserved the option to oppose specific moves toward independence on principle, he abjured the use of force to keep the empire whole. He was unequivocal in his public commitment to 'the full right of separation from Russia of all nations and nationalities, oppressed by tsarism, joined by force or held by force within the borders of the state, i.e., annexed'. At the same time, he argued that the goal of the proletarian party was the creation of the largest state possible and the rapprochement (*sblizhenie*) and eventual merging (*sliianie*) of nations. Such a goal was to be reached, not through force, but voluntarily, by the will of the workers.[10]

Lenin understood the need for alliances with the peasants and the non-Russians, and he was convinced that the approaching international socialist revolution would make the movements for land and statehood largely irrelevant. Acutely aware that the weakness of the central state gave new potency to movements for autonomy and separation from the empire, as well as the spontaneous resolution of the land question by peasants, Lenin staked out a clear position supporting both processes. By doing so, he distinguished the Bolshevik programme of national self-determination from both that of the Provisional Government and those of the successive anti-Bolshevik 'White' movements of the civil war.

Immediately after taking power, the Bolsheviks set up the People's Commissariat of Nationalities under Joseph Stalin and issued a series of declarations on 'the rights of the toiling and exploited peoples', 'to all Muslim toilers of Russia and the East', and on the disposition of Turkish Armenia. Most importantly, with little real ability to effect its will in the peripheries, the Soviet government made a strategic shift in response to the growing number of autonomies, and accepted by January 1918 the principle of federalism. As they launched an attack on Ukraine, the Bolsheviks announced that they recognized the Central Executive Committee of Soviets of Ukraine as 'the supreme authority in Ukraine' and accepted 'a federal union with Russia and complete unity in matters of internal and external policy'. By the end of the month the Third Congress of Soviets resolved: 'The Soviet Russian Republic is established on the basis of a free union of free nations, as a federation of Soviet national republics'. Both federalism and national-territorial autonomy were written into the first Soviet constitution, adopted in July 1918. As Richard Pipes has noted, 'Soviet Russia...became the first modern state to place the national principle at the base of its federal structure'.[11]

In the ferocity of the civil war, many communists, particularly those in the peripheries or of non-Russian origin, opposed Lenin's principled stand in favour of national self-determination, fearing the dissolution of the unitary state. As early as December 1917, Stalin argued that the freedom of self-determination should be given only to the labouring classes, not to the bourgeoisie. At the Eighth Party Congress in March 1919, Bukharin supported Stalin's position and tried to divide the national from the colonial question. Only in those nations where the proletariat had not defined its interests as separate from the bourgeoisie should the slogan of 'self-determination of nations' be employed. Lenin's formula, he claimed, was appropriate only 'for Hottentots, Bushmen, Negroes, Indians', whereas Stalin's notion of 'self-determination for the labouring classes' corresponded to the period in which the dictatorship of the proletariat was being established.[12] Lenin answered Bukharin sharply:

> There are no Bushmen in Russia; as for the Hottentots, I also have not heard that they have pretensions to an autonomous republic, but we have the Bashkirs, the Kyrgyz, a whole series of other peoples, and in relation to them we cannot refuse recognition.

All nations, he reasserted, have the right to self-determination, and Bolshevik support for this principle would aid the self-determination of the labouring classes. The stage of a given nation as it moved from 'medieval forms to bourgeois democracy and on to proletarian democracy' should be considered, he stated, but it was difficult to differentiate the interests of the proletariat and the bourgeoisie, which had been sharply defined only in Russia.[13]

The final resolution of the Congress was a compromise between Lenin's tolerance of nationalism and the more militant opposition to it. Maintaining the principle of national self-determination, the resolution went on to say: 'As to the question who is the carrier of the nation's will to separation, the RKP stands on the historico-class point-of-view, taking into consideration the level of historical development on which a given nation stands'.[14] The Bolsheviks reached no consensus on nationality policy, and the conflict between those who, like Lenin, considered the national agenda of non-Russians and those who, like Stalin, subordinated the national to the 'proletarian' continued until the former's death and the latter's consolidation of power within the party. On the ground, communists themselves decided who was the carrier of the nation's will, and after the initial recognition of independence for Finland, Poland, the Baltic republics and (for a time) Georgia, few other gestures were made toward 'separatists'.

Toward the end of 1919, while reflecting on the factors that had led to Bolshevik victory in 1917, Lenin turned to Ukraine to underscore the importance of tolerance in nationality policy. Reviewing the Constitutent Assembly election results, in which Ukrainian SRs and socialists outpolled the Russian SRs, he noted: 'The division between the Russian and Ukrainian Socialist Revolutionaries as early as 1917 could not have been accidental'. Without holding that national sentiments are fixed or permanent, he suggested once again that internationalists must be tolerant of the changing national consciousness of non-Russians, which, he was confident, was part of the petty bourgeois vacillation that had been characteristic of the peasantry throughout the civil war.

> The question whether the Ukraine will be a separate state is far less important [than the fundamental interests of the proletarian dictatorship, the unity of the Red Army, or the leading role of the proletariat in relation to the peasantry]. We must not be in the least surprised, or frightened, even by the prospect of the Ukrainian workers and peasants trying out different systems, and in the course of, say, several years, testing by practice union with the RSFSR, or seceding from the latter and forming an independent Ukrainian SSR, or various forms of their close alliance…
>
> The vacillation of non-proletarian working people on *such* a question is quite natural, even inevitable, but not in the least frightful for the proletariat. It is the duty of the proletarian who is really capable of being an internationalist…to leave it to the

non-proletarian masses *themselves* to *get rid* of this vacillation as a result of their own experience.[15]

A moment of truth, 1920: fighting imperialism with nationalism

As the strategic situation improved for the Bolsheviks and their allies by the summer of 1920, the 'national-colonial question' was put squarely on the agenda. The British were leaving the Russian periphery, and the communists had gained their first foothold south of the Caucasus with the relatively easy Sovietization of Azerbaijan in April. The balance of forces in Central Asia and in Transcaucasia was clearly in favour of the Soviets, even though Georgia and Armenia remained independent. The Soviets established direct links with the Kemalist nationalists in Anatolia, effectively squeezing the South Caucasian republics between them. On 26 April, Kemal sent an official communication to Moscow expressing his appreciation of Moscow's fight against imperialism and his readiness to take upon himself 'military operations against the imperialist Armenian government' and to encourage Azerbaijan 'to enter the Bolshevik state union'.[16] In May, Soviet troops and the Persian revolutionary Kuchuk Khan established the Soviet republic of Gilan on the southern coast of the Caspian Sea, and though the situation in Persia remained extraordinarily fluid, the government at Tehran appeared prepared to distance itself from the British and open negotiations with the Soviets. With Denikin defeated, Kolchak dead, and the Red Army marching against Pilsudski's Poland, the latter half of 1920 turned out to be a high point of revolutionary enthusiasm and direct Bolshevik promotion of the revolution in the East.

Several themes repeatedly reasserted themselves in the discussions around the national-colonial question in 1920, both at the Second Congress of the Communist International and the Baku Congress of the Peoples of the East. The first was Lenin's leitmotivs that had haunted his writings since 1914 – the relationship of capitalist imperialism and the revolutionary crisis in both the advanced and the colonial world. Besides the one billion people living in colonial and semi-colonial states, and another quarter-billion living in Russia, since the war Germany, Austria and Bulgaria, he argued, had been relegated to 'what amounts to colonial status'. The 'super-profits of thousands of millions form the economic basis on which opportunism in the labour movement is built'.[17] This dependency of the capitalist metropole on the colonial and semi-colonial world was recognized by all communists, but some non-European communists, like the Indian M. N. Roy and 'many comrades in Turkestan' (referred to by the Iranian delegate Avetis Sultanzade at the Second World Congress), went further and argued that the revolution in Europe required a revolution in the East.

A second theme was the failure of the Second International to address the colonial issue in a revolutionary manner. Lenin, Roy, Sultan Zade and others portrayed the Social Democrats as Eurocentric reformers, willing to support movements toward self-government in the colonies but reluctant to back revolutionary efforts. Communists, on the other hand, recognized the need for collaboration between revolutionaries in Europe, America and Asia, and took pride in the multi-racial representation in the Comintern meetings.

A third dominant theme was the historic difference between bourgeois democracy, supported by the Social Democrats of Europe, and soviet democracy, and the strong sense that a new historical epoch had opened that had rendered parliamentarianism obsolete.[18] In his 'Preliminary theses on the national-colonial question', Lenin began with the distinction between formal bourgeois democracy, which grants all under juridical equality to all, "property owner and proletarian, expolitor and expolited," and Soviet democracy, which recognizes the real meaning of the demand of equality', which requires the abolition of classes.[19] Bourgeois democracy also disguised the exploitation of weaker nations by the stronger, though the imperialist war of 1914–18 had exposed this hypocrisy. Only a common struggle of all proletarians and labouring people of all nations could overthrow the rule of the landlords and bourgeoisie.

Yet another theme was the nature of the future socialist state, a grand multinational federation not unlike the Russian Socialist Federative Soviet Republic (RSFSR). Federation, Lenin maintained, was the advanced form for the full unity of the toilers of different countries. Federation already had shown its utility in practice, both in the relations of the RSFSR with other soviet republics (Hungarian, Finnish and Latvian in the past; Azerbaijani and Ukrainian in the present) and, within the RSFSR, in relations with the nationalities that earlier had not had either state existence or autonomy (for example, the Bashkir and Tatar autonomous republics in the RSFSR). It was essential to work for a tighter federative union, both politically and economically, but at the same time, Lenin cautioned, full recognition of the rights of nations and minorities, including the right to separate states, had to be supported.

Differences in tone and direction arose in discussions of appropriate strategies to win over the masses of the East. In his original theses delivered to the Second Comintern Congress, Lenin had argued that 'all communist parties must aid the bourgeois-democratic liberation' in backward countries with feudal or patriarchal relations. While fighting against clerical reaction and medieval elements, against Pan-Islam and other movements that attempt to unite the liberation movement while strengthening the khans, landlords, mullahs, etc., communists must support the peasant movement against landlords by forming a 'provisional alliance' with bourgeois democracy of the colonies and backward countries. When Lenin submitted his theses to his comrades, he met resistance to his provisional alliance with the national bourgeoisie. Lenin assured the doubters that 'the alliance with the peasantry is more strongly underlined for me (and this is not completely equal to the bourgeoisie)'.[20] Most vociferously, Roy disputed Lenin's support of the national bourgeoisie and argued that Lenin was mistaken to believe that the national liberation movement had the significance of the bourgeois democratic revolution. Though as yet an unproven revolutionary, Roy (as he tells us in his memoirs)

> pointed out that the bourgeoisie even in the most advanced colonial countries, like India, as a class, was not economically and culturally differentiated from the feudal social order: therefore, the nationalist movement was ideologically reactionary in the sense that the triumph would not necessarily mean a bourgeois democratic revolution. The role of Gandhi was the crucial point of difference. Lenin believed that, as the inspirer and leader of a mass movement, he was a revolutionary. I maintained that, as a religious and cultural revivalist, he was bound to be a reactionary socially, however revolutionary he might appear politically.[21]

Lenin was impressed by Roy's arguments. Other delegates 'whispered, mostly in awe, that the Indian upstart had dared question the wisdom of Lenin and cross verbal swords with him, with the master of polemics. But Lenin's attitude [Roy remembered] was very kind and tolerant'.[22] After several private discussions with Roy and a general debate in the Commission on the national-colonial question, Lenin admitted that his views had been changed by Roy's challenge. Roy argued that foreign domination constantly obstructed the free development of social life and that, therefore, the revolution's first step must be the removal of this foreign domination. But the struggle to overthrow foreign domination, rather than underwrite the aims of the national bourgeoisie, should smooth the path to liberation for the proletariat of the colonies.

Roy distinguished more clearly than Lenin the two opposing movements in the colonial world: 'The bourgeois-democratic nationalist movement, which pursues the program of political liberation with the conservation of the capitalist order; [and] the struggle of the propertyless peasants for their liberation from every kind of exploitation'.[23] Communists must not allow the former movement to dominate the latter and must ally with and support the latter. Lenin eventually conceded that communists should support 'national-revolutionary' movements but withhold support from reformist movements based on collaboration of the colonial and the metropolitan bourgeoisies. In the absence of a proletariat, as in Turkestan, the Communist Party must take over the leading role 'in order to awaken independent political thinking and political action'.[24]

The essence of Roy's critique of Lenin was preserved in the final version of the thesis. Colonial revolutions, though they would not be communist in their first stages, were not fated to move through a bourgeois-democratic phase. Capitalist development was not necessary for every people.

> Theoretically the Communist International must also declare and explain that with the help of the proletariat of the advanced countries the backward countries can arrive at soviet organization and, through a series of stages, and even avoiding the capitalist system, can arrive at Communism.[25]

Communists preferred, of course, nationalist movements in which peasants would act independently of the bourgeoisie and form soviets or other councils of the exploited. But even in this euphoric moment, when the anti-imperialist struggle seemed to be reaching a crescendo and it seemed possible to leap over the capitalist stage, a certain sobriety and caution kept the communists from cutting themselves off from the actual nationalist movements in the colonial world and taking a disastrous left turn.[26]

In the debate at the Second World Congress, opponents to the Lenin/Roy compromise attacked from both the left and the right. Sultanzade, an Armenian founder of the Communist Party of Iran, called for the creation of 'a purely communist movement in opposition to the bourgeois-democratic one'.[27] Serratti of Italy opposed the theses as class-collaborationist and, instead of support of national liberation movements of the bourgeoisie, proposed using them instrumentally for the purposes of a social revolution. Connolly of Ireland, on the other side, pleaded that the Communist International 'encourage and support every movement that strives to weaken the imperialist powers and to advance the growing world revolution'. Communists in Ireland had no choice but to favour the nationalists who favoured an independent bourgeois-democratic Irish state; otherwise they faced political isolation. Ismael Hakki Pasha similarly argued that the Kemalist movement in Anatolia was 'the best answer to the ruthless exploitation to which Turkey is subjected by the countries of the Entente'.[28] The Dutch communist Maring (Sneevliet), who had witnessed a religious national movement Sarekat-Islam in Java that combined anti-imperialism with social antagonism, agreed with the Lenin/Roy strategy: 'There is the necessity of working together with the revolutionary nationalist elements, and we are only doing half the job if we deny this movement and play at being doctrinaire Marxists'.[29] And his Dutch comrade Wijnkoop agreed that the revolutionary action of the masses had to be supported whether or not it was socialist. Communists should struggle against the importation of capitalism into non-capitalist countries, however, for the penetration of capitalism was not a necessary precondition for the transition to socialism.

The final resolution stated that

> the Communist International should accompany the revolutionary movement in the colonies and the backward countries for part of the way, should even make an alliance with it; it may not, however, fuse with it, but must unconditionally maintain the independent character of the proletarian movement, be it only in embryo.

Although the exact nature of the cooperation between nationalists and communists was not spelled out, the Lenin/Roy position allowed for provisional common efforts limited by the communists' ultimate promotion of the social revolution.

Though he held on to his principle of national self-determination, Lenin's adjustment to Roy's formulation had a political effect similar to the move by Stalin and Bukharin to consider the stage that a nation had reached. Both undermined the authenticity of the claims of nationalism and removed the restraints that Lenin had previously proposed. These more revolutionary positions pushed the communists to a leadership in the peripheral and colonial struggles that hardly corresponded to their real power in these regions. In the absence of a significant proletariat, in situations where the only viable revolutionary movement was one that communists could not bring themselves to support wholly, the party became a surrogate proletariat. Instead of being engaged in the actual revolution, which was anticolonial and led by nationalists or ethnosocialists, the party constructed a reading of the political moment that allowed them extraordinary freedom and left them open to precisely the charges of Russian expansionism of which Lenin had warned. The great advantage of the theses adopted by the Congress lay in their ambiguity about the actual tactics to be adopted in any concrete situation.

To implement the strategy of expanding the revolution in the East, the Comintern had decided to organize a Central Asian Bureau in Tashkent and organize a Congress of the Peoples of the East to be held in Baku, the newly liberated capital of Soviet Azerbaijan. An appeal to come to Baku was directed to 'the enslaved masses of Persia, Armenia, and Turkey'. The Congress has rightly been described as an inebriated display of revolutionary millenarianism, impractical and poorly planned from the beginning. Excessively rhetorical, it reflected the enthusiasms and style of its chief organizer, Grigorii Zinoviev, and has been vividly memorialized in Warren Beatty's film, *Reds*, largely for its fatal effects on the American communist John Reed. Roy dubbed the Congress 'Zinoviev's circus' and refused to attend, despite pressure from Zinoviev, Radek and Chicherin. More than 2,000 delegates, primarily from Caucasia and overwhelmingly Muslim, attended.[30] In his opening address Zinoviev reiterated the recently adopted positions of the Comintern. He declared that 'in China, India, Turkey, Persia, and Armenia it is possible and necessary to begin fighting directly for a Soviet system', because the Russian Revolution had made it possible for the East to move beyond the stage of capitalism. Communists would support nationalist revolutionaries like Kemal in Turkey, even though their policies were not communist, and would 'wait for a real people's revolution to rise'. He ended with a call for 'a true people's holy war' against both imperialism and capitalism.[31]

Much of the discussion at the Congress focused on the nationalist resistance in Turkey and the two still-independent Transcaucasian republics, Georgia and Armenia. The Armenian republic, which was ruled by the nationalist and anti-communist Dashnaktsutiun, was savagely attacked by Comintern leaders, among them Karl Radek and John Reed, and the orientalist V. M. Pavlovich (Veltman), who labelled it an Entente base that impeded Soviet Russia from aiding the Kemalist movement in Anatolia. The Turkish delegates were divided between Kemalists and deposed leaders of the Ottoman Empire, like Bahaeddin Shakir and Enver Pasha, both of whom had engineered the deportations and genocidal massacres of Ottoman Armenians just a few years earlier and now defended the struggle of the Turkish nationalists against Entente imperialism. Despite the efforts of the Turks to display their revolutionary credentials and disassociate themselves from the Turkish bourgeoisie, the Congress offered only cautious support to their movement. In the resolution presented by the Hungarian communist Bela Kun, Kemalism was characterized as a movement 'directed only against foreign oppressors' that 'would not in the least signify the emancipation of the Turkish peasants and workers from oppression and exploitation of every kind'.[32]

The Baku Congress, lauded as the first congress of the peoples of the East, turned out to be the last as well. The export of revolution proved far more difficult than had been imagined. Lenin publicly praised the Congress, but privately he was dismayed by Zinoviev's unbounded enthusiasm for the nationalists. 'Don't paint nationalism red', he admonished.[33] Within a few months the Armenian republic, facing an invasion by the Kemalist Turks, capitulated to the Bolshevik forces stationed on its border as the lesser evil. In February 1921 the Red Army drove the Mensheviks out of Georgia. Both of these Transcaucasian 'revolutions' were far more artificial and external than had been the collapse of Azerbaijan in April 1920, where Bolsheviks enjoyed considerable support from Baku workers. Though at first the Armenian communists agreed to work with the Dashnaks and Lenin preferred some accommodation with the Georgian Mensheviks, in both cases the moderates were quickly eliminated and purely communist political orders were established. In Transcaucasia, at least, no real attempt was made to implement the more cautious aspect of Comintern strategy, namely limited cooperation with non-communist nationalists. Rather, the more militant reading of that strategy, advancing as soon as possible to communist direction of the movement, was adopted. But in Armenia and Georgia, where there was no significant support for Bolshevism, the party remained an isolated political force until time, inertia and coercion brought grudging acquiescence from the population.

In Turkey the Kemalists swept to victory by defeating Armenian and French resistance in Marash and Greek and Entente efforts to occupy parts of western Anatolia. Here an anti-imperialist nationalism carried out its own limited cultural revolution, while the communists, many of whom were killed off by the Kemalists, were prevented from developing the social revolution. In Persia the Gilan movement lasted until the fall of 1921, but Kuchik Khan broke with his communist supporters, arresting and executing Haidar Khan (one of the Iranian delegates to the Baku Congress). Both in Turkey and Persia, Soviet Russia's shift toward establishing diplomatic relations with the governments in Ankara and Tehran left the revolutionary movements in those countries, both nationalist and communist, without the kind of open and direct support they had had earlier. Soviet Russia withdrew its troops from Persia, and Kuchik Khan was left to the mercies of Reza Khan.

The first phase of the Comintern's involvement with the peoples of the East was over by late 1921. The revolutionary wave had receded, and the Soviet government began to see itself as one state among many, albeit with a different historical role. The link between the national question within the USSR and the anti-imperialist struggle abroad became more tenuous. Both in its domestic nationality policies and in its anti-imperialist foreign policy, the experience of the Soviet leadership demonstrated a series of concessions and adjustments of theory to reality, of desire to necessity, and of ideology to pragmatism. Bolsheviks were a minority party representing a social class that had nearly disappeared in the civil war. With no political or cultural hegemony over the vast peasant masses and with exceptional vulnerability in the non-Russian regions, the communist parties moderated their own leap into socialism. The years of the New Economic Policy (1921–8) were a period of strategic compromise with the peasantry in both Russia and the national republics, a time of retreat and patience awaiting the delayed international revolution. It was also a time of greater accommodation to the non-Russian peoples of the periphery. National cultures were promoted; native languages taught; and local cadres were elevated into positions of power, displacing Russians over time.

Until his last active days Lenin continued to advocate caution and sensitivity toward non-Russians, whereas many of his comrades, most notably Stalin and Orjonikidze, were less willing to accommodate even moderate nationalists. In several republics, leaders of defeated parties were quickly removed from power and driven into exile; but other former members of the nationalist or moderate socialist movements were integrated into the communist parties and state apparatus. Soviet decolonization was unique in that it preserved the shape and territorial boundaries of most of the empire it replaced. Instead of disintegrating at the end of the civil war, the new Soviet state reintegrated the periphery, now subordinated to an ostensibly internationalist metropole with a radical developmentalist agenda. The Bolshevik project involved the building of a federated state that would both nurture the nations within it, raise the borderlands up to the cultural and economic level of the centre, and thus forge new loyalties to the ideals of the socialists. The pragmatic gradually won out over the purely ideological. Perhaps most ominously, in the light of a resistant reality in which the inevitable movement toward communism appeared stalled, the gap widened between the actual practices of Bolsheviks and the inflated rhetoric that disguised them. The language of national liberation and anti-imperialism remained a potent discursive cloak under which an empire of subordinated nations was gradually built.

Notes

1 Parts of this essay appeared earlier in Ronald Grigor Suny (1993) *The Revenge of the Past: Nationalism, Revolution, and the Collapse of the Soviet Union*, Stanford: Stanford University Press; and in Suny, 'Nationality policies', in Edward Acton, Vladimir Iu. Cherniaev and William G. Rosenberg (eds) (1997) *Critical Companion to the Russian Revolution, 1914–1915*, Bloomington and Indianapolis: Indiana University Press, 659–66.
2 *Novoe vremia*, no. 14734, 23 March 1917; translated in Robert Paul Browder and Alexander F. Kerensky (eds) (1961) *The Russian Provisional Government 1917: Documents*, vol. I, Stanford: Stanford University Press, 212–13.
3 *Rech'*, no. 108, 10 May 1917; translated in Browder and Kerensky, *The Russian Provisional Government*, I, 317.
4 William G. Rosenberg (1974) *Liberals in the Russian Revolution: The Constitutional Democratic Party, 1917–1921*, Princeton: Princeton University Press, 63.
5 *Ibid.*, 18–19.
6 Oliver H. Radkey (1958) *The Agrarian Foes of Bolshevism: Promise and Default of the Russian Socialist Revolutionaries, February to October 1917*, New York and London: Columbia University Press, 40.
7 Browder and Kerensky, *The Russian Provisional Government*, I, 334–5.
8 The strength of nationalist versus socialist parties varied from nationality to nationality. Nationalists or socialist nationalists were strongest among the

Armenians, Finns and Poles; less strong among Ukrainians, Estonians and Latvians; and even less powerful among Lithuanians, Belorussians, Georgians and the Muslim peoples. For a comparative account of nationalism and socialism during the Russian Revolution, see Suny, *The Revenge of the Past*, particularly 20–83.

9 'We say to the Ukrainians', wrote Lenin,

> as Ukrainians, you can run your own lives as you wish. But we extend a fraternal hand to the Ukrainian workers and say to them: together with you we will fight against your and our bourgeoisie. Only a socialist alliance of labourers of all countries eliminates any ground for national persecution and fighting.
> (V. I. Lenin [1958–65] *Polnoe sobranie sochineniia* [henceforth *PSS*] vol. XXXV, Moscow: Izdatel'stvo politicheskoi literatury, 116)

10 From the brochure *Zadachi proletariata v nashei revoliutsii (Proekt platformy proletarskoi partii)*, written in April 1917, first published in September (V. I. Lenin, *PSS*, XXXI, 167–8).

11 Richard Pipes (1964) *The Formation of the Soviet Union: Communism and Nationalism, 1917–1923*, Cambridge MA: Harvard University Press, 11.

12 *Vosmoi s'ezd RKP (b). Mart 1919 goda. Protokoly*, Moscow: Gosudarstvennoe izdatel'stvo politicheskoi literatury, 1959, 46–8.

13 *Ibid.*, 52–6.

14 *Ibid.*, 397–8.

15 V. I. Lenin, *PSS*, XL, 20; V. I. Lenin, (1960–70) *Collected Works*, vol. XXX, Moscow, 271.

16 Richard G. Hovannisian, (1973) 'Armenia and the Caucasus in the genesis of the Soviet-Turkish entente', *International Journal of Middle East Studies* IV: 147.

17 V. I. Lenin (1991) 'Report on the world political situation and the basic tasks of the Communist International', in John Riddell (ed.) *Workers of the World and Oppressed Peoples, Unite! Proceedings and Documents of the Second Congress, 1920*, New York and London: Pathfinder Press, 108–9.

18 *Second Congress of the Communist International: Minutes of the Proceedings*, London: New Park, 1977, 11.

19 'Pervonachal'nyi nabrosok tezisov po natsional'nomu i kolonial'nomu voprosam', V. I. Lenin, *PPS*, XLI, 161–8.

20 Stalin, in a letter of 12 June 1920, wrote to Lenin that he ought to include the idea of confederation as the transition step bringing different nations into a single political unit. The Soviet Federation (RSFSR) was appropriate for the nationalities that had been part of the old Russia, but not for those that had been independent. He noted that differences between the federative relations within the RSFSR and between the RSFSR and other soviet republics did not exist or were so few that they mean nothing ('net, ili ona tak mala, chto ravni-aetsia nuliu') (Lenin, *PPS*, XLI, 513). This idea was later brought up in Stalin's notion of autonomization. Stalin's letter is available in an English translation in Xenia Joukoff Eudin and Robert C. North (1957) *Soviet Russia and the East, 1920–1927: A Documentary Survey*, Stanford: Stanford University Press, 67–8.

21 *M. N. Roy's Memoirs*, Bombay: Allied Publishers, 1964, 379.

22 *Ibid.*, 380.

23 *Second Congress of the Communist International*, 117.

24 *Ibid.*, 110–12.
25 *Selected Works of M. N. Roy, Volume I, 1917–1922*, ed. Sibnarayan Ray, Delhi and New York: Oxford University Press, 1987, 113.
26 *Second Congress of the Communist International*, 133–5.
27 *Ibid.*
28 *Ibid.*, 143–5, 148–9.
29 *Ibid.*, 154.
30 *Pervyi s'ezd narodov Vostoka*, Petrograd: Kommunisticheskii internatsional, 1920; *Congress of the Peoples of the East: Baku, September 1920: Stenographic Report*, trans. and annotated by Brian Pearce, London: New Park, 1977.
31 *Congress of the Peoples of the East*, 23–7.
32 *Ibid.*, 55–6, 76–83.
33 *M. N. Roy's Memoirs*, 395.

References

Terry Martin (2001) *The Affirmative Action Empire: Nations and Nationalism in the Soviet Union, 1923–1939*, Ithaca NY and London: Cornell University Press.

Richard Pipes (1964) *The Formation of the Soviet Union: Communism and Nationalism, 1917–1923*, Cambridge MA: Harvard University Press.

Yuri Slezkine (1994) *Arctic Mirrors: Russia and the Small Peoples of the North*, Ithaca NY and London: Cornell University Press.

Ronald Grigor Suny (1993) *The Revenge of the Past: Nationalism, Revolution, and the Collapse of the Soviet Union*, Stanford: Stanford University Press.

Ronald Grigor Suny and Terry Martin (2001) *A State of Nations: Empire and Nation-making in the Age of Lenin and Stalin*, New York and Oxford: Oxford University Press.

15

ISLAMIC RENEWAL AND THE 'FAILURE OF THE WEST'

John O. Voll

The contemporary resurgence of Islam involves a dramatic re-evaluation of the West. At the beginning of the twenty-first century, many Muslims believe that the West has failed, not just in moral terms but in material terms as well. This attitude represents a new stage in the long interaction between Western and Muslim societies. This evolution of Muslim evaluations of the Western experience spans the era of imperialism and nationalist response, providing both the foundations for initial responses and the basis for many of the intellectual and political dynamics of the post-decolonization era.

The concept of the 'failure of the West' changes the orientation of reformist thought. As a concept, it plays an important role in the logic of Islamic revivalist thinking in the contemporary era. It makes it possible to ignore or reject Western models, thus transcending older nationalist attitudes, while affirming the validity of the authentic Islamic message in the context of the modern and postmodern world.

The modern and contemporary Islamic experience has many dimensions. A number of factors influence the developing modes of expression and the forms of Muslim life. The belief that the West has failed is only one of many dimensions of the movements of Islamic resurgence. However, it is worth examining this aspect in more detail, keeping in mind that it is only a part of a larger context. Such an analysis can provide a basis for understanding some of the specific forms and ideas involved in the current phase of Islamic renewal. It is important to have sociological profiles of 'resurgent Muslims' and quantitative data on the social composition of various movements, but it is also useful to attempt to understand the conceptual frameworks as well.

The concept of the failure of the West has a role in the logic of the Islamic revival. For some, it provides a reason for the return to Islam, while for others it helps to provide confirmation for the affirmation of Islam. However, no movement of Islamic renewal in the modern era ignores the West. Reformers may view the West in a positive fashion and others may call for a rejection of Western ideas, but the context of

modern world history makes it impossible to avoid making some evaluation of the West.

Islamic renewal has a long history within the Muslim experience. In
principle, *tajdid* (renewal) does not depend upon the existence of a challenge from the Western world; it has occurred in many times and places
before the expansion of the West.[1] However, in the modern situation,
Western influences have a global impact. If Islamic renewers are to
change their social orders, they must present an evaluation of the role of
the West and of the nature of modern Western civilization, but such an
evaluation is not the only aspect of *tajdid* in the modern world. The positive content of the ideology of Islamic renewal remains based, as it has
always been, on the Quran and the Sunnah (traditions and practice) of
the Prophet. Nevertheless, the application of the basic Islamic principles
does not take place in a vacuum. As Abul Ala Maududi notes, the first
step in the programme of Islamic revival must be the 'diagnosis of the
current ailments: to examine thoroughly the circumstances and conditions of the time'.[2]

Evolution of Muslim attitudes toward the West

During the modern era, the attitudes of reformers, renewers and revolutionaries in the Muslim world have changed in terms of their evaluations
of the nature of modern Western civilization. There never is a single,
monolithic vision of the West, but at any given time, there is a dominant
view that sets the tone for the most influential evaluation of the Western
experience in the Islamic context.

During the past two centuries, despite wide diversities due to local
conditions, it is possible to see a gradual evolution of the dominant tone
of Islamic renewal and its reaction to the West. In the eighteenth century,
'the West' as a concept or conceptual entity played little or no role in the
thinking of the leaders of major movements of renewal. The basic context
was described in terms of the interaction of belief and unbelief, or of true
Islam and corrupted Muslim practice. In areas where contact with the
West was limited, such a position remained possible well into the
modern era. 'Modernity' and Western ideas were not consciously seen as
challenges, and – if they were considered at all – were treated in a traditional manner as simply different manifestations of the old enemies,
unbelief and unacceptable innovation. In this context, there was little
place for 'nationalist' definitions of identity or nationalist-style responses
to attack. The eighteenth-century tradition of renewal was replaced with
varying rates of speed, again depending upon local conditions, by movements of reform, revival and response that were clearly conscious of the
West.

In the nineteenth century, the major feature of this consciousness was that somehow the West had succeeded – and this success was frequently compared to the apparent weaknesses of the Muslim world. There were some movements of militant opposition to European expansion that maintained the older conceptualization of the conflict as being between belief and unbelief. However, these were soon militarily defeated and efforts were begun to work to create more effective responses. In many areas, major efforts were made to reform institutions of society and reshape intellectual formulations in accord with a positive evaluation of the Western experience. There was little in these efforts that can be thought of as a 'nationalist' response. The major reform programmes of Muhammad Ali in Egypt, for example, were more for dynastic than 'national' purposes.

By the end of the nineteenth century, movements of Islamic modernism were emerging as the dominant force in Muslim intellectual life. Islam, in this context, was increasingly defined as in accord with modernity and basic Western ideas. The process of the development of Islamic modernism and the adaptation to the new situation, in the context of a favourable evaluation of the West, has been described in detail by a number of scholars. The general tone of the development is seen in Albert Hourani's discussion of Muhammad Abduh's major concerns: Abduh

> was not concerned, as Khayr al-Din [an Ottoman reformer of the mid-nineteenth century] had been in a previous generation, to ask whether devout Muslims could accept the institutions and ideas of the modern world; they had come to stay, and so much the worse for anyone who did not accept them. He asked the opposite question, whether someone who lived in the modern world could still be a devout Muslim.[3]

In the movements of the late nineteenth century, there is a spirit of renewal which has ties to earlier efforts. However, this *tajdid* took place within the framework of a sense of the success of the West, not its failure. In parallel movements of the time that represent the beginnings of nationalism in Muslim societies, there was an even stronger sense of the need to adopt Western modes in politics and society.

While some Muslim intellectuals were relatively uncritical in their positive evaluation of Western civilization, total cultural assimilation was neither practically feasible nor ultimately desirable for most Muslims. Clearly, Western society was not perfect, and neither naive observers nor Western ethnocentric propaganda could make it so. As a result, by the beginning of the twentieth century, the positive evaluation of the West began to be tempered by a view that discriminated between positive and negative aspects of modernity and Western civilization. In the Arab world, for example, the intellectuals of the nineteenth century 'Awakening' believed that they were proclaiming the dawn of a new age. In the serious thinking before World War I, the intellectuals 'were primarily reacting to the challenge of European civilization. They perceived the West as a model from which one was to borrow the good and reject the bad'.[4] A very common theme in this era of positive evaluation of the West was to see the material culture of the West as desirable while rejecting aspects of Western morality. Among many thinkers the distinction is clearly presented between the materially successful West and the morally superior East.

The positive evaluation of Western civilization remains clearly visible throughout much of the twentieth century. One of the most outspoken intellectuals in this regard is Taha Husayn, who has been described as 'the writer who has given the final statement of the system of ideas which underlay social thought and political action in Arab countries for three generations'.[5] In *The Future of Culture in Egypt*, he stated:

> In order to become equal partners in civilization with the Europeans, we must literally forthrightly do every thing that they do; we must share with them the present civilization, with all its pleasant and unpleasant sides.…My advocacy of contact with and imitation of the way of life that has brought progress and pre-eminence to the Europeans does not mean that I approve of their evils.…Obviously then I am pleading for a selective approach to European culture, not wholesale and indiscriminate borrowing.[6]

In the period between the two world wars, there was a growing awareness of the imperfections of the Western model. 'The Islamic intelligentsia became aware that within the Western world itself there were profound criticisms of that civilization and that the Western model which so many Muslims had tried to emulate was itself breaking down'.[7] In many ways, however, this new awareness of the problems of Western civilization continued to be a form of accepting the success of at least part of the Western experience. This is visible in the fact that much of the new awareness was expressed in terms strongly affected by 'successful' Western self-criticism rather than in more authentically Islamic terms. In the political and ideological realm, the failure of the West was most frequently described in the terms of Western-influenced radicalism or Western-stimulated nationalism. While major studies of global nationalism speak of 'the revolt against the West' at this time, this revolt was 'a rejection of western domination' that had special power because of 'the assimilation by Asians and Africans of western ideas, techniques, and institutions, which could be turned against the occupying powers'.[8] Most

of the major nationalist leaders in the Muslim world were relatively secularist 'Westernizers' in terms of their vision of the desired society. Some
of the most important examples of this are Mustafa Kemal Ataturk
(Turkey), Sa'd Zaghloul (Egypt), Sukarno (Indonesia), and even Jinnah of
Pakistan. The strongest critique of the West in terms of values came from
more explicitly Islamic groups, like the Muslim Brotherhood in Egypt or
the Jamaat-I Islami in South Asia, and these were relatively marginal in
terms of nationalist politics and political power in the middle decades of
the twentieth century.

The established political elites were frequently displaced in the years
following World War II, and the older intellectuals, who had been
profoundly influenced by Western liberalism, gave way to new generations of thinkers. However, the new generations of the 1950s and 1960s
differed from the older ones, not in replacing the older sense of the
'success' of the West by a sense of the 'failure' of the West, so much as by
accepting different aspects of Western civilization as models or inspiration. From the perspective of global history, communism and radical
socialism is as much a Western model as liberalism and capitalism, and
Lenin as much a product of the West as Woodrow Wilson. Radical
nationalism in the 1960s rejected Western hegemony, but not necessarily
Western modernity in one of its forms.

In the period since World War II, the continuing interaction between
Islam and the West can be seen as an overlapping series of disassocia-
tions. A key element is a growing redefinition of the West and the
elements of Western civilization that can be judged as failures.
Ultimately, this has led to a major reorientation of the fundamental questions involved in the dialogue between the West and Islam. The
evolution of the early questions which Albert Hourani suggested as basic
involved the change from 'Can a devout Muslim be "modern"?' to
Abduh's issue of whether or not a modern person could still be Muslim;
in both cases there is an assumption that the West provides the most
effective model of the modern. However, in the second half of the twentieth century, this assumption was seriously challenged, both within the
West and in areas such as the Muslim world. In many ways, one of the
basic questions now is whether or not any Western model is effective for
survival in the contemporary world. The failure of communism and the
Soviet Union as the exemplar of the Western 'radical model' highlighted
the issue and the questioning of the effectiveness of the 'nation-state',
which had been the fundamental concept for nationalism, gave further
emphasis to the doubts about the old Western ways of doing things. As a
result, an important conceptual element in the Islamic resurgence of
recent years is the realization that it is a legitimate question to ask: 'Can
the West survive in the contemporary world?'.

The sequence of perceived failures of the West provides part of the foundation for the new Islamic awareness. This sequence has been described in many ways. The two world wars and the global depression of the 1930s raised basic doubts about the ability of the West to survive, after which the ineffectiveness of programmes that 'borrowed the good' from the West continued the process. Liberal constitutionalism, various forms of capitalist economic systems, and party-parliamentary systems all exhibited severe weaknesses in the context of Muslim countries. The revolutions and movements of the 1950s and 1960s represent a rejection of these systems and, in many ways, reflect a belief in the failure of those aspects of Western civilization. However, the new radicalism was strongly influenced by other Western models. Socialism, communism and various forms of Marxist analysis played an important role in the emerging consciousness. By the end of the 1960s, many Muslim intellectuals were willing to judge even these aspects of the West as failures. Both the various programmes of radical socialism, such as Nasser's in Egypt, and the monarchically forced programmes of Westernizing modernization, such as the shah of Iran's so-called White Revolution, failed to meet the needs of Muslim societies. Strong critiques developed within the Islamic community.

These new critiques were not always clearly Islamic in sentiment, but they were profoundly anti-Western in a relatively new way, in that they portrayed the Western models as dangerous because of their own inherent weakness. Some of the most articulate of these new critics of the late 1960s were Iranian. Jalal Al-i Ahmad coined a new term in naming the disease of early generations of reforms who blindly copied the West as *gharbzadegi* ('Weststruckness'). Ali Shariati wrote more broadly ranging critiques and provided important intellectual foundations for the later Islamic revolutionary movement in Iran.

Early in the 1970s, some of the last elements of the perceived Western successes were undermined. For a long time, non-Western intellectuals had been willing to admit that at least in terms of material advancement and power, Western civilization was successful. These last spheres came to be seen in a very different light during the 1970s.

In terms of sheer military power, the prestige of the West was undermined in the years following World War II. The abortive Anglo-French invasion of Egypt in 1956 and the French defeat in Algeria, along with the dismantling of the old European empires, showed that the old imperialists had lost their positions of military dominance. Then, the defeat of the United States in Vietnam pointed up the military weaknesses of even the superpowers. During the 1970s, this vision was reinforced. All of the Westernized military might of the shah could not prevent the Islamic revolution in Iran, while the Arab-Israeli war of 1973 did away with the illusion of the invincibility of Israel – another Westernized military power. Even the Russians were not able to subdue their small and militarily weak neighbour, Afghanistan. In the spring of 1986, the United States appeared to feel the need for the largest possible American battle fleet to mount a small bombing raid on the capital of Libya. The vision of Western military success created in the days of imperial expansion was now clouded, and in this military area as well, one could now perceive a failure of the West.

Similarly, the material riches of the West and the strength of its economic systems had been widely accepted as demonstrating the success of the Western models, but the growing economic difficulties of the major developed economies tarnished that image. The revolution of global economics created by the transformation of the world oil market intensified this disillusionment. While much of the non-Western world remained economically weak, the tremendous transfer of wealth in the 1970s to oil-exporting countries, many of which are Muslim, changed the economic perception of the world: 'The oil boom had shown the vulnerability of the West more dramatically than anything in the past five centuries. By confirming Islam in the eyes of many, it prepared the way for the Islamic movements of the 1970s'.[9] The drop in world oil prices in the mid-1980s did not change the image of the vulnerability of the Western economies, since the leadership of the United States seemed at least as concerned by falling oil prices as the leaders of the major oil-exporting countries. The image of US and general Western dependency on oil from Muslim countries was strengthened by the willingness to commit huge military and financial resources in the Gulf War of 1990–1. Economics became another area in which there was a perceived failure of the West.

Finally, one of the fundamental ideals behind the process of Westernization – the idea of 'development' – was being questioned in a variety of ways throughout the globe. The concern about the destruction of the natural environment that followed development in Western societies, the growing belief that underdevelopment in non-Western societies was related not to inherent backwardness but to the very process of development itself, and a questioning of the social and human consequences of the processes of industrialization and urbanization, are examples of the profound issues raised by the contemporary situation in the West. For observers both within and outside of the West, it has become possible to ask whether or not development, as it has been understood in the past, is a legitimate strategy for survival in the contemporary world. This doubt about development has become a dimension in the question of whether or not the West can survive modernity.

Within this broad historical context, the theme of the failure of the West is part of many of the major intellectual movements of recent years. Within the West as well as in other parts of the world, the concept of the failure of the West has shaped the logic of intellectual formulations and reformist hopes. Within the Islamic world, the concept is part of the logic and vocabulary of movements of resurgence. It is an element that has influenced the possible forms of expression and logic of current manifestations of Islamic renewal. Utilization of the concept of the failure of the West marks a significant change in the logic of reformist thought in the Islamic world.

Implications of the idea of the failure of the West

The concept of the failure of the West makes it possible to distinguish certain aspects of the current mood of Islamic renewal from earlier modern Muslim reform and renewal efforts. The concept has provided a kind of liberation in a number of ways. The content of the message of Islam remains constant, but the form and mood of *tajdid* and the modes of expression are freed from certain limitations that had bound the terminology and style of earlier modern Muslim reformers.

The first area where the impact of the idea of the failure of the West is visible is in terms of the changing nature of the target audience, or effective partners in the dialogue involved in Islamic renewal. Earlier reformers tended to operate within the limitations imposed by 'hoping to obtain a favorable verdict from the invisible jury of the West'.[10] Frequently, this jury was not so invisible. Early modernist thinkers such as Muhammad Abduh and Jamal al-Din al-Afghani argued directly with Western critics of Islam. Many of the important works of such reformers were clearly in the genre of apologetics, trying to persuade this invisible jury that Islam could meet intellectual and practical standards set by Western concepts. Instead of the Islamic tradition itself giving rise to the basic ideas of reform, Western ideas tended to define the areas of concern.

The failure of the West, however, liberates contemporary Muslim thinkers from many of these constraints. Such failure makes it possible to see the judgments of Westerners as less relevant. Instead of having to accept the basic analytical framework of Western thought as the definition of the ground rules for the dialogue, the failure of the West makes it possible to disagree with even that basic conceptual framework. While earlier reformers, for example, felt a responsibility to persuade those Western scholars who studied Islam of Islam's virtues, the conceptual framework of orientalism itself can now be criticized on the basis of more authentically Islamic values. The work of the traditional Western orientalists is increasingly seen as a reflection of Western ethnocentric values.

Starting from the Islamic concept of *tawhid* (the absolute one-ness of God), contemporary Muslim scholars have worked to redefine basic academic disciplines in terms of moral obligation and value-laden scholarship. They argue, for example, that older Western ideas of value-free or objective analysis in the social sciences are not only impossible but undesirable. In this way, a more clearly Islamic orientation for social science scholarship is possible. Such scholars, convinced of the intellectual failure of the West, are not as sensitive as their predecessors to criticisms from the West based on Western assumptions. The concept of the failure of the West has liberated Muslim intellectuals from constraints imposed by the intellectual formulations of an outside 'jury', and the way is thus opened for a positive rather than a defensive orientation in the presentation of Islamic values. This change has had an impact upon the mode of Islamic expression during the current resurgence.

Under these new conditions, the most important partner in dialogue became other Muslims. The failure of the West had changed at least some of the terms of the dialogue of reform among Muslims. By liberating intellectuals and political leaders from the pressure to persuade Westerners, the concept opened the way for discussion in which the Islamic tradition could play a more significant role. This was in turn reinforced by the achievement of political independence and the resulting necessity for creating independent policy. It was already apparent to some observers in the mid-1960s that the basic dialogue for the new leaders, intellectuals and policy makers

> is not with the West; it is with their fellow citizens. They are judged internally by their performance and in the light of a shared ideology....It is becoming evident that the Arab-Muslim intelligentsia feel and argue that an Islamic meaning to modern society is feasible, that Islamic solutions to objective contemporary problems are possible.[11]

The discussions of the Western-oriented modernists were elite phenomena that by the late 1960s could be described as symptoms of 'Weststruckness'. However, as has long been noted, when concern for renewal is more broadly inclusive of the Muslim masses, the terms of the dialogue become more clearly Islamic. Concerning the development of nationalism, for example, in the 1950s Wilfred Cantwell Smith pointed out that

> the driving force of nationalism has become more and more religious the more the movement has penetrated the masses. Even where the leaders and the form and the ideas of movement have

been nationalist on a more or less Western pattern, the followers and the substance and the emotions were significantly Islamic.[12]

When the Western pattern itself is seen as a failure even the elite can move, as they have in recent years, to transform the form and ideas into a more clearly Islamic pattern. This modification in the attitude of the elite opens the way for a more significant and meaningful interaction between the educated classes and the majority of the population. In a context where the fundamental concept for nationalism, the 'nation-state', is being questioned, old-style more secular nationalisms falter in the face of more Islamically oriented conceptualizations of what the desired polity should be. Increasingly, Muslims are speaking in more non-national terms, like those used by a cosmopolitan Islamic scholar born in South Asia, educated in North America, and teaching in Southeast Asia:

> Muslim society needs to change as it did under its Prophet; in his time the *ummah* [the community of Muslim believers] replaced tribal identity; today it needs to replace the nation-state identity. Nation-state identity does not need to be abolished; rather like the early Muslim community [that did not abolish tribal identity], modern Muslims need to change the hierarchy of their identities.[13]

In this vision, clearly the old era of imperialism and nationalism has little relevance.

The movement toward more authentically Islamic solutions to social problems and to the needs for renewal is thus strengthened by the ability of the educated elite to go beyond the concepts and goals set by the old intellectual domination by the West. One of the basic problems in implementing the ideas of the old modernists was that they assumed 'as the final objective an ideal determined by considerations external to their own society'.[14] The perception of the failure of the West makes it possible to define basic ideals and solutions in ways that may not coincide with Western solutions, but which are more appropriately Islamic. It also makes it possible to judge the progress toward those goals by standards other than those set by Western ethnocentric observers.

The second general area of the impact of the concept of the failure of the West follows from this discussion: the concept frees Muslim thinkers from the domination of certain specifically Western concepts involved in interpreting modernity. *Secularism* is the most significant of these concepts. Because of the specific conditions of the emergence of modern society in the West, secularism was believed to be a critical element in the process of modernization. It was widely believed that 'the secularization of the polity is in many respects a prerequisite for significant social change'.[15] The specific implications of this view for traditional religions were usually clearly spelled out:

> The secularization of the polity, like the secularization of culture and society, is a process which has moved inexorably since the breakup of the traditional religio-political system....While religion, a mass phenomenon in traditional societies, can play a useful role in transitional societies in making politics meaningful to the apolitical masses, the general forces of secularization of culture and society will in the long run erode its political effectiveness also.[16]

Within the Islamic world, secularism was an important part of the adjustments to the modern context. Albert Hourani has noted the importance of a positive evaluation of secularism in reformist thought in Syria and Lebanon during the first half of the twentieth century. The movement of secularization in that area, he has pointed out, 'springs from the belief of many Arab thinkers that the superior strength and stability of Western society is due to the limitations which have been imposed upon the action and influence of religion'.[17]

The adaptation of political organization was carried furthest in Turkey, where an officially secular state was established after World War I. In the programme of the Republican People's Party adopted in 1935, the secularist rationale is clearly spelled out:

> As the conception of religion is a matter of conscience, the Party considers it to be one of the chief factors of the success of our nation in contemporary progress, to separate ideas of religion from politics, and from the affairs of the world and of the State.[18]

While few other states were as explicitly secularized as Turkey, secularist thinking was important elsewhere, and few modernizing states became rigorously Islamic in the first half of the twentieth century. In the years following World War II, avowedly secularist, although not anti-religious, ideas were popular and influential among the educated elites. A relatively extreme but widely read expression of this perspective was presented by Khalid Muhammad Khalid, who concluded that one

> should remember that the faith should continue as its Lord wishes – with prophecy not kingship, with guidance not government, with preaching rather than the whip. Its separation from

politics and its soaring above politics is the best agent for maintaining its purity and its perfection.[19]

Muslims have been liberated from the persuasiveness of this line of argument by the conviction that the West has failed. One dimension of the revival of the 1970s is the substantial decline in the persuasiveness of the idea that secularism is necessary for the modernization of Muslim states. In the experience of Middle Eastern countries, progress toward the goals of modernization is not inevitably accompanied by secularization.

Contemporary discussions follow at least two lines – one attacking the idea of secularism as contrary to the Islamic sense of unity, and another advocating the virtues of a society in which faith in not separated from other aspects of life. Both of these are, not unexpectedly, part of the presentations of clearly fundamentalist thinkers who, throughout the twentieth century, have maintained a tradition of opposition to secularism. However, in addition to the traditional fundamentalists, most major Muslim intellectuals with a thoroughly modern education have abandoned or at least substantially modified their advocacy of secularism. One concrete example of the new mood is the change in the views of Khalid Muhammad Khalid, a major spokesman for secularism in the years following World War II. In 1981, he showed a significant change in his views, publishing a book advocating state implementation of Islamic law. It should be noted that even in the West, some of the scholars who defined 'secularization theory' have now said that the theory is 'essentially mistaken'.[20] The only clearly identifiable groups in the Muslim world maintaining explicitly secularist positions are those that still accept the success of some type of Western conceptual model. Such cases are usually found among the openly Marxist secularists and communists, or the 'true believers' like the leaders of the Turkish military.

The spectrum of backgrounds and positions of those who have been liberated from the domination of the ideas of secularism and who affirm the non-secularist Islamic tradition is very broad. There is, however, remarkable unanimity on this issue among contemporary Islamic thinkers who disagree vigorously on a wide range of other subjects. The key element in this is a renewed emphasis on the concept of *tawhid* – the one-ness of God – and the implications of this one-ness for all of life.

A brief sampling of positions from a variety of people illustrates the non-secularist unanimity among contemporary Muslims with significantly modern experience and education who might, in previous years, have been relatively secularist in their approach. The shift away from the secularist positions is most dramatic among what might be termed the radical segment of the spectrum of thought in the Islamic world. In previous years, positions of social and intellectual radicalism were most likely to include secularist views.

Ali Shariati presented one important articulation of an Islamic radicalism that presented a *tawhidi* rather than a secularist viewpoint. He rejected the separation of various realms of human life as exploitative and opposed to Islam:

> the very structure of *tawhid* cannot accept contradiction or disharmony in the world....Contradiction between nature and metanature...science and religion, metaphysics and nature, working for men and working for God, politics and religion...all these forms of contradiction are reconcilable only with the worldview of *shirk* – dualism, trinitarianism or polytheism – but not with *tawhid* – monotheism.[21]

This perspective provides a foundation for important tendencies within the contemporary Islamic reformist movement in Iran. Similar positions can be seen in the intellectual radicalism of the 1980s in the Arab world. Again, before the belief in the failure of the West, many of these thinkers might have adopted a more secularist position as a part of their intellectual radicalism. For example, while the Egyptian philosopher, Hassan Hanafi, is thoroughly familiar with Western philosophy and objects to the 'rituals' of many traditional Muslim fundamentalists, his philosophical position is basically *tawhidi* rather than secularist. This position provides the basis for a 'revolutionary theology'. According to Hanafi,

> A reactionary theology divides Man into two parts: body and soul, as it divided the World into two parts: Temporal and eternal....[However, in a revolutionary theology] there is one World, one action and one life....The only world is this world where Man exists. The spiritual is the temporal and the temporal is the spiritual....A revolutionary religion does not have any cults. Devotion to God is expressed by devotion to Man. Cult is not symbolic but every act in the daily life is a cult.[22]

These perspectives affirm basic Islamic positions. *Tawhid* is a fundamental Islamic concept that has always been a part of *tajdid*, or Islamic renewal. However, one dimension of this affirmation of *tawhid* is that the secularist model, as it has been defined by Western experience, is seen as having failed. In this way, the concept of the failure of the West provides an important reinforcement for the reappropriation of Islamic themes. The perception of the failure of the West makes it possible to argue that the Western model has failed and the *tawhid* provides the foundation for a more effective way of coping with the challenges of contemporary history. This is true, as has been seen, not only in traditional fundamentalist thought but also in some of the significant contemporary radical Muslim formulations. Secularism can be labelled not only as unbelief, but also as ineffective.

It then becomes possible to identify a third area in which Islamic thought is liberated by the concept of the failure of the West. The concept makes it possible to divorce modernity from Western models and precedents. Non-Western modernity becomes both intellectually conceivable and practically possible. Western ideas and systems are still important in the dialogue, but they are now conceivable as simply one among a number of competing models of potentially equal efficiency. The old debate over whether or not a modern person could still be a devout Muslim tended to assume that the modern person was basically Westernized, there being an implicit equation between modern and Western. The perceived failure of the West makes it possible to break that old assumed identity, and the basic issue becomes reformulated in terms of which models provide the most effective form of modernity. Now Islamic modernity competes with Western modernity, and the concept of the failure of the West strengthens the affirmation of Islam as the more effective model for modernity.

This has a number of implications for the forms taken by the current Islamic renewal. One of the most important of these is a vindication of the fundamentalist style of Islamic experience. Although there is often disagreement about the use of the term *fundamentalist*, and although fundamentalism has taken a variety of forms, the style of Islam often called fundamentalist has in recent years clearly experienced a significant revival. At least part of the reason for the revival is that this style of Islam is the one least affected in the modern period by the idea of the success of the West. As a result, in the context of an awareness of the failure of the West, Muslim fundamentalists have the most coherent and fully developed models currently available.

For many years, many educated Muslims rejected the fundamentalist models as reactionary. As long as the West was viewed as the major successful model of modernity, most specifically Muslim reformist efforts were aimed at showing the compatibility between Islamic and modern Western ideas. Any perspective that rejected these assumptions, such as the fundamentalist viewpoint, could be viewed as an obstacle to progress. This can be seen in the debates between nationalists and Islamists in the 1920s and 1930s, when old-style fundamentalists argued that nationalism was un-Islamic because it placed the sovereignty of the nation above the sovereignty of God.

When Islamic and Western models came to be seen as competitive formats for modernity, and when it could be argued that the West had failed, the Islamic fundamentalist perspective gained popularity. In the final quarter of the twentieth century, growing numbers of people in Muslim societies identified themselves with movements and ideas that emphasized the validity of 'the Islamic solution'. An Islamist party won national elections in Algeria and was only prevented from coming to power by a military coup in 1992; and even in Turkey, the Islamically identified Welfare Party won a plurality of the national elections of 1995, and its leader, Necmettin Erbakan, became Prime Minister for a short period in 1996–7. By the beginning of the twenty-first century, Islamic perspectives had moved from the periphery to the mainstream of politics throughout the Muslim world, and this was usually not seen as a rejection of modernity as such, but rather an affirmation of the possibility of an Islamic modernity that did not simply copy the West.

The fundamentalist format of the resurgence of Islam at the end of the twentieth century should not be understood as the only possible alternative. *Tajdid* has taken many forms in Islamic history. A history of *tajdid* written by a modern Muslim fundamentalist describes a number of leaders of renewal who are not clearly fundamentalist in style, such as al-Ghazali, the great medieval mystic. Renewal has come through the efforts of synthesizers and adaptationists and individualist charismatic leaders, as well as fundamentalists. However, the fundamentalist style of *tajdid* was the least affected by the discrediting of Western models. It represented a clear alternative to earlier modern reform efforts. In this the importance of the eighteenth-century heritage is visible. During the eighteenth century, fundamentalist reformism was defined without reference to the West. This legacy has provided an important foundation for continuity with significant past experiences, paving the way for more broadly based support in the present. The clearest example of this is the Wahhabi experience in Saudi Arabia and the activist movements in a number of places that are called 'Wahhabi'.

In the process of transition from an Islamic modernism that accepts the success of the West to a more fundamentalist Islam that perceives the failure of the West, there has been a reinterpretation of the actual meaning of Islamic fundamentalism. When adaptationist Islamic modernism was clearly in the ascendancy, fundamentalism was regarded as an anachronism. At best, it was considered an unrealistic attempt to recreate the conditions of the seventh century; at worst, it was claimed that the aims of the fundamentalists were 'to arrest development and progress and to deprive the people of their hard-won gains, acting as agents of imperialism and reaction....It has gone even further and attempted to make religion seem to contradict science, knowledge and progress'.[23] Such a rejection of fundamentalism was strengthened by the assumption that modernization involved at least some significant aspects of Westernization and by a simple definition, often inaccurate, of fundamentalism as a rejection of all elements of modernity. In a context where secularism was a powerful force, the reaffirmation of the traditional religion was assumed to be inherently anti-modern. Once Westernization and modernization came to be seen as two separate (if related) phenomena, Muslims were free to examine the fundamentalist positions in a new light.

The attempt to picture modern Muslim fundamentalists as simpleminded utopians who want to restore the conditions of the seventh century is inaccurate. For those who were willing to take the teachings of twentieth-century fundamentalists seriously, this has long been apparent. In his analysis of the ideology of the Muslim Brotherhood, Richard Mitchell, for example, notes that the Ikhwan issued 'a call to return to Islamic principles and not a literal return to the seventh century; those who say this are confusing [in the words of Sayyid Qutb] "the historical beginning of Islam with the system of Islam itself"'.[24] This type of approach is clearly appealing in the contemporary context of defining an authentically Islamic modernity.

By liberating Muslims from the belief in secularism as a necessary part of modernization, and by making possible a distinction between Westernization and modernization, the concept of the failure of the West strengthened the appeal of fundamentalist Islam. It is possible to challenge Westernization measures on the basis of Islamic principles without automatically being considered anti-modern. Such challenges are now being made in the context of the contemporary competition among the various models of modernity. In the context of the failure of the West, the renewed popularity of the fundamentalist style stems from contemporary perceptions rather than from traditional reasons alone.

By the final decade of the twentieth century, new lines of debate and discourse were emerging. In these new debates, many of the old arguments of the era of modernism and reform have been left behind. The core of the old discussions was defining the relationship between Islam and the West in the framework of issues involved in the processes of modernization and development. However, by the 1990s, old arguments about whether or not one could be both 'modern' and a true Muslim were replaced by affirmations of the validity of Islam as the world-view for the contemporary age.

Two important bases for discourse are involved in these new debates: one is the articulation of a militant, absolutist position that ignores many of the issues of the old debates about relations between Islam and the West and simply affirms the superiority of Islam. The most visible presenter of this position is Usama bin Ladin. The second position builds on the old discussions and then goes beyond them, in the context of advocating a 'dialogue of civilizations' as the means for defining the future of Islam in the contemporary world. This position has been most fully articulated by Muhammad Khatami, President of the Islamic

Republic of Iran. An important part of the logic and discourse of these two very different leaders is their assessment of the West. Neither view the West as a successful model to copy, but both articulate their calls for action in terms of relations with the West in a new mode that goes beyond the old debates of modernism.

Usama bin Ladin emerged in the 1990s as a key figure in the development of an extreme, absolutist Muslim worldview that viewed the West not simply as materialist or imperialist, but as representing Satan in the contemporary world. In this world-view the nature of the struggle now goes beyond the relations between Islam and modernity or Islam and the West, and becomes a more stark and cosmic struggle between true faith and unbelief. In his pronouncements and recruiting films, Bin Ladin spends little time on issues of cultural clash or morality. He concentrates on the issue of power. Like Satan, the modern West appears to have overwhelming power, but it is here that his argument overlaps with the logic of the 'failure of the West'. The West's apparent power can be defeated and its weakness revealed through the acts of terrorism organized by Bin Ladin and his followers. In this line of reasoning, and especially through this line of action, Bin Ladin went beyond the logic of Islamic renewal and fundamentalism into the realm of the violent extremist fanatics of world history.

Muhammad Khatami, Iran's president, provides an important example of the continuing evolution of Islamic renewalist thought that remains within that tradition. A highly visible reformist perspective is being articulated by Khatami, who has been elected, and then re-elected, in two startling electoral victories (in 1997 and 2001). He advocates a 'dialogue of civilizations' as an alternative to those who see relations between Islam and the West in terms of 'the clash of civilizations'. Khatami brings together most of the major elements involved in the new logic of Islamic resurgence. He sees the contemporary world as a competitive arena that has been dominated for some time by Western civilization. However, he argues that now 'Western civilization is worn out and senile' and facing the crisis of civilizational decline.[25] He sees the new Islamic approach represented by the Islamic Revolution in Iran as being in competition with the West. Attempts by the West to continue its global political domination by 'adapting neocolonialism to the new age'[26] must be opposed. However, the West has achieved much and, Khatami argues, that 'we can only think of our revolution as giving rise to a new civilization if we have the ability to absorb the positive aspects of Western civilization'.[27] The failure of the West thus opens a great opportunity: 'As Western civilization becomes increasingly worn out and senile, humanity is today searching for a new vision for its future, awaiting a new civilization which is more capable of meeting its material and spiritual needs and wants'.[28] This perspective represents an important culmination of the tradition that started with the conviction that the West had succeeded, and passed through the time of Western-style nationalism that opposed Western colonialism. The concept of the 'failure of the West' makes a new post-nationalist (and post-fundamentalist) vision possible.

Notes

1 John O. Voll (1983) 'Renewal and reform in Islamic history: *Tajdid* and *Islah*', in *Voices of Resurgent Islam*, ed. John L. Esposito, New York: Oxford University Press, 32–47. See also John O. Voll (1999) 'Foundations for renewal and reform: Islamic movements in the eighteenth and nineteenth centuries', in *The Oxford History of Islam*, ed. John L. Esposito, New York: Oxford University Press.
2 Abdul A'la Maududi (1976) *A Short History of the Revivalist Movement in Islam*, trans. al-Ash'ari, Lahore: Islamic Publications Limited, 38.
3 Albert Hourani (1962) *Arabic Thought in the Liberal Age, 1798–1939*, London: Oxford University Press, 139.
4 Hisham Sharabi (1979) 'Islam, democracy and socialism in the Arab world', in *The Arab Future: Crucial Issues*, ed. Michael C. Hudson, Washington: Center for Contemporary Arab Studies, Georgetown University, 96.
5 Hourani, *Arabic Thought*, 326.
6 Taha Hussein (1954) *The Future of Culture in Egypt*, trans. Sidney Glazer, Washington: American Council of Learned Societies, 15, 17.
7 Seyyed Hossein Nasr (1980) 'Islam in the Islamic world: an overview', in *Islam in the Contemporary World*, ed. Cyriac K. Pullapilly, Notre Dame IN: Cross Roads Books, 8.
8 Geoffrey Barraclough (1967) *An Introduction to Contemporary History*, Baltimore: Penguin Books, 159, 161.
9 Daniel Pipes (1980) ' "This World is Political!": the Islamic revival of the seventies', *Orbis* 24(1) (spring): 22.
10 Ibrahim Abu-Lughod (1966) 'Retreat from the secular path? Islamic dilemmas of Arab politics', *The Review of Politics* 28: 475.
11 *Ibid.*
12 Wilfred Cantwell Smith (1957) *Islam in Modern History*, Princeton: Princeton University Press, 75. This phenomenon was also noted in the 1940s by H. A. R. Gibb. See Gibb (1947) *Modern Trends in Islam*, Chicago: University of Chicago Press, 119.
13 Abdullah al-Ahsan (1992/1413) *Ummah or Nation? Identity Crisis in Contemporary Muslim Society*, Leicester: The Islamic Foundation, 152.
14 Gibb, *Modern Trends*, 104.
15 Donald Eugene Smith (1971) *Religion, Politics, and Social Change in the Third World*, New York: The Free Press, 3.
16 *Ibid.*, 3–4.
17 A. H. Hourani (1946) *Syria and Lebanon, A Political Essay*, London: Oxford University Press, 81.
18 Quoted in Smith, *Religion, Politics*, 66.
19 Khalid Muhammad Khalid (1963) *Min Huna Nabda'*, Cairo: Mu'assisah al-Khanji, 184.
20 Peter L. Berger (1999) 'The desecularization of the world: a global overview', in *The Desecularization of the World*, ed. Peter L. Berger, Washington DC: Ethics

and Public Policy Center, 2.

21 Ali Shari'ati (1979) *On the Sociology of Islam*, trans. Hamid Algar, Berkeley: Mizan Press, 86.

22 Hassan Hanafi (1977) *Religious Dialogue and Revolution*, Cairo: The Anglo-Egyptian Bookshop, 207–9.

23 'Report by the Legislative Committee of the UAR National Assembly on the Republican Law regarding the Moslem Brotherhood', in *Arab Political Documents 1965*, Beirut: American University of Beirut, n.d., 453.

24 Richard P. Mitchell (1969) *The Society of the Muslim Brothers*, London: Oxford University Press, 234.

25 Mohammad Khatami (1998) *Islam, Liberty, and Development*, Binghamton: Binghamton University, Institute of Global Cultural Studies, 53.

26 *Ibid.*, 56.

27 *Ibid.*, 68.

28 *Ibid.*, 66–7.

Further reading: Islamic critiques of the West for the period after the 1960s

Jalal Al-e Ahmad (1982) *Gharbzadegi* ('Weststruckness') trans. John Green and Ahmad Alizadeh, Lexington KY: Mazda.

Ali Shari'ati (1980) *Marxism and Other Western Fallacies: An Islamic Critique*, trans. R. Campbell, Berkeley: Mizan Press.

Seyyed Hossein Nasr (1976) 'The Western world and its challenges to Islam', in Khurshid Ahmad (ed.) *Islam: Its Meaning and Message*, London: Islamic Council of Europe, 222–5.

Maryam Jameelah (1971) *Islam and Orientalism*, Lahore: Mohammad Yusuf Khan.

Bruce M. Borthwick (1979) 'Religion and politics in Israel and Egypt', *The Middle East Journal* 33(2): 145–63.

16

THE DIALECTICS OF DECOLONIZATION

Nationalism and labour movements in post-war French Africa[1]

Frederick Cooper

Patterns of decolonization are particularly difficult to unravel because we know the endpoint: the emergence of the independent state from colonial rule. It is tempting to read the history of the period from 1945 to 1960 as the inevitable triumph of nationalism, and to see in each social movement taking place within a colony – be it of peasants, of women, of workers, or of religious groups – another piece to be integrated into the coming together of the nation. What is lost in such a reading are the ways in which different groups within colonies mobilized for concrete ends and used, as well as opposed, the institutions of the colonial state and the niches opened up in the clash of new and old structures. Whether such efforts fed into the attempts of nationalist parties to build anticolonial coalitions needs to be investigated, not assumed. In this chapter, I will show that, at the very moment that the distinct but related struggles of labour movements and parties became increasingly powerful in the mid-1950s, a direct clash emerged between the principle of class struggle and African unity.

The clash is important not just for its place in the history of twentieth-century Africa, but for the implications it had for what kinds of Africas would be imaginable in the post-colonial era and what kinds of Africas would be excluded from political debates. Beyond that, the clash is an instance of a profound conflict of aspirations that the end of colonial rule did more to reveal than to resolve: for some, the end of empire meant that impoverished and oppressed people could share in the universal good, could aspire to a generally defined minimum standard of living, could insist on certain rights, as workers, as citizens, as women, as individuals. But for others, liberation had a different meaning – as an expression of aspirations that were specific to Africa, that postulated a notion of community against the pretensions of universal progress. In such an argument, universality was a mask for Eurocentrism, a confusion of Europe's peculiar history with standards that Europe expected the rest of the world to meet, an assumption that European categories like 'class' or 'rights' displaced African ideas of affinity. Yet as African labour movements were among the first to learn, the very insistence on the primacy of 'African' community can constitute a denial of solidarities and differences that people experience in their daily lives.

I will focus on one sort of social movement, labour, and on a particular example, the transition of the French West African labour movement from a class-centred, internationalist organization from roughly 1945 to 1955 to a nationalist organization that insisted that workers subordinate their own concerns, interests and collective awareness to the emerging national struggle. As much as this is a story of the ambivalent relationship of two sorts of movements in a colony, it is also a story of a complex engagement of an African labour movement and a colonial state: how workers' collective actions forced officials to rethink their conceptions of labour as much as their policies, how workers seized the new colonial discourse and turned attempts to articulate control to claims to entitlements, and how the colonial state finally began to move away from the implications of the universalistic language in which it had asserted its authority. Ironically, France found relief from such demands by reaching an understanding with the nationalist parties, whose vision of African autonomy promised an end to insistence on wages and benefits equal to those of European workers. My goal is thus an interactive, dynamic analysis of the relationship between the political strategies and discourses of a colonial regime and social and political movements within African colonies.

The national question and the labour question

The metanarrative of anticolonial triumph takes two forms. One, the narrative of social mobilization, shows that inchoate, often local, resistance to colonial rule which had been evident since the conquest, was channelled into a unified anticolonial movement in the years after World War II by Western-educated intellectuals. Mobilizing African teachers, clerks, workers and peasants, working through organizations ranging from ethnic associations to groups of market women to alumni of secondary schools, and bringing people into modern political parties, the post-war leaders forged a movement that attacked head on the racist construction of the colonial state and claimed its territory, its symbols and its institutions to bring material progress and a sense of national identity to the people of each African colony.

The second metanarrative is the revolutionary one, denying legitimacy to the modernizing national elite as much as to the colonial regime. Frantz Fanon argued that wage workers, aspiring only to the privileges of white workers in the colony, could not consistently challenge colonial dominance. Rather, it would be peasants and the lumpen proletariat who would spearhead the struggle, for only they were willing to face up to the absolute denial of identity that colonialism necessarily entailed, and to use violence to end it. Fanon was not in fact a nationalist, and had little sympathy for the rhetoric of racial unity or the invocation of symbols of the African past that 'bourgeois nationalists' found easy to embrace as they set themselves up as brokers between African 'tradition' and post-colonial 'modernity'. His imagined future was actually a reversal of an imperialist past: ' "The last shall be first and the first last". Decolonization is the putting into practice of this sentence'.[2]

These metahistories of decolonization imply particular readings of colonialism itself. The first version accepts the image of progress associated with Western education, the expansion of markets, and global linkages, but insists that colonialism blocked the path, which could only be cleared by national liberation, hence a focus on social struggles in colonies insofar as they led to and were subsumed in the national struggle. The second version sees colonialism as destructive at every level, the only possible change a total reversal of a political and social order.

The irony of Fanon's position is that his quest to define the True Anticolonialist allows colonialism, by the logic of inversion, to define the only politics to which he can accord legitimacy. That different groups among a colonized population might bring their own histories and their own interests to a complex engagement with colonial power, is lost in a powerful rhetoric that not only demands a singular focus but also delegitimates any other kind of contestation.

[...]

Colonial power and African labour

[...]

Late nineteenth-century imperialism justified itself by playing up tyranny and slaving on the African continent, insisting that only the benevolent exercise of European power could bring the continent into a world of peaceful commerce and social and cultural progress. Early colonial regimes at times took seriously the reformist implications of such arguments, but immediately ran into the consequences of the limited spatial and cultural domains over which they could exercise effective power, and the necessity for alliances with the very people whose tyranny they had pledged to uproot. In effect, colonial regimes had to link themselves to the attempts of a wide range of African elites to establish their own hegemonies and protect or enhance their own resources. [...] By the 1920s, Great Britain and France were downplaying their 'civilizing missions' and trying to portray their compromises and weaknesses as sound policy, termed 'indirect rule' or 'association'.

The strongest attempts to use African labour in new ways, such as labour recruitment in Upper Volta or Kenya, actually deepened regimes' reliance on indigenous intermediaries to do their dirty work. Colonial regimes had to foster chiefs' ambitions and at times restrict their own, for fear that excessive demands for labour or over-zealous sub-imperialism on the part of chiefs might undermine the stability of rural authority.

Colonial officials went a long way to convince themselves that Africa was a continent of 'tribes', that its people were deeply and immutably immersed in the social relations of the village and the polities of defer-ence to chiefly authority. They were therefore anxious about the emergence of social categories that fell outside their boundaries. Such people were often called 'detribalized', and they included mission converts and educated Africans – the very minds imperial powers seemed to be colonizing – and wage labourers, the necessary condition of a capitalist future. The political language of colonial states was thus only capable of labelling such people by what they were not – it could not think through what they were.

[...]

The problem was that the systems of authority articulated and legiti-mated through local authorities could not handle the extent of social change that the uneven development of colonial economies entailed. Cities, commercial pathways, mines and other sites not easily contained in the idea of 'traditional Africa' were to prove especially troublesome, precisely because colonial officials did not want to think of Africans as belonging there. Colonial regimes would swing back to the universal-istic, change-oriented project, only to find that this hegemonic ideal was even more contradictory and even more open to subversion than the fragmented idioms of rule of the 1920s and 1930s.

Colonial authority challenged

Colonial states had created a system vulnerable to challenges in precisely those areas they did not want to think about. However unimpressive and uneven efforts to build imperial economies in Africa were, colonial regimes had created islands of wage labour production as well as nodes on commercial networks, through which cash crops produced by peasant farms and the narrow range of European commodities sold by European firms passed.

Colonial regimes were able to diffuse the strains of the depression of the 1930s into the countryside, but the revival of export production reconcentrated African labour and led to the first wave of strikes in the British copper mines of Central Africa and in some railroad and port centres. In much of British Africa, World War II – when Britain had little to supply to African workers and much to demand of them – led to endemic labour crisis, forcing officials to raise wages and, more importantly, to think seriously for the first time about the category of labour. French Africa, relatively isolated after the fall of France, had rather different wartime experiences, but labour protest caught up soon after the war ended, in a period when exports were increasing, labour forces were growing, and urban inflation was rampant.

The post-war strike wave took place in a changed political and economic context. France and Great Britain, their economies in shambles and their ability to sell their own products for foreign exchange cruelly limited, saw their tropical colonies as the only way they could save the franc, the pound, and national autonomy from the new hegemon on the international horizon, the United States. India was going, Indochina was threatened, and officials said in so many words that Africa was their great hope, its underdeveloped state itself a sign of how much its productive capacity could be improved. Ideologically, the great war against conquering tyrannies – and the language of 'self-determination' that emerged in the propaganda wars against Hitler – put colonial powers on the defensive, and the Soviet Union was eager to attack colonialism while the United States was less than eager to defend it.

In this context, the two leading colonial powers had to articulate a compelling justification for what they were doing in the colonies. The idea of 'development' simultaneously promised that Africa would make an enhanced contribution to production – saving the empires – and that Africa would receive the benefits of the technical knowledge and newfound ability to plan, as well as whatever capital these powers could afford to invest. The developmental initiative was both an assertion of a coherent and unified rationale for the continuation of colonial rule, and a process in which Africans could join in their own interests but under government direction.

[…]

The continued strikes in Africa were both a disruption of the economic project and an embarrassment to the ideological one. They represented a telling instance of the 'powerless' making the 'powerful' reconfigure both ideology and the apparatus of government. […] Both governments found that the subcontracted power structure and the subcontracted and multiple hegemonies they had elaborately constructed in rural Africa meant nothing in the workplace. The perceived loss of control had a double effect on the exercise of power in colonial regimes in this critical conjuncture. First, African strike action diminished within the bureaucracy the once-dominant provincial administrators who knew their natives and had long tried to keep Africans inside their 'tribal' categories in favour of a rising generation of technocrats whose interventions were rooted in the universalities of European social engineering. Labour officers and *inspecteurs du travail* became key actors. Second, the need to reassert control in mines, railways, ports and cities disciplined officials to take their new hegemonic project seriously and to make a closer effort to articulate that project with the intimacies of actual social life. Trying to think of ways to get Africans back to work, officials turned to the precedents they thought they knew: the efforts to tame class conflict in Europe itself.

In British Africa, the series of crucial, dramatic strikes in the few key mines and communications networks in Central, West and East Africa on which the colonial economy depended, which lasted from 1935 until the late 1940s, led to a slowly growing recognition that the labour question was a reality that had to be faced. In French Africa, the ideological journey from the peculiarity of the African to the universality of the worker was a surprisingly fast one. On the eve of the Dakar general strike of 1946, the governer-general still thought it was possible to have development without proletarianization. But a series of strikes in the port that began in December 1945 with minimal labour organization turned into larger union-led strikes in early January. By mid-January, a general strike lasting eleven days emerged out of a moment that was part carefully planned strike, part mass urban collective action. The unions came together in a citywide organization that brought in civil servants, clerks in commercial establishments, bakery workers, skilled workers, dockers, and manual labourers in a variety of trades. Market women refused to sell anything to white customers. A daily mass meeting became the focus of organization and sense of collective empowerment. The unions demanded 'equal pay for equal work and output', a minimum wage three times that of official calculations, equal rates of indemnities for family obligations and local cost of living for civil servants, and union participation in classifying jobs. Colonial officials were constrained from using their most obvious old weapon – the colonial army – because of their belief that Africans were a naturally rural people and that wage workers would desert the city if handled too roughly, because of concerns that violence in a highly visible city would be an international embarrassment, and because of their new hope that if treated as a modern man the African worker might eventually act like one. The governor-general, symbol of colonial power, telegraphed Paris in despair that he saw no way to get Africans back to work.

In the heat of the strike, officials called in a form of knowledge that was familiar to them in the metropole but which had not appeared relevant to the colonies. Inspector Masselot, an expert in labour affairs, was flown in from Paris, and he set about negotiating with commercial workers, with metalworkers, and with government workers in different unions. He brought with him model collective bargaining agreements based on a form standardized in France: the contracts – with significant wage increases at the bottom and wider increments at the top – eventually induced workers, group by group, to peel away from the general strike. The general strike lasted eleven days, the strike movement as a whole two and a half months. At its end, most workers were considerably better off, the unions that had organized the strikes had become self-confident, and the more privileged government workers who had struck alongside their brethren had acquired such benefits as family allowances. Not only were the monetary victories substantial, but by conceding that low-level civil servants receive family allowances – even if not at rates equal to those of French officials or the small number of African 'évolués' in the senior ranks – the government was in effect admitting that the needs of an African worker were of the same kind as those of a European worker. The myth that Africans were not really workers fell before the strikers' insistence on equal pay for equal work and the labour specialist's belief that French models of industrial relations could solve problems anywhere. Masselot saw this not so much as a victory for labour as the advent of a new approach to managing African society: 'There is a technique in organizing work, as with anything, and it cannot be improvised'.[3]

The process of channelling a wide conflict into specific, negotiable issues was soon institutionalized within the Inspection du Travail in French West Africa. These techniques – and the entire fabric of French claims to be 'assimilating' or 'developing' Africans – were promptly turned by African labour leaders into claims to entitlements. Even during the first strike wave, one labour leader rendered his opposite number in the administration speechless at a bargaining session by commenting, 'Your goal is to raise us to your level; without the means we will never get there'.[4] Over the years, African trade unionists used the rhetoric of imperial policy and the institutions of French industrial relations to claim the emoluments won by metropolitan workers.

Collective action continued to make clear that African voices would not just set off a rethinking of the labour question in colonial bureaucracies, but would make themselves heard over the details of each dispute. The Dakar strike was followed by the massive railway strike in all of French West Africa from October 1947 to March 1948. This strike of some twenty thousand workers revealed that the combination of union organizing and the networks among railway workers could bring about collective action over a vast space, and the union showed its determination to exercise its voice concerning the details of a programme of 'stabilizing' and restructuring work organization. Meanwhile, such issues as minimum wages were at the centre of citywide general strikes in Conakry, Guinea, and Cotonou, Dahomey. The strike wave in British Africa also continued – the Gold Coast mines and railways in 1947, Dar es Salaam, and, again, Mombasa in 1947, the riots in the Gold Coast in 1948. These strikes were deeply rooted in the conjuncture of the post-war years. French West African wage labour forces were small – perhaps 2 or 3 per cent of the total population – and concentrated in transport, commerce and government (plus scattered mines, the agricultural processing industry in Senegal, and plantation agriculture in Guinea and the Ivory Coast). But the narrowness of colonial economies gave them considerable power: a few nodal points (Dakar, Conakry, Abidjan, Cotonou, and the railway lines extending inland from those points) were essential to the all-important import-export trade and to government services. Yet at this time, the wage spectrum was narrow and provided little incentive to stay in a particular job. The strikes of the late 1940s followed linkages within a workforce that was poorly attached to specific jobs, that was involved in networks linking city and country, but that nonetheless vitally needed wages to survive.

[...]

In the French case, the approach that Inspector Masselot had taken in the 1946 general strike acquired a strong institutional base within the Inspection du Travail. 'Since May 1946', stated the next annual report on labour in French West Africa, 'the constant preoccupation of the Inspection du Travail has been to avoid the repetition of events of the same nature and to bring about...the conclusion of a package of collective bargaining agreements discussed in an atmosphere of mutual comprehension'.[5]

Officials came to think trade unions were a good idea, since an orderly process of negotiation could be carried out with them. The idea of masses of cheap labour power circulating among jobs and between workplace and village lost it appeal, for it was this seemingly amorphous nature of an urban labour force that was blamed for the fact that strikes rapidly became general strikes. Officials set about attaching workers to particular occupational categories and fracturing the almost uniform low level of wages through substantial raises to workers in the most vulnerable sectors. They began to talk of 'stabilization', of making a career, not just a few months of employment, attractive to African workers.

And officials soon began to think that the labour force had to be reproduced in a different way. The old model of the worker – and officials thought almost exclusively about male workers – as a single man who need only be paid an individual subsistence, leaving the costs of maintaining households, raising children, and caring for anyone not actually at work to a village economy increasingly peopled by women, seemed to be reproducing the wrong kind of workforce. Now, they wanted workers to be socialized and acculturated to urban life and industrial discipline from childhood.

As the drive to turn the African worker from unruly primitive into industrial man accelerated in the late 1940s, colonial officials read the significance of 'tradition' in increasingly negative terms. Such an African was no longer a quaint figure whose well-being and cultural integrity the wise colonial ruler was to maintain, but an obstacle to progress. This was why the brutality of colonial regimes in the 1940s and 1950s – beyond the occasional detention of 'agitators' – was usually aimed at people whose dissidence could be conceptualized as atavistic, as the dangerous violence of primitive people. Such was the case in the terror unleashed against rural rebels in Madagascar in 1947 and Kenya in 1952, even as British and French regimes handled 'modern' forms of protest with considerably more diffidence. Indeed, as the governor of Senegal made clear in his post-mortem on the 1946 strike, the fear that a spreading strike could extend to 'the most remote corners of the bush' was very much in officials' minds, and a reason for handling strikes with care and trying to mark them off as *labour* disputes solvable through orderly procedures, rather than as challenges to colonial power that could not be so clearly bounded.[6] The quest for the modern African was not limited to the field of labour: cautious attempts to bring selected Africans into European-modelled political institutions, and to make African agriculture more scientific, were being made. But the labour question struck in the most visible and vulnerable parts of empire, and forced officials to come to grips with the concrete realities of Africans acting in ways that transcended the old boundaries of control.

The discourse described above represented an effort to reassert control. Organized around a single vision of progress in a European image, focused on specific institutions and practices, it represented a hegemonic project couched in universalistic language. But even before the notions of stabilization and reproduction had been fully spelled out, African labour leaders were trying to seize the discourse. They turned a language of social engineering into a language of entitlement, seizing on the desperate hope of officials that Africans would behave in predictable ways to claim that wages and benefits should also be determined on a European model.

From working class to nation: trade unionism in French Africa

What made the demands of labour particularly powerful was that they were set forth within disciplined, effective strike movements and that they were posed in the very rhetorical structure on which French officials placed their claims to legitimate rule over their subjects. In the general strike of 1946 and several subsequent strikes, unions won substantial gains and acquired the confidence to demand more. Even as officials tried to divide workers by occupation and rank, the victories of some encouraged others to try, while the fledgling organizations of workers focused demands on the state itself for a *code du travail* that would set minimum standards of wages and working conditions for all wage workers.

This was also a demand that officials thought paralleled their own desire for a clear map – based on French labour codes – of what industrial relations were supposed to be. Such a code had to apply to workers of all races, unless France wished to undermine its own claim, made in response to critics of its empire, that Overseas France was an integral part of France itself, and the presumption of a non-racial code raised the stakes of the debate over how the universal worker would be defined. Business groups saw the danger, but could not jettison either the rhetoric of imperial unity, depending as they did on the protection of the colonial state, or the rhetoric of regulation, for they too wanted industrial relations channelled into predictable directions. So they could only plead that the special conditions of the colonies be taken into consideration in drafting the code.

Meanwhile, worker organizations began to affiliate with the rival labour federations into which unions in France itself were grouped, and by far the most popular was the Conféderation Générale du Travail (CGT), closely linked to the French Communist Party (PCF). The CGT's efforts in the colonies have been the subject of some scholarly debate, and the organization's claim to have assisted colonial proletariats has been challenged by scholars who insist that the CGT was in its own way imperialist. [...] The condescending attitude of CGT officers, and their insistence that only French communists could lead colonized people on the path to socialism, caused them to miss the paramount importance of nationalism to the people of the colonies.

But this argument itself assumes that a historical judgment can be passed on the basis of a discussion that took place in France. At the same time, the argument naturalizes nationalism – treating it as an inevitable drive toward a future of political independence, as a train that one either boards or misses. Whatever the limits of the vision of CGT leaders in France, African trade unionists could use the institutions of the CGT and the legitimacy it had in French politics in their own ways. By associating themselves with the CGT, African trade unionists not only let colonial officials think that their approach to work issues was fundamentally modern and progressive – modelled on France – but reminded them that claims to universalism could take more than one form.

In practice, the CGT-affiliated unions in French West Africa traced a number of campaigns in different colonial cities, with uneven but significant success, for higher wages and other benefits, while they developed a French West Africa-wide organization to mobilize politically for the *code du travail*. The CGT unions insisted throughout the late 1940s and 1950s that their fundamental goal was 'equal pay for equal work', and indeed equal benefits for equal work.

Given the universalistic, non-racial definition of the wage labourer, the costs of whatever guarantees workers won could be high. The elevated stakes of the debate over the *code du travail* caused it to drag on for six years, until November 1952. Its final passage came after a one-day, highly effective general strike throughout French West Africa, organized by all the trade union federations and spearheaded by the CGT. The code guaranteed all wage workers a forty-hour week, paid vacations, and other benefits: it guaranteed the right to organize unions and, with certain restrictions, the right to strike: it created consultative bodies in the state apparatus with union representation. The code pronounced in principle for wage workers to receive family allowances to help them raise children.

It did all this for a strictly bounded workforce – wage labourers only. The officials' assumption that wage workers were male was so ingrained it was only occasionally commented on, and the trade unions' version of 'equal pay for equal work' was focused on a comparison of male bread-winners across the races. The code was quite explicit in focusing only on workers who received a wage. So-called customary labour – which included most labour done by women as well as most of the forms of labour on African farms that shaded into tenancy – was left to an African world that officials did not have to probe. This realm, in fact, was where several leading African politicians, like Léopold Senghor and Félix Houphouët-Boigny, were building political machines, and they were content to keep the *inspecteurs du travail* from asking too many questions there.

The African deputies to the French National Assembly in Paris had played an active role in the debate, and their threats to drop their support for the code if certain provisions that they cherished were left out had swayed some metropolitan politicians who feared polarization and a new strike wave.

This was the high point of cooperation between the leaders of African political parties and the trade unions. Earlier, the leading political activists had retained a certain distance from the labour movement: Lamine Guèye, then the leading Socialist politician in Dakar, had sat out the 1946 strike and accordingly earned the contempt of the strikers. Senghor and Houphouët-Boigny had at times seemed more concerned with the damage the railway strike of 1947–8 was doing to commerce than with helping the railwaymen achieve victory, and Houphouët-Boigny was credited by the French labour inspectors with persuading the railwaymen in his territory, the Ivory Coast, to give up the strike two months before the rest of the workers settled. The leading politician from the Soudan, Fily Dabo Sissoko, conspired with French officials to split

Soudanese railwaymen off from their Senegalese brethren on the crucial Dakar-Niger line, a move that failed ignominiously when the railwaymen whom Sissoko thought of as his clients ignored his call to break the strike. Houphouët-Boigny remained distrustful of the labour movement, although Senghor, *after* the railway strike, moved to bring its leaders into his party's orbit, pushing Ibrahima Sarr, the hero of 1947–8, into an elected office. But in the strike wave of 1946–8, it was clear that electoral mobilization and labour mobilization were two processes, with considerable tension between them. After the victory of 1952, the tension would soon become manifest again.

The most interesting figure in this regard is Sékou Touré of Guinea. He had been a humble clerk in the French bureaucracy and made his start in a civil servants' union. He became leader of the Guinean national federation of CGT unions and led a bitter general strike, largely over the government's setting of the minimum wage, in 1950. This gave him a reputation throughout CGT circles, and he was one of the prime movers behind the strike of November 1952 for the code. He more than anyone in the early 1950s stood for CGT trade unionism: aggressive tactics, detailed demands for one after another of the perquisites enjoyed by French workers, and the rhetoric of proletarian internationalism. He was a true *cégétiste* (CGTist). There were curious sides to his political persona even then: outside of union matters, he cooperated with the more conservative Houphouët-Boigny, and within the CGT he was a rival of the Soudanese leader Abdoulaye Diallo, who had the inside track in internationalist circles, having become a vice-president of the leftist World Federation of Trade Unions (WFTU). But at the time of victory in the struggle for the code, Sékou Touré seemed fully committed to making the French working class the reference point for the aspirations of African workers. When the code was voted he directed his union leaders, '*Responsable*, your bedside reading is the *Code du Travail*, which you can never study enough'.[7]

When business interests tried to stall implementation of key provisions of the code and the government temporized, another French West Africa-wide strike movement materialized, while in Guinea Sékou Touré led a strike lasting sixty-seven days and resulting in acceptance of the labour movement's interpretation that a key article of the code entitled workers to a 20 per cent increase in the minimum wage. This strike, officials admitted, was a 'remarkable personal success' for Sékou Touré. He took a less personal interest – but the CGT and other unions were in any case well prepared – in the next great campaign culminating in 1956, for family allowances for wage workers. By then, strike threats were sufficiently intimidating to get the government to make the necessary concessions before the scheduled strike took place. The union movement in French West Africa had at that time signed up an impressive 36 per cent of the region's 500,000 wage workers.

But already the politics of African trade unionism were shifting, with Sékou Touré leading the new direction as he had led the old. In 1953, the year of his triumph in the Guinea strike, Sékou Touré ran for the territorial council, the principle legislative body at the level of the individual colony. He was not the only trade unionist to realize that labour offered a launching platform for politics, but that it was no more than that. In fact, the precision with which the *code du travail* defined the working-class – and the partial success of union efforts at raising voices and government efforts at stabilizing the labour force – meant that the population with a direct interest in labour's success was narrower than it might have been in the days of the amorphous labouring mass. Houphouët-Boigny was explicit in downplaying workers as a political base; the relatively well off farmers who constituted his own base may not have been more numerous, but their networks of tenancy, clientage and affiliation penetrated much more deeply into the Ivory Coast's rural population. Sékou Touré seems to have begun by following Houphouët-Boigny's tutelage in his political career, and in those years he kept his union activity compartmentalized so as not to antagonize his patron.

Herein lies the best way for understanding the shift in the French labour movement from a predominantly internationalist (or *cégétiste*) orientation to a nationalist one. Most writing on the subject of the anti-metropolitan turn among African trade unionists does not consider any explanation necessary: the nationalism of the African masses is self evident. But there is not much evidence that this turn originated among the rank and file. There is, on the contrary, evidence that the shift came from above, from labour leaders anxious to enter the political arena, and that as they did so, the autonomist labour movement they had spawned itself became subject to rank-and-file pressures for old-style demands, for higher wages and for equality with metropolitan workers. For someone like Sékou Touré, electoral support required mobilizing people of diverse interests through multiple networks of organization and affiliation and finding a language of broad appeal. The language of the labour movement had, since the war, urged African workers to cast their gaze toward French workers and demand entitlements accordingly. It was, of course, filled with attacks on colonialists, but above all on colonialists who had not lived up to the assimilationist and universalist rhetoric of French imperialism. The peasant or pastoralist in rural Guinea had no French person whose entitlements were a relevant basis of comparison. Yet peasants and pastoralists had much of the structure of colonial society to feel constricted by. The common denominator that a budding politician in the early 1950s could mobilize was not equality but reactions to the colonial state itself, however diverse the common base of grievances might be.

Even at the height of his trade union militancy, Sékou Touré reportedly remarked that support for him in his first electoral campaigns 'is not solely due to the progressive ideas which I defended; it is the consequence of the affection which a part of the Guinean masses hold for me, because I am the descendant of an illustrious family'.[8] The search was on for building multiple bases of support and finding an idiom of affinity that went beyond class-based appeals.

It was thus, while workers were still engaged in struggles for equal wages and family allowances, that some labour leaders in French West Africa began to try to disaffiliate their organizations from their metropolitan connections and turn them into truly African organizations – with changed slogans and mobilizing ideologies – that could be used in broad political struggles.

[...]

Sékou Touré became the most articulate spokesman of the new African trade unionism. He argued that the fundamental issue was African unity in the struggle against imperialism. The old rhetoric of equality, like that of class struggle, was gone. Indeed, Sékou Touré insisted, 'although the classes of metropolitan and European populations battle and oppose each other, nothing separates the diverse African social classes'. Because of the common identity of Africans, there was no need for a plurality of trade unions. The claim to unity and uniformity came in the same breath.[9] He joined other labour leaders in founding in 1957 a specifically African federation of trade unions, UGTAN (Union Générale des Travailleurs d'Afrique Noire). UGTAN debated the issue of class struggle, and refused a proposal that the organization act not only against 'white colonialism but also against Africans who exploit their racial brothers, like the planters of the Ivory Coast'. Instead, delegates – with considerable unease and disagreement – insisted that the liquidation of colonialism should 'take pride of place over the class struggle'.[10]

[...]

In 1956 the context in which the African struggles for power and for social justice intersected underwent a dramatic change. The French government, frustrated in its efforts to shape economic and social change in its own way, fearing a second Algeria, and seeking to distance itself from all the demands for parity that followed from its assimilationist and universalist imperial ideology, pulled back. Developmentalist thinking, in the end, did not offer an answer to the question that had bedevilled Africa's conquerors for over sixty years: how to harness the resources and labour power of the continent. The French government redefined political institutions under the *loi cadre* (framework law), devolving effective government (except for foreign affairs, defence, etc.) to the individual territories, operating under elected legislatures, a 'vice-président du conseil' chosen by the party controlling the legislature, and African ministers. Most decisions and budgets were devolved from the federations (French West Africa and French Equatorial Africa) to the territories (Senegal, Ivory Coast, Dahomey, Niger, etc.).

France made it clear that the civil service in each territory, with certain transitional provisions, would be the responsibility of each government: if government workers were to get any more perquisites, the territorial legislatures would have to raise the money to pay for them. The effect of this was to put the French reference point at one remove from African civil servants and workers. The civil service unions realized quickly that 'territorialization' threatened the rhetorical and institutional basis for all their demands. But the tide was against them: African politicians were eagerly seeking the legislative and executive offices, and trade union leaders were prominent among them.

French officials thought they had got themselves out of the trap that their own rhetoric and CGT organization had got them into. As one political observer noted, as soon as trade union leaders won office they would be in the same position as their French predecessors in facing workers' demands for new entitlements, and – having to pay the bills – they would offer 'meagre satisfaction'. Workers would be held in check by 'their respectful fear of local African authorities, who will not lack the means to make their point of view prevail'.[11] It would now be African trade unionists who would fall into a trap baited by their own nationalism and sprung by the takeover of state institutions by ambitious men of power.

French officials guessed right: as African politicians, including those of trade union background, moved into state offices, they would seek to tame the labour movement. Trade union leaders did well in the 1957 elections. In eight of the nine territories of French West Africa, trade union leaders were named minister of labour or minister of the civil service, and seven of these eight were UGTAN members. Sékou Touré became vice-président du conseil in Guinea. Even Diallo gave up his communist connections and his communist rhetoric to join the government in the Soudan. The level of strike activity went down, and UGTAN itself intervened to cool off some strike movements. This soon led to considerable tension from the rank and file, whose interests in the old demands of equality with French workers, higher minimum wages, better benefits, and guarantees against the loss through territorialization of already-won privileges were now threatened by the very success of anti-colonial politics. A particularly long and bitter strike – entailing riots, imprisonments and deaths – took place in Dahomey, in which a militant rank and file stood opposed to a government labour minister who was himself a CGT and UGTAN veteran, with the union caught in between. As the dispute dragged on to only partial resolution, a pro-labour speaker at a rally commented, 'It was easier to obtain satisfaction from a European *inspecteur du travail* than it is now from an African minister'. The minister, for his part, was trying to turn his comrades' discourse about African-French equality and universal standards of labour policy into a discourse on the scarcity of local resources.[12]

Sékou Touré, as he moved toward power, told trade unionists that the game had changed, and they now would have to fall in line to express the unity of the African personality and the unity of the anti-imperialist struggle. A strike against 'the organisms of colonialism', was one thing,

> but when it is directed against an African government, it affects African authority....Trade unionism for trade unionism's stake is historically unthinkable in current conditions, trade unionism of class just as much....The trade union movement is obligated to reconvert itself to remain in the same line of emancipation.

[...]

Coming on the eve of Guinean independence, the words were chilling, and one of Sékou Touré's collaborators and rivals in years of trade union action, David Soumah, already understood the implications: 'A unity which stifles the voice of free trade unionism sets back the emancipation of the labouring masses instead of facilitating it'.[13]

Sékou Touré practised what he preached, beyond the expectations of French officials who had thought him a useful tool against universalistic trade unionism. He led Guinea out of the French empire in 1958, rejecting de Gaulle's programme for close Franco-African relations during the devolution of power. He duly set about consolidating his personal authority and that of his henchmen, repressing – among other groups – any vestige of autonomous trade unionism. Unions were forcefully amalgamated into a single confederation, which was in turn subordinated to Sékou Touré's political party as Guinea became a single-party state. As one commentator put it, 'Trade unionism was forbidden to trade unions', and the unions became 'an organization of the party for the control of the masses'. When Sékou Touré humiliated the teachers' union and jailed some of its leaders during their pathetic attempt in 1961 to secure a pay raise, it was clear that unions as an organism to advance members' interests had no place in this kind of political independence.[14]

Guinea – presided over by a former trade unionist – represented an extreme in the extent of government destruction of union rights and organizations. In places like Nigeria, Ghana, Zambia or Senegal, unions struggled more successfully to remain a part of political and social life. [...] But co-optation of the top layer of union leadership and considerable repression of the base in many countries reduced the room for manoeuvre they had seized during the post-war decade. Veterans of the labour movement in Senegal refer in interviews to trade unionists taking off the *le boubou syndical* in favour of *le boubou politique* – trading in the robes of union power for the robes of political office, asserting that the unions contributed to political struggle but only became the 'auxiliaries' of political parties even as many trade union leaders were co-opted into the government. Senegal's prime minister in 1958 dismissed trade unionists' concerns as 'secondary'. Later, the leader of the railway strike of 1947–8, Ibrahim Sarr, who was never jailed by the French, was imprisoned by the government of Senghor for his role in trying to forge a populist political movement in 1962, and the most influential Senegalese in UGTAN, Alioune Cissé, who had been able to lead a nationalist labour organization without running foul of the colonial police, served time in jail in 1968 for his role in a general strike.

Repression and co-optation must be understood in relation to the politics of patronage: labour leaders were never pure embodiments of proletarian solidarity, but people inserted in diverse webs of affiliation. They could fit into wider structures of political mobilization or else use their own connections to tie working-class communities into rival structures – hence the central importance to new regimes of fracturing the class-based potential of the labour movement while incorporating its leaders and its component parts into structures of patronage. Even before coming to power, political-cum-labour leaders within UGTAN were trying to bring about an ideological shift within the labour movement that would put the claim to state power at the apex of political relationships, focusing on workers' relationship with a nationalist leadership rather than their solidarity among themselves. The French move in 1956 to put significant resources in the hands of elected African politicians fundamentally changed the context of party-union relations. However much nationalist sentiments among the labour rank and file evolved from 1946 to 1956, the sharp break in 1956–8 reflected the shift of state resources from a colonial power to African political leaders, eager to turn their complex political networks into an effective political machine. The new rhetorical strategies would be underscored by the new resources, yet the aspiring leaders' sense of the fragility of their position made them anxious to eliminate rival modes of organizing collectively and rival ideologies of mobilization.

There was, of course, a case to be made that African trade unionists had done well enough in the final years of colonialism that they should have exercised restraint in the early years of independence, but the government of Guinea, for one, was not calling for a debate over priorities. Sékou Touré's version of unity and anti-imperialism – and other regimes similarly posited 'development' as a national goal that no one could legitimately oppose – refused debate as it proclaimed that the dialectic of nation and class had been resolved in favour of the former. The irony of this pattern of decolonization was that the vision of a unified Africa that animated political rhetoric in the mid-1950s, and which Sékou Touré and others used to shift attention from 'equal pay for equal work', was itself lost. As African leaders consolidated power in their respective territories – focusing patronage, repression, and political symbolism within the borders they inherited – the possibilities of cooperation within francophone West Africa faded, and UGTAN soon ceased to function.

Conclusion

[...]

African labour movements, as their leaders became caught up in the quest for state power, fell into an ideological trap. It became more difficult for them to assert that the metropolitan standard for wages and benefits should apply to all workers, or indeed to frame their political position around the notion that workers existed both within the nation and across the globe and that the condition of 'the worker' posed problems that required specific attention, both within and among nations. The tension between workers' claims as workers and Africans' assertions of political rights as Africans was, during the 1940s and early 1950s, a creative and empowering one. But when 'nation-building' became a state project and national identity was held to subsume all other forms of affiliation, that tension was pushed from the arena of politics.

[...]

The forms of post-colonial states and the attitudes they projected in their moment of triumph may seem to represent the imposition of a European conception of political and social questions: francophone African states let the French *code du travail* be the blueprint for their labour legislation, just as they maintained colonial bureaucracies and expanded the modernist architecture of colonial cities into a symbol of national sovereignty. The colonial code's contribution to defining a sharp boundary between the working class and all those excluded from the legislation's purview continued, in the form of invidious distinctions between a regulated 'formal sector' and an 'urban informal sector' of self-employed or irregularly employed people unprotected by legislation and subject to harassment for unlicensed activities. [...] The failings of decolonization, it might seem, lie in the way colonial regimes, even as their sense of command failed, determined the institutional and discursive parameters for future social policy.

Such an argument would miss two crucial points. First, the bounded and regulated labour force did not emerge full blown from the late colonial imagination, but came about as colonial state and African labour movements struggled with and influenced each other. The discourses of stabilization, unionization, and industrial relations were brought to

Africa only when Africans forced the labour question onto the imperial agenda. The labour movement thought it could achieve material gains for its members by operating within the system the colonial governments were moving toward and by insisting that all workers, regardless of race, be treated as equals within it. Both sides, as they negotiated and struggled with each other, immersed themselves ever more deeply within a discursive structure that treated wage labour as a universal construct, and both tried to use that structure for different ends.

Second, the hegemonic project of post-war imperialism, passed on to post-colonial states, never did confine Africa into its developmentalist categories. Instead, it narrowed into a gatekeeper's ideology. In taking over capital-city institutions, African governments soon learned how thin was the wave of 'nationalism' that had carried them into office, and how much they had merely taken over a sovereignty often better defined by its linkage to organizations overseas than within the territory of the state. Some scholars have even argued that such states exist largely by virtue of their international recognition – their seats in the United Nations, and above all their being the locus for administering aid programmes. [...] The gate, of course, faces inward as well, and administering the juncture of local structures and the international economy represents a potent source of jobs and patronage. But now that the universalistic claims of development theories have failed to remake economy and society, these processes serve to maintain a tottering, constricted apparatus rather than to form the basis for the further penetration of a hegemonic ideology much beyond the site of the gatekeeper's tollbooth. Within the national boundaries, African leaders have had to make and remake their political bases by whatever means they could, building on the particularistic ties that the universalities of modernity were supposed to diminish. The crisis of African states is not attributable to too much modernity or too little: uncovering its origins and its meanings requires a much deeper probing of pathways taken and pathways missed, of possibilities and constraints in global systems that are themselves changing and contested.

For a time, the labour movement was able to achieve significant material rewards and a sense of empowerment by turning the colonial state's assertion of its modernizing role into claims to the standards and resources of a European state. For a time, the debate between labour leaders who wanted to continue to claim entitlement in similar terms and those who wished to envelop the movement in struggles for political independence, brought out issues and tensions in social and political movements that were important to confront. But when one sort of movement – which claimed a singular and exclusive role for the nation state – insisted that all other movements be subsumed under it, the possibility of creative tension and fruitful debate was lost. African politics would benefit from confronting those tensions and that debate again.

Notes

1 Frederick Cooper (1997) selections from 'The dialectics of decolonization: nationalism and labor movements in postwar French Africa', in Frederick Cooper and Ann Laura Stoler (eds) *Tensions of Empire: Colonial Cultures in a Bourgeois World*, Berkeley: University of California Press, 406–36. Please see the original for a fully referenced version of this essay.
2 Frantz Fanon (1966) [1961] *The Wretched of the Earth*, trans. Constance Farrington, New York: Grove Books, 30.
3 Masselot to Minister of Colonies, 23 February 1946. AP 960/syndicalisme, Archives d'Outre-Mer (AOM), France.
4 Transcript of a meeting between union leaders and officials of the Government General, St Louis, 15 January 1946, K 405 (132), Archives of Senegal (AS).
5 Inspection du Travail, AOF, Annual Report, 1946, p. 74.
6 Governor, Senegal, to Governor-General, 9 February 1946, incl. Governor-General to Minister, 23 March 1946, AP960/Syndicalisme, AOM.
7 Quoted in R. W. Johnson (1970) 'Sékou Touré and the Guinean Revolution', *African Affairs* 69: 351.
8 Sûreté, Renseignements, 5 October 1951, 17G 272, AS.
9 Senegal, Sûreté, Renseignements, 21 February 1956, 21G, 215, AS.
10 Governor, Dahomey, to High Commissioner, 22 January 1957, K 421 (165), AS, reporting on the UGTAN conference in Bamako.
11 FWA, IGT, 'Note sur l'evolution du syndicalisme in A.O.F', 19 April 1957, IGT 11/2, ANSOM.
12 Dahomey, Renseignements, October 1957–April 1958, 17G 588, AS; Governor, Dahomey to Minister, 30 January 1958, AP 2189/12, AOM.
13 Sékou Touré, exposés to conference of the RDA, 2 February 1958, Centre de Recherche et de Documentation Africaine, PDG (9)/dossier 7; David Soumah, report to Congress of CATC, 10–12 November 1958, 17G 610, AS.
14 Claude Rivière (1975) 'Lutte ouvrière et phenomène syndical en Guinée', *Cultures et Développement* 7: 53, 73–5.

Further reading

Bayart, Jean-François (1993) [1989] *The State in Africa: The Politics of the Belly*, London: Longman.
Chafer, Tony (2002) *The End of Empire in French West Africa*, Oxford: Berg.
Conklin, Alice (1997) *A Mission to Civilize: The Republican Idea of Empire in France and West Africa, 1895–1930*, Stanford: Stanford University Press.
Cooper, Frederick (1994) 'A conflict and connection: rethinking colonial African history', *American Historical Review* 99: 1516–45.
——(1996) *Decolonization and African Society: The Labor Question in French and British Africa*, Cambridge: Cambridge University Press.
Delanoue, Paul (1983) 'La CGT et les syndicats d'Afrique Noire', *Le Mouvement Social* 122: 103–16.
DeWitte, Philippe (1981) 'La CGT et les syndicats d'Afrique Occidentale Française (1945–1957)', *Le Mouvement Social* 117: 3–32.

Fanon, Frantz (1966) [1961] *The Wretched of the Earth*, trans. Constance Farrington, New York: Grove Press.

Hodgkin, Thomas (1957) *Nationalism in Colonial Africa*, New York: New York University Press.

Marseille, Jacques (1984) *Empire colonial et capitalisme français: Histoire d'un divorce*, Paris: Albin Michel.

Martens, George (1979) 'Industrial relations and trade unionism in French-speaking West Africa', in Ukandi G. Damachi, H. Dieter Seibel and Lester Trachtman (eds) *Industrial Relations in Africa*, New York: St Martin's Press, 16–72.

Morgenthau, Ruth Schachter (1964) *Political Parties in French Speaking West Africa*, Oxford: Clarendon Press.

Zolberg, Aristide (1966) *Creating Political Order: The Party States of West Africa*, Chicago: Rand McNally.

17

SOCIAL CONSTRUCTION OF IDEALIZED IMAGES OF WOMEN IN COLONIAL KOREA

The 'new woman' versus 'motherhood'[1]

Jiweon Shin

In contemporary Korea, motherhood is much respected and glorified. What Chizuko Ueno states about Japanese motherhood can also be applied to Korea; according to Ueno, the word 'mother' connotes 'a cultural representation rather than a clearly defined female sub-group'; an idealized crystallized personification which is characterized by 'devotion to children, parental affection, and self sacrifice'.[2] However, motherhood is not the only virtue that has been expected of women historically, nor is the modern cultural construct of motherhood inherent in women. As Edward Shorter states, '[g]ood mothering is an invention of modernization'.[3] Different sociopolitical conditions require different roles for women, and the image of an ideal woman is constructed and reconstructed as an ongoing process according to society's needs at any given era. Research in this field argues that a society requires and endorses certain types of women depending on its stage of modernization, industrialization, and/or international/political environment. This is clearly reflected in late nineteenth- and early twentieth-century Korea.

Prior to the 1870s, the traditional image of Korean women can be described as primarily that of procreation: the foremost responsibility of married women was to bear sons to continue the family lineage. But this role changed during the Enlightenment period (1876–1910), when the image of the 'educated mother' emerged as a new ideal. After Korea's annexation by Japan in 1910, the feminist image of *shin yosong* (new womanhood) emerged, and Korean society became infatuated with this new ideal. But by the late 1920s, it had become the target of severe criticism from conservative Korean intellectual circles and the Japanese colonial government. *Mosong* (motherhood) was asserted to be the proper role model for Korean women, and by the early to mid-1930s, 'motherhood' was established in the public sphere as a sort of officially correct ideal. This image differed from earlier images of motherhood in that it was linked to nationalistic ideology rather than the traditional

Confucian roles of daughter-in-law or wife. Moreover, it was largely a response to Japanese imperialism. By the mid-1930s, the image of women as mothers raising an enlightened next generation for the sake of national well-being was firmly established in Korea.

This chapter argues that the image of motherhood in contemporary Korean society has its roots in the colonial period, when the construction of this version of motherhood was conditioned by strong nationalism and a vigilant Japanese colonialism. The research is based on an analysis of women's journals that were published by leading intellectuals and were intended to shape and direct the nation toward modernization and independence. These journals basically come from two distinct time periods: pre-1910 or post-1920. Although modern publishing began in Korea in the 1890s, and the first women's journal appeared in 1906, Japanese annexation in 1910 was followed by a decade of severe censorship of all Korean media as a part of the colonial power's policy of ruthless repression. But after the March First Movement in 1919, the biggest nationalistic political event in colonial Korea, Japanese policy shifted, and the publication of journals and newspapers resumed in the 1920s and thenceforth flourished. Women's magazines reappeared, but their content continued to change as the political and social situation under colonialism developed.

The beginning of the public discourse on women can be traced to the 1890s, when the image of 'educating mothers' began to appear. Confucian ideology, which stressed the inferior position of women, dominated Korea until the late nineteenth century. Women were regarded as inferior to men, and obedience, subjugation, chastity and endurance were considered the highest virtues that they could attain, while education was reserved exclusively for males. Women were regarded as merely ignorant and subordinate, and even the 'seven bases for divorce' (unfilial behaviour toward parents-in-law, failing to bear a son, gossiping, stealing, jealousy, improper conduct, and disease) which had formed the fundamental code of conduct for women during the Yi Dynasty (1392–1910), did not contain any reference to education.

In the arranged marriage system, women were primarily significant for producing sons and as cheap labour. In this patriarchal marriage system, any close link between a husband and wife was neither meaningful nor encouraged. The most important family relationship for a married woman was with her parents-in-law, not with her own children nor her husband, since the foremost responsibility of women was to serve them. But as Korea came under increased military pressure from Japan in the last decade of the nineteenth century, some leaders questioned whether the country could afford to maintain this traditional female role in an increasingly hostile international environment.

As the military threat increased and aggressive Japanese colonialism expanded into Northeast and Southeast Asia, Korean intellectuals and political leaders opposed this aggression in many forms. These included the struggles within the Choson imperial dynasty to reinstate its fading power; memorials were made to the throne from Confucian literati which pleaded for a more effective defence policy. 'Righteous armies' were formed by both Confucian literati and common people, with anti-Japanese guerrilla warfare reaching a peak in 1908. Political and social movements sought internal institutional and political change to preserve national independence, and publications (including newspapers) sought to raise the social and political consciousness of the people. Progressive elites also sought to foster a contemporary, nationalistic culture to instil modern education and nationalism within the people.

In this socio-historical context, Korean intellectuals began to realize the importance of women's education for this struggle, and in the 1890s initiated the *Kaehwa Undong* (Enlightenment Movement). Pak Yong-hyo, one of the progressive political leaders of the time, mentioned several women's issues for the first time in an official petition to the King in 1888. These included abolishing the legality of domestic violence against women, establishing equal opportunity of education for boys and girls above the age of six, banning child marriage and concubinage, and permitting widows to remarry.

These issues, however, were not circulated in public until the *Tongnip Shinmun* (the *Independent*), the most influential daily newspaper of the time, began to advocate women's rights for equal education in 1896. Through a series of editorials, *Tongnip Shinmun* argued that if women were not given a proper education, half of the Korean population would remain ignorant, thus jeopardizing the education of future generations. Hence the neglect of women's education would ultimately result in a deterioration of the national well-being. The paper also encouraged women to fight for more education, and rights:

> So we are urging you, women of Korea, to strive for high educa-
> tion, conducting yourselves in an exemplary manner to become
> models for men. In this way not only will you gain rights prop-
> erly due you, but guide ignorant men in the right direction.[4]

Tongnip Shinmun tried to foster social consensus on the necessity of educating women, and succeeded in gaining the attention of both the government and public. Its efforts bore fruit in several significant ways. In 1908, the first law on women's education, the Article on Public High Schools for Women, was proclaimed by the government, and in the same year the first government girls' high school was founded. Intellectuals' emphasis on the importance of women's education increased during the first decade of the new century, as various segments of the Korean intelligentsia attempted to educate the people and mobilize nationalist opinion, while Korean sovereignty eroded, since the government did not have the resources to reorganize and redirect an effective defence.

By this time, *Kajong Chapji* (*Home Journal*), published from 1906 to 1908, was circulating the novel idea that mothers should be responsible for the education of their children at home. This approach emphasized the importance of women's education for the sake of the next generation who would be responsible for the nation's fate in the hostile international political environment. *Kajong Chapji* also attempted to enlighten the people by first changing their attitudes regarding sons:

> To those with sons, when you love and raise your sons, do not expect any payback from them; do not consider them as yours. Instead, consider them as social resources, and raise them as such. When your sons make great contributions to this society, the society will reward you properly.[5]

This was a major break with past views of motherhood. Raising children, especially sons, was the only guarantee for support in retirement, and thus filial piety was considered a primary virtue. Encouraging people to give up their privileges as parents, and to consider their sons more as social resources, was thus a significant departure from tradition. Yet within this revolutionary view, women were still regarded as being important only for educating their sons at home.

In the realm of domestic education, however, it was asserted that women – rather than their husbands – should have indisputable authority in educating their children. In 1906, *Kajong Chapji* declared:

> For children's education, women's role is far more important than men's. Since men are busy earning money outside home, they do not have enough time to spend with children. On the other hand, women give birth to children, breast-feed them and raise them with their own hands. Until children reach the age of twenty, when they go out into society as adults, they are under the direct influence of their mothers....If mothers are intellectual, smart, sincere, and socially conscious, children will grow to be as such....If women get married and raise such wonderful children, those children will again be wonderful parents. In this way, this nation will be full of good people and will prosper. Therefore, we can say that *women are the teachers of the whole nation.*[6]
>
> (emphasis added)

This idea of giving enormous significance to women's education attained popularity among the intellectuals, and they founded over fifty women's schools during the Enlightenment period. Although many of these private schools suffered from lack of adequate financial support, they helped to generate widespread enthusiasm for learning among Korean women. By 1910, educating daughters had become an established custom for middle- and upper-class Koreans. Official records show 7,000 women students in Seoul in 1907; by 1910, 2,230 private schools were registered, and it was estimated that there were as many unregistered schools. The notion that women were the teachers of the whole nation was a further step away from the idea that women were primarily responsible for children's education at home, and it is far beyond the Confucian view of women as mere procreators.

Following Japan's forced annexation of Korea in 1910, the role of women in Korean society changed once again. The first decade of Japanese colonial rule 'has been called the "dark period" (*amhukki*) because of the repression of political and cultural life in the colony'.[7] Political organizations were dismissed and the right of public assembly was abolished; the publication of newspapers, magazines and books was strictly controlled and censored. The slightest sign of political opposition was crushed by military force; intellectuals and nationalist leaders were put under police surveillance, and the Japanese colonial educational system provided Koreans with only minimal, basic learning with the goal of moulding them into loyal and obedient subjects. Japanese was taught as the 'national language', and Korean became the second language; colonial education likewise aimed to implant ambivalent attitudes toward Korea's culture, history and heritage.

This repressive colonial policy and social atmosphere changed after 1918. Following World War I, US president Woodrow Wilson declared the principle of humanism and respect for the self-determination of peoples in the post-war settlement. Korean nationalists considered Wilson's principles as a basis to prepare a nationwide nationalistic protest and to proclaim the independence of Korea. National leaders in exile, religious leaders and moderate nationalists combined their resources to prepare the Declaration of Independence. On 1 March 1919, this was proclaimed in Seoul by so-called 'national representatives', and a copy was dispatched to the Japanese governor-general.

Non-violent demonstrations and nationwide rallies were then staged over the following months, in which more than a million people participated. The Japanese overlords reacted with their customary imperial brutality; Korean nationalists estimated that the subsequent repression resulted in over 7,500 deaths and approximately 15,000 injured, with some 45,000 arrests made between March and December of that year.

The severity of this repression meant that the Japanese colonial administration's authority was severely damaged; by June, the government in Tokyo had begun to realize that a policy change was inevitable.

Admiral Saito Makoto was appointed as a new governor-general, and the colonial administration was reorganized. This new strategy brought out a new style of colonial rule in Korea: Saito's reform was known as the 'Cultural Policy' or 'Cultural Ruling'. Various controls in cultural, political and social aspects were altered, and the discriminatory educational system, restrictions on freedom of the press, and restrictions on organizations were either removed or greatly improved. The Cultural Policy provided an environment for Koreans to forge a cultural and political renaissance in the 1920s. Although publications were still supposed to be censored, hundreds of popular magazines and specialized journals appeared, and Korean national leaders were developing their own 'cultural nationalism' in a more relaxed colonial atmosphere. Thus the 1920s blossomed into a radical and progressive age for every aspect of Korean society, including women's issues.

The new stage of the public discourse on women revolved around the concept of *shin yosong* (new woman), which had originally meant women who received education from newly established Western-style schools, called *shin kyoyook* (new education); these 'new women' were those who gained the new education. Those who were opposed to them were the 'traditional women', meaning all those – regardless of age – who stuck to the old ways. The 'new women' were easily distinguished from 'traditional women' by their appearance: they wore Western-style clothing, with suits and shoes, or the modernized version of *hanbok* (traditional Korean dress), and either cut or permed their hair.

However, appearances alone were not enough to be a 'new woman', and they were expected to espouse both a new philosophy and a new way of life. 'New womanhood' was defined in the first issue of *Shin Yosong* (*New Woman*) in 1923 as 'characteristics of women who have found their real, inner individuality', which was central to this new identity of the 1920s; women were thus advised to discard their traditional collective identity, to discover their own individual personalities, and to reject the old, false, pathological identity and all hypocritical, face-saving customs that the old society had demanded which limited their freedom. To become a true 'new woman', they had to be reborn.

Educated women were taught that without first discovering their inner selves through this intense revolution from within, they did not deserve to be called 'new women'. 'Traditional women' depended solely on their husbands; 'new women' were supposed to guide their own fates. A radical new code of conduct for women was clearly suggested. According to the July issue of *Shin Yosong* in 1926, the first thing that 'new women' should do was destroy all negative remnants of the past:

Recently people hear a lot about women's education, women's liberation, equality, and freedom. But you [Korean women] should not be satisfied, since nothing has been changed and you are not respected enough as whole selves. You should make fierce efforts to become complete human beings and to be treated as such....You must burn everything from the past in your mind and create a new mind, new thought, and a new personality. Things from the past cannot be improved; they should be eradicated.[8]

For women who wished to remake themselves into 'new women', three suggestions were offered: first, women should develop self-respect. In the past, women did not have an opportunity to assert their identities as autonomous people; their identities were simply subordinated to those of men. To recover their individuality, they had to realize their value as human beings. Second, women should liberate their thoughts; without free will, they could not cultivate an individuality separate from that of men. Third, women were strongly advised to cultivate both financial and mental independence. However, these recommendations were accompanied by an acknowledgement that Korean society at that time did not provide women with a favourable environment in which to achieve these goals. But they were advised not to give up, and to at least strive to achieve both financial and spiritual independence.

By 1925, *Shin Yosong* was advocating absolute equality for women, and their education was thus perceived as a necessity. However, this educational agenda aimed at creating 'new women' and was therefore different from the earlier ideal. The Enlightenment period stressed only the necessity for women to educate the next generation. But by the 1920s, it was understood that women themselves should contribute to society, and their social participation was viewed much more favourably. This perspective became the basis of the concept of the 'new morality'.

In addition, the Western model of the nuclear family became idealized during the 1920s, and intellectuals criticized the traditional arranged marriage system as barbaric and inhumane. They wanted to liberate Korean women, stressing that the foremost condition for marriage should be love, and romantic love and marriage based upon love received eager endorsements. In 1924, *Shin Yosong* stated that: 'For human beings, marriage is not just for procreation. Marriage makes life beautiful and sacred; it satisfies the spiritual desires of people. And the indispensable element for a great marriage is love. Then what is love?'. The author then quotes Ellen Key: ' "Love cannot be defined solely by body or spirit. Love is the elegant unity of mind and body. Sensation should not oppress the spirit; the spirit should not expel the sensation. True love exists only when body and spirit are combined" '.[9]

Feminists thus audaciously challenged the traditional conventions of marriage and morality, arguing that as long as there was love, any kind of relationship was moral. For them, even a legal marriage was considered as immoral if love did not exist between a husband and a wife. According to the new morality, marriage was defined as true love – the unity of mind and body – and such a marriage was considered sacred regardless of its legal status.

Challenges were also made to the traditional female virtues of virginity and absolute chastity, and feminists argued that chastity was merely a tool of a patriarchal social order to suppress and control women.

> Chastity was applied only to women, who were forced to follow this rule, even to the extreme of forfeiting their lives for violating it. Men, who are the beneficiaries of this system, can believe and easily claim that 'chastity is the essence of a good woman', yet it is truly both degrading and ironic that women should believe in this myth. It is only a coerced moral concept, and should not be considered to be an obligation. It is a sick ideology that was only established by men with power to monopolize women's minds and bodies.[10]

The feminists thus suggested a new concept of chastity, as a relative concept, a chastity that could be renewed over and over with new lovers.

Along with this radical view on gender equality, feminists also recommended a new, progressive type of marriage. They argued that both husband and wife should continue to work after marriage, property should be equally divided between the husband and wife, and that women should be financially independent, and have the right to divorce. Henrik Ibsen's play *A Doll's House* and the works of Ellen Key were frequently quoted. Kim Maria's poem succinctly represents the spirit of feminism that prevailed in the 1920s:

Come out, Friends!

The darkness is alive.
Even for us, who are lost in the dark,
The darkness is alive.
Friends, get up, and come out
This is not the time to be in a dark room.
Nor is this the time to agonize over traditions.
Look, isn't the road visible?
Do not hesitate and come out.

Out of your beautiful silk dress,
Out of the tide of your vanity
Out of your high, arrogant tower,

Friends, come out.

Can't you hear?
The weak voices of hunger, echoing in the dark.
Wake up from your idle dream,
Throw away your vanity.
Friends, come out fast,
Hasn't the time already come?[11]

In contrast to these feminists, there were also conservative groups of 'new women', though their influence was much weaker. They cherished the traditional domestic role of women and the charm of the old feminine role. What they wanted was equal status for women at home, and they continued to stress women's education as preparing them to be good 'educating mothers'.

In the late 1920s, strong reaction set in against the progressive 'new women' agenda in conservative Korean intellectual circles and among the older generation who advocated the Confucian social order. In addition to the practical difficulties of getting education and finding employment, marriage was the biggest problem for the 'new woman'. Those who graduated from the high schools had nowhere to go; changes in the social structure and labour markets were not fast enough to include all these highly educated women. These 'new women' had to face the gap between their ideals and hard social realities, yet even achieving compromises could he difficult.

Due to the traditional custom of child marriage, most of the educated men whom 'new women' wished to marry already had wives and children. This lack of eligible men, combined with the radical perspective of 'new women' on chastity and morality, encouraged most 'new women' to became mistresses or 'second wives'. Combined with an extraordinary growth in the divorce rate over a very short time, this trend elicited severe criticisms against the 'new women' and the leaders of feminist opinion. Even the term 'new woman' began to acquire the connotation of promiscuity, or of being a high-class call girl. The term 'modern girl' replaced 'new woman', and intellectual women no longer wanted to be categorized as the latter. Instead they began to designate themselves as *intelli yosong* ('intelligent' or 'intellectual' women). By the late 1920s, the term 'new woman' was regarded as disgraceful. Thus, during the decade of Japanese reform, the Korean view of culturally progressive women underwent a dramatic change.

The emphasis on the self that was promoted for women during the decade of Japanese reform did not sit well with nationalists, who called upon all Koreans – and especially women – to devote themselves to maintaining Korean culture and identity in the face of Japanese oppression. For women, this meant a return to the emphasis on selfless motherhood, this time in the service of the nation, and it was directly related to actions taken by the Japanese colonial authorities. By the early 1930s, Japan's military had expanded its influence, both at home and abroad. Japan renewed its imperial interests in Manchuria, setting up the puppet state of Manchukuo in 1931. Korea was its strategic stepping-stone, and was integrated into Japan's plan for dominating Northeast Asia, with a greater mobilization of Koreans to support its political and military goals. This change brought about the end of the Cultural Policy in Korea. In 1931, the new governor-general Ugaki Kazushige devised a more stringent policy to wipe out Korean cultural autonomy and to carry out a more rapid cultural, historical and political assimilation of the Korean people into the Japanese empire. A new education policy in 1934 enforced the intensified teaching of Japanese language, history and ethics, as well as demanding a compulsory pledge of allegiance from all imperial subjects; the Korean language was prohibited. After 1937, all Korean organizations were disbanded and Japanese colonial policy henceforth specifically focused on tightening control over the social and cultural aspects of Korean society. The Japanese attempted to force Koreans to become loyal, obedient imperial subjects, with an intensive mobilization of both people and economic resources to serve Japanese colonial interests.

These developments provided the basis for a dramatic change in Korea's domestic atmosphere, which in turn strongly affected the ideals of the image of Korean women. The changes in colonial policy, especially those aimed at erasing Korean culture and national identity and assimilating Koreans under Japanese subordination, created an enormous sense of national crisis among Korea's nationalist leaders and people. They were now confronted with a historic juncture in the face of the imminent obliteration of their unique national identity and cultural heritage. This crisis superseded all other issues, including the feminist discussions and leftist activities that had prevailed in the 1920s. Thus to show concern for women's status or feminist issues was regarded as extremely selfish, unpatriotic and anti-nationalistic.

This social reaction created an alternative image of the ideal woman; instead of the 1920s' progressive image of the 'new woman', from the early 1930s a new conservative idealization of women as mothers began to emerge. By the mid-1930s, this new ideal of 'glorified motherhood' had become firmly established. The very same authors who had promoted the ideal of female individuality in the 1920s were now praising the virtues of motherhood. Now the highest, most beautiful goal for women was to become good mothers so that they could give their love and soul to the next generation:

The most wonderful goal for a woman lies in becoming a good mother. By becoming a mother, she transmits the long cherished love and the beauty of her deepest heart, of her soul, to a new generation. Let's devote all of our lives and beings to our children. After all, the highest goal and ideal for a woman is to give her love and soul to the next generation. For a woman, the very reason to live in this world is to become a good mother.[12]

Practically every issue of *Shin Yosong* and *Shin Kajong* (*New Home*) was flooded with poems, essays, short stories and articles that praised 'motherly love', which was typically characterized by selfless sacrifice and the endless devotion of women to their children. 'My mother', 'A letter to my mother', 'Thinking about my mother', 'At my mother's grave', 'A song for my mother', 'Missing my mother', are typical examples of these contributions. Good mothers were those who dreamed of their children's beautiful future, wove the clothes of hope for their children, and endured the endless pain of sacrificing everything they had for their children.

This 'sacred motherhood' was justified and supported by nationalism, since the nation's urgent political crisis called for sacrifice. Many Koreans considered it inappropriate to waste time arguing for the rights and status of women, when the fate of the whole nation was at stake. In her article, 'Choson [Korea] needs mothers like this', Whang Shin-tuk asserted that Korea needed mothers who could raise tomorrow's nation-builders and transform today's misery into a prosperous future.

What, then, were the virtues such mothers should have? Whang Shin-tuk specifically set out the following four qualities. First, mothers should be determined to carry out what they believe in; they needed to have a critical understanding of rapidly changing social issues, and the strength of will to put their ideas into practice. Second, mothers should be progressive and keep up with social changes so that they could raise informed, strong children to become tomorrow's heroes. Korean mothers should be able to discard corrupt customs and conventions and construct new ones to build a better Korea. Third, mothers should keenly understand Korea's current situation, since this was the environment in which their children would grow up. Mothers should thus know in what direction Korea needed to go, and accordingly influence their children so that they could also help to change that environment as they matured. Finally, mothers should sacrifice themselves, discard self-centred vanity, and educate themselves to contribute to the well-being of the country. After all, the future of Korea rested upon the mothers' shoulders, since each and every baby would become one of tomorrow's nation-builders.

Mothers were said to be the flowers and the stars of the nation; the ones who should give their children the true soul of Korea; and they should thus bear the burden of serving their country. Raising children at home was therefore considered the supreme nationalist virtue for women:

> The most important thing for a nation is to have the next generation
> To hear and raise sons and daughters
> Nothing can he compared to mothers' pain, endurance and love
> ...
> Mother's love is endless love
> Do you have appreciation?
> Dedicate it all to your mother
> Do you have words of praise?
> Present it all to your mother
> Those who gave us our flesh and blood
> Love, sacrifice, endurance, diligence
> Mothers gave all these to us
> They are our mothers
> Our sacred mothers
> They are also mothers of our nation.[13]

In addition to these neo-conservative ideals of motherhood, women were expected to be good wives. The image of equal companionship in marriage in the 1920s was replaced by that of a housewife who likes to clean and decorate her home, and who always smiles at and perfectly understands her husband. Having a job or being financially independent was no longer encouraged for married women. A wife was supposed to be the source of strength for her husband, her family and the nation, and was even described as 'an angel with an apron'.

The material analysed in this study shows that ideal images of woman in Korea went though radical changes between the 1890s and the 1930s. The image of 'educating mothers' in the Enlightenment period before 1910 was an enormous break from the traditional image of the 'procreating mother'. Yet the image of the 'educating mother' was superseded by the 'new woman' of the 1920s, whose foremost goal was to find and express her individuality. Nationalistic reaction to the changed colonial environment in the 1930s, however, brushed away all such feminist issues, and instead constructed a new ideal of women as strong mothers keenly aware of the political situation of the nation, who would raise the next generation accordingly. By the mid-1930s, this new image of motherhood was firmly established for Korean women; mothers were supposed to sacrifice themselves for their children and for the nation. They would raise the enlightened next generation, which was the only hope for Korean society to reclaim its national autonomy.

The colonial threat to the national identity thus eclipsed the calls for Korean women to define and develop a feminist agenda, since the national interest always came first. As Bonnie Oh (1982) indicates, feminism and the women's movement in Korea 'did not arise from a crisis of *conscience* which sought to rectify a basic inequity within a society, but from a response to the external threat, and sought to ensure national survival'.[14]

These two opposing ideologies, colonialism and nationalism, thus shaped social, political and cultural conditions that constructed and imposed ideal images of women that shifted according to society's changing needs. The 'educating mothers' ideal in the Enlightenment period was superseded by the 'new woman' of the 1920s, which finally gave way to the 'selfless motherhood' ideal of the 1930s. Ironically, both the colonialist and nationalist ideologies, though for different reasons, seemed to direct the image of women toward the 1930s' 'selfless motherhood' ideal. By the mid-1930s, this latter image of motherhood was firmly established and strongly promoted to Korean women by nationalistic leaders as well as by the Japanese colonial government. The motherhood image was also approved by conservative circles in Korean society. However, if colonialism regulated and affected societal factors that limited the possible path of women's self-image, the subtle content of the image was more strongly influenced by nationalism. The 1930s' motherhood ideal was on the surface agreeable to the colonial government, who were attempting to make docile and submissive subjects out of Koreans; yet in reality, this constructed image of motherhood embraced a strong, covertly patriotic spirit.

The image of 'selfless motherhood' became the basis of today's ideal of Korean motherhood. By considering these transitions of the idealized image of Korean women, we can confirm Ueno Chizuko's conclusion that 'Motherhood is neither nature nor culture. It is a historical product, subject to historical change'.[15]

Notes

1 Jiweon Shin (2002) 'Social construction of idealized images of women in colonial Korea: the "new woman" versus "motherhood"', in Tamara L. Hunt and Micheline R. Lessard (eds) *Women and the Colonial Gaze*, New York: New York University Press, 162–73.
2 Chizuko Ueno (1996) 'Collapse of "Japanese mothers"', *US-Japan Women's Journal*, English supplement no. 10: 3–5. Masami Ohinata (1995) 'The mystique of motherhood', in Kumiko Fujimura-Fanselow and Atsuko Kameda (eds) *Japanese Women*, New York: The Feminist Press, 205.
3 Edward Shorter (1975) *The Making of the Modern Family*, New York: Basic Books, 168.
4 Editorial, *Tongnip Shinmun (The Independent)*, 21 April 1896, cited in Bonnie Oh (1982) 'From Three Obediences to patriotism and nationalism', *Korea Journal* 22(7): 42–3.
5 *Kajong Chapji* (1906) 1(3).
6 *Kajong Chapji* (1906) 1(4).

7 Carter J. Eckert *et al.* (1990) *Korea Old and New: A History*, Seoul: Ilchokak Publishers.
8 Myung-ho Kim (1926) 'Directions for modern women', *Shin Yosong*, July, 17–18.
9 'Three conditions of marriage', *Shin Yosong*, May 1924, 15–16.
10 'The streams of the feminist movement', *Shin Yosong*, February 1925, 7.
11 Kim Maria, 'Come out, friends!', *Shin Kajong*, April 1933.
12 Cha-young Noh, 'Maternal love and eternal stars', *Shin Kajong*, March 1934, 127.
13 Kwang-su Lee, 'Mother', *Shin Kajong*, April 1933, 155.
14 Oh 1982: 37–55.
15 Ueno 1996: 18.

References and further reading

Choi, Sook-Kyung (1986) 'The formation of women's movement in Korea: from the Enlightenment period to 1910', in *Challenges for Women*, Seoul: Ewha Women's University Press.

Cumings, Bruce (1984) 'The legacy of Japanese colonialism in Korea', in Ramon H. Meyers and Mark R. Peattie (eds) *The Japanese Colonial Empire, 1895–1945*, Princeton: Princeton University Press, 478–96.

Eckert, Carter J., Ki-Baik Lee and Michael Robinson (1990) *Korea Old and New: A History*, Seoul: Ilchokak Publishers.

Gelb, Joyce, and Mirian L. Palley (1994) *Women of Japan and Korea: Continuity and Change*, Philadelphia: Temple University Press.

Kendall, Laurel (ed.) (2002) *Under Construction: The Gendering of Modernity, Class, and Consumption in the Republic of Korea*, Honolulu: University of Hawaii Press.

Kendall, Laurel and Mark Peterson (eds) (1983) *Korean Women: View from the Inner Room*, New Haven: East Rock Press.

Kim, Elaine H. and Chungmoo Choi (eds) (1998) *Dangerous Women: Gender and Korean Nationalism*, New York: Routledge.

Kim, Yung-chung (ed.) (1976) *Women of Korea: A History from Ancient Times to 1945*, Seoul: Ewha Women's University Press.

Oh, Bonnie B. (1982) 'From Three Obediences to patriotism and nationalism', *Korea Journal* 22(7): 37–55.

Shin, Gi-Wook and Michael Robinson (eds) (1999) *Colonial Modernity in Korea*, Cambridge MA: Harvard University Press.

Shin, Jiweon and Muta, Kazue (1998) 'The "new women" and the creation of modern sexuality: a comparative analysis', *Shiso* no. 886: 89–115.

Ueno, Chizuko (1996) 'Collapse of "Japanese mothers"', *US-Japan Women's Journal*, English supplement no. 10: 3–19.

Yoshiaki, Yoshimi (1995) *Comfort Women: Sexual Slavery in the Japanese Military During World War II*, New York: Columbia University Press.

18

NATIONAL DIVISIONS IN INDOCHINA'S DECOLONIZATION

Stein Tønnesson

Introduction

'Decolonization' can be defined as the process by which a subordinated territory becomes a sovereign and independent state. For a territory to be successfully decolonized, four essential conditions must be met: a government must be created locally which can act on behalf of the whole population; the colonial power must transfer its sovereignty formally and in practice to this government; the local government and the colonial power must agree on the extension of the new national territory; and finally, the new state must receive international recognition and membership of the United Nations.

If the above definition is applied, then Indochina's decolonization, which started in 1945, was not complete until 1975–6, when the 'Vietnam War' ended in the creation of three communist regimes, each represented in the United Nations. An international conference in Geneva in 1954 had affirmed the national sovereignty of French Indochina's three successor states – Vietnam, Cambodia and Laos – but their territories continued to be contested by rival regimes and armed movements, and some local governments reverted to foreign domination. Indochina's decolonization is therefore best seen as a process lasting from 1945 to 1976.

The two most obvious reasons for the drawn-out and conflictual character of Indochina's decolonization are, first, that France clung more firmly to its empire than the other colonial powers in Southeast Asia; and second, that the United States decided to support France and its local collaborators in Vietnam rather than the Viet Minh, the leading nationalist force, and eventually took over the French role in trying to repress the Indochinese revolution. This essay does not purport to refute these explanations, but argues that they are insufficient. An additional explanation will be sought in the inability of the Indochinese elites, in particular the Vietnamese, to establish a minimum of national consensus concerning institutions, territory and international alignment.

The essay will discuss how basic questions of national profile and identity were left unresolved through the various phases of Indochina's decolonization, how the local elites failed to establish national unity, how they fought each other, and how some of them continued to invite foreign domination. The main characteristic of Indochina's decolonization is no doubt its extreme degree of violence. This cannot be blamed solely on the policies of France and the USA. The two imperial powers could act as they did because there were groups within the Indochinese nations who were willing – even eager – to collaborate. Inside the 'long wars of resistance' against French colonialism and US imperialism there were civil wars between Vietnamese, Cambodian and Laotian groups, sects and regimes.

First, the main phases in the process should be summarized. It started in March 1945, when Japan detached Indochina from French colonial rule and encouraged the monarchs in Hue, Phnom Penh and Luang Phrabãng to proclaim their independence. Next, there were local revolts in the aftermath of the Japanese capitulation of August 1945, leading to the establishment of new governments. The return of French forces in late 1945 led to a drawn-out guerrilla war. France then initiated a controlled, gradual transfer of power to new collaborator regimes. By January-February 1950, Vietnam, Laos and Cambodia had gained international recognition, but it took until 1953–4 before they were given the normal attributions of independent states. The next twenty years, which encompass the 'Vietnam War' (1959–75), was characterized by the territorial division of Vietnam, and the internationalization of a civil war in South Vietnam.

This civil war had started already during the war against France. While France had negotiated the terms of decolonization with its collaborators in Viang Chan (Vientiane), Phnom Penh and Saigon, a broad communist-led national movement (the Viet Minh) had waged a 'war of national resistance' in defence of the Democratic Republic of Vietnam (DRV), which had been created in 1945. Because of solid local support, and because the Viet Minh was able to capture or assassinate many collaborating village leaders, the DRV retained control of most of the countryside and prevented the establishment of an effective French-sponsored regime. In Laos and Cambodia, the traditional monarchies enjoyed more popular support, so the French were able to manage a more convincing controlled decolonization.

In 1953, Cambodia gained full independence. Laos became independent at the same time, but by contrast to Cambodia it remained a member of the French Union, a new 'voluntary association' of former French colonies. An international conference in Geneva 1954 agreed on the terms for an armistice between the belligerent forces in Indochina, and declared that this should 'allow Cambodia, Laos and Vietnam to exercise henceforth, in full independence and sovereignty, their role in the pacific community of nations'. Peace would be instituted on the basis of 'respect for the independence and sovereignty, unity and territorial integrity of Cambodia, Laos and Vietnam'. Vietnam, however, was temporarily divided in North and South Vietnam, under separate, hostile regimes. Cambodia and Laos gained membership of the United Nations in 1954, but Vietnam had to wait till 1976, after South Vietnam had been defeated by North Vietnam and its southern allies in the Vietnam War. Laos and Cambodia were dragged into the war, and were also split between anti-communist governments and communist-led guerrilla movements. After the communist takeover of all three Indochinese states in 1975–6, a new Socialist Republic of Vietnam strove to establish a special, almost colonial-type, relationship with similar regimes in Laos and Cambodia.

Background: inside Indochina

The term 'Indochina' has two meanings. At first it was a European name for the lands between India and China, a space now commonly referred to as 'continental Southeast Asia' (Burma, Thailand, Laos, Cambodia and Vietnam). In the second half of the nineteenth century, after 'Indochina' had gained currency as a geographic notion, France colonized its eastern part. This became 'French Indochina', meaning 'the French part of Indochina' as opposed to the British and Siamese parts. Later, the term 'Indochina' became synonymous with 'French Indochina'. Thailand and Burma were rarely referred to as Indochinese, and in the 1940s became part of a region called 'Southeast Asia'. This essay uses 'Indochina' in the conventional way, as encompassing the territories of today's Vietnam, Laos and Cambodia.

However, French Indochina did not consist of three, but five territories, which had been colonized at different times: Cochinchina (1862), Cambodia (1867), Annam and Tonkin (1884) and Laos (1893). Before colonization there were a number of princely states in the area with loosely defined borders. By far the largest and most powerful was Dai Nam (Great South), also sometimes called Dai Viet (Great Viet), Viet Nam (Viet South) or An Nam (Peaceful South), which since 1802 had been ruled by the Nguyen dynasty from the imperial city of Hue.

The pattern of French colonization in the second half of the nineteenth century forms the background for the painful questions that the three main ethnic groups in Indochina (Viet, Khmer and Lao), as well as a range of smaller ethnic groups, had to struggle with for the next hundred years.[1] The Cambodian state and the several principalities that existed in today's Laos were weak and easily subdued by the French, and some of the local elites saw French protection as preferable to domination by

Siam or Dai Nam (Vietnam). Soon, however, the Khmer would discover that the French were more intrusive than the Thai or Viet had ever been. For the French it was not enough to gain tribute from the local princes. They set out to educate, employ and tax the locals. The French also stimulated Viet immigration into Cambodia and Laos, since the Viet were found to be more efficient traders, troops and civil servants than the Khmer and Lao. Thus under French auspices, Laos and Cambodia were drawn away from Siam while receiving a steady stream of Viet, and also Chinese, immigration.

France did not administer the five colonies independently, but as subunits of an Indochinese Union, which was created in 1897 with Hanoi as capital. This meant that the former lands of Dai Nam, although all primarily populated by ethnic Viet, were partioned in three. The Khmer were also divided into a majority population in Cambodia and a minority population in Cochinchina. On their part, the Lao living east of the Mekong were separated from their brethren on the west bank, who were gradually assimilated in Thailand. The French administered the east bank Lao, together with the highland populations to their east and north, in a new unit called 'Laos', the French plural of the ethnic term 'Lao'. Out of Indochina's five territories the French set out to create a modern colonial state, using forced labour to construct roads, railroads and ports. Telegraph lines were laid out, new schools and prisons built. The governor-general of the Indochinese Union did his best to make the colony economically viable by extracting taxes on salt, alcohol and opium, and encouraging exports of rice and rubber.

In the French-directed Indochinese Union the local governments, while being deprived of their independence, gained increasing power over the inhabitants. There had always been tension between the villages and government officials. Both the French and the city-based local elites saw the village elders as backward, attached as they were to local customs and autonomy. A kind of triangular relationship emerged between tradition-bound village authorities and courtly officials, the new educated classes in the cities, and the French colonial regime. The French would sometimes support the local conservatives as a way to obtain peasant loyalty, while on other occasions encouraging the younger modernizers. Cochinchina, by contrast to the protectorates of Annam, Tonkin, Cambodia and the Lao principalities, was a directly ruled French colony with legal status as French territory. It developed a vibrant commercial life and a highly unequal distribution of land, and rapidly became a hotbed of new religious and political sects and parties. The protectorates remained more closely attached to indigenous traditions.

The formation of French Indochina created new conditions for identity formation. The superior energy of an impatient and arrogant France impressed, inspired and humiliated the locals, and instilled in them a sense of shame, mixed with hopes of a new beginning. From the setup of the Indochinese Union in 1897 to the Greater East Asian War of 1937–45, Indochina remained firmly under French control. After the failure of the anti-colonial struggles in the 1880s and 1890s, the most independent-minded mandarins sought refuge in scholarship or low-level administrative posts. Their offspring would often become leading revolutionaries. Around 1900 a Darwinian-inspired sense of inferiority held ground among intellectuals. The white race had reached a superior stage, and Asians would have to go through a process of regeneration in order to catch up. Japan's victory over Russia in 1905 and the European war of 1914–18 provoked the first changes of attitude. The 'superior' whites were beaten both by Japan and by each other, and they cynically exploited their colonies instead of living up to promises of local development. Close to 100,000 Indochinese were shipped to France to serve, together with Africans, as factory workers or cannon fodder in the European war, and in Indochina the heavily taxed opium trade became the favoured method of funding the colonial administration. This stimulated revolts and the founding of secret societies. In the 1920s and 1930s two new religious sects were formed in Cochinchina, the syncretic Cao Dai and the Buddhist Hoa Hao, and also a number of nationalist parties. A basic conflict emerged between those who sought national emancipation through collaboration with France and those who organized clandestine networks in preparation for a chance to revolt. In 1930, in connection with the disastrous social effects of the world depression, there were new revolts, this time under the leadership of nationalists and communists with modern doctrines and organizational skills acquired through participation in international revolutionary networks. However, the revolts were violently repressed. The same repeated itself in 1940, when the communists in Cochinchina and a Japan-inspired nationalist group in Tonkin each tried to carry out an insurrection and were severely repressed. Even in the 1941–4 period, when the French Vichy government allowed Japan to occupy Indochina militarily and exploit it economically, the French colonial government continued to control the local populations and repress local nationalism, including some pro-Japanese groups.

The division of Indochina into five constitutive parts had a great impact on local politics. As inhabitants of a directly administered French territory, the Cochinchinese enjoyed the greatest intellectual and political freedoms; a small minority were even allowed to hold elections for representative institutions. A Constitutional Party emerged, but the French neither repressed it nor bowed to its demands. Thus it gained neither success nor martyrdom and hence no widespread following. Hue remained the centre of Viet court politics. The French lost an opportunity to open a path to decolonization here when the young emperor Bao Dai took up his reign in 1932. He formed a reform cabinet and tried to carry out new policies, but the local French advisors would not give up their prerogatives. Bao Dai's new minister of the interior, the young Catholic Ngo Dinh Diem, resigned in protest, and the emperor withdrew to an indolent life. Hanoi, the capital of Tonkin (and the Indochina Union), held an intermediate position between cosmopolitan Saigon and traditional Hue. Tonkin was a separate protectorate, under the nominal rule of an imperial delegate representing the Hue-based emperor. In practice both Tonkin and Annam were governed by a French 'superior resident', but the cities Hanoi, Haiphong, Tourane (Da Nang) and Vientiane (Viang Chan) had a separate status. Hanoi was close to China, and it was here that the French built Indochina's only university.

Luang Phrabāng and Phnom Penh remained centres of traditional courtly politics, quite like Hue, while Viang Chan, the administrative capital of Laos, became a city dominated by Viet officials and Chinese shopkeepers. Some of the poorest peripheral provinces of Annam and Tonkin, and also the area around the Mekong Delta, became hotbeds of communism. Nghe An province in northern Annam produced an . impressive number of communist leaders. Saigon had a plethora of parties, and the Cochinchinese countryside was divided into regions dominated by either the Cao Dai or Hoa Hao religious sects, or communist groups.

The French colonial regime played an equivocal role as far as national emancipation was concerned. On the one hand, the schools and media encouraged an overarching Indochinese identity, which was eagerly embraced by Viet immigrants in Laos and Cambodia. The French tried to knit Indochina together through communication networks, shared administrative services, and an all-Indochinese indigenous advisory council. On the other hand, the French also encouraged separate identities for each of Indochina's constituent parts. In Cambodia, Annam and the kingdom of Luang Phrabāng, the local monarchs became the focal points of French-sponsored local traditionalism, while Cochinchina and to a lesser extent Tonkin developed a cosmopolitan or 'modern' culture. In the protected monarchies, the idea was to gradually develop autonomous nationhood, under French tutorship. Meanwhile in Cochinchina, and also the towns with a separate status, some members of the local elite were granted French citizenship. Together with the French *colons* (local residents) they elected their own representatives to the French National Assembly. The French *colons* however, were jealous of their racial prerogatives. The more farsighted reformers among the colonial administrators had to fight against the petty interests and ingrained racism of the *colons* and government officials, and were never able to stimulate the emergence of a moderate indigenous nationalism of the Indian Congress kind.

Indochinese nationalists often disagreed among themselves, or were uncertain, as to the territorial extent of their nation and its ethnic scope. Some dreamed of an independent all-Indochinese Republic, to be liberated not only from France but also from old habits and kings. This was the vision of modernists in Cochinchina, of ethnic Viet officials serving the colonial administration in Laos and Cambodia, and of activists learning socialist doctrines abroad. For internationally minded communists it was natural to adopt an all-Indochinese rather than a narrow ethno-national approach. In the beginning, however, there was much confusion within the communist movement. Among the first organized groups, one adopted 'Indochina' in its name, another 'An Nam' and a third 'Viet Nam'. In 1930, on the instructions of the Comintern, the name became 'Indochinese Communist Party' (ICP). The ICP soon became a strong political force among the Viet, and also to some extent the Chinese minorities (Hoa) in all parts of Indochina. It recruited very few members among the Lao and Khmer.

Several nationalist leaders had a strong feeling for history, and wanted to link up with traditions from the former Lao kingdom of Lan Xang, the Khmer kingdom of Angkor and the ancient Viet dynasties. The debates about the extension and character of nationhood had not been resolved by 1937, when Japan initiated its war with China, in pursuit of a Greater Asia. Some Indochinese groups, such as the Cao Dai and Hoa Hao sects, and also some political parties, would sympathize with Japan, as an example of a vigorous Asian nation, while the Viet Nam Quoc Can Dang (VNQDD) – a party inspired by the Chinese Guomindang – and the communists sided with China against Japan. All of them hoped, although in different ways, that the war in Asia would give them a chance to liberate themselves from France.

A veteran communist leader, who had left Indochina as a young man in 1911 and become one of the Comintern's main organizers in Asia, travelled from Moscow to southern China in 1938. He crossed into Indochinese territory in 1941, shortly after the French had quelled the communist insurrection in Cochinchina, and around this time started to use the pseudonym Ho Chi Minh. Until 1940, the ICP leadership had been based in Cochinchina. Now a new clandestine leadership was established in Tonkin, and guerrilla groups were formed in the border region to China. In this period, when anti-fascists everywhere were utilizing nationalist symbols, Ho Chi Minh skilfully grafted international communism onto a nationalist historiography of Viet struggles against foreign oppression, and organized a formula for national insurrection. The key term in his formula was not 'Indochina' (Dong Duong), but 'Viet Nam'. By using 'Viet Nam' in the name for a new league of national liberation, 'Viet Nam Doc Lap Dong Minh' (Viet Minh), Ho Chi Minh was able to ground his movement in a nationalist version of Viet history.

He also moved closer to the VNQDD and gained support from Chiang Kai-shek's Chinese government, who remained in control of the Indochinese border. The Viet Minh established itself with a secret head-quarters in a cave just inside Tonkin. Here, leaflets and clandestine newspapers were produced and sent southwards. In 1942, Ho Chi Minh wrote the first version of his long poem *Lich su nuoc ta* ('Our history') which – at least in its later editions – ended with the prediction of a national revolution in 1945.

Breaking out

During the period of Japanese occupation, the dilemma of collaboration or revolt presented itself in a new way. There were now two collabora-tive options: France and Japan. The monarchs and their courts in Hue, Phnom Penh and Luang Phrabāng remained under French protection until March 1945, and with basis in the authoritarian conservatism of the Vichy regime, which collaborated with Germany, the French did their best to enhance the authority of the monarchs over their populations. After the Japanese coup of March 1945, which eliminated the French colonial regime, the Emperor of Annam and the King of Cambodia swiftly shifted sides, proclaimed themselves independent from France, and let Japan take over as protecting power. The King of Luang Phrabāng was less eager to join up with Japan, and later received much praise from France for his loyalty.

There were three parties who considered both Japan and France as enemies: the pro-Chinese VNQDD and Dong Minh Hoi, and the communist ICP. All of them operated from sanctuaries in Guomindang-controlled China. Under the Viet Minh formula, and by establishing an alliance with the other two parties, the communists were able to build a highly effective organization in northern Indochina, and to obtain assis-tance from Chiang Kai-shek and also US and British agencies. After the March 1945 coup, the Japanese released most political prisoners from the French jails, thus providing the Viet Minh with highly dedicated orga-nizers who spread out and established revolutionary cells. Meanwhile, Emperor Bao Dai and his new national government were unable to do anything effective to prevent a famine in north central Vietnam, which cost the lives of up to a million people. Ho Chi Minh, who now moved down from the hills to be closer to the Red River Delta, planned to carry out a national insurrection in convergence with an Allied invasion of Indochina, and fight alongside the Allies against Japan in the same way as the French communists had done in France. The invasion never came, but when the Japanese surrender was announced in August 1945, Vietnam had its 'August Revolution'. Local groups seized power in all the main towns of Cochinchina, Annam and Tonkin. Revolutionary governments were established in Hanoi and Saigon. Ho Chi Minh moved into Hanoi and became leader of a provisional government. The government that Japan had installed in Hue resigned. Emperor Bao Dai abdicated and was driven in a car to Hanoi together with the young Laotian Prince Suphānuvong, who at that time worked in Vietnam. By the time they arrived in Hanoi, Ho Chi Minh had proclaimed the independent Democratic Republic of Vietnam (DRV) on 2 September. Bao Dai was invited to serve as Supreme Advisor to the republican government, and Suphānuvong and Ho Chi Minh formed a life-long friendship.

Ho Chi Minh and Suphānuvong agreed that the new Democratic Republic should encompass only the three Viet lands, and that Laos should be considered a nation of its own, which would have its own revolution. Whereas the Viet Minh had strong appeal in all of the three Viet lands, it did not arouse much enthusiasm in Laos and Cambodia, except among the local Viet minorities. In Vietnam the pro-Japanese parties had been sidelined, but in Cambodia and Laos the formerly pro-Japanese leaders Son Ngoc Thanh and Phetxarāt retained the initiative in anti-colonial politics. There was no August Revolution in Laos and Cambodia. The difference between the political trajectories of the three main ethnic groups in Indochina forms the background for Ho Chi Minh and Suphānuvong's decision to consider Vietnam and Laos (and by implication Cambodia) as separate nations, although all three would need to cooperate in preventing the return of French colonialism.

By early September 1945, all three Indochinese countries had new independent governments, but none of these had been internationally recognized. In Laos, a small French military force had survived during the whole of the Japanese period, and was now able to reinforce French power in some of the cities. It could build on the pro-French attitudes of the King. The French troops in the other Indochinese countries had been disarmed, and continued to be held in Japanese captivity, while the troops who had fled to China when they came under Japanese attack in March, now lived under precarious conditions with no means of returning either to a hostile Tonkin or a mountainous Laos. The Allies had, moreover, decided to give Chiang Kai-shek's China the responsibility for occupying northern Indochina and disarming the Japanese troops there. In the South, the Allies had charged Britain with the same task. The British rearmed the French prisoners-of-war and helped de Gaulle to send some of his best divisions to reoccupy southern Indochina. Thus the populations in Cochinchina, south Annam, southern Laos and Cambodia would have to face French reconquest much earlier than those in the north, who instead had to endure the presence of a large Chinese occupation force.

Being divided

Only two to three years after the successful and immensely popular revolutionary breakout from French Indochina, the Vietnamese nation allowed itself to be divided in two hostile camps, one betraying the Democratic Republic and entering a French-directed effort towards gradual decolonization, the other aligning itself with communist China and the Soviet Union. The division of the Vietnamese nation dragged the whole of Indochina into a process of civil war and foreign intervention, and led the Laotian and Cambodian nations to also be divided.

The split among the Viet was based on opposite answers to a tortuous question: collaborate or resist? In the beginning there was a general will to resist, almost a national consensus, but the propertied classes, much of the urban population, some of the highland ethnic minorities, the Catholics, Cao Dai and Hoa Hao after a few years ceased to support the communists. They either went into passivity or sought an arrangement with France. Nevertheless, the Viet Minh was able to retain an alliance between a tightly knit group of dedicated intellectuals, some of the highland ethnic minorities and, notably, a great number of peasant leaders with strong village-based political support. In Cambodia and Laos, the resistance forces (Khmer Issarak and Lao Issara) were weaker, so the French could recruit new government officials and reconstitute a viable state. Most Khmer and Lao accepted or passively tolerated their government's collaboration with France. Thus the French were satisfied to see a 'return to normality'. In Cambodia the French had arrested prime minister Son Ngoc Thanh on 12 October 1945, without meeting serious resistance.

Laos developed its own national polity, in a tense relationship with France, and with mostly non-violent internal power struggles. A process of gradual decolonization was on its way. Once having re-established control of the two countries, France was eager to honour the loyalty of the local populations by offering them autonomy and democratic institutions. Cambodia and Laos could then be held out as examples of the generosity and farsightedness of the new France. *Modus vivendi* agreements were signed with Cambodia in January and with Laos in August 1946, and institutional reforms, including the adoption of constitutions, were announced. Multi-party elections were held in both countries from 1947 onward, but the electorates disappointed France by tending to prefer the most impatient nationalist parties.

Until the 1950s the populations of Cambodia and Laos were not engaged in internal warfare. Political opponents were not in the habit of killing each other. The national divisions in Indochina had their origin in Vietnam. By January 1946, British and French forces had crushed all open resistance in Cochinchina, but the communists and other nationalists in

Cochinchina and south Annam reorganized to form a guerrilla army, harassing the French occupation forces and intimidating or assassinating the most notorious collaborators. In the north, the Chinese occupants tolerated Ho Chi Minh's national government, which claimed to represent all three Vietnamese 'regions': *Bac bo* (northern region; Tonkin), *Trung bo* (central region; Annam) and *Nam bo* (southern region; Cochinchina). For Ho Chi Minh's government, and for all Vietnamese nationalists across the political spectrum, the three regions constituted an indivisible 'Vietnam'.

The Chinese were not the only ones to tolerate Ho Chi Minh's government. Chiang Kai-shek also obliged the French, through astute tactics, to enter an agreement with Ho Chi Minh. On 28 February 1946, a Sino-French agreement was signed whereby France gave up all of its special treaty rights in China. In return, China agreed to withdraw its troops from northern Indochina, and also to facilitate French reoccupation. A huge French invasion force sailed north from the ports of southern Indochina in order to land in the port city of Haiphong. The French made ready to seize Hanoi by force, and to pacify northern Indochina in the same way they had done in the south. However, the Chinese troops were still in place. Their commanders, no doubt operating on Chiang Kai-shek's orders, refused to stand idly by while France took Tonkin by force. Instead the Chinese put pressure on the French and Ho Chi Minh to reach an agreement. Ho Chi Minh formed a new government of national union and demanded recognition of Vietnam's independence and unity. When confronted by the risk of war with China, the French commander decided he had to cut a deal with Ho Chi Minh, almost at any cost. The invasion force could not turn around, but had to land in Haiphong on 6 March.

Only hours before the landing, a French representative and the president and vice-president of the DRV signed an agreement in Hanoi. It recognized 'Vietnam' as a 'free state' (*état libre*) within the French Union, and stipulated that a referendum on national unity, i.e. the inclusion of the French colony Cochinchina in the free state of Vietnam, should be held. The main Vietnamese concession in the 6 March 1946 agreement was to allow the temporary establishment of French military garrisons in the north. For the DRV, the agreement was a significant victory. It enhanced the government's national legitimacy and gave it a semi-recognized status. Ho Chi Minh would now represent the Vietnamese nation *vis-à-vis* France. The role of China in obliging France to sign the 6 March accord was not known at the time. In the international press it was falsely interpreted as a sign of French liberalism, and for a short period the French were praised for being more liberal and farsighted than the Dutch in Indonesia.

The 6 March agreement was a significant victory for the Vietnamese national idea of unifying Tonkin, Annam and Cochinchina (but not Laos and Cambodia) into a unitary nation. Few doubted that in a referendum, a great majority in Cochinchina (Nam bo) and Annam (Trung bo) would opt for national unity, and accept inclusion in the DRV. This was anathema to France – also to the French socialists – for several reasons. One was that in the French perception, Cochinchina retained its legal status as French territory. The French protectorates could change status through negotiations, but Cochinchina could only be ceded by a quali-fied majority decision in the French National Assembly and Senate. Another reason was that the unification of Tonkin, Annam and Cochinchina ran counter to a French plan to remould the Indochinese Union into an Indochinese Federation, consisting of five units. This plan had been prepared by the most reform-minded members of the Colonial Ministry, and had been declared as official French policy by General de Gaulle's provisional French government on 24 March 1945. If Indochina consisted of five units, France could preside over the Federation as a mediating judge ('arbitre de tous'), sorting out differences between the various states. If, however, Vietnam were to be unified, it would domi-nate the Federation. Then it would be difficult for France to play a mediating role.

While negotiating with Vietnam from April to September 1946, France refused to follow up its pledge to hold a referendum, and generally treated Ho Chi Minh's government as representing only the northern half of Vietnam. Meanwhile the French High Commissioner, who resided in Saigon, initiated his own rival decolonization process in the South. From June to September 1946, he encouraged the creation of a separate Cochinchinese Republic, with its own president, and convened a confer-ence of representatives from Laos, Cambodia, Cochinchina, south Annam, and also a recently established autonomous highland minority region, to establish the institutional framework for an Indochinese Federation.

Thus two overlapping institutional frameworks for decolonization were established in parallel: On the one hand there was a locally consti-tuted free republic which claimed to represent the whole of Vietnam if not Laos and Cambodia, and who negotiated officially with the French government. On the other hand the French high commissioner was constructing a five-state federation under French administration and local representation, in which Tonkin for the time being did not partici-pate. Cambodia had been under full French control since October 1945, Laos since April-May 1946, but the French soon discovered that the Khmer and Lao were less than happy with the federal concept. They feared that strong federal institutions would in the short run prolong French colonial domination and in the long run become a vehicle for Viet hegemony. Thus they opted for as much local autonomy as possible. The French had expected support for its federal project from the more cosmopolitan and economically developed populations of Cochinchina, but here French power was compounded by an increasingly active guerrilla movement, and also by the general popularity of the Vietnamese national idea.

What triggered the outbreak of the Indochina War in December 1946 was the failure of Cochinchinese separatism. The small and disparate group of Francophiles who agreed to serve in the government of the separate Cochinchinese Republic were ridiculed in the Saigon media, who largely supported Vietnamese unity. By October 1946 it was clear to all that Ho Chi Minh commanded authority also in the South, and that the Cochinchinese government was despised, inept and powerless. In November, the Cochinchinese president committed suicide. This provoked a sense of crisis among French decision makers. Cochinchina was the main foundation of French power. It had been the first region to be colonized, the only area to create an economic surplus, and was meant to serve as the cornerstone of the Federation. Now French power was about to erode. A decision was therefore made by the French government in Saigon to confront the Viet Minh in the north in a hope that a 'psychological shock' would make the local intelligentsia, both north and south, understand that their only option was to take part in the Federation. The collection of customs duties, the French argued, would be a federal prerogative; none of the five states should be allowed to have its own customs service. To enforce federalism, the French deliberately provoked a conflict over customs in the northern port of Haiphong, seized the city in a brutal military offensive, and subsequently provoked a crisis in Hanoi that forced the Vietnamese government to react.

On 19 December the Vietnamese army and militia retaliated with an ill prepared and badly coordinated attack against the local French forces. Some forty European civilians were assassinated, 200 taken as hostages, and there was an outcry in France. The result was an immediate French counter-offensive leading to full-scale war. France rapidly took control of all the main towns in the north. But the effect on the local intelligentsia was the opposite of what the French had expected. Only a tiny minority were shocked into collaboration. Many joined up with Ho Chi Minh's forces in the countryside, and for a long time even outspoken anti-communists remained politically passive. The initial reaction to the outbreak of war was thus a demonstration of national unity in defence of the DRV.

This unity gradually eroded from 1947 to 1949. In conjunction with the onset of the Cold War internationally and the victory of Mao's Red Army in China, the Vietnamese nation allowed itself to be divided. It was this division that so strongly hampered the decolonization process. If all of

Vietnam's main religious and political groups had continued to refuse collaboration, and had demanded the reinstitution of Ho Chi Minh as president, France would eventually have been obliged to give in. Then the communists would have got the upper hand, but Ho Chi Minh might not in that case have aligned himself as completely with Mao and Stalin as he did later. He knew the international communist movement intimately, and would probably have guarded his national independence if he had not been forced to depend on China for support. If, on the other hand, the vast majority of Vietnam's village leaders and educated classes had turned away from Ho Chi Minh in 1947–8, and opted for a decolonization strategy similar to that of Laos and Cambodia, then France would have come under strong local and international pressure for granting genuine independence. Indochina could then have achieved independence, while remaining a part of the French Union and allowing a certain level of French cultural, economic and military influence. However, this was not possible. Ho Chi Minh was too popular, the Viet Minh too well organized, and there was no other leader who could seriously challenge President Ho's legitimacy.

The decolonization of Indochina was delayed for the same reason as in British Malaya: division and struggle between communist and anti-communist forces in the domestic arena. In Malaya the division followed ethnic lines, the British allying themselves with the Malay Muslim majority in defeating the ethnic Chinese communists. In Indochina the French could not defeat the communists, despite allying themselves with the main representatives of the Khmer and Lao, with several highland minority populations, the Cao Dai and Hoa Hao sects, the gangster syndicates of Saigon, a class of wealthy Viet landowners and a plethora of Viet anti-communist groups. The reason why France lost its war in 1954 was, first, the strong legitimacy that Ho Chi Minh had won for himself and the Viet Minh movement during 1945–6; and second, the fact that Vietnam bordered on China so the Viet Minh could receive massive support from the People's Republic of China once Mao gained control of the provinces bordering Vietnam in early 1950.

How did Vietnam's fateful division come about? Not in the way that France had hoped for in 1946. Cochinchinese separatism remained weak, and the Cochinchinese Republic did not fare much better in 1947–8 than it had in 1946. Already in 1947, the French had to concede the defeat of the Cochinchinese experiment and let the Cochinchinese Republic enter a process of formally merging with the rest of Vietnam. The Cochinchinese leaders now established an alternative, non-communist government for all of Vietnam, and sought contact with former Emperor Bao Dai. In 1949 the French government agreed to cede Cochinchina to this new Vietnam, a decision accepted by the French Senate in February 1950. The division of the Vietnamese nation thus no longer took the form of a split between separate regions or territories, but instead between two rival regimes claiming the same territory.

Two men played the leading roles in dividing the Vietnamese nation: former emperor Bao Dai and the Catholic mandarin Ngo Dinh Diem. Bao Dai was a weak character, but at French and Cochinchinese instigation he agreed to form a new regime, based on a broad but loosely organized anti-communist alliance, which lasted from 1949 to 1956. Ngo Dinh Diem was a strong-willed leader who ousted Bao Dai in 1955, sent the French packing, invited US aid, and destroyed the broad local alliance that had sustained Bao Dai's government. Diem created an authoritarian, military state in South Vietnam, based on the country's Catholic minority. Diem's state enjoyed formal independence, but in practice came to depend on the USA.

The origin of Diem's state was the so-called 'Bao Dai solution'. After Bao Dai's abdication in August 1945, he served as supreme advisor to Ho Chi Minh's government, and was sent on a mission to China in April 1946. He stayed abroad and entered into talks with French representatives. In these talks, Bao Dai had to compensate for his lack of national legitimacy by extracting more concessions than Ho Chi Minh had been able to when he negotiated. Bao Dai demanded that the French use the term 'independence' and endorse the formal inclusion of Cochinchina in Vietnam. By May 1948, the French were ready to yield the necessary concessions in principle, and signed an agreement with Bao Dai which included the terms 'independence' and 'unity', but the French did not yield real powers. The legal status of the three Indochinese states was now altered to that of so-called 'associated states'.

The French aim was now to form a new all-Vietnamese government through negotiations with and between various non-communist groups. Some important leaders, such as Diem, stayed out of the game, but many other nationalist leaders of less stature took part in the Bao Dai solution. The French were also able to benefit from conflicts between the communist Cao Dai and Hoa Hao guerrillas in the south. Most of the Cao Dai and the Hoa Hao had broken off relations with the communists and now found a place within Bao Dai's state. On 8 March 1949, an agreement was signed between the French president and Bao Dai, which stipulated that Cochinchina would become part of an independent State of Vietnam. Bao Dai then returned to Vietnam, but not to the imperial capital of Hue. Instead he took up quarters in Saigon and became a 'head of state'. Never before had he ruled Saigon, and the population there did not care much for him. There were no enthusiastic crowds to greet him, and in practice the French continued to run the country. The State of Vietnam did not, like Cambodia and Laos, have a national assembly or independent financial means. The British and US governments were unimpressed by Bao Dai, but supported his regime as a lesser evil. They refused to recognize the State of Vietnam until the French Senate had ratified the agreement to grant it unity and independence. The United Kingdom and the USA then recognized the independent states of Vietnam, Laos and Cambodia on 7 February 1950.

In the meantime the DRV had been recognized by China and the Soviet Union. The Bao Dai solution pushed Ho Chi Minh into the arms of Mao and Stalin. After the outbreak of war in December 1946, Ho Chi Minh had used Bangkok and Rangoon as his main diplomatic outlets and had appealed to the USA, Britain and other countries for help. But it became more and more difficult for communists to cooperate with non-communist nationalists. After a right-wing coup in Thailand in late 1948, the Viet Minh and the Lao Issara were deprived of Thai support. At the same time, Soviet policy became more hard-line. The Vietnamese communists were targeted for criticism in Moscow because the ICP had been formally dissolved in 1945, and because the DRV government had failed to carry out land reforms. By 1949, however, the Red Army was winning the civil war in China, and Mao was eager to expand the Chinese revolution to neighbouring countries. Inside Indochina the ICP was now reconstructed; new members were recruited, and there was an increasing emphasis on ideology. The United States was now also increasingly demonized in Viet Minh propaganda. In 1949, DRV forces provided assistance to Chinese communist guerrillas fighting the Guomindang on the other side of the border, and in mid-January 1950, presumably at Mao's invitation, the DRV officially recognized the People's Republic of China. Beijing responded, on 18 January, by recognizing the DRV. At this time Mao was in Moscow to negotiate the Sino-Soviet treaty of alliance, and on 30 January Stalin followed the Chinese initiative and also recognized the DRV. The ICP now eagerly discussed how to stimulate revolts against the French-sponsored regimes in Laos and Cambodia, and decided it would be best to appeal to the independent national feelings of the Laotians and Cambodians. It was decided to have separate parties for each of the three states. At a party congress in 1951, the ICP changed its name to the Vietnam Workers' Party (Lao Dong). A Cambodian party was founded shortly afterwards, while the Laotians had to wait until 1955 before they got their own revolutionary party.

If formal international recognition were to be sufficient proof of decolonization, then Indochina's decolonization was completed in January–February 1950. Yet this is not normally considered the date of independence. The DRV, although recognized by the socialist camp and commanding widespread support in the Vietnamese villages, was not yet in possession of any major city. The State of Vietnam was independent in name only, and the French also continued to control key functions in Laos and Cambodia. For these two countries, the date of independence is normally said to be 1953, when France 'perfected' the independence of Laos and Cambodia by transferring full sovereignty (except over defence planning). For Vietnam, the year of full independence is normally set at 1954. On 24 June of that year, after the French military defeat at Dien Bien Phu, a new treaty was signed between France and Bao Dai, similar to that which had been signed by Laos. This happened while the Geneva conference was in session. At this conference the royal governments of Laos and Cambodia and Bao Dai's State of Vietnam were represented, and there was also a delegation from the DRV that included representatives of the Pathet Lao and a Cambodian Liberation Movement. On 21 July the conference ended with the signing of armistice agreements between the forces of the DRV, the Pathet Lao and the French Union, involving a temporary division of Vietnam along the seventeenth parallel and the regrouping of Pathet Lao forces in two provinces of northeastern Laos. French forces would be withdrawn from North Vietnam, and DRV forces would withdraw from Cambodia, Laos and South Vietnam. The agreement also stipulated that there would be elections in Laos 1955, and in all of Vietnam before July 1956.

Studies of Soviet and Chinese archives have shown that the Soviet and Chinese communist leaders expected the promise of national elections to be kept. Thus the Soviets and Chinese put pressure on their Vietnamese comrades to aim for peaceful national reunification, and refrain from any armed struggle against the French and the Bao Dai regime after Geneva. France had committed itself to arrange for national elections, but France now lost control of South Vietnam. During the Geneva conference Bao Dai had taken a decisive step towards real independence by asking the staunchly anti-French Ngo Dinh Diem to form a new government. Diem used support from the United States to build his own personal power, ousted Bao Dai in 1955 and refused to take any steps towards the holding of nationwide elections. In view of the risk that Ho Chi Minh might win such elections, Washington chose to support Ngo Dinh Diem's policy.

Since 1953, the Vietnamese communists had been carrying out radical land reforms in the north and instituting a more Soviet-style government. This provoked social conflicts, leading to much loss of life, and to an apology from Ho Chi Minh in 1956. The result of these policies was to weaken the ability of the DRV to speak on behalf of the whole Vietnamese nation, and to facilitate the nationally divisive policies of Ngo Dinh Diem.

Inviting recolonization

In the period 1955–62, Ngo Dinh Diem ran his personal dictatorship in South Vietnam, with a narrow social basis. Economically his state depended on the USA, and his army could not operate without US advice. Although it was not Diem's intention, the effect of his actions was to instigate the recolonization of South Vietnam by the USA. It is a paradox that Diem, who had been made premier in 1954 because of his strong nationalist credentials, was the man who cemented the partition of the country.

By appealing to US anti-communism and its scepticism towards France, Diem pulled the USA into Vietnam. Most of the literature describes Diem as a tool of American policy. It was as much the other way round. Diem knew Vietnam intimately. He had been playing cat-and-mouse with the French and the communists for many years. Washington had little knowledge of Indochina, particularly in the 1950s when the main Asia experts had been forced to resign from the State Department because they were suspected of pro-communist leanings. Diem had left Bao Dai's cabinet in protest in 1932. In 1944–5 he had been ready to form a government with Japanese backing, but seems to have been too demanding, so the Japanese turned away from him. Shortly after Bao Dai's return to Vietnam, there were negotiations with Diem for the creation of a new government. Just as in 1945, however, he was too demanding. He now wanted to replace French with US aid, and left for a long stay in America. Here he used his Catholic connections to build support for a political solution that would at once be anti-colonialist and anti-communist. His chance came in 1954, when France lost its decisive battle with Viet Minh forces at Dien Bien Phu. Diem returned to Saigon and was able to persuade Bao Dai, with US backing, to grant him full authority as new head of government.

After assuming power, he drew in the USA by inviting aid and advice. This made him powerful enough to expel all remaining French forces and advisors, and to organize a referendum to depose Bao Dai and proclaim himself head of state. In the spring of 1955 he launched a risky all-out attack against the groups who had sustained Bao Dai's regime: first the Binh Xuyen (a gangster syndicate in Saigon), then the Cao Dai and Hoa Hao. Through swift military action he succeeded in crushing his enemies, and then ousted Bao Dai. Diem subsequently almost succeeded in crushing the communist party in the south, but the local communists were still not permitted by Hanoi to resume armed struggle.

Diem came across as an anti-communist hero in the United States. In the process, however, he had alienated most other groups, and came to rely heavily on the Catholics who had left the north and settled in the south after the partition of Vietnam in 1954. His power depended on fear. With US help he created a kind of regime that would be unacceptable to Americans once its true character was known. Americans were insensitive to atrocities committed against suspected communists, but when non-communist Buddhist protesters were subjected to similarly brutal repression, there was an outcry in the US and international media. Washington asked Diem to liberalize his regime, carry out land reforms, and allow basic freedoms. Diem ignored the advice.

Diem's policy was to enforce his own power, while relying on US support. His political isolation forms a stark contrast to the policies of cautious national bridge-building pursued by the leading statesmen of Cambodia and Laos at that time. King Norodom Sihanouk, who had welcomed the French back in October 1945, was also no democrat. In 1952–3 he severely curtailed the power of the party politicians and took personal leadership of the political struggle for independence, but his government had far more national legitimacy than Diem's. Sihanouk abdicated in 1955, left the throne to his father, and formed his own political party, which gained massive support in national elections. Sihanouk, who remained the country's real leader, adopted a neutral stance in the Cold War and took part in the Bandung conference of non-aligned countries in 1955. At Geneva in 1954, when Vietnam was divided in two, and the Pathet Lao obtained a regrouping zone in northeastern Laos, Sihanouk managed to prevent the Khmer Issarak from gaining any recognition. Sihanouk's repressive internal policies alienated the people who would later form the political basis of the Lon Nol regime in the period 1970–5 and the Pol Pot regime in 1975–8, but for a long time these groups remained marginal. Cambodia's unity was made to depend on Sihanouk's person, and in the end this was not enough. Yet Sihanouk managed for a number of years to pursue his balancing act both internally and externally. He remained attached to France, forged close relations with China, and secretly allowed the DRV to import arms through a Cambodian port. Ngo Dinh Diem and the United States, of course, despised his neutralist policy.

In Laos, the main protagonist of neutralism and national unity was Prince Suvanna Phūmā. He managed to establish a succession of coalition governments in Viang Chan, with representatives both of the pro-Western aristocrats in the southern part of the country, the traditional royalty in Luang Phrabāng (he himself belonged to the royal family), and the leftist Pathet Lao faction of Prince Suphānuvong. Repeatedly, however, their coalitions broke down, and in the late 1950s and early 1960s, Laos was a hot spot in Cold War diplomacy, leading to a special Geneva settlement on Laos in 1962. With the escalation of the Vietnam War, Suvanna Phūmā's policy became impracticable. The North Vietnamese army took control of the areas closest to Vietnam, which were crucial to the transportation networks that linked North Vietnam to the main battlefields in the south (the 'Ho Chi Minh Trail'). In Viang Chan the government was dominated by right-wing politicians and their US advisors, so Suvanna Phūmā became a figurehead.

A comparison between Sihanouk, Suvanna Phūmā and Diem shows the difference between conditions in the three non-communist states of

Indochina. Sihanouk led a nation that was under his control. Suvanna Phūmā strove to keep together a weak nation with many centrifugal forces. Diem was trying to wield absolute power in a society where he had little support, and where a strong communist movement was aided by a Chinese-supported government in Hanoi. If Diem had pursued a policy of national reconciliation, he would have faced the risk of playing into the hands of his main enemy. This, in addition to Diem's autocratic personality and visceral anti-communism, may explain his policy of national division.

By 1959, after years of severe repression, the communists in South Vietnam were finally authorized by Hanoi to resume armed struggle. They formed the National Front for the Liberation of South Vietnam (NLF), which soon gained support from non-communist groups alienated by Diem's policies. The NLF's mounting guerrilla campaign rapidly undermined the Saigon regime. By late 1963 the Americans had lost their patience with Diem and gave the green light for a military coup in which he and his brother were assassinated. This resulted in the formation of a moderate military regime, which came under French influence and probably wanted to adopt a policy similar to those of Sihanouk and Suvanna Phūmā. The Americans suspected the new Saigon leaders of seeking contact with Hanoi. This was anathema to Washington, who encouraged another coup, led by a young officer. It took place in January 1964. The new government was so weak that in practice the Americans took over the administration of the country. Thus South Vietnam had been effectively recolonized by the USA. This forms the background for the escalation of the Vietnam War in 1964–5, leading to the bombing of North Vietnam and the introduction of half a million American troops.

The United States never planned to colonize South Vietnam. The American involvement happened in the same way that so many territories had been colonized by Europeans in the previous century. Factional struggles within African or Asian countries led the weaker party to seek aid from powerful Europeans. With aid came advice, and when the locals failed to heed advice or to safeguard Western interests, the Europeans started to manipulate local politics. Eventually they would take full control and encompass the new territories within their empires, either as directly ruled colonies or protectorates. By the 1960s the imperial idea had been discredited worldwide, not the least through American efforts. Thus the American domination of South Vietnam, which was soon expanded to include Laos and in 1970 even Cambodia, was always portrayed as assistance to independent states. In reality, however, it was informal colonization.

The USA did not take up the old French plans for a federation of the Indochinese states, but wanted to economically integrate the non-communist countries along the Mekong River (Thailand, Laos,

Cambodia and South Vietnam) in order to create a vibrant growth area in continental Southeast Asia, and isolate north Vietnam. The USA had to fight an enemy who saw the whole of Indochina as one battlefield, with a vast north-south land-based transportation system through Laos and Cambodia (the Ho Chi Minh Trail). In its effort to destroy this communication system, the United States were able to use airfields in Thailand, and aircraft carriers in the South China Sea. By 1964 the United States found itself in the same situation as the French in 1946. The regime it sustained in Saigon was falling apart because of its incapacity and a mounting communist insurgency. In their desperation the Americans followed the same impulse as the French: They brought the war to the north. Where the French had used a customs conflict to legitimize their conquest of Haiphong in November 1946, the Americans used a naval incident in the Gulf of Tonkin in August 1964 as a reason for beginning the bombing of North Vietnam. For fear of provoking a Chinese invasion like that of Korea 1950, the USA did not, however, occupy any territory north of the seventeenth parallel.

Just as the French capture of Haiphong and Hanoi in 1946 had failed to provoke a 'psychological shock' forcing the Vietnamese into compliance, US bombing also failed to break the will of North Vietnam. Instead, the bombing galvanized the fighting spirit of the population, who readily sent their young men south to fight and die with the NLF. US bombing also provoked a decision by the post-Khruschev regime in the Soviet Union to contribute massive aid to the DRV, and added wind to a wave of worldwide anti-Americanism. By 1968–9 even the American public had turned against the war, and the USA was forced to negotiate with Hanoi and pursue a policy of decolonization, called 'Vietnamization'. Negotiations dragged on for four years until the Paris accords were finally signed in 1973. Meanwhile the administrative capacity of the Saigon regime improved, and the government of Nguyen Van Thieu gained gradually more leverage in relation to the US 'ambassador' and commanding general. Thus, to some extent, the policy of decolonization was successful.

To make Hanoi negotiate, the USA was obliged to periodically halt the bombing of North Vietnam. In order to continue the demonstration of US resolve, and to try and block the NLF's use of Cambodian territory, the USA put increasing pressure on Sihanouk's Cambodia. After Sihanouk had been deposed in a right-wing coup in 1970, the USA launched a devastating bombing campaign in the eastern part of the country. Until then, Sihanouk had successfully maintained national unity under his neutralist formula, keeping special relations both with France and China, although he had not been able to avoid the creation of a guerrilla force, the *Khmer Rouge*, who cooperated with the Vietnamese communists. The coup in 1970, which led General Lon Nol to power, dealt a deathblow to

Cambodian national unity. The result was to create a favourable situation for the Khmer Rouge, who could now fight in the name of Sihanouk, recruit thousands of soldiers, acquire better arms, and initiate larger offensives. After the Paris accords, South Vietnam was therefore not the only regime in Indochina to be threatened by a mounting communist insurgency. The same was the case in Cambodia and Laos, although the Vietnamese put brakes on the armed struggle in the Lao lowlands, since the highlands played such a significant role for supplying the struggle in South Vietnam. The military commanders in Hanoi had always considered Indochina as one battlefield, and their intention was to liberate the Laotians and Cambodians alongside the Vietnamese. Hanoi had, at least officially, given up the idea of establishing a formal Indochinese Federation, but between the three brotherly peoples, there would continue to be a 'special relationship'.

Vietnamization

To colonize other countries went against the dominant ideology in the United States. The Americans had themselves fought a war of national liberation, and there was full consensus in the USA to condemn colonialism as such. Only for a short period at the beginning of the twentieth century did the US tend towards a 'manifest destiny' of possessing territories abroad and subordinating other peoples. This quickly gave way to the principle of national self-determination, which formed a crucial part of US ideology during the First World War of 1914–18 and the World War that began with the Japanese onslaught on China in 1937 and ended in 1945. After 1918, US policy played a significant role in ensuring national independence for the countries of the dissolving Habsburg and Ottoman empires. In 1945, the USA hosted the foundation of the United Nations, which was based on the principle of national sovereignty, and in 1946 fulfilled the promise of granting independence to the Philippines. Subsequently, each time the US entered into a colonial-type relationship through attempts to assist or rescue a non-communist regime, this was conceived as assistance to an independent state. This held the United States back from establishing a formal empire.

The term 'Vietnamization', which was Richard M. Nixon's slogan when campaigning for the US presidency in 1968, represented an implicit realization that the southern half of Vietnam had become a virtual US colony.[2] There is good reason to consider 'Vietnamization' and 'decolonization' as synonymous, although Nixon of course did not. In the American decolonization of South Vietnam, the Paris accords of 1973 form a crucial juncture, since they involved the withdrawal of US troops. Even before the accords, however, the number of troops had been drastically reduced. After 1973, although still receiving substantial economic and military aid and advice, South Vietnam became more autonomous. This further revealed the inherent weakness of the regime, which fell apart with amazing speed when subjected to North Vietnam's massive spring offensive of March and April 1975.

The formation of Democratic Kampuchea in 1975, the 1976 unification of North and South Vietnam in the Socialist Republic of Vietnam (SRV), which led to Vietnamese membership of the United Nations, and the formation of the Laotian People's Democratic Republic in 1976, form the end of the decolonization process in Indochina. Hanoi's subsequent domination of southern Vietnam should not be considered colonization, since this was not a relationship between nations but regions within the same nation. Nevertheless, it needs to be said that the so-called 'national unification' was a unification of national territory, not of people or minds. Tens of thousands of losers were placed in re-education camps, and in 1978–9 there was an exodus of ethnic Chinese, of city-based Viet upper classes, and of those who had served under the Saigon regime. They left their home country on small boats and became known as 'the boat people'. Many drowned, while the survivors settled around the world. Thus a Viet diaspora was formed that would retain the memory of the Saigon regime. A resourceful minority had been excluded from the Vietnamese nation. Thus the history of national division did not end.

Conclusion

This essay has sought to address the question of why the decolonization of French Indochina took longer and was more violent than the decolonization of most other territories in the decades after 1945. There are two standard answers. The first is that France held more stubbornly onto its empire than did other colonial powers, a fact also proved in Algeria. The second is that the decolonization process in Indochina became embroiled in the Cold War, thus leading the United States to first support France and later replace it in its colonial role. These arguments are both valid, but it has been argued here that the length and violence of Indochina's decolonization must also be explained by local factors. The first such factor is the division of the Vietnamese nation between those who remained loyal to the Democratic Republic of Vietnam, which Ho Chi Minh had proclaimed in 1945, and those anti-communist groups who opted for collaboration with France or invited US domination. The other local factor was the unresolved relationship between the three countries of Indochina. On the one hand, they were increasingly recognized from all sides as independent countries. On the other hand, both France and the Vietnamese communists had plans to federalize Indochina, and for logistical reasons, Indochina was always seen as one battlefield. What allowed the decolonization process to reach its end was the fall of the non-communist regimes in Phnom Penh, Saigon and Vian Chang in 1975–6, but even then the relationship between the three Indochinese countries was not resolved. Vietnam wanted a 'special relationship'. This was acceptable to the Laotian communist leaders, but not the Khmer Rouge, who instead sought support from China. The result was ten years of post-colonial warfare in Cambodia. Only with the end of the Cold War in the late 1980s did the former French Indochina cease to be a political bloc, so the three independent countries of Vietnam, Cambodia and Laos could join Southeast Asia and the world, and face the challenge from globalization.

Notes

1 This essay uses the terms 'Viet', 'Khmer' and 'Lao' for the ethnic majority groups in Vietnam, Cambodia and Laos, and 'Vietnamese', 'Cambodians' and 'Laotians' for the nationals of the three states. Thus a Viet who has taken French citizenship and given up his Vietnamese nationality will remain Viet, but not Vietnamese. On the other hand a Vietnamese citizen who is ethnically Chinese (Hoa) will be Vietnamese, but not Viet.
2 The French had used the same term when they tried to give Bao Dai a greater share in the responsibility for warfare in 1953. Charles-Robert Agéron (1991) *La décolonisation française*, Paris: Armand Colin, 90.

Further reading

Agéron, Charles-Robert (1991) *La décolonisation française*, Paris: Armand Colin.

Bradley, Mark Philip (2000) *Imagining Vietnam and America: The Making of Postcolonial Vietnam, 1919–1950*, Chapel Hill: University of North Carolina Press.

Brocheux, Pierre and Daniel Hémery (2001) *Indochine: La colonisation ambiguë 1858–1954*, 2nd edn, Paris: la Découverte.

Cesari, Laurent (1995) *L'Indochine en guerres 1945–1993*, Paris: Belin.

Chandler, David P. (1991) *The Tragedy of Cambodian History: Politics, War and Revolution since 1945*, New Haven: Yale University Press.

Clayton, Anthony (1994) *The Wars of French Decolonization*, London: Longman.

Devillers, Philippe (1952) *Histoire du Viêt-Nam de 1940 à 1952*, Paris: Seuil.

Duiker, William J. (1996) *The Communist Road to Power in Vietnam*, 2nd edn, Boulder: Westview.

Goscha, Christopher E. (1999) *Thailand and the Southeast Asian Networks of the Vietnamese Revolution, 1885–1954*, Richmond, Surrey: Curzon/NIAS Press.

Kiernan, Ben (1985) *How Pol Pot Came to Power: A History of Communism in Kampuchea, 1930–1975*, London: Verso.

Marr, David G. (1995) *Vietnam 1945: The Quest for Power*, Berkeley: University of California Press.

Qiang Zhai (2000) *China and the Vietnam Wars, 1950–1975*, Chapel Hill: University of North Carolina Press.

Stuart-Fox, Martin (1996) *Buddhist Kingdom, Marxist State: The Making of Modern Laos*, Bangkok: White Lotus.

——(1997) *A History of Laos*, Cambridge: Cambridge University Press.

Tønnesson, Stein (1987) *1946: Déclenchement de la guerre d'Indochine*, Paris: l'Harmattan.

——(1991) *The Vietnamese Revolution of 1945: Roosevelt, Ho Chi Minh and de Gaulle in a World at War*, London: Sage.

Tønnesson, Stein and Hans Antlöv (eds) (1996) *Asian Forms of the Nation*, Richmond, Surrey: Curzon/NIAS Press.

Young, Marilyn B. and Bob Buzzanco (eds) (2002) *A Companion to the Vietnam War*, Malden MA: Blackwell.

19

COLONIAL FORMATIONS AND DEFORMATIONS

Korea, Taiwan and Vietnam[1]

Bruce Cumings

A debate has emerged about the sources of economic growth in South Korea and Taiwan: did it all begin around 1960, when both had miniscule per capita incomes but somehow launched themselves onto a trajectory of export-led growth, or do the origins of growth push back further, into the legacies of Japan's colonial rule? That debate also bears on the export-led plans of a different former colony, at a very different time: Vietnam in the 1990s.

First we need to know what a 'colonial legacy' is, and why colonial history is still such a neuralgic point in East Asia today. I take a *colony* to have been one way of organizing territorial space in the modern world system, one that obliterated political sovereignty and oriented the colonial economy toward monopoly controls and monopoly profits (even if done differently by the various imperial powers), and a *legacy* to be something that appears to be a follow-on to the different historical experiences of colonialism. 'Legacy' is a term that can be good, bad or neutral: the legacy of a rich family might be seen as good, an alumni legacy to an entering freshman class bad, and a railroad running from Hanoi to Saigon neutral, good, or bad depending on one's point of view. As it happens, the comparative 'points of view' afforded by our three cases are very different, offering much food for thought about nationalism, resistance, development and modernity. I will examine colonial legacies for their utility in explaining the post-war growth of Taiwan, Korea and – in a curious way – Japan itself; and the virtual opposite in Vietnam, namely, the thirty years of war and revolution that was the prime post-colonial 'legacy' of the French.

The nationalist point of view is that there is no such thing as a good colonial legacy, and therefore the contribution of imperialism to growth was zero, really minus-zero: for example, Korean historiography (South and North) sees anything good or useful deriving from Japanese colonialism as incidental to the ruthless pursuit of Japanese interests; even if a railroad from Pusan to Sinûiju is useful, a railroad built by Koreans, for Koreans, would have been better. Furthermore, without the Japanese, a

278

native railway system would still have been built: Koreans assume that Japan aborted their drive for modernity, rather than merely distorting it.

Taiwanese, on the other hand, have tended to look upon their colonial experience with Japan as a reasonably tolerable and efficacious interlude between ineffectual Ch'ing Dynasty rule and rapacious Chinese Nationalist rule. A political scientist's sojourn in Taiwan as late as 1970 found nostalgia for the Japanese era at every turn. Japan held Taiwan longer than any of its colonies, from 1895 to 1945: did Japan do something here that it did not do in Korea? Or did it do the same thing, with a very different native response?

The French took a long time to colonize Vietnam (from 1856 to 1885) and then held onto it until 1945. There followed a thirty-year war. At the end of that war, in 1975, Vietnam was one of the most impoverished nations in the world. Meanwhile South Korea, North Korea and Taiwan were all mid-1970s success stories of economic development. Vietnamese planners soon found that Soviet-style development schemes emphasizing heavy industry were inapplicable to a country still primarily agrarian, contrasting their low starting point in the late 1970s with North Korea's in 1945, or China's in 1949. Today Vietnamese planners look to South Korea and Taiwan as models of 'export-led development'. Did this different outcome have anything to do with the nature of French colonialism, as contrasted with Japanese? Or did the thirty-year war bequeath a backward economy?

I will argue in this chapter that the differing colonial experiences of these three nations did make a big difference in their post-war development. It is a complex argument, however, because Taiwan and Korea got the same type of colonialism with very different results, because each of these three nations had different pre-colonial experiences, and because two of them (South Korea and Taiwan) got all the benefits of post-colonial American hegemony, while Vietnam and North Korea got all the drawbacks of being objects of post-colonial American hegemony. Primarily, though, I want to make the case that the 'East Asian model' of capitalism, so widely discussed these days, has deep historical roots and cannot be understood merely as an outcome of salutary policy packages that encouraged 'export-led development'. It is in many ways, as I will argue briefly at the end of this chapter and at more length elsewhere, an East Asian adaptation of the nineteenth-century European (continental) conception of the state and its relation to the national, industrial economy, in a world system of dog-eat-dog competition.

The modern and the colonial

At the onset of colonial rule, Taiwan and Vietnam were backward by almost any measure of modern or industrial development. Vietnam was purely agrarian; Taiwan had a mini-spurt of development in 1885–91, followed by a four-year lapse and then absorption by Japan. Korea, however, had begun to 'modernize' on the usual indices in the 1880s, with mixed results by 1905 when Japan began its protectorate, but certainly more progress than was to be found in Taiwan or Vietnam. Angus Hamilton, for example, found Korea in 1904 to be 'a land of exceptional beauty' and Seoul much superior to Beijing.

There was for him 'no question of the superiority' of Korean living conditions, both urban and rural, to those in China (if not Japan). Seoul was the first city in East Asia to have electricity, trolley cars, and water, telephone and telegraph systems all at the same time. Most of these systems were installed and run by Americans: the Seoul Electric Light Company, the Seoul Electric Car Company, the Seoul 'Fresh Spring' Water Company, were all American firms.

Schools of every description abounded in Seoul – law, engineering, medicine. Hamilton noted that King Kojong wanted personally to supervise all public business; he was, Hamilton thought, a progressive monarch who had chosen well from the models put before him by the West and Japan. The period since the opening of the country had afforded Koreans countless opportunities 'to select for themselves such institutions as may be calculated to promote their own welfare'.[2]

This is powerful evidence supporting the Korean claim that their route to modernity was not facilitated by Japan, but derailed and hijacked. Still, note the indices that the American Hamilton chooses to highlight: electricity, telephones, trollies, schools, cleanliness, consumption of American exports. If we find that Japan brought similar facilities to Seoul and Taipei, do we place them on the ledger of colonialism, or modernization? The Korean answer is 'colonialism' and the Japanese and Taiwanese answer is 'modernization'.

Tim Mitchell has a better answer to this question, which is to address 'the place of colonialism in the critique of modernity':

> Colonising refers not simply to the establishing of a European presence but also to the spread of a political order that inscribes in the social world a new conception of space, new forms of personhood, and a new means of manufacturing the experience of the real.[3]

Following Michel Foucault, Mitchell examines British colonialism in Egypt as a matter of a 'restrictive, exterior power' giving way to the 'internal, productive power' demanded by modernity, a disciplining that produces 'the organized power of armies, schools, and factories', and above all the modern individual – 'constructed as an isolated, disciplined, receptive, and industrious political subject'.

There is much more to be said here, but if we put things this way, with a conception of Foucauldian power and Foucauldian modernity, then there is no fundamental distinction between second phase (i.e. late-nineteenth-century) colonialism and the modern industrial project itself, and thus – at this level of abstraction – no basic distinction between Japanese colonialism, American hegemony, and South Korean, North Korean or Taiwanese modernization. At the least, none of these national discourses of modernity can tell you what's wrong with the precise timing of the factory punch-clock or the railway timetable or the policeman's neighbourhood beat; they just differ over the auspices of their introduction and their effects on national sovereignty. Every political entity just mentioned, but above all Japan, put its citizens through a regimen of public education that seemed perfectly designed to develop the industrious political subject, with the vices of self-surveillance and repression that Mitchell analysed for British Egypt.

The Vietnamese, however, find nothing good to enter on the colonial or the modernization ledger: the literature of anti-colonialism shouts itself hoarse over French exploitation, the French literature almost always takes to task its own colonization project and the 'industrious political subject' never appeared, with French education more likely to create the industrious political rebel (e.g. Ho Chi Minh in Paris, 1921). The French were not 'late' colonizers in Indochina, tying the colonies to metropolitan industrialization efforts: like the Portuguese in Africa since the sixteenth century, they preferred to spend comparatively little money – just enough to keep the colonial settlers happy, the rice, rubber and tin flowing, and the natives pacified.

And here we see the undeniable legacy (and the irony) of Japanese colonialism: they were imperialists but also capitalists, colonizers but also modernizers, every bit as interested as a Frederic Taylor in laying an industrial grid and disciplining, training and surveilling the workforce. Threatened by the modern project in the form of Western imperialism, after 1868 the Japanese internalized it, made it their own, and imposed it on their neighbours: a highly disciplined, rational, almost Weberian type of colonialism, but one that was ultimately irrational because it could not last over time without creating its own competitors, and thus its own grave. (The best symbol of this is the Korean-owned, spanking new textile mill in Manchuria that came onstream just in time to fall into the hands of the Russians in August 1945.) Above all they imposed the modern project *on themselves*, late in world time, with all the attendant uprootings, distortions, self-disciplines and self-negations, fractured outcomes and moth-toward-a-flame terrors that mark modern Japan's history, and still play upon the national psyche (Hiroshima and Nagasaki being the obvious but also ultimate reference points). Modernity was an inorganic growth, and the Japanese in their internal self-colonization have always known it.

Japan's most important and most recalcitrant colony: Korea

Among Koreans, North and South, the mere mention of the idea that Japan somehow 'modernized' Korea calls forth indignant denials, raw emotions, and the imminent sense of mayhem having just been, or about to be, committed. For the foreigner, even the most extensive cataloguing of Japanese atrocities will pale beside the bare mention of anything positive and lasting that might have emerged from the colonial period. I do not wish to argue that Japan 'developed' Korea, or that post-war South Korea owes its growth to Japan. I wish instead to contrast the different retrospective optics of the people of Korea and Taiwan on Japanese imperialism, and to mark the differences between Japanese and French imperialism.

The critical difference between Korea and Taiwan begins with Korea's millenium-long history of continuous, independent existence within well recognized territorial boundaries, combined with a startling ethnic homogeneity and a pronounced ethnic, linguistic and cultural difference from its neighbours (in the case of neighbour Japan, a difference compounded by 250 years of mutual isolation after the wars of the 1590s). Colonial difference ends with the stunningly dissimilar Japanese policy toward Koreans in the harshest days of the Pacific War, when millions of Koreans were forcibly relocated to Japan, Manchuria and northern Korea for hard labour in mines and factories – or in the worst case, for sexual slavery. By contrast, Taiwan was never a nation, never had a central state before the 1890s, put up marginal resistance to Japan's entry, and even upon Japan's 1945 exit a mere handful of Taiwanese had left the island for Japan or the empire (30,000, most not forcibly mobilized), or even their native village for Taipei. I see this dissimilar outcome in the years 1935–45 to have been the reason for Korea's combination of development and under-development and the key to its resulting post-war turmoil and civil strife, but have written much about this elsewhere, and merely highlight it here. The point is that within five years of Japan's departure, Japan's colonial effort had left the Taiwanese complaining about Chinese Nationalist 'pigs', South Koreans with gnawing respect/hate feelings toward Japan, and a state organized totally as an anti-Japanese entity called North Korea.

With that said (and with no illusions that Korean nationalism is hereby appeased), we can highlight important continuities between the pre-war and post-war political economies of Korea, continuities which began in the 1920s. Unlike Taiwan, Korea had an integral role in Japan's 'administrative guidance' of the entire Northeast Asian regional economy. Korea was a bridge linking the metropole with hinterland economies, and it is also from this point that we can date Japan's specific brand of architectonic capitalism that has influenced Northeast Asia down to the present.

Japan entered a period of economic stagnation after World War I, and generally pursued free trade and political liberalization at home, and less repressive colonial policies in both Korea and Taiwan. When we turn to Korea in this period, however, we can see the kernel of a subsequent logic – the logic of administrative guidance. In the government-general's Industrial Commission of 1921, the first-time planners called for supports to Korea's fledgling textile industry and for it to produce not just for the domestic market, but especially for exports to the Asian continent, where lower Korean labour costs would give its goods a price advantage. This was by no means a purely 'top-down' Japanese exercise, for Koreans were part of the Commission and quickly called for state subsidies and hothouse 'protection' for Korean companies. The nurturing of a Korean business class was a necessity if the new policy of 'gradualism' (adopted after the March 1st independence uprisings in 1919) was to have any meaning, and this was in effect its birthday party – although a controversial one (three days before the Commission opened, two bombs had been lobbed into the government-general building). Japan had much larger ideas in mind: Korean industry would be integral to the overall planning being done in Tokyo, and would require some protection if it were to accept its proper place in 'a single, coexistent, co-prosperous Japanese-Korean unit'.

Also visible at this early point was the developmental model of state-sponsored loans at preferential interests rates as a means to shape industrial development and take advantage of 'product cycle' advantages, yielding firms whose paid-in capital was often much less than their outstanding debt. Businessmen did not offer shares on a stock market, but went to state banks for their capital. Strategic investment decisions were in the hands of state bureaucrats, state banks and state corporations (like the Oriental Development Company), meaning that policy could move 'swiftly and *sequentially*', in Meredith Woo's words, in ways that subsequently and indelibly marked South Korean development in the 1960s and 1970s.

The Great Depression delayed full implementation of this model, but by the mid-1930s this sort of financing had became a standard practice. The key institution at the nexus of the colonial model was the Korean Industrial Bank (*Chōsen Shokusan Ginkō*), the main source of capital for big Korean firms; by the end of the colonial period about half of its employees were Korean. Meanwhile Seoul's Bank of Chōsen played the role of central bank and provisioned capital throughout the imperial realm in Northeast China. It had twenty branches in Manchukuo, served as fiscal agent for Japan's Kwantung Army, and also had an office in New York to vacuum up American loans for colonial expansion. On the

side it 'trafficked in opium, silver and textile smuggling', and participated in the ill-famed Nishihara Loan, designed to buy off Chinese
opposition to Japan's 'twenty-one demands' – about nineteen of which
bit off pieces of Chinese sovereignty (Woo 1991: 23–30). Most important
for Korea, however, was the Industrial Bank's role under Ariga
Mitsutoyo (1919–37) in 'jump-starting Korea's first industrial and
commercial entrepreneurs, men such as Min T'ae-shik, Min Kyu-sik, Pak
Hông-sik, and Kim Yôn-su'.

By 1936 heavy industry accounted for 28 per cent of total industrial
production in Korea, quite unlike Taiwan, and more than half a million
Koreans were employed in industry – a figure that had tripled by 1945.
Industry expanded in Korea at double or triple the rate in Taiwan (Table
19.1).

Table 19.1 Koreans employed in industry within Korea, 1923–43

Year	Number of persons	Index of increase
1932	384,951	100
1936	594,739	154
1940	702,868	183
1943	1,321,713	343

This table excludes mining and transportation, which employed tens
of thousands more, and does not count the millions of Koreans labouring
outside the country in the 1940s. By 1943, the production ratio between
Korea's heavy and light industry had become equal. Nor is it really the
case that northern Korea had all the big factories and the South only light
industry; in the middle of the war the South surpassed the North in
machine building, electric machinery, heavy vehicles, mining tools, and
the like. Thus Korea's industrial revolution began in earnest during the
last fifteen years of Japanese rule.

Hermann Lautensach, no apologist for colonialism, was much
impressed by the rapid development of Korea in the late 1930s. Here was
an 'obvious, indeed astonishing success', even if the development was
'oriented toward the needs of the empire'. This, combined with a succession of excellent harvests in 1936–8, yielded the notion of a 'Korean
boom': with 'the rapid development of all of Korea's economic
capacity...a certain amount of prosperity is beginning to enter even the
farmer's huts'. The northeast corner of Korea, long backward, was 'expe-
riencing an upswing unlike any other part of Korea', mainly because of
its incorporation into Manchukuo trading networks.[4]

There is much more to be said, but given space limitations I would direct the reader to my previous work on colonialism in Korea and go on to Taiwan and Vietnam. I will merely conclude this brief account with the comment that post-war South Korea, far from being an anti-colonial entity, often contained virtual replicas of Japanese forms in industry, state policies toward the economy, education, police, military affairs, the physiognomy of its cities, and its civic culture (such as it was). Newspapers were identical in form to Japan's, if not in content; South Korean schools were museums of colonial practice until the early 1980s, down to the black uniforms, pressed collars and peaked hats which every male student wore.

North Korea was an anti-colonial entity *par excellence*, but in its haste to deny everything Japanese it created mirror-image institutions, beginning with the emperor-like leader principle, the corporate political system, the leader's ubiquitous *chuch'e* ideology, and the establishment of the leader/emperor's birthday as a national holiday. Even some of P'yôngyang's wretched excesses, like the botanist-produced orchids and begonias christened 'Kimilsungia' and 'Kimjongilia', have their counterpart in Japanese practice. Instant experts will never know this, of course; only prolonged experience with post-war Korea yields knowledge of just how far the Japanese got under the Korean skin. Of course, in comparative perspective this is hardly surprising, and few Koreans could ever match (nor did they want to) the accomplished assimilationism of other colonized peoples the world over, from Angolans in Lisbon to Vietnamese in Paris to Americans at the court of King George. Such evidence only surprises us in the context of post-war Korean nationalism.

Japan in its model colony, Taiwan

In the recent literature on the East Asian 'NICs', much has been made of Taiwan's manifold difference from Korea: a less intrusive state, light industry, no big *chaebôl*, more small business and family enterprise, continuous export-led development, more egalitarian distribution, less nationalism, less hatred of the Japanese. Fine: but if this is true, it has been true not since the vaunted Rostovian 'takeoff' of the 1960s, but since the 1920s or the 1930s.

Gustav Ranis, for example, argued that the typically dispersed and rural character of Taiwan's industrialization effort was a key reason for its quick growth; it reduced the high costs of urbanization, helped labour-intensive industries (with low-cost rural labour, etc.), and led to rational economies of scale. This explains the relative smallness of various firms, and the relatively less centralized nature of Taiwan's capitalism as compared to Korea. But this was also true throughout the colonial period. The Japanese had dispersed Taiwan's transportation network such that it was well connected and articulated with the main ports of Kaohsiung, Keelung and Hwalien. This existing infrastructure then greatly aided 'the heavy export of domestic raw-material-intensive products in the 1950s and early 1960s', and also facilitated the location of new Export Processing Zones.[5]

Table 19.2 Exports as percentage of gross value of production

1922	1929	1937
44.7	46.3	49.4

If Taiwan was a fine example of export-led industrialization (ELI) after 1960, it was in the colonial period as well: it really has had a kind of ELI throughout its industrial history. In 1911–15, the average annual total of exports was 63 million yen; in 1926–30 the average was 252 million yen. 1920s growth was clearly export-led (Table 19.2). Kublin calls the increase in exports during the 1920s 'literally astounding', but it quickly went higher. From 1935 to 1937 exports were about half of the net national product (with imports at 40 per cent of NNP); Kublin wrote that 'these very high ratios' were not regained 'until the 1970s'. Foodstuffs were the most important export in the mid-1930s; they retained 'a dominating position' in the 1960s and 1970s. Scott simply calls Taiwan's exporting in the 1960s and 1970s 'a return to normal', with the ratio of imports and exports as a percentage of GDP being 38 per cent in 1935–7, and 38 per cent again in 1975. This was the fourth highest ratio in the world in the mid-1970s, but it was fourth highest in the 1930s as well – and both Taiwan and Korea were higher than Japan (Table 19.3).

Table 19.3 Estimated per capita value of foreign trade circa 1939 (US dollar equivalents)

	Year	Imports	Exports	Total
New Zealand	1939	109	127	236
British Malaya	1939	61	72	133
Australia	1938–9	67	64	131
Taiwan	1937	16	23	39
Korea	1939	15	11	26
Japan proper	1939	10	13	23
Philippines	1939	8	10	18
Burma	1938–9	5	12	17
Thailand	1938–9	4	5	9
Indochina	1937	3	4	7
China	1939	0.85	0.25	1.1

While *Time* magazine and others were lauding the Taiwan miracle in the late 1960s, the natives were telling a political scientist that their situation had been better in the late 1930s. The only sectors in which production increased per capita between 1939 and 1965 were citrus, cement, electricity output, and fish. As for Taiwan's vaunted egalitarian income distribution, land and wealth distribution actually became 'more equal' between 1931 and 1950, before the effects of land reform were felt. In a complete contrast with Korea, many tenants moved into the owner-tenant category. Greenhalgh found 'significant continuity in the distribution of income and wealth' from the middle of the Japanese period into the 1950s.[6] Other sources describe the late 1930s and early 1940s as 'Taiwan's period of greatest material progress', as Taiwan became second only to Japan in East Asian industrialization. All this evidence illustrates the extraordinary leg-up that Taiwan had, not from the onset of ELI in the early 1960s, but from the colonial experience in the 1930s.

Japan also taught its colonies how to export while protecting the domestic market. As in South Korea, Taiwan's market was nearly closed during the first phase of import-substitution industrialization (ISI). The state imposed strict import controls in the spring of 1951, along with a highly pegged exchange rate; high tariffs, tight import licensing systems and 100 per cent deposits paid in advance by importers, were prevalent for many goods. These controls yielded effective premiums above the actual cost of imports, ranging from 48 per cent on wheat flour and 33 per cent on cotton yarn to 100 per cent on ammonium sulphate, 275 per cent on soda ash and 350 per cent on woollen yarn. Meanwhile state officials rode herd on ISI producers: in 1954 K. Y. Yin, vice-chair of the Taiwan Production Board from 1951 to 1954 and later the minister of economic affairs, well known for promoting domestic glass, cement, plastics, plywood and of course textiles, in 1954 ordered some 20,000 Taiwan lightbulbs smashed in a park in Taipei, and then announced that he would liberalize imports if the quality of local lightbulbs did not improve within three months.

Much like Japan's pre-war industrial programme, Taiwan industrialized on the back of its peasantry. The colonial state mobilized resources through a complex maze of land taxes, squeezing what Rong-I Wu called 'a massive fund for industrialization' out of the countryside, while offering very generous tax policies toward private savings and capital formation. Taiwan did the same thing in the early 1960s when export-led industrialization took off, becoming a tax heaven for exporters (five-year tax holidays and many other incentives).[7]

The financing of industrialization also mimicked Japan and Korea. The leading student of Taiwan's colonial economy placed much emphasis on the state's financing and harnessing of investment for the industrial boom in the mid-1930s: 'Bank credit was made available for new investments at low fixed interest rates. Subsidies were granted widely to induce old firms to enter new fields. Corporations were spared the burden of taxes'.[8] A specialist on post-war Taiwan's financial system acknowledged that Taiwan 'inherited a relatively advanced banking system', especially the rural credit cooperatives, farmers' associations and post office savings deposit systems. In 1949 the Chinese Nationalists' Central Bank of China, established in 1928, was suspended and did not return until 1961; thus Taiwan's financial system was essentially colonial in origin, and not relocated from the mainland. Although Taiwan had no central bank from 1949 to 1961, the largest commercial bank, the Bank of Taiwan, performed central banking functions – issuing currency notes, handling the state's business, etc. This bank's main mechanism to influence the economy was its control of interest rates on bank deposits and loans, a control that Lundberg calls 'more or less complete'. With a small bond market and virtually no stock exchange (although one was founded in 1962, it wasn't active until the mid-1980s), most financing came through the state. Big corporations got most of it, especially the state companies inherited from Japanese colonialism. After the switch to ELI, the state financed low rates of interest for exporters.

What about nationalism and resistance to the Japanese in Taiwan? There was hardly any: the Japanese pacified the island within five months, meeting some resistance in the south but almost none in the north. The only recalcitrants thereafter were aborigines in the mountains (who remain recalcitrant today, not to colonialism but to modernity). Even after the March 1st Movement in Korea and the May 4th Movement in China, an observant American traveller noted that some Taiwanese wore Japanese clothes, whereas 'I cannot recall ever having seen a Korean in *geta*s and kimono'. There was a big 'independence question' in Korea, he wrote, but 'Independence, if it is ever considered at all in Taiwan, is evidently regarded as hopeless, not even worth thinking about'.[9] Kublin wrote that 'it would be misleading even to imply that Taiwan was shaken by this tide of change' after World War I, except for a bit of labour organizing in the late 1920s; thereafter until 1945 'Taiwan was practically devoid of any unrest'.[10]

Quiescent Taiwan nonetheless got the same ubiquitous national police system that Korea got, instituted in 1898 by the paradigmatic Gotö Shimpei – the colonizer as rigorous administrator rather than swash-buckling conqueror. This is how Patti Tsurumi described the new police system:

Under Gotö the police became the backbone of regional adminis-tration. In addition to regular policing duties, the police supervised the collection of taxes, the enforcement of sanitary measures, and works connected with the salt, camphor and opium monopolies....They superintended road and irrigation improvements, introduced new plant specimens to the farmers, and encouraged education and the development of local industries.[11]

Taiwan's Chinese settlers, far from resisting, appreciated Gotö's reforms; even Sun Yat-sen himself found it difficult to organize on the island. American travellers liked what they saw, too:

Taihoku [Taipei] gives one a queer, almost an uncanny feeling, after months in China; for here all is orderliness in complete contrast to Chinese disorder on the other side of the channel, a Prussian exactness which Prussia never matched....The Nipponese, it is quickly impressed upon such a visitor, hate any suggestion of irregularity as bitterly as the Chinese seem to love it.[12]

Gotö's ubiquitous policing structure was erected on top of the traditional Chinese system for local surveillance, the *paochia*: ten families formed a *chia* and ten *chia* formed a *pao*. The *pao* had 100 families or about 500–600 people; at the end of 1938, for example, there were 53,876 *chia* heads and 5,648 *pao* heads (or *paochiang*). Interestingly, all of these leaders were elected by members of the *chia* or *pao*, even if they required approval by province governors and chiefs of districts. The Japanese, of course, made the *paochia* system far more efficient: its functions were every bit as extensive and total as the post-war Chinese communist and North Korean local *tanwei* (*tanûi* in Korean) committees. The *paochia* reported births and deaths, recorded and controlled 'all movements of persons in and out of its area along with [monitoring] the conduct of the permanent residents', implemented Japanese health and sanitation regulations, mobilized labour details, disseminated information about crops, seeds and fertilizers, collected many local taxes, and aided the police in every way. The colonizers liked this hybrid Sino-Japanese system so much that they 'kept the regulations in full force throughout the entire span of their rule', and an American in 1954 called this a 'most efficient' system of 'refined' coercion. More to our point, it was a Japanese fulfilment of the British (and Benthamite) project of omnipresent surveillance that the British themselves never quite perfected in Egypt.

All in all, colonial Taiwan was a project that American academics could only applaud in the heyday of modernization theory.

In many ways Taiwan continued to be a colony after the mainlander debauch in the late 1940s, with Nationalists monopolizing executive government and political positions, and taking over the many state-owned enterprises. The Nationalist political elite took over industrial assets that Japan had controlled; the economic power of the Taiwanese elite – always much greater during colonialism than Chinese historiography admits – was quickly 'stripped away'. Like the Japanese period, the economy was open to the natives (mostly for small business) but politics was closed. Unlike the Japanese, carpetbagging Chinese bankrupted the carefully regulated economy within a year of 'liberation'.

The Nationalists were never politically well organized on the mainland, but they quickly came to appreciate Japanese innovations, and added their overbearing centralism to the ubiquitous grassroots structures of the colonial period. As specialists have noted, even the carefully manipulated local elections that the KMT allowed 'remained back-stopped by the same pervasive police network through which the Japanese had controlled the island', with Nationalist secret security agencies added on 'for good measure'. A minority of mainlanders monopolized politics and the state, controlled the means of violence, and used 'thorough police repression' to hold onto power.

Vietnam: colonization without development or modernity

The French took a long time to colonize Vietnam and to propel it forward toward even the most exploitative forms of capitalist enterprise. Beginning in 1859, the French navy occupied parts of southern Vietnam or Cochinchina, which took almost a decade; the French seized other outposts, establishing themselves at the mouth of the Mekong River but only moving inland slowly. In the early 1880s the French invaded central and northern Vietnam (Annam and Tonkin) and finally obliterated Vietnamese independence in 1885. Their colonization of Vietnam, however, was incidental to their desire for a southern point of entry to China.

Once they got control the French primarily encouraged extractive economic activity, oriented toward exports of agro-mineral products. The transportation and communications infrastructure developed accordingly, shaped by the export trade in rice, rubber, tin and other commodities; Vietnam's extensive riverine landscape made canal-building and dredging much more cost-effective than the road and railway network that the Japanese built in Korea and Taiwan. Large natural resource companies like Michelin monopolized economic activity, with the main colonial state function being to facilitate the movement of commodities out of Vietnam. The state served the interests of the colonizers' exporting by building the necessary routes to the sea, and organizing a franc bloc and tariffs to protect export-oriented production.

In effect French policies introduced a money economy without much else, tying Mekong Delta rice prices to the world market and thus upsetting the annual peasant 'round of time' and drowning marginal subsistence farmers; the result was major unrest in 1940 and 1941, and an unbeatable Viet Minh insurgency by the late 1940s. A mere glance at the transportation network discloses French goals (or their absence): quite irrationally, Vietnam's longest rail line and asphalt road ran side-by-side along the coast, recapitulating existing (and more economical) sailing routes and veering away from the most developed parts of Vietnam to run through miles of empty rural areas until it got to China.

An obsession with cost-effective administration by the relatively small colonial government left Vietnamese villages mostly self-sufficient and autonomous, unlike Japanese penetration to the lowest levels of administration in Korea and Taiwan. The colonizers tended to maintain rural order with periodic punitive military campaigns, not with Japan's constant presence and surveillance (although the French did mobilize village informants to monitor their brethren and report miscreants to the authorities.) Another way to save money was to buy off collaborators with large land grants, a practice also found in Korea and Vietnam but without subsequent French programmes to rationalize land arrangements or develop agriculture scientifically. Instead of a central colonial budget and financial pump-priming of industry, the French had local budgets for the three regions of Vietnam and financed them through state monopolies of customs, duties, stamps, salt, alcohol and opium. The state's revenue extraction was much lower than in Korea or Taiwan, particularly from the multitude of agricultural producers; instead of controlling and reducing the opium trade, as the Japanese did (particularly in Taiwan, where its use was extensive), the French encouraged it – early on, it was their most lucrative colonial enterprise.

The general French emphasis on monopoly control and coercion without corresponding investment in human capital can best be seen in the constant recourse to corveé labour for so-called 'public works' projects. The Haiphong-Laokay railway, for example, was completed in 1904–6 only with five separate labour drafts totalling almost 30,000 labourers, and such practices continued into the 1930s. When they weren't organizing great corveé projects, the French relied on seasonal migrations of labourers to and from the rubber and tin plantations, yielding a large, uneducated, underemployed, unskilled or semi-skilled labour force. Both these forms of labour mobilization were rarely used by the Japanese in Korea and never in Taiwan; massive 'corveé' might describe the forced labour by Koreans in the war years, but in a typically Japanese, highly organized fashion. Long estimates that perhaps 200,000 Vietnamese out of a total late-1930s population of over 20 million were workers, but large numbers were unskilled seasonal migrants, with 40,000 alone in the rubber industry and another 49,000 in mining.

The one period of real development in Vietnam was the 'roaring 20s', when after 1924 the French poured capital into Indochina. Still, the main direction was toward plantation agriculture, above all rubber but also rice, sugar cane, tea, cotton and other goods, and to the transportation and communications overheads necessary to move the goods out of the country. Martin writes that by the 1930s 'Indochina had become the most immensely exploited of all European colonies in Asia', but extraction was still mostly from primary-product processing; he notes that even in the 1920s boom the colonial state was not so important, but more like an appendage of metropolitan French interests. In the 1930s Vietnamese communist and nationalist organizers achieved an extraordinarily rapid and sustained mobilization of peasants for radical activity, something that never occurred in Taiwan; in Korea radical organizers in the 1930s did well in those counties and border areas away from the purview of the central state, but not elsewhere.

France was full of its *mission civilatrice* after World War I, and sought to put its cultural stamp on Vietnam – above all in an educational system designed to turn out an elite of Vietnamese *assimilados*, not a mass of industry-ready workers. Thus we find fully Francophile Vietnamese elites like 'Emperor' Bao Dai, who retired to a villa outside of Paris, people who were non-existent in Taiwan and Korea outside of rank collaborationist circles. (Perhaps Korea's Prince Yi, vegetating with a Japanese wife in his Akasaka residence after 1910, might be comparable, but no one thought him fit for leadership after 1945; meanwhile by 1947 Dean Acheson and Dean Rusk saw Bao Dai as Vietnam's anti-communist 'white hope'.) As a rule the French paid little attention to education – there were more teachers in Vietnam before the French arrived than after they left; the schools could assimilate a small stratum of the natives, but did not foster the industrial and administrative skills that Japanese disciplines produced. In the early 1930s there were about 28,000 Vietnamese in elementary schools, compared with more than 300,000 Taiwanese; Taiwan had 8 million people, Vietnam 20 million.

The 1920s did witness something never seen in Korea, however: local elections, beginning in 1921 for village councils (which continued until 1941 when Bao Dai abolished them). This was merely one more way in which the French left (or created) space for traditional autonomy or contemporary resistance at the level where most Vietnamese lived, the rural villages, leaving an enormous gap between city and countryside. Instead of fostering the development and differentiation of Vietnamese society, French colonialism tended to preserve the hierarchy of social relationships in the rural hinterlands, with the state and the trading companies at the top, French businessmen and local agents in the middle, and the mass of the people consigned irrevocably to the bottom.

Quite unlike Taiwan, the French inhibited even 'the most meager forms' of small business, much of the middle-level commerce was in Chinese hands (rice mills and the like), and poor peasant interests tended to vector horizontally rather than vertically, given the general absence of prospects for upward mobility. As Jeffrey Paige, Ngo Vinh Long and others have shown, of course, such a political economy has a tendency to promote peasant revolution – an important point, but one that bears no restatement given the punctuation of Vietnam's thirty-year war from 1945 to 1975.

French investment of all types dropped off rapidly after the Great Depression began, and by the end of the 1930s the global war had started – a war which eventually loosened the French grip on Vietnam. European settlement (never very high and much smaller than Japanese settlement in Korea and Taiwan) dropped off to nothing; the colonizers stopped building railroads (they had never built many, anyway), using existing roads or new ones with motorbus conveyances. Martin speaks of 'colonial nonindustrialization' in the 1930s, in complete contrast to the way in which Japan used its colonies to industrialize itself out of the depression.

The French brought forth a plan for the industrialization of Indochina in 1938, including the fostering of chemicals, automobiles and textiles, which might have brought its policies close to the combination of *étatisme* and *dirigisme* that the Japanese had pioneered in Korea and Taiwan. But the plan was deemed impractical and they were still debating what else to do when World War II broke across their horizon and borders, placing a premium on the rubber and minerals that France had always extracted from Vietnam. Meanwhile, Japan had opted for an integral colonial development strategy as early as 1921, as we have seen.

Northeast Asia's modern/colonial/developmental project

What, then, is the East Asian 'developmental model'? Since many people have written about this subject before (myself included), let me just sketch briefly the Northeast Asian model of political economy, which we find in Japan and its colonies by the mid-1930s if not earlier, and then successively in post-war Japan, South Korea and Taiwan (with many mirror-image reflections in North Korea). Since pre-modern Japan had a very different political system from Korea or China (feudal-style parcelized sovereignty vs. centralized agrarian bureaucracy), and since other post-colonial nations do not demonstrate the characteristics outlined below (e.g. the Philippines, Vietnam, Indonesia, Burma or India), it seems reasonable to think that modern and colonially imposed

Japan had a good deal to do with this difference – although the main point for this paper is more modest, namely that post-war economic successes in Northeast Asia have roots going back well before the Rostovian period of 'take-off' in the early 1960s. Let's have a sketch of this regional bureaucratic-authoritarian industrializing regime (or BAIR, as I have called it):

1   A *bureaucratic* state, drawing upon native Confucian statecraft and civil service, modified by modern Weberian (usually German or French) models; centralized *national capitals* which are administrative, commercial and transportation-communication nerve centres with populations dwarfing other cities (Tokyo, Seoul, Taipei, P'yŏngyang); little or no local autonomy (centre-appointed officials down to county or lower levels), national administrative and policing systems.

2   *Education of the masses* necessary to create the disciplined proletariat, secretariat and saliarate requisite to the BAIR; corresponding de-emphasis on higher education (the university as playground and networking site). For example, in Korea and Taiwan, about 70 per cent of schoolchildren getting elementary education by the late 1930s (contrasted with 2 per cent of Vietnamese in elementary school in the 1930s).

3   Effective *surveillance* of that same mass by every means necessary. In all of these societies there is a Great Leader, be it the Emperor in Japan, maximum Great Leader or General in South Korea (Rhee, Park, Chun, Roh), the Great Leader/emperor in Taiwan (Chiang Kai-shek and Chiang Ching-guo), and the Great Leader/emperor in North Korea (Kim Il Sung and Kim Jong Il). While post-war Japan has a democratic constitution (with authoritarian tinges), authoritarian constitutions, national police, the registration of all citizens, meaningless elections, the absence of civil and political rights, many secret police and intelligence groupings, extremes of torture and thought reform for dissidents, close neighbourhood surveillance by police and resident families – all prevailed in these societies, especially in the pre-war period.

4   *Metaphysical ideology of national essence*: Pre-war and post-war Japan, North and South Korea, and Taiwan have all had a metaphysical political ideology emphasizing national *difference* and anti-liberalism or anti-Westernism. (Korean, Japanese and Chinese scholars all read and commented upon the same neo-Confucian texts 150 years ago, which is the common point of origin.) Ultimately these doctrines seek an obliteration of liberal politics in favour of an organic conception, or the merger of state and society such that 'civil society' barely exists.

5   *Political economy of administrative guidance and neo-mercantilism*: state-centred direction of economic activity, state-accumulated and provisioned capital, relying in the early stages on maximum extraction from a peasant economy, a state-guided product cycle through stages of industrialization, import-substitution followed by exporting followed by secondary and tertiary import-substitution and subsequent exporting, 'getting prices wrong' as means of strangling domestic consumption and capturing foreign markets, a highly protected domestic market, national or cartelized industries (railways, roads, steel, chemicals, electricity, banks, etc.); no labour unions or corporatized labour.

6   Involvement in closely linked *regional* political economy: this was true *a fortiori* of Japan's regional empire in the 1930s and 1940s, but also re-imposed in modified form after American-sponsored changes beginning in 1947 (George Kennans' reverse course and Dean Acheson's 'great crescent', with a decade-long delay caused by Kim Il Sung's attempt to break this developing system in 1950 – see Cumings 1984). Japanese economic influence had been re-introduced in South Korea and Taiwan by the mid-1960s, and is being re-introduced in North Korea and Manchuria in the 1990s.

Conclusion: *Staatswissenschaften*, the state science of late industrialization

Our discussion thus far, whether we know it or not, has indulged in a kind of science unknown in America: what nineteenth-century Germans called *Staatswissenschaften*, or state science (as distinct from, say, social science). When Itö Hirobumi came back from Germany and quipped, 'I understand the secret of the state, now I can die a happy man', it was first of all because he had met Lorenz von Stein, author of the classic text *Der Begriff der Gesellschaft und die soziale Geschichte der Französischen Revolution bis zum Jahre 1830*. As Immanuel Wallerstein argues, von Stein understood 'society' to be a concept of *Staatswissenschaft* because it has meaning primarily 'in the antimony, society/state'. For von Stein, society and state were not simply linked inextricably in meaning, but fused in a number of senses: for example, states decide who constitutes the citizenry ('civil society'); more powerfully, if for Hegel the monarch embodied the state and vice-versa (a different fusion), the novelty of the French Revolution was that after it, the state embodied the popular will (or should). The question then becomes, who embodies (or creates, or knows) the popular will?

American rhetoric is not the rhetoric of mid-nineteenth-century Germany or twentieth-century Japan, Korea or China. The latter were drawn inexorably toward state science, whether of the von Stein or the

Leninist or the Park Chung Hee variety. Sooner or later all the Northeast Asian nations fashioned states worthy of the battle of late industrialization, and all of them did so in conditions ranging from the complete absence to the overwhelming presence of hegemonic American ideology (1930s Japan vs. 1960s Japan, North Korea vs. South Korea, post-1949 China vs. post-1949 Taiwan).

The meaning of 'state-building' in Northeast Asia's fused state/societies is that recourse to the state comes first, followed by conscious or unconscious attempts to create industry, and then and only then 'society', that is, the groups requisite for and appropriate to contemporary imaginings of 'modernity'. The space may have been semi-peripheral or, more accurately, in heaven-sent or carved-out breathing spaces of the world (uncolonized Northeast Asia circa 1850–1910; indulgent America's part of Northeast Asia circa 1945–70, revolutionary-nationalist East Asia circa 1945–75), but the time was 'late', with imperial and industrial antagonists breathing hotly on the neck. Nothing concentrates the mind more than grand opportunity combined with overwhelming danger. In some ways East Asia has meant industrialization without enlightenment, a crude adoption that strikes at the heart of Western civilization: behold, they took the baby and not the bathwater.

A state science of late industrialization, however, is not hegemonic ideology. It cannot take the world as its oyster and reckon for the whole. It takes the world as its octopus and reckons for the parts. To put it another way, Northeast Asia, beginning with Japan, has not exported universals. It has consumed Western universals only to pass that which it did not want – the supreme and unforgivable insult. Our universals have been British universals, artefacts of England's pre-eminence after Waterloo. The mid-nineteenth century was not merely England as the workshop of the world, but England as the ventriloquist for the world (especially the American world). Germany was the *bête noire* of this world, shamelessly copying the inventive wizardry of the English and then dumping the shabby results in British markets. The German and Japanese consciousness was the mirrored reflection of hegemonic thought: a replicative consciousness in search of an elusive perfection, through which the particulars could become not hegemonic, not dominant, but merely equal.

The difference between American and East Asian experience, then, is quite breathtaking: here, replication of the British model thus to supersede, there selective replication of continental experience thus to pass muster. The first, being hegemonic in intent, was holistic; the second, being egalitarian in intent, was particular. Inevitably the latter would fasten upon *technique* stripped away from *Weltanschauung*, and give you *kokutai*, *chuch'e*, and the insoluble *t'i-yung* problem. If internally the state would create 'the modern', auto-disciplined subject, externally it would defend the terrain against the hegemonic power, its products and its world-view.

In Japan and South Korea the United States fashioned liberal constitutions (albeit with the requisite loopholes in the precarious ROK), but Taiwan got martial law and in all three countries the inter-war bureaucrats continued apace as if nothing had happened. In North Korea and Taiwan the constitutions were Leninist. But the central bureaucrats endured, and no doubt will endure.

Still, the central experience of Northeast Asia in the twentieth century has not been a realm of independence where autonomy and equality reigned, but with enmeshment in another web, as we have seen: the hegemonic web. This web had a spider: first England/America, then America/England, then war and defeat, then unilateral America, then (about 1975 down to the present), trilateral America. Japan, South Korea and Taiwan industrialized mostly within this web. North Korea and China defined themselves as outside the web, thereby endowing the web with overriding significance – and so they structured their states to resist enmeshment. Japan, South Korea and Taiwan have thus had states 'strong' for the struggle to industrialize, but 'weak' because of the web of enmeshment: they are semi-sovereign states. North Korea had a state 'strong' for industrialization, and 'total' for hegemonic resistance. But as the century ends, it, too is being drawn into the web; and so is, finally, Vietnam. Heir to French exploitation and Ho Chi Minh's revolution, it now wants to discipline itself thus to follow in the wake of 'the NICs'. Better that it had invited the Japanese to colonize it.

Notes

1   An expanded and fully referenced version of this essay may be found in my (1999, 2002) *Parallax Visions*, Duke University Press.
2   Angus Hamilton (1904) *Korea*, New York: Charles Scribner's Sons, 8, 11–24.
3   Timothy Mitchell (1988) *Colonising Egypt*, Berkeley: University of California Press, ix.
4   Hermann Lautensach (1988) [1945] *Korea: A Geography Based on the Author's Travels and Literature*, trans. Katherine and Eckart Dege, Berlin: Springer-Verlag, 204–7, 383, 386–7.
5   Gustav Ranis (1979) 'Industrial development', in Walter Galenson (ed.) *Economic Growth and Structural Change in Taiwan: The Postwar Experience of the Republic of China*, Ithaca NY: Cornell University Press, 222–5.
6   Susan Greenhalgh (1988) 'Supranational processes of income distribution', in Edwin Winckler and Susan Greenhalgh (eds) *Contending Approaches to the Political Economy of Taiwan*, Armonk: M. E. Sharpe, 70–1.
7   Rong-I Wu (1971) *The Strategy of Economic Development: A Case Study of Taiwan*, Louvain, 191.
8   George W. Barclay (1954) *Colonial Development and Population in Taiwan*, Princeton: Princeton University Press, 28–9.

9 Harry A. Franck (1924) *Glimpses of Japan and Formosa*, New York: The Century Co., 183–4.
10 Hyman Kublin (1973) 'Taiwan's Japanese interlude, 1895–1945', in Paul K. T. Sih (ed.) *Taiwan in Modern Times*, New York: St John's University Press, 336.
11 E. Patricia Tsurumi (1967) 'Taiwan under Kodama Gentarö and Gotö Shimpei', *Papers on Japan*, vol. IV, Cambridge MA: Harvard University, East Asian Research Center, 117–18.
12 Franck, *Glimpses*, 144.

Further reading

Barclay, George W. (1954) *Colonial Development and Population in Taiwan*, Princeton: Princeton University Press.

Cumings, Bruce (1984) 'The origins and development of the Northeast Asian political economy', *International Organization*, winter.

Eckert, Carter J. (1991) *Offspring of Empire: The Koch'ang Kims and the Origins of Korean Capitalism*, Seattle: University of Washington Press.

Gragert, Edwin H. (1994) *Landownership Under Colonial Rule: Korea's Japanese Experience, 1900–1935*, Honolulu: University of Hawaii Press.

Mendel, Douglas (1970) *The Politics of Formosan Nationalism*, Berkeley: University of California Press.

Murray, Martin J. (1980) *The Development of Capitalism in Colonial Indochina (1870–1940)*, Berkeley: University of California Press.

Lautensach, Hermann (1988) [1945] *Korea: A Geography Based on the Author's Travels and Literature*, trans. Katherine and Eckart Dege, Berlin: Springer-Verlag.

Mitchell, Tim (1988) *Colonising Egypt*, Cambridge: Cambridge University Press.

Myers, Ramon H. and Mark R. Peattie (eds) (1984) *The Japanese Colonial Empire, 1895–1945*, Princeton: Princeton University Press.

Ngo Vin Long (1973) *Before the Revolution: The Vietnamese Peasants Under the French*, Cambridge MA: MIT Press.

Robinson, Michael (1988) *Cultural Nationalism in Colonial Korea, 1920–25*, Seattle: University of Washington Press.

Vien, Nguyen Kac (1975) *Tradition and Revolution in Vietnam*, trans. Jayne Werner, Ithaca NY: Cornell University Press.

Winckler, Edwin and Susan Greenhalgh (eds) (1988) *Contending Approaches to the Political Economy of Taiwan*, Armonk: M. E. Sharpe.

Woo, Jung-en (1991) *Race to the Swift: State and Finance in the Industrialization of Korea*, New York: Columbia University Press.

INDEX

Ivan IV 176
Ivory Coast 225, 228, 231, 232

Jalal Al-i Ahmad 204
Jamal al-Din al-Afghani 206
Japan 2, 3, 4, 6, 7, 15, 22, 141;
capitulation (1945) 254, 260; China
284; colonial legacy 278; colonialism
240-1, 279, 281, 293; consciousness
296; economic stagnation 283;
education 281; empire 13, 16;
imperialism 7, 282; Indochina 254;
industrialization 60, 85, 297; Korea
278, 280, 282-3, 291, 293; Kwantung
Army 283; Manchukuo 248;
Manchuria 248; Meiji Restoration
(1868) 6-7; Russo-Japanese War
(1904-5) 2-3, 119, 257; Second World
War 119; Shantung 119; Sino-
Japanese War (1937) 259, 274;
Taiwan 279, 280, 283, 285-90, 291,
293; twenty-one demands 284; USA
and 297; Vietnam 270
Java 192
Jewish Agency 166
Jewish Bund 181

Kajong Chapji 242
Kalmyk steppe 179
Kampuchea 275
Kang Yu-wei 128
Kaohsiung 286
Kashmir 13, 168, 170
Katanga 62
Kautsky, Karl 102-3
Kazan 176
Keelung 286
Kemal Ataturk 119, 189, 192, 194, 195,
203
Kemal Pasha 184
Kennan, George F. 295
Kennedy, John F. 159
Kenya 159, 160, 221, 226
Kerensky, Alexander 182
Key, Ellen 245, 246
Keynes, John Maynard 153
Keyserling, Hermann 88
Khalid Muhammad Khalid 209-10
Khayr al-Din 201
Khiva 177
Khmer Issarak 262, 271

Khmer Rouge 273, 274, 276
Khrushchev, Nikita 59, 157
Khuzistan 62
Kiev 183
Kim Il Sung 294, 295
Kim Jong Il 294
Kim Maria: 'Come out, Friends' 246-7
Kim Yön-su 284
Kin Tartars 27
King, Martin Luther 149
Kirman 62
Kojong, King 280
Kokoshkin 180
Kolchak 189
Korea 15, 26; administration 291;
Choson imperial dynasty 241; civil
war 140; colonial legacy 278-98;
Cultural Policy 244, 248;
deportations 282; economic
development 278-97; education 241-
3, 250, 281, 285; Enlightenment 239,
241, 243, 245, 250; Industrial
Commission (1921) 283;
industrialization 284, 297; Japan
and 278, 280, 282-3, 291, 293; March
1st Movement 240, 283, 288; mining
284; modernization 281, 282;
motherhood 239-52; nationalism
282; 'new woman' 239-52; North
281, 285; railways 278-9, 284, 290;
sexual slavery 282; South 281, 285;
USA and 297; women 239-52; Yi
dynasty 240; see also Korean War
Korean Industrial Bank 283, 284
Korean War 155, 273
Kublin, Hyman 286, 288
Kuchuk Khan 184, 189, 195
Kun, Bela 194
Kuomintang, see China
Kurds 13
Kuusinen, Otto 182
Kuwait 60
Kwang-su Lee: 'Mother' 250
Kyrgyz Inner Horde 179

Lagos 159
Lao Issara 262, 268
Laos 256, 272, 274, 276; Britain and 268;
Chinese immigration 256; civil war
254, 262; communists 255; France
and 268-9; Geneva settlement (1962)
271; independence (1953) 254;

Thoreau, Henry David 92, 97
Thucydides 69
Tibet 13
Tilak, B. G. 126-7
Time 287
'To All Muslim Toilers of Russia and
  the East' 184, 187
Tokyo 136
Tolstoy, Leo 92, 97
Tongnip Shinmun 241
Tonkin, see Vietnam
Tourane, see Da Nang
Touré, Sékou 229, 230, 231, 232, 233,
  234, 235
Tours Congress 31
Toynbee, Arnold 11
trade unions: Africa 226-35
tradition 33, 34, 35, 40, 71, 72-3
Transcaucasia 179, 189
tribalism 13, 19, 61
tribute 27, 256
Truman Doctrine 140, 154
Truman, Harry S. 131, 136, 139, 140,
  154, 156, 160
Tsurumi, Patti 288-9
Tunisia 43; Destour party 120; Senussi
  uprising 4
Turkestan 189, 192
Turkey 24, 192, 193, 194; Arab
  nationalism and 119; Britain and
  154; Cyprus invasion (1974) 164,
  166; France and 119; Greece and
  119; nationalism 194; Republican
  People's Party 209; Revolution
  (1908) 119; Welfare Party 213; see
  also Ottoman Empire

U Nu 7
Ueno, Chizuko 239, 251
Ugaki Kazushige 248
Uganda 159
Ukraine 180, 182, 183, 184, 185, 186,
  187, 190
Ulster, see Ireland
Union Générale des Travailleurs
  d'Afrique Noire 231, 232, 234, 235
Union of Soviet Socialist Republics 3,
  7, 9, 176-98; Afghanistan 204-5;
  Africa 119, 159, 222; All-Russian
  Constituent Assembly 181, 182;
  Asian empire 103, 123, 155; Baltic
  states 188; Bashkirs 187; Bolsheviks

121, 128, 177, 181, 182, 183-4, 185,
  186-7, 194, 195, 196; Central Asian
  Bureau 193; civil war (1918) 183,
  184, 186; collapse (1989) 16, 164, 173;
  Communist International 8, 29, 102,
  189, 190-1, 192, 193, 194, 195;
  Communist Party 192; Congress of
  the Peoples of the East 189;
  Constituent Assembly 179, 182, 183,
  188; constitution (1918) 187;
  cosmopolitanism 28; Cuba 58;
  Czechoslovakia (1968) 110;
  development 34; Eighth Party
  Congress 187-8; federalism 183-9;
  Finland 178, 181, 182, 183, 186, 188;
  First All-Russian Congress of
  Soviets 182-3; First World War 24-5,
  59; five-year plans 34; Gilan 189;
  hotline 59; India and 142; inorodtsy
  179; Islam 190, 194; Japan and 60;
  Jews 186; Kadets 179-80, 183;
  Kyrgyz 187; Liberals 177;
  Manchuria 281; Mensheviks 182,
  194, 195; nationalism 185; New
  Economic Policy (1921-8) 195; Party
  of Socialist Revolutionaries 180;
  People's Commissariat of
  Nationalities 186-7; Petrograd
  soviet 180, 182, 183; Poland 180,
  181, 182, 186, 188; Provisional
  Government 178-9, 180, 182, 183,
  186; purges 34; Red Army 184, 188,
  189, 194; Revolution (1905) 24, 119;
  Revolution (February 1917) 178,
  180; Revolution (October 1917) 8,
  24, 30, 33, 34, 91, 173, 176-98; Russo-
  Japanese War (1904-5) 2-3, 119;
  Second World War 33; Sino-Soviet
  treaty 268; Slavic people 27; Social
  Democrats 181, 190; Suez 58; teddy-
  boys 70; Third Congress of Soviets
  187; tsars 176-8; Vietnam 268, 269,
  273; 'White' movement 186;
  zemstva 179; see also Cold War
United Kingdom, see Britain
United Nations 14-15, 77, 131-51, 160,
  165-6, 167, 170, 236, 253, 255, 274;
  Economic Commission for Asia and
  the Far East 59; Food and
  Agriculture Organization 59;
  Implementation Force (IFOR) 168-
  70; United Nations Educational,